The Working Class in American History

Editorial Advisors

David Brody
David Montgomery
Alice Kessler-Harris
Sean Wilentz

A list of books in the series appears at the end of the book.

Labor Leaders in America

Labor Leaders in America

Edited by
Melvyn Dubofsky
and
Warren Van Tine

UNIVERSITY OF ILLINOIS PRESS
Urbana and Chicago

Library of Congress Cataloging-in-Publication Data

Labor leaders in America.

(The Working class in American history)
Includes bibliographies and index.
1. Trade-unions—United States—Officials and
employees—Biography.   I. Dubofsky, Melvyn, 1934–   .
II. Van Tine, Warren R. III. Series.
HD8073.A1L33   1987   331.87'33'0922 [B]   86-4368
ISBN 0-252-01327-1 (cloth)
ISBN 0-252-01343-3 (paper)

Contents

Introduction   ix
Melvyn Dubofsky and Warren Van Tine

1. William H. Sylvis and the Search
for Working-Class Citizenship   3
David Montgomery

2. Terence V. Powderly, the Knights of Labor,
and Artisanal Republicanism   30
Richard Oestreicher

3. Samuel Gompers and the Rise of American
Business Unionism   62
John H. M. Laslett

4. Eugene V. Debs: From Trade Unionist to Socialist   89
Nick Salvatore

5. William D. "Big Bill" Haywood: The Westerner
as Labor Radical   111
Joseph R. Conlin

6. William Green and the Ideal of Christian Cooperation   134
Craig Phelan

7. Rose Schneiderman and the Limits of
Women's Trade Unionism   160
Alice Kessler-Harris

Contents

8. John L. Lewis and the Triumph of
Mass-Production Unionism   185
Melvyn Dubofsky and Warren Van Tine

9. Sidney Hillman: Labor's Machiavelli   207
Steven Fraser

10. Philip Murray and the Subordination of the Industrial
Unions to the United States Government   234
Ronald Schatz

11. A. Philip Randolph, Black Workers,
and the Labor Movement   258
William H. Harris

12. Walter Reuther and the Rise of Labor-Liberalism   280
Nelson Lichtenstein

13. Jimmy Hoffa: Labor Hero or Labor's Own Foe?   303
Estelle James

14. George Meany: Labor's Organization Man   324
Robert H. Zieger

15. Cesar Chavez and the Unionization of
California Farm Workers   350
Cletus E. Daniel

Notes on Contributors   383

Index   387

Introduction

Melvyn Dubofsky and Warren Van Tine

In the middle of the 1980s, as once before in the mid–1920s, the American labor movement seems beset by enemies on all sides. Once again politicians, business people, and workers themselves find little to laud in the nation's trade unions. Sixty years ago a president declared the business of America to be business; the leading corporations effectively blended the open shop and welfare capitalism; and millions of new workers in the mass-production, basic industries and the emerging retail and service sectors rejected unionism. In absolute numbers and more so as a proportion of the gainfully employed, trade unionism dwindled in size. In the 1920s as in the 1980s, moreover, the term *labor leader* became a mark of opprobrium, and many citizens dismissed trade union officers as "labor bosses."

As part of a collaborative effort first to explain the paralysis of the labor movement in the 1920s and then to prescribe a cure for its ailments, the labor educator and journalist J. B. S. Hardman wrote a fictional essay to illustrate why many of the labor leaders he had known personally had evolved from idealistic dreamers into more cautious bureaucrats.[1] Hardman introduces his fictional creation, XYZ, the president of the Asbestos Workers' International Association, as he sails on the SS *Atlantic* to an international labor gathering in Europe. XYZ is "a safe and sane progressive" heading a "forward-looking union." He is traveling to Europe not so much to participate in the exchange of ideas—like most American labor leaders he does not take international conferences too seriously. Rather, he is exhausted from the daily routine of union administration and seeks time to think and take stock of the post–World War I developments in America. Setting up the trip, like most everything else involving the union, has taken extensive "political patching and gluing." This XYZ expects, for he is a

realist. "Ambition," he believes, "is the real driving force in any movement. There are no movements free of politics. . . . Politics is no fitting
occupation for saints, and union politics is human politics." Yet XYZ also
has ideals. "At times knee-deep in the mud of union-politics," Hardman
relates, "he never ceased to think of larger aims and, yes, even ultimates."
But XYZ is tired!

One night, while XYZ stands alone on deck gazing through the mist at
the waves, a vision of his younger self (HYS) appears. The setting is
fifteen years earlier, and HYS, having just been nominated for the union's
district presidency, is addressing the cheering delegates. The speech ex-
udes energy and idealism. "We want to make great headway," HYS thun-
ders. "We want to improve conditions. But we also want to create a new
condition. . . . This being our aim, what, then, is our method?" The democratic process, HYS declares firmly. "Real unity implies equality. It does
not follow from the acceptances of equality, however, that we reject leadership. . . . But leadership is not bossism. Leadership is a give-and-take
arrangement. . . . This is the democracy of a fighting army."

HYS's words stir XYZ deeply. They had been his sentiments fifteen
years ago, before he became burdened with union responsibilities, but he
is not sure they are his views today. Mulling over what he said then and
what he now believes, he closes his eyes to think. Again a vision appears,
this time of himself and HYS in a heated conversation.

"Look what you have made of me," HYS exclaims. "Is that what I meant
to grow into?"

"Why, a leader of labor, that was your dream," responds XYZ.

"No, old man," HYS counters, "you are not a leader of labor, you are a
labor leader. . . . One is a fighter, the other a professional."

"But labor is not an army in the field," the older man replies. "Labor is
a part of the state. It must have its own competent administration."

Again the younger self disagrees. "Leaders of labor are generals of armies constantly in action. . . . I wanted to be of service to the labor movement, not a specialist in the art of manipulating the conditions of labor
employment." And he criticizes XYZ for abandoning democracy.

"I am as loyal to the movement as ever," XYZ protests, "but . . . but I
have no longer that youthful confidence in the rank and file, in the mass of
people. They don't really want to be led, and so one must drag them."

"Benevolent oligarchy," HYS snaps back and then shifts the argument.
"The function of your power is bargaining," he observes. "Buying and
selling. . . . You buy subordination, coherence. You sell labor to employers. . . . Labor is the commodity you sell. Like hot dogs. . . . Your or-

ganizations have become part of the system, props of the system, upholders of the unshakable order of privilege and exploitation."

To this the older labor leader responds philosophically: "People accept what life offers to them. . . . People have more food, better clothing, better housing today than they ever had before. People nowadays think less of the day ahead. . . . They dream not, they grab. . . . When you grab, you grab as much as you can, and you are more fearsome about holding on to what you have grabbed than about acquiring more." "This is Babbittry applied to labor," HYS retorts. "I will grant you that the size of most people's vision is in inverse ratio to the food they hold in their stomach. But what of it? We are not to inherit a movement, but to build it. . . . If we set out to do nothing else but to hold on to what we are certain of, we will never get anywhere. You have abandoned democracy in the name of efficiency. Idealism you decry because that upsets your hunt for the immediate and tangible. Dissatisfaction with things as they are you describe as indulgence in fruitless opposition. And thus your labor movement breaks down. It ceases being a striving, fighting force. . . . You have identified yourself with the organization which you are called on to lead, to such a point that you cannot think of the movement without you leading."

This last charge startles XYZ out of his fantasy. Yet the vision has helped him realize how much he is trapped in a vicious circle. "The union," he muses, "is the queerest compound of contradictions. Its accepted vocabulary is that of a militant venture. But, in point of fact and in terms of what its members want it to be, it is a business enterprise all through. It is supposed to be nonpolitical, if not apolitical. Why, it is the most political of all things! It carries the gospel of rebellion, and it suppresses opposition within its own ranks with an iron hand, ruthlessly."

The dilemma, XYZ concludes, is inherent in the need for organization to correct grievances and alter society. "Organize to cohere, for without cohesion action is impossible. And then—corrupt, divide, play both ends against the middle—to keep the organization going. It is a maddeningly vicious circle," XYZ ponders, "but labor must break the circle through, if it is to breathe, to live, to be its own fulfillment."

Hardman's imaginary dialogue between XYZ and his younger self introduces various themes that are relevant to understanding the broad sweep of American trade union history as well as the careers of individual labor leaders. As the essays that follow demonstrate, the years after the Civil War witnessed a transformation of union leadership from a calling to a career and of its exemplars from missionaries to professionals. Early labor leaders sacrificed personal security, comfort, and well-being to create a labor movement that would, they dreamed, produce a freer and more equal society. As unions grew larger, more stable, and more powerful, however, the second or third generation of labor leaders acquired job security, lush perquisites, and professional lifestyles. Some now saw the labor movement as a means for personal aggrandizement. Democratic practices within unions, always in tension with the need for organizational discipline, further weakened under the demand for administrative efficiency and a large bureaucracy to handle the union's daily business in an increasingly technical society.

Changes is labor-management relations strongly influenced the emergence of careerism within the labor movement. Over time trade unions and employers moved to accommodate their conflicting interest through a form of antagonistic cooperation. Founded to fight employers in the interest of workers, unions sometimes came to serve management in the search for labor peace, higher productivity, and social harmony. Like XYZ, many labor leaders no longer sought "to create a new condition"; they settled for modest improvements within the existing system.

These changes are reflected in the lives and careers of the labor leaders discussed in this volume. Those who became heads of individual unions often found themselves behaving much like big-city political bosses— granting favors to cement a working coalition, playing upon individual ambitions, and restraining rank-and-file initiatives to maintain organizational stability as well as their own positions of power.

Moreover, several leaders, like XYZ, commenced their union careers filled with an idealism that over time they tempered in the name of realism as they sought to advance unionism in a barely tolerant, and at times openly hostile, business-dominated society. John H. M. Laslett, for instance, traces Samuel Gompers, founder and president for almost forty years of the American Federation of Labor (AFL), from his involvement with socialist ideas as a youth to his advocacy of a restrictive "business unionism" as he aged. Likewise, Steve Fraser reveals that Sidney Hillman, head of the Amalgamated Clothing Workers (the union for which Hardman worked) lost part of his original idealism as he labored to gain stability and security for his members, the labor movement, and the nation. Nelson Lichtenstein tells a similar story for Walter Reuther. Introduced to socialism by his father and considered a young militant in the 1930s, Reuther, like Hillman, gradually evolved into a proponent of a modern liberalism that, in Lichtenstein's words, "would link union power with government authority in what many historians today would label a 'corporative' framework designed to reorganize American capitalism within a more stable and humane framework." None of these leaders, it should be noted, became arch-conservatives; all remained liberals and promoted humanitarian ideals, however much their social vision diminished.

The lives of other labor leaders covered in this book reveal that XYZ's experiences were not universal. Some, like John L. Lewis, Philip Murray, George Meany, and Jimmy Hoffa, were not notably idealistic when young. Others were actually driven by circumstances from a limited view of unionism to a broader challenge to the economic system. David Montgomery documents well how William Sylvis, the leading spirit of the National Labor Union, expanded his critique of the emerging corporate-capitalist society and came to recognize the need to mobilize black and women workers in order for the labor movement to be effective. Eugene V. Debs initially accepted the established order and pleaded for caution in trade union circles. Yet, as Nick Salvatore shows, the realities of an expanding corporate capitalism educated Debs to ever more radical positions—first as a champion of a wider-based industrial unionism and then as the nation's best known apostle of socialism. The realities of class warfare in the Rocky Mountain West, as Joseph R. Conlin argues, had a similar impact on William D. "Big Bill" Haywood. Interestingly, just as those whose vision narrowed still remained liberal, those who became radicalized did so while proclaiming their adherence to traditional American values.

XYZ's dialogue with his younger self, then, acquaints us with some basic themes in American labor history. The authors of the following essays, however, have pushed beyond Hardman's perspective of 1928 to examine issue that were either not significant at that time or to which he was not as attuned as contemporary scholars. All the contributors writing on leaders prominent from the 1930s onward, for example, had to confront the relationship between the labor movement and the expanding power of the state. In our own essay, we trace United Mine Workers president John L. Lewis's curious courtship with the state as he oscillated from advocating Herbert Hoover's policy of voluntary associationalism under government guidance in the 1920s, to championing enlarged government powers during the New Deal, to condemning the Imperial Presidency, bureaucratic government, and restraints on free enterprise in the 1940s and 1950s. In his essay on Philip Murray, Ronald Schatz shows how Lewis's successor as the Congress of Industrial Organizations' (CIO) president chose a different course and steadily increased his commitment to strong labor ties with the Democratic party and a paramount role for the state in labor-management affairs. Of all the labor leaders considered in this volume, however, Sidney Hillman, as Fraser depicts him, made the fullest effort to link the labor movement to an active state. Hillman became so wedded to that end that many critics charged that he evolved from being labor's representative in government to being the government's spokesperson to labor. By midcentury the state had become so entwined in the internal affairs of unions as well as collective bargaining that AFL-CIO president George Meany, as Robert H. Zieger documents, spent much of his time representing unionism on Capitol Hill and at the White House. And Teamsters president Jimmy Hoffa, as demonstrated by Estelle James, had to devise ingenious strategies to sidestep restrictive labor laws.

The following essays also reveal how the new labor history has informed the old art of biography, for the authors are sensitive to the importance of working-class culture in weaving the various threads of the labor movement. Laslett's observation that Gompers' values were rooted "in the political and economic environments in which he grew to maturity" is applicable to most of the subjects in this book. Montgomery, for example, ties the unions that emerged in the 1860s and early 1870s to the practical experiences of workers on the job. Richard Oestreicher links Terence V. Powderly and the Knights of Labor to the community-centered culture from which they emerged. And Craig Phelan argues that the Christian idealism common among many workers at the turn of the century influenced William Green's behavior as AFL president in the 1920s and 1930s. All of the authors insist that ideology—broadly defined—has been an important force in shaping the behavior of the leaders considered.

Finally, several of the essays in this collection address the fact that women, blacks, Hispanics, and other minorities have had a much more limited role in the labor movement than white male workers. William H. Harris examines the sometimes futile efforts of A. Philip Randolph, the most prominent black leader to arise in this country, to make the AFL more responsive to black needs. In her essay on Rose Schneiderman, a leader of the Women's Trade Union League, Alice Kessler-Harris surveys efforts to bring women into the union fold and Schneiderman's growing realization that to advance the interests of working women state power must also be used. Finally, in his essay on the only surviving labor leader treated here, Cletus E. Daniel traces Cesar Chavez's struggle to build a successful farm workers' union upon the culture of California's largely Chicano agricultural population.

As a group, the essays show that labor leaders were as much the products of their circumstances as the shapers of a new order, as much the servants of their followers as the unchallenged commanders of union armies. The essays also demonstrate that by the mid-twentieth century a diversified and segmented labor force thrust to power leaders of quite different characters and beliefs. On the one hand, Jimmy Hoffa (as portrayed by Estelle James) and George Meany (as analyzed by Robert H. Zieger) could practice an unabashed "business unionism," which in Carl Sandburg's words appealed "to the dictates of the belly." Moreover, that appeal had a wide and firm popular base among workers and trade unionists. On the other hand, Sidney Hillman, Walter Reuther, Philip Murray, and Cesar Chavez could promote a "social reform unionism" that appealed to the heart as well as the stomach, the mind as much as the fist. And they, too, found their loyal and devoted followers. Finally, we see such mavericks as John L. Lewis, Eugene V. Debs, and William D. Haywood whose changing beliefs and aims spanned the spectrum from business to revolutionary unionism.

Despite the diversity apparent among the labor leaders, the workers they led, the unions they built, and the policies they advocated, certain common themes emerge clearly from the essays. First, almost all the labor leaders, including the most radical, had to contend with the reality of the increasing institutionalization of the movements they led, what the political scientist Robert Michels referred to as the "oligarchical imperative." As a rule, labor leaders devoted as much effort to strengthening the unions they built (which often meant creating self-perpetuating oligarchies of officers) as to transforming external reality. Associated with this was the need to sublimate charismatic forms of leadership to more routinized, rationalized, and bureaucratized modes. John L. Lewis, Walter Reuther, Sidney Hillman, and Samuel Gompers proved especially adept at making that adjustment. Terence V. Powderly, William D. Haywood, A. Philip Randolph, and Cesar Chavez were less successful. As charismatic leaders, they proved their ability to build movements among the least likely recruits. Yet they were less successful in translating their talent for mobilizing masses into the creation of stable institutions. This is shown most graphically by the persistent organizational problems of Chavez's farmworkers' union, which even today is not assured of stable survival. A few of the labor leaders never had to face issues of that sort. William Green, Philip Murray, George Meany, and even Jimmy Hoffa came to power in already institutionalized settings. Each in his own way, and Green least successfully, used the existing structures of union power to magnify both his own influence and that of the movement he led. And, finally, there is the anomalous case of Eugene V. Debs, who transformed himself from a typical official in one of the railroad brotherhoods into a charismatic leader. Yet the more charismatic Debs became the more attenuated was his relationship to a stable workers' organization. Clearly, then, charismatic labor leadership and the ability to build stable unions conflict as often as they coincide.

A second common theme, already alluded to above, also pervades the essays. Union power came increasingly to depend on the assistance of a benevolent state. This required labor leaders to woo influential allies outside the labor movement. For Randolph and Chavez that meant appealing to a civil rights constituency; for Schneiderman, feminists; for Reuther and Hillman, the creation of a secular liberal-labor coalition; for Green and Murray, a more religiously inspired alliance; for Gompers and Meany, friends in Congress, the White House, and the permanent federal bureaucracy. Those labor leaders less adept at winning influential allies in the community or in government—Debs, Haywood, Hoffa, and occasionally Lewis—often found themselves and their movements victimized by the state.

A century of diversified labor leadership, partly charismatic and partly routinized, partly idealistic and partly mundane, partly romantic and partly practical, has bequeathed to the 1980s a legacy of institutionalized, bureaucratized unions. Although the unions of the 1980s are larger, wealthier, more stable, and led by professionals as compared to those of the 1880s, they are in some respects even more dependent on a friendly state and in need of influential allies in the broader nonunion community.

The individuals discussed in this volume have been selected because of their importance as architects of the American labor movement or as representatives of certain major themes and developments. Each essay surveys the subject's life and career while highlighting a particular thesis or conjuncture important to the history of American workers. The authors, all recognized authorities on their subjects, have each sought to present the latest historical wisdom on the topic in clear, intelligible language. At the end of each essay, the author provides bibliographic notes, listing other materials on the subject that can be found in most college libraries. We hope that readers will find these essays an enlightening introduction to the study of working-class history and an enticement to learn more.

Acknowledgments. We wish to thank Richard Wentworth of the University of Illinois Press for his encouragement and assistance in carrying this project into final form.

Bibliographic Note

1. J. B. S. Hardman (ed.), *American Labor Dynamics* (1928), pp. 149–68. For stylistic purposes, we have quoted without excessive use of ellipses.

Labor Leaders in America

William H. Sylvis and the Search for Working-Class Citizenship

1

David Montgomery

In 1828, when William Sylvis was born in the town of Armagh, it consisted of some thirty buildings nestled among the mountains of western Pennsylvania only a few miles from the Connemaugh River. His parents had but recently moved there in hopes that the building of the western division of the Pennsylvania Canal along the Connemaugh might provide work for an experienced wagon maker. Nicholas Sylvis's ancestors had come from the German Palatinate to Pennsylvania in the 1730s and through subsequent generations had scraped together a living by hard work at farming or mechanical trades. His wife, Maria Mott Sylvis, spoke of her family's prominence in New Jersey's revolutionary conflicts of half a century before. Memories of the battles working people had fought for survival, for their nation, and for citizenship were their legacy. The rugged terrain through which the canal and its railroad portage were built failed to provide Nicholas Sylvis the steady customers he needed to support his family, so he moved east to Mauch Chunk, where another canal linked the anthracite fields to Philadelphia, bringing the coal that heated most of the city's homes.

In 1835 Irish immigrants who unloaded coal from the canal boats began a strike, which gathered the support of shoemakers, printers, building workers, blacksmiths, and others in such numbers as to culminate in a citywide general strike for higher wages and the ten-hour working day. For more than a year after this strike a General Trades Union assembled delegates from more than fifty unions of artisans, laborers, and even factory operatives from mill villages at the nearby falls of the Wisahickon, to support each other's strikes and formulate a common program of action. The movement produced remarkable leaders, like John Ferral, William English, and Thomas Hogan, who spoke not just for the weaving, shoemaking, and printing trades from which they had sprung but also for all those who produced society's growing wealth but enjoyed so little of it. Thirty years later William Sylvis evoked their memory in summoning his own molders' union to fight for the eight-hour day. Unfortunately, the General Trade Union and the accompanying unions that had made Philadelphia the leading center of workingmen's agitation did not survive the depression of 1837–43. Twenty years would pass before a new movement, created by another generation of workers and based on the growing industrial trades rather than ancient handicrafts, would emerge in Philadelphia.

During those years, as William Sylvis grew to manhood, his father experienced a fluctuating fate not uncommon to early nineteenth-century artisans. Nicholas became a partner at building canal boats in Mauch Chunk, failed, moved back to the west bank of the Susquehanna to open a wagon shop, failed again, then during the long depression years left his family for months on end searching for wagons to build or repair. Young William was sent to the homestead of a prosperous farmer and Whig state legislator from Lycoming County to earn his keep at chores and field work. There, at age eleven, he had his first instruction at a rural schoolhouse. More important, he had access to his master's library and began to devour the books, which were to reappear in his later speeches in the partially digested form typical of the self-educated individual. No oration by Sylvis was complete without passages lifted from Thomas Malthus, Nassau Senior, Henry Carey, and especially John Stuart Mill. Along with the prevailing political economy, he also imbibed the gospel of self-improvement. His teenage commitment to the temperance cause and to teaching in Methodist Sunday schools remained with him the rest of his life. The most justly famous of all his speeches, his rousing appeal at the Iron Molders' national convention in 1865 for workers to act for themselves, voiced as its central theme: "It is not what is done for people, but what they do for themselves, that acts upon their character and condition."

Although young Sylvis was far away from the vibrant artisans' culture and politics of Philadelphia, the countryside in which he grew up was dotted with sawmills, primitive mines, canal and railroad construction, and ironworks. Less than eighteen miles to the east of his mother's home was the Montour Iron Works of Danville, whose 3,000 workers in 1860 made it then the largest ironworks in the country. Further east the anthracite fields were penetrated by deep shafts and capped by numerous tipples by the 1850s. Along the banks of rivers that wound into the western hills were many small ironworks still smelting ore with charcoal.

Such furnaces not only poured pig iron but also had forges where smiths pounded out axes, shovels, and saws, and foundries where anything from

Archives of Labor and Urban Affairs, Wayne Sate University

frying pans to canal lock hinges might be cast. The founder of such a works contracted with the owner to produce all these wares, usually at specified prices per item. His assistant, the keeper, also had to learn the arts of smelting, molding, smithing, and supervising helpers and laborers. All these arts were ancient and preliterate. In the late 1840s a master workman taught an apprentice, who then journeyed from one furnace to another increasing his knowledge.

That is how William learned to make molten iron flow into the molds he had devised with sand rammed just right around wooden patterns, so as to fabricate the ironwares his mind had conceived. Usually he was employed as a journeyman; once he and another molder rented and worked a foundry of their own for a year. Invariably he moved on—to Half-Moon Valley, Union, Hollidaysburg (with its new Pennsylvania Railroad repair shops, soon to rank among the largest in the world). At age twenty-three he married fifteen-year-old Amelia Thomas, and soon they produced sons, who were named after heroes: Henry Clay, Oliver Perry, and Lewis Clark Sylvis. Two years after his marriage, however, he had decided that the best future for an ironworker lay in Philadelphia itself, and there the family went.

The iron trades of Philadelphia, Cincinnati, New York, Troy, Pittsburgh, and other metal fabricating centers were much more specialized than those of Half-Moon Valley. Their smelting was done in far-off furnaces close to coal deposits and then shipped as pig iron to the cities rolling mills and foundries. New crafts flourished in urban centers: puddlers and rollers to make rails and bar iron; machinists to cut and fit metal components of steam engines, reapers, and power looms; blacksmiths to shape and anneal boiler plates, anchors, and couplings with their sledges and trip hammers; and molders to make liquid iron assume a thousand different shapes. Iron beams and columns for building construction, gear wheels, huge ship propellors, and small hinges all were cast by molders, as were the potbellied stoves in which city-dwellers burned anthracite coal.

During prosperous times well-trained and experienced journeymen in all these trades could and did move freely and often from one employer to another in search of better earnings, experience at new kinds of work, less obnoxious bosses, or simply to take some time off. Many molders contracted with employers to fabricate castings at a specified price, recruited their own helpers, brought their own hand tools, sieves, and bellows, and even paid weekly rent for the floor space on which they worked.

By 1860 the heavy immigration of the previous decade and the relative ease of entry into the trade combined to make a majority of molders in most urban centers Irish and German born. Due to the fixed capital investment required for working iron, most urban molders worked for large firms, especially in the manufacture of railroad locomotives and steamships. Physical exhaustion and injuries struck down journeymen so frequently that Sylvis's chronic illness and death at age forty-one were not uncommon experiences. Still, skillful men could command sufficiently high wages in the 1850s that many did save up to buy meat markets, saloons, or shoe stores. Some of them even became employers. More common among molders was the practice of establishing their own cooperative foundries. Starting in Cincinnati in the 1840s, the establishment of cooperatives spread widely over the upper Ohio River valley in the 1850s and 1860s and was enthusiastically endorsed by the molders' union after the Civil War.

The Trade Union Cause

The high demand for iron molders and their products also had less beneficial effects. Employers tried to hold onto their skilled hands by forcing them to contract for a year at a time, by withholding much of their earnings, and by paying them in store goods rather than cash. They tried to replenish the journeymen's ranks by flooding their foundries with apprentices and helpers. Whenever possible, they subdivided molders' tasks. Because the art of molding depended on the ability to ram sand to just the right density throughout the mold, often around complex patterns and in shapes and sizes that required a wide variety of approaches, it took years to train an all-around journeyman. But little time was needed to train a man or boy to pack a single, simple pattern again and again. In the manufacture of stoves, where Sylvis found work in Philadelphia, molders were assigned and paid by the individual plate rather than by the whole stove. They were encouraged to hire helpers (called "bucks," after the Berkshire farm youth among whom the system originated) to fashion molds for simpler parts under a journeyman's supervision, whereas the latter finished off the molds, made the more complex ones, and received the pay for the total output. Journeymen were thus encouraged to run their own little sweatshops within an employer's foundry while recruiting partially-trained novices to compete with them for future jobs.

Simultaneously the nature of molders' payment underwent a subtle but fundamental change. Although some molders, like those experts who worked in groups to pour huge castings, were paid by the day, most were paid by the piece. By the later 1850s, however, the price per piece was no longer based on the value of the product, as it had been for rural founders or early stove molders, but rather was based on the prevailing local daily earnings. When a new pattern appeared in a shop, a few castings were made from it under the foreman's eye in order to determine how long they took. The price per piece was then fixed simply by dividing the daily earnings a molder competent to perform it could get on the local market by the number of parts he could make in a day. In other words, piece work was transformed into a form of payment for the worker's time rather than his product. "Wages are gauged," observed molders' union leader H. J. Walls, "not by the value of the services done, or the product of such labor, but by the present necessities of the laborer." Still, piece-work payment tempted molders to increase their own output, thus maximizing their employers' return on their hired labor, and invariably piece rates were reduced when scurrying molders earned more per day than would be needed to hire their replacements.

Molders could stem the ruinous tide of competition only by regulating their own behavior—by thinking and acting collectively. Two years after Sylvis arrived in Philadelphia, a molder in the large Liebrandt and Mc-Dowell foundry threw his "rammer into the sand heap and with a terrible oath, swore [he] would not make another mold at such prices." After he approached every other man in the shop, all walked out on strike, and a month later they formed the Journeymen Stove and Hollow-Ware Moulders' Union of Philadelphia.

It was not until 1857, when a general economic crisis made wage cuts rampant, that Sylvis joined his first strike and was subsequently admitted to the union. Having joined, however, he threw his boundless energy into the tasks of bringing all the city's molders into the organization and of communicating with unions of the trade in other cities for the purpose of establishing a national union. Thirty-two delegates from nine different unions gathered in Philadelphia on July 5, 1859, and drafted plans for the National Union of Iron Molders. At the formal founding convention early in 1860, Sylvis was made treasurer, and he wrote the preamble to the union's constitution.

The preamble's rhetoric bore Sylvis's personal imprint, but the ideas it expressed resembled those found in many trade union declarations of the late 1850s. It began by observing that those in possession of capital had used it "to monopolize particular branches of business, until the vast and various industrial pursuits of the world had been brought under the immediate control of a comparatively small portion of mankind." This "concentration of wealth and business tact" was potentially beneficial to humanity because it contributed "to the most perfect working of the vast business machinery of the world." Experience had shown, however, that the potential benefits of industrial growth had not been shared by "the poor of humanity." The reason, simply, was that "WEALTH IS POWER . . . a power too often used to oppress and degrade the daily laborer." The impoverishment of workers by the wealth they had created forced them to grapple with the question: "What position are we, the Mechanics of America to hold in Society? Are we to receive an equivalent for our labor sufficient to maintain us in comparative independence and respectability, to procure the means with which to educate our children and qualify them to play their part on the world's drama, or must we be forced to bow the suppliant knee to wealth, and earn by unprofitable toil a life too void of solace to confirm the very chains that bind us to our doom?"

Thus while celebrating the promise of rising productivity, Sylvis noted that its fruits were aggrandized by those who already possessed capital and then used to diminish the incomes and independence of their employees. The only remedy was for molders to organize, think, and act on their own behalf, "to rescue our trade from the condition into which it has fallen," to secure it against "further encroachment, and to elevate the moral, social and intellectual condition of every Moulder in the country."

Delegates to the 1860 convention denounced piece work, the employment of "bucks," and unrestricted employment of apprentices. They also voted Sylvis out of the national treasurer's office. The combined impact of protracted hard times and the outbreak of civil war, however, subsequently destroyed the new organization, and no convention at all met in 1862. It was Sylvis who persuaded twenty leaders of locals in the United States and Canada to come to Pittsburgh in January 1863 and to try again (this time naming themselves the Iron Moulders' International Union [IMIU]), and they elected him their president. He was now thirty-four years old and described by a newsman as "a medium-sized man, strongly built, of florid complexion, light beard and moustache, and a face and eyes beaming with intelligence." He wasted no time in demonstrating the qualities for which he soon became famous: an ability to chart a clear course of action amid the confusion of daily experience, a way of analyzing the problems faced by workers in terms that linked their everyday experience to passages lifted from the most eminent social commentators of the day (often exposing the latter's errors), and a rousing style of oratory, which workers demanded to hear repeatedly.

Above all, he drove himself mercilessly. With only $100 borrowed from the Philadelphia local, he made a four-month tour of northern foundries after his election to office, talking to molders as they worked, in meeting halls, in their homes, and on the streets. Scarcely had he returned home to help with a protracted strike in Philadelphia than he set out again—then once more before the year was out. As a result of his efforts thirty-three functioning unions sent delegates to a convention in Buffalo in January 1864, and seventeen others reported by mail. Sylvis was reelected president and authorized a salary of $600 per year, which he used the next year to organize thirty-eight more locals and to bring the total union membership to 6,000 of the estimated 9,200 journeymen molders in the country by January 1865. Although the union was most solidly organized along the Hudson valley from New York to Troy, its impact on wages was greatest in the booming economy of the Ohio valley, where most of its strikes were won quickly.

The purpose of the IMIU, according to its constitution, was to "determine the customs and usages in regard to all matters pertaining to the craft." This was done by means of shop committees, strike relief, regulation of apprentices and helpers, and traveling cards. Battles over piece rates were fought by shop committees, which learned to deal with both foremen and *hogs* (overzealous molders). The international union accumulated a strike fund out of the members' dues and used it to sustain workers who walked off their jobs in order to enforce shop committees' decisions. Sylvis described that fund as the key to the organization's success. "When we can have on hand and constantly at our command, a sufficient amount of money to carry us through any and all emergencies that may arise," he said in 1864, "strikes will cease to have any existence." Union rules limited apprentices to one per shop, plus one for each ten journeymen, and they outlawed the Berkshire system by allowing no molder more than one helper. The traveling card linked locals by providing the mobile molder with evidence of his commitment to the obligations of membership, among which was a prohibition against approaching any prospective employer for a job without first getting the approval and advice of the shop committee.

Through all these means the molders regulated their own behavior, in the knowledge that only if all of them acted according to the group code could they prevail against the power of their employers to hire, fire, and fix piece rates. To enforce that code, in Sylvis's view, required incessant agitation and organizational discipline. He argued for strict regulation of strikes, to make them less numerous and more effective. He urged powerful locals not to push their wages too high above those of competing regions, lest they invite employers to counterattack. When his sense of organization was pitted against members' hunger for earnings, however, he often lost, and having lost, he resorted to an increasingly authoritarian style of leadership.

The Boston convention of January 1867 found the IMIU at its zenith (boasting 8,615 members) but confronted by a formidable employers' counterattack. Although commodity prices had begun to decline slowly after the end of the Civil War, the wages of molders and other skilled trades continued to be pushed upwards by aggressive strikes. Ominously for the molders, however, their wages to the west of Pittsburgh had risen to the vicinity of $5.00 a day, while those in the Hudson valley remained around $3.25. Consequently stoves from Troy sold in Cincinnati at prices that threatened the survival of the Queen City's founders. The union's remedy was equalization, and its Troy locals had opened a campaign in early 1866 for an increase of fifty percent in their wages. Hardly had they raised the demand, however, when more than eighty employers formed the American National Stove Manufacturers' and Iron Founders' Association, proclaimed their intention to "control our own workshops, and to manage our own business," and posted notices in foundries east and west announcing "that we will proceed at once to introduce into our shops all the apprentices or helpers we deem advisable, and that we will not allow any Union Committee in our shops, and that we will in every way possible free our shops of all dictation or interference on the part of our employees."

In handling the crisis of 1866, Sylvis well earned labor editor Andrew Cameron's description of him as a "Napoleonic genius." He ordered locals back to work in order to frustrate the employers' scheme for a nationwide lockout, kept the pressure of competition from Pittsburgh on obdurate employers in Cincinnati, and as far as possible, isolated the strike in the Troy region. The union's constitution gave no authority to the president to act like a general, and neither did it authorize him to assess every working member five percent of his earnings between April and June to aid the strikers, yet he did just that. By year's end the manufacturers' association had been roundly defeated. National organization and centralized strategy had safeguarded the workplace power of 8,000 molders.

Delegates to the January 1867 convention, however, had no occasion to celebrate. Not only had the employers' assault turned back the Troy wage demands, thus maintaining the perilous east-west differential, but also reports from all over the land at the new year noted falling prices, closing businesses, mounting unemployment, and wage reductions. Miners, textile workers, shipbuilders, farm laborers—virtually everyone but urban construction workers—received notice of lowered wages. The many workers who struck in protest were usually replaced by the unemployed. Sylvis responded by sending a secret circular to all molders' locals advising them that preserving their organization was more important than upholding their wage rates. He advised western locals to reduce their wages voluntarily by thirty percent until prosperity returned. Only in Pittsburgh, where locals had already sacrificed their needs to the general good in 1866

11

and where employers had now initiated a lockout that lasted the entire year, did Sylvis authorize a strike to preserve existing wage rates. This time his strategy did not work. Cincinnati founders not only cut wages by forty percent but also announced that new piece rates henceforth would be fixed by foremen "without dictation from any shop committee." The Cincinnati union leaders led a revolt against Sylvis's efforts to lower their wages and sparked a general refusal along the Ohio valley to accept any reductions. While strikes spread throughout the West and parts of the East, apprentices and helpers in large numbers reported to their jobs and were joined not only by unemployed American molders but also by scores of strikebreakers recruited in Germany and Belgium by United States consulates. Soon the union's proverbial strike fund dried up; union members who were at best working part-time could not pay assessments. By year's end the international union's membership had fallen from 8,615 to less than 5,000, and influential locals, such as those in Cincinnati and Pittsburgh, could exercise little control inside the foundries. The decline continued until 1870, when membership was scarcely 3,800. Only after that point did molders again participate in the general upsurge of unionism that lasted until the depression of 1873. Widespread reassertion of collective control over foundry practice did not come until the 1880s.

When the battered union's next convention assembled in Toronto in July 1868, Sylvis controlled the platform as never before. His opening report was by far the longest speech he had ever made to convention delegates, and in it he excoriated his absent foes for their refusal to follow his instructions during the previous year. The union's long and costly strikes, he declared, had spent its funds and exhausted its membership to no lasting benefit. Workers and their employers faced each other like hostile armies in the field, and what workers won in good times they lost in bad.

The apparent failure of the union to attain the goals Sylvis had prescribed for it in his preamble to the 1859 constitution now led him to a more radical conclusion. Labor's only remedy, he concluded, was to attack the fundamental cause of the workers' suffering: the wages system. The union should build on the example already provided by members in Troy, Pittsburgh, Somerset, and elsewhere, who put their funds into cooperative foundries and became their own collective employers. The time had come, he concluded, "to abandon the whole system of strikes" and make cooperatives "the foundation of our organization."

Although the union subsequently tightened its control of strikes, it by no means abolished them. It did, however, amend its constitution to encourage cooperatives, institute a voluntary assessment for capital stock, and change its name to the Iron Molders' International Co-operative and Protective Union. The idea was neither new nor chimerical. Sylvis had urged the delegates to the 1867 convention to start cooperatives, and more than twenty foundries were established by the union during the 1860s. One in Somerset, Massachusetts, remained in business and paid its molders dividends until 1891. Two circumstances made Sylvis's 1868 speech significant, however. First, Sylvis faced only feeble opposition at the convention. Second, he had come to the Toronto convention by way of a special meeting of the National Labor Union (NLU) in New York. There he had emerged as the dominant figure of that organization (despite the fact that he was not yet one of its elected officers), a committed foe of the social system that made some men the employees of others, and the stanch advocate of allying labor to middle-class reformers through the NLU.

The National Labor Union

Iron molders were always well represented at national labor congresses from 1866 through 1874. Sylvis himself was involved in the discussions that prepared the way for the congress of 1866 in Baltimore where the National Labor Union was founded, although illness prevented him from attending that gathering himself. He worked closely in Philadelphia with like-minded trade unionists, among them William Harding of the Coach Makers and Jonathan Fincher of the Machinists and Blacksmiths, and after the war he broadened his circle to include John Siney of the anthracite miners; C. Ben Johnson, a labor-oriented journalist from Sunbury, near which Sylvis had grown up; Richard Trevellick, the ship carpenter and later Sylvis's successor as NLU president; and William Jessup, who was the corresponding secretary of the most powerful trade union body in the country, the New York City Workingmen's Union. In 1867 Sylvis joined Chicago's Andrew Cameron as coeditor of the nation's most influential labor newspaper, the *Workingman's Advocate*.

The variety of occupations and communities represented by these men bears witness to the remarkable size and scope that the union movement achieved immediately after the Civil War. The best estimates of union membership place its peak at about 300,000 workers on the eve of the depression of 1873—a number that would not be reached again until 1885. Some thirty-four national and international unions were formed between 1859 and 1873. Their membership and strength fluctuated constantly, and some proved short lived. Nevertheless, the appearance of so many unions reveals that by the 1860s large portions of the United States has become industrialized. Almost 5 million Americans were wage earners in industry, commerce, and agriculture. With the growth of industry and the emancipation of the slaves, American had become a nation of employees. Four million of its wage earners were in industry, more than any other country in the world except England. It is equally noteworthy, moreover, that the National Labor Union, Britain's Trades Union Congress, the General German Workers Association, and the International Workingmen's Association (or First International) all emerged within four years during the 1860s.

The American working class made its presence felt far more in the social and political life of industrial towns than in national politics. The NLU, in fact, was never much more than a series of annual congresses to which workers' organizations of several types sent delegates. It had no executive structure at all until Sylvis created one in 1869, and the administration he constructed was designed more for electoral politics than for the coordination of unions' economic struggles. Nevertheless, the National Labor congresses were representative of the country's trade union leadership between 1866 and 1870 and again between 1873 and 1874. Molders, miners, printers, cigarmakers, bricklayers, carpenters and joiners, shoe workers, tailors, machinists and blacksmiths, painters, woodworkers, and coopers were regularly represented, and most other important unions, except those of locomotive engineers and telegraphers, showed up occasionally. Corresponding secretaries were elected from each state. Some of them, like William Gibson of New Haven and William Jessup of New York, worked ardently to build the organization; others did little. The first president was John C. C. Whaley, a proofreader in the Government Printing Office and a prominent figure in the typographical union. For all its frailities, the NLU was a workers' organization—the first enduring, nationwide institution created by the American working class.

The NLU's initial program was drafted after the Baltimore congress and published as the *Address of the National Labor Congress to the Workingmen of the United States*. It was both a call for governmental action and an outline of what working people should do for themselves. It espoused four basic ideas. First, through workers' efforts, eight hours should be made "by legal enactment, a day's work in every state." Second, through cooperatives and through the distribution of public lands to settlers, the tools of production should become the property of "those that have the ability and skill to use them." Third, all workers should join trade unions so as to have "an equal voice with the employer in determining the value of the labor performed," and unions should better regulate apprenticeship, use strikes only "as a *dernier* resort," and encourage the negotiation of grievances with employers. Finally, white workers had to recognize that slavery was

14

gone and that their behavior would determine whether blacks became "an element of strength or an element of weakness" for the labor movement. "What is wanted then," the address concluded, "is for every union to help inculcate the grand, ennobling idea that the interests of labor are one; that there should be no distinction of race or nationality; no classification of Jew or Gentile, Christian or Infidel; that there is but one dividing line— that which separates mankind into two great classes, the class that labors and the class that lives by others' labor."

Although the NLU itself exerted little influence on the events of 1866– 68, local trade unionists did expand their organizations, cultivate cooperatives, and do battle for the eight-hour day. There were even scattered instances of strikes undertaken jointly by white and black workers, most notably among Philadelphia's brickmakers; but far more significant was a rapid growth of black trade unions, mostly in the South. Illinois, Connecticut, Missouri, Wisconsin, New York, and California all enacted laws during 1867 making eight hours "a legal day's work," and the next year Pennsylvania joined their ranks, while a petition campaign organized by Whaley and the NLU helped persuade Congress to make eight hours the working day for employees of the federal government.

None of these laws substantially affected business practices. In fact, the depressed economic conditions of 1867 intensified employers' resistance to any reduction of working hours. A decisive battle had been fought in Chicago, where five to six thousand marchers organized by forty-four local unions staged a festive parade to celebrate the inauguration of the legal eight-hour day on May 1, 1867, only to find that "capital had its back up" in defiance of the new law. A week-long strike of most trades was climaxed by a march of laborers through the congested Bridgeport district of the city, shutting down all workplaces, clashing violently with police, and prompting the mayor to call in the Dearborn Light Artillery to patrol the city. Although many strikes, among them those of molders and machinists, dragged on into June, the combined force of military occupation and thousands of men in search of work produced total defeat for the strikers. For the rest of the century the actual day's work was to remain far longer than the "legal day's work"; even the federal government ignored its own law.

At the National Labor Congress of 1868, however, William Jessup sounded an optimistic note. "With the coming of Spring a revival of trade took place, causing a demand for labor," he reported. "Our unions again revived, and many trades demanded a return to the wages formerly received, which, in most cases, was acceded to." The president of the Plasterers' International Union told its July convention: "The utility and

15

importance of Trades Unions becomes more apparent each day." Union growth was clearly again on the upswing, despite the pessimistic prospects of the molders; Pennsylvania's anthracite miners and Massachusetts' shoe workers had unions of formidable strength by 1870; and Jessup could then boast that New York State had some three hundred fifty labor organizations, the largest numbers of which had been formed by shoe workers, molders, bricklayers, and cigarmakers, in that order. In 1872 New Yorkers were to unleash the most formidable labor struggle of the epoch. Trade unions and eight-hour leagues of building tradesmen, furniture workers, and metal tradesmen brought about 100,000 of the city's 150,000 workers out on strike during May and June. They faced furious opposition by employers, who declared that "the spirit of communism [was] behind the movement." Even this strike movement eventually failed to win much reduction of hours for its participants, however, and the depression that began the following spring and lasted most of the rest of the decade largely destroyed the union gains of 1868–73.

The 1868 National Labor Congress shared the year's spirit of optimism, but its debates and resolutions emphasized political action, not strikes. At the first congress in 1866 delegates had adopted by a three-to-two margin a resolution calling for "a National Labor Party, the object of which shall be, to secure the enactment" of federal and state eight-hour day laws "and the election of men pledged to sustain and represent the interests of the industrial classes." Although nothing was done to implement this resolution, and President Whaley exhibited at best tepid support for the labor party idea during his two years in office, trade unionists in several areas did plunge into the electoral arena in a variety of ways. In Boston they nominated their own candidates for Congress but made a pathetic showing at the polls. In Connecticut during the state elections in the spring of 1867, a workingmen's convention mobilized effective support for the Democrats' gubernatorial candidate through its own independent organization. Not only did the Democrat win, but a dozen worker candidates for the legislature also won office and set the stage for the speedy enactment of the state's eight-hour day law. During the following summer, the trade assemblies of local unions in Pittsburgh and Cincinnati proved to be effective political machines. The Pittsburghers put their candidate in the mayor's office, and the Cincinnatians sent Samuel F. Cary to Congress. In both these cases the labor platforms had stressed primarily local issues, and the major parties had reasserted their control during the presidential elections of 1868. The party formed by workers in the mining and glassmaking town of La-Salle, Illinois, however, had a major impact on the NLU and on Sylvis's career.

The intellectual leader of the LaSalle movement was Alexander Campbell, a businessman, writer, and former mayor of the town. He had entered into the national debates over banking and currency provoked by the Civil War crisis and published a plan for the abolition of all banks, so that only the federal government could issue currency. This money (called *greenbacks*) was to be available directly to consumers and investors at nominal rates of interest and freely convertible into low-interest bonds so that its value might remain stable.

Campbell's plan captured the imagination of a local antimonopoly association and of the area's coal miners' union. It seemed to promise not only a means by which capital could easily be made available to those who wished to enter or expand business operations, but also a remedy for exploitation, poverty, and economic crises. The power of private banks over the money supply and the rate of interest, Campbell argued, allowed the capitalists who owned them to appropriate the surplus created by other people's labors. Moreover, it was because the banks siphoned off so much of the national product that workers and their employers had to war with each other over what was left. Only with the establishment of a "true American, or people's monetary system" could trade unions function securely and cooperatives prosper, Campbell and his colleagues concluded, and only through this system could the economy grow without recurrent trade crises.

Campbell's writings appeared in the *Workingman's Advocate* in 1866 and won Sylvis's hearty approval. Soon Sylvis's own articles were reproducing Campbell's arguments at length and finding in them an explanation for the difficulties faced by his union. He wrote, for example: "In many instances, the employer, to keep his works going, must borrow money, and must pay more interest for the use of it than his return in profit; to save himself, he reduces wages; the workmen, not being able to see where the true difficulty is, go on a strike—the works are closed, and the employer and workman go to ruin together."

When Campbell and the LaSalle miners brought their plan to the 1867 National Labor Congress in Chicago, it won the hearty approval of the important Committee on National Labor Organization and was included in its lengthy report and appended to its renewed call for a national labor party. There was virtually no opposition from the assembled trade unionists, and Sylvis's close identification with the proposal magnified his importance on the floor of the congress. The "Napolenic genius" of the previous year's strikes and coeditor of the nation's leading labor paper now had a plan—a program for the whole labor movement—to which to attach his energy and skills. Although Whaley was reelected president of the

17

NLU, and although the ineffective structure of the NLU remained intact, it was committed to a new political course, and Sylvis was taking over as its navigator.

The logic of the new course dictated that the NLU should broaden its appeal to people who agreed with its program even if they were not trade unionists and that it should not sit out the election of 1868. Vice-presidents Gibson and Henry Lucker (a German-American tailor from New York City) joined Trevellick and Sylvis in publicly urging Whaley to act on both these needs. In June 1868 Whaley responded by inviting "a few friends of labor reform" to a special advisory council in New York, on the eve of the Democratic party convention. Because this was not a regular congress of the NLU, participants did not need credentials from labor organizations. Whaley, Sylvis, Lucker, Jessup, and other familiar trade unionists were joined by a remarkable array of people described in the Boston *Daily Evening Voice* as "the intelligent 'middle classes' . . . who are not capitalists or otherwise selfishly involved in the present order of things." They included, along with Campbell, veteran politicians who had fallen out with the Republican or Democratic party, businessmen with years of political involvement (like Horace H. Day), and the leaders of the woman suffrage movement (Susan B. Anthony and Elizabeth Cady Stanton). All of them had for one reason or another concluded that the major parties had lost their reforming zeal and that the National Labor Union offered the most promising vehicle for the realization of their own ideals. Although these reformers were ignorant of trade unions, if not openly hostile to them, they were all enthusiastic about workers' self-organization, cooperatives, and political partipation, and they were enthralled by the greenback plan. The trade unionist who best understood them and most excited their admiration was Sylvis.

When the officers of the NLU returned to New York in late September for their regular convention, the representatives of "the intelligent 'middle classes'" took their seats among the assembled union delegates. Political action, currency reform, and cooperatives provided the dominant topics of debate, and the constitution was amended to create both an executive committee to direct NLU affairs between congresses and a structure of state labor unions adapted to the political divisions of the federal system. For the first time, women and the problems of working women played prominent parts in NLU debates despite the caustic reactions of some New York building tradesmen to the presence of Elizabeth Cady Stanton. The discussion of the platform closed with a rousing oration by Sylvis on behalf of currency reform. After a straw vote, Whaley declined to run for reelection. Sylvis was unanimously elected president of the National Labor Union.

Citizenship

Two circulars mailed out by the president of the NLU immediately after the close of the 1868 congress left no doubt that Sylvis was in command. The task before labor, he announced, was the "organization of a new party" for the purpose of wiping from the statute books "obnoxious laws" that fattened a "moneyed aristocracy" and putting "practical laws for the preservation and encouragement of the deserving" in their place. He summoned the country's trade unions to help establish a new monetary system, which "would so change the whole face of society as to do away with the necessity of trades-unions entirely." Because "the evils under which we groan . . . are the results of bad laws," they can be cured only "by a repeal of those laws, and this can only be done through political action."

Sylvis's cultivation of state labor unions and his appointment of a committee to work with Congressman Samuel F. Cary on legislation in Washington raised the framework for the National Labor Reform party that his successor Trevellick ultimately completed in 1872. Even in New York, where many trade unionists grumbled about the admission to the NLU of people "in no wise connected with labor" and were left cold by Sylvis's fixation on currency reform, a state labor union led by Alexander Troup provided the mechanism for widely supported political action in 1869 and 1870. But Sylvis was not content to organize only in the North. In February 1869 he set out for one more whirlwind organizing tour—one which proved to be his last. His target was the South.

Here Sylvis faced the most profound questions of his career. He had often thought and spoken about the American republic, about slavery, and about race before, but he had always done so within an intellectual framework taught him by prewar political leaders. Now he had to rethink those questions as a postwar working-class leader. The transition was not easy to make.

Sylvis had come of age in a country where 4 million blacks were held in slavery. Adult slaves alone clearly outnumbered white wage earners in America until the census of 1850. The Democratic party, to which he and his father had been ardently loyal, had unswervingly supported the right of each state to determine its own social institution and underscored this defense of southern slavery by relentlessly repeating that America was a "white man's country." There is no indication, moreover, that Sylvis had every wavered in his devotion to these prewar Democratic tenets.

The crisis of the Union caused him to act on these beliefs and, for the first time, to reconsider them. Abraham Lincoln, a Republican who was hostile to slavery in his rhetoric and pledged to bar its extension into the

19

western territories, was elected president of the United States. In response states of the Deep South began to withdraw from the federal Union and then, in February 1861, held a constitutional convention to form a new country of their own. Sylvis and his workmates in Philadelphia's metal-working enterprises were profoundly alarmed. A series of even larger meetings to which shops and unions around the city sent delegates organized a massive parade on Washington's birthday and established the Committee of Thirty-Four to coordinate a nationwide workingmen's campaign to restore the disintegrating federal union and to dispel the rising menace of a civil war. Sylvis was its corresponding secretary, and he wrote that under "the leadership of political demagogues and traitors, the country is going to the devil as fast as it can." His conclusion and that of the committee was: "unless the masses rise up in their might and teach their representatives what to do, the good old ship will go to pieces."

Two aspects of this movement deserve notice. First, it represented the first time wage earners had mobilized to intervene on their own behalf and through their own organizations in the affairs of state. "Our political machinery is out of order; mechanics must repair it," read a popular placard in one parade. Furthermore, the proposals it advanced were lifted from conservative Buchanan Democrats: to enact the Crittenden Compromise to guarantee slavery forever, to partition the territories into free and slave regions, and to secure the capture and return of fugitive slaves. From this perspective, enemies of the nation were the abolitionists. Only their defeat could secure the unity and prosperity of the United States. The working class had thus made its political debut attired in borrowed and worn-out ideas.

Leadership of the country and of Philadelphia itself was assumed by a Republican party that gradually committed the machinery of state not only to military reconquest of the secessionist South but also to the emancipation of the slaves, to the extension of full citizenship rights to all adult males, to the promotion of industrial growth through private enterprise, a free market system within the restored national boundaries, and tariff protection against outside competition, and to the firm use of the government's police and military powers against any threats to that system. Workers were mobilized to support this project, first in volunteer armed companies raised by people of prominence in their communities and often raised within factories by the owners and overseers, and later by federal conscription. Provost marshalls who were assigned the task of enforcing conscription locally used their powers in St. Louis, Louisville, and Pennsylvania's coal fields to break strikes and cleanse their districts of working-class agitators. Enthusiastic legislators in Illinois outlawed strikes, and others tried to do the same in New York, Pennsylvania, and elsewhere but were stopped by the vigorous response of the state's union movements.

Sylvis left only a fragmentary record of his own reactions to these events. He helped assemble a militia company shortly after the outbreak of war, clearly believing, like most other workers, that whatever else happened the nation had to be held intact; but he soon abandoned that martial effort because he and his mates disliked the colonel who was put in command. A year later, during the campaigns that ended with the battle of Antietam, he and other molders in the Liebrandt and McDowell foundry (which had also been an important center of the 1861 workers' peace movement) mustered themselves into a new regiment and marched off to Maryland. Their war ended quickly after a ludicrous episode: their panic-striken colonel surrendered the whole regiment without firing a shot one dark night—to a returning patrol of his own men. Although his colleagues Fincher, Cameron, and Uriah Stephens (later founder of the Knights of Labor) offered qualified support to the Republicans, Sylvis never ceased to despise that party as long as he lived. Many other workers not only shared his distaste but also carried their hatred into the streets in bloody riots and insurrections in New York, Troy, Buffalo, and elsewhere triggered by the 1863 draft act.

The "draft riots" took place just before Sylvis set out on his second famous organizing tour of 1863, and he visited many of the Hudson valley centers of violence. Typically, however, Sylvis had his mind fixed on a single objective: to organize the molders. Later, in a powerful speech to the union's convention of January 1865, he analyzed the connection between his unionizing efforts and the revolutionary changes through which the country was passing. While "armed treason and rebellion threatened our institutions with destruction," he said, "while the proud and opulent of the land were plotting the downfall of our Government, the toiling millions stood like a wall of adamant . . . between the country and all its foes." Even while the workers sacrificed lives and fortune for the republic, he continued, a "spirit of centralization" had encouraged military suppression of the working class and the dissemination of "monstrous" economic doctrines. "What would it profit us, as a nation," he asked, "to preserve our institutions . . . save our Constitution, and sink the masses into hopeless ignorance, poverty . . . and utter dependence on the lords of the land?" He concluded by arguing that popular "governments must depend upon the virtue and intelligence of the masses," and they, in turn, could be safeguarded only by the actions of the masses themselves, that is, through trade unions and cooperatives. Given what Sylvis called "a war of classes,"

21

the self-organization of working people became their only guarantee of meaningful citizenship.

But what of black citizens? They had wrenched themselves out of bondage by taking advantage of the war to desert plantations en masse, by demanding and often winning the payment of wages by their masters, and by enrolling in the Union armies (which 179,000 did). The Emancipation Proclamation and the Thirteenth Amendment, which was ratified by the end of 1865, gave legal sanction to the demolition of chattel slavery. From the large demonstrations of urban blacks for civil rights and the suffrage in 1865–66 through the drafting of new constitutions for the southern states between 1867 and 1869, an emerging network of black social organizations supported mass political involvement. In cities such as Richmond, Mobile, and Memphis, that activitiy was spearheaded by workers rather than by the still minute black middle class. In Richmond, where the black population had doubled between 1860 and 1865, societies of domestic servants and tobacco factory workers were especially prominent. Many of the black marchers demanding the vote in 1866 were grouped by trades. Black dockworkers, tobacco workers, ship caulkers, plasterers, hod carriers, wagoners, coopers, brickmakers, and molders formed unions of their own in the urban South in the late sixties. Many of them also established their own cooperative workshops.

A large black working class was taking shape, and it seemed to be moving on much the same path as that chosen by white workers. This development was recognized in the NLU's 1867 *Address to the Workingmen*, in which it was declared that "the interests of labor are one" and there would be "no distinction of race or nationality." Nevertheless, two enormous obstacles blocked any speedy fusion of the white and black union movements. First, most white trade unions implicitly or explicitly barred blacks from membership. Virtually no unions had admitted blacks before the Civil War, and few of them seemed in a hurry to open their doors after emancipation. White trade unionists usually argued, as did one Richmond carpenter, that "the dark sea of misery" around them threatened to take all the jobs at lower wages if the unions did not bar blacks physically from the work sites. The coopers and quarrymen of Richmond disagreed; they argued that only a common stand of both races for the same union wages could fend off the destructive impact of competition between the races, and they formed some of the country's first biracial unions. When the question was put to the 1867 National Labor Congress, Alfred Phelps of New Haven pointed out that though he believed blacks should be admitted, most members of his carpenter's union did not. The Committee on Colored Labor that he chaired at the congress could only report: "we find the subject involved in so much mystery, and upon it so wide a divergence of opinion amongst our members" that discussion should be postponed until the next convention.

Second, the fundamental political demands of all blacks for civil rights, for the right to vote, to hold governmental offices, to attend schools, and to receive protection against vigilante violence depended on loyalty to the Republican party. White workers of Baltimore, Richmond, and other southern cities were bound by ties almost as strong to the Democrats (or Conservatives, as they usually called themselves then in the South). The Conservatives cultivated the allegiances of upwardly mobile white mechanics and of immigrant societies, preached a common interest of worker and employer in their cities' economic recovery, denounced independently minded workers' organizations as Republican-inspired, suppressed "illicit" interracial gatherings with the municipal police, and tirelessly preached the doctrine of white supremacy. The effectiveness of this formula for attaching white workers to the political leadership of the Conservatives was evident in the solid vote against a labor party cast by southern delegates to the 1866 National Labor Congress and in the allegedly "nonpolitical" posture of Richmond's trade assembly of white unions, the Mechanics' Union.

Sylvis himself fell into the Conservatives' ideological trap during the first stops on his 1869 tour of the South. He hailed every sign of business growth, reported enthusiastically on conversations with antediluvian politicians like Duff Green who admired the greenback plan, denounced the Freedman's Bureau for retarding recovery by feeding "lazy loafers," and was scandalized in Alabama by the sight of racially-mixed juries and a white politician who allowed his daughters to "entertain young [N]egro gentlemen in their parlors." Wilmington, North Carolina, he reported, was "completely under the control of the [N]egro; there is no money, consequently no business, no enterprise."

Nevertheless, as he had often demonstrated, Sylvis was able to learn, and he never forgot his mission. He visited foundries and union locals with his customary enthusiasm, chartered locals of the NLU, and in Wilmington met for the first time with blacks and invited them into the organization. "Careful management, and a vigorous campaign, will unite the whole laboring population of the South, white and black, upon our platform," he wrote from Augusta, Georgia. "The people down here, white and black, will be a unit on the great money question, because everybody is poor, and ours is a war of poverty against a moneyed aristocracy."

Sylvis died July 27, 1869, four months after his return from the South, but the fruits of his labors were plainly visible when delegates gathered in his home city for the opening of the National Labor Congress on September 4. Among the 102 delegates (the largest number ever gathered in the history of the NLU) were ten from former Confederate states, six of them iron molders. Moreover, eight black workers were seated, the first ever at an American national labor convention. Five of them came from Philadelphia and were building laborers, and the others were from Baltimore. One, Ignatius Gross, was a molder. Another Baltimorean was Isaac Myers, a ship caulker who had founded a dry dock company, financed by the black community, to employ craftsmen who had been violently driven from the city's shipyards by white workers after emancipation.

It was Myers who gave the most comprehensive speech on behalf of the black delegates. In his address, which the press said was "much applauded," he praised the memory of Sylvis and hailed the NLU for "taking the colored laborer by the hand and telling him that his interest is common with yours." He went on to stress the common interests of workers of both races in organization, good wages, and shorter hours, but he emphasized the point that white workers who barred blacks from employment erected an impassable barrier in the path toward unity. "If American citizenship means anything at all," Myers explained, "it means the freedom of labor, as broad and universal as the freedom of the ballot." Moreover, he saluted President Grant as "a strong friend" of the country's workingmen, who was "thoroughly endorse[d]" by the "colored men of this country."

These propositions made it clear that, although black trade unionists had decided to participate in the NLU, they were also going to establish a national organization of their own. Myers returned to the National Labor Congress of 1870 along with two other blacks, and when the Industrial Congress of 1873 revived the national movement, Richmond's black tobacco workers were prominent participants, and one of them (Warwick J. Reed) was elected its first vice-president. Meanwhile a black labor congress had met in December 1869, with Myers in the chair, and had established an organization that also called itself the National Labor Union. Its purposes were to combat the exclusion of blacks from trades, to encourage black trade unions and cooperatives, and to support the Republican party while urging it to provide the former slaves with schools and with land redistributed from southern plantations.

If the blacks who participated in the NLU had other ideas than Sylvis's of what was needed to secure the workers' citizenship, so did the white women. The four women who were seated at the 1868 National Labor Congress were unmistakably from the "intelligent 'middle classes,'" as they spoke openly of their real estate and servants. Susan B. Anthony, Elizabeth Cady Stanton, Mary A. MacDonald, and Mary Kellogg Putnam were all concerned with the exclusion of women from American public life—with their inability to vote or to run for office and with their legal and social subordination to their husbands. The failure of the Republicans to support women's struggles had alienated the suffragists from men whom they had once considered allies. Not only had the Fourteenth Amendment establishing national citizenship rights been enacted with the qualifying phrase "male," but also New York, Connecticut, Michigan, and Kansas had all rejected amendments to their state constitutions that would have enfranchised women during 1867. In January 1868 Stanton and Anthony had participated in founding the *Revolution*, a paper dedicated to "educated suffrage, irrespective of sex or color." Conspicuous in their platform, however, was also a demand for "Greenbacks for money. An American System of Finance." Currency reform was no passing fancy; it occupied many columns of the *Revolution*, which also declared: "The principles of the National Labor Union are our principles." Moreover, delegate Putnam was the daughter of the earliest advocate of greenbacks, Edward Kellogg.

Stanton chaired the Committee on Female Labor at the 1868 congress and presented a report that urged women "to learn trades, engage in business, join labor unions, or form protective unions of their own, secure the ballot, and use every other honorable means to persuade or force employers to do justice to women by paying them equal wages for equal work." Although the report was roundly praised from the floor, many delegates demanded that the words "secure the ballot" be eliminated. They were, and the report as amended was adopted. This by no means marked the end of the women's role. Not only did they participate vigorously in the debates as a whole, but they also proposed Kate Mullaney, leader of the collar starchers' union of Troy, for second vice-president, and she handily won the election even though she was not at the congress. Mullaney's victory was short lived, however, because both vice-presidents could not come from the same state, and Henry Lucker of New York had already been elected first vice-president. Nevertheless, on the last day of the congress the delegates empowered Sylvis to appoint Mullaney "assistant female secretary" charged with organizing women workers.

Two questions had thus overlapped in the congress' deliberations: the social and political rights of all women, and the earnings and organization of wage-earning women. They had been disposed of in significantly different ways. Paradoxically, although no wage-earning women were present and Mullaney herself confessed that she was "under the idea that female delegates would not be admitted," women's economic needs proved to be the subject most readily understood by the male delegates. Women were no strangers to the American workplace. According to the census of 1870, 25.8 percent of all nonagricultural wage earners were women (1,281,700). To be sure 902,000 of them were domestic servants, the largest single occupational group recorded by the census. Still, one out of every ten industrial wage earners was a woman, and most daughters of the working class expected to work for wages at least until they married and raised children. Moreover, many women working in the textile, paper, and shoe industries had longer tenure on the job than the highly transient male operatives. A significant minority of New England's working women, in fact, either never married, married quite late in life, or were widowed young. The myth of "domestic bliss" had little relevance to their experience and thinking.

Sylvis was one of many male trade unionists who found it much easier to understand the economic needs of women wage earners than women's protests against their subordination in marriage and political life. He had married twice, both times to women in their teens whose lives quickly became devoted to the raising of children. His first wife seems to have seen him mostly when he was ill or recuperating from an organizing trip, and she died when she was only twenty-four. "Woman," Sylvis asserted unhesitatingly, "was created to be man's companion, not his slave," but the proper place for that companionship was as "queen of the household." There she might exercise the moralizing and comforting influence that was her "true worldly mission." Even his ardent plea for the eight-hour day was couched in terms of reuniting the family from which long hours of toil had kept the man—"a little time transferred from the busy workshop to the quiet family circle." The worst of all vultures, he proclaimed, were those men who drove their wives into the labor market.

Nevertheless, he called upon the labor movement to champion the demands of the woman who was in the workshop. "If we leave her behind, capital will not be slow to unsex her, and place her in many of the channels of labor now occupied by us," he warned the molders in 1867. "She must have the same inducements, and derive equal benefits from the reform we are striving to accomplish, to make ourselves secure." He envisaged two ways that man, "her natural protector," could aid the struggles of working women. One was to encourage unions and cooperatives of the type Kate Mullaney led among the collar laundry workers of Troy. The other was to boycott and hold up to public opprobrium those bosses who shamelessly exploited their female employees. Women workers were far more favorably impressed by the first tactic than by the second. Many of them did join unions, especially in the shoe and printing industries, but a woman whose denunciation led to a boycott of her employer was simply fired.

Moreover, in the same speech Sylvis called explicitly for woman's suffrage. Six months earlier he had written cautiously in the *Molders' Journal* that a "limited female suffrage" might help reform society. Women, he had then argued, should be allowed to vote on "all questions involving a moral issue," such as liquor licensing, the use of tobacco, and the reduction of working hours; but he did not explain how this was to be accomplished within a system of representative government. Now, in his 1867 convention speech, Sylvis saluted the leadership of no less radical a Republican than Senator Benjamin F. Wade of Ohio, long a champion of women's rights, and called for the admission of women to the suffrage, to higher education, and to the whole realm of public involvement.

Sylvis's advocacy of active citizenship for women never persuaded the NLU, but it did encourage a close working relationship with Stanton, Anthony, and the *Revolution* group during the last years of his life. When vigorous objections to the seating of Stanton as representative of the Women Suffrage Association of America were raised by some New York building trades delegates to the 1868 NLU congress, Sylvis vigorously and successfully defended her right to a seat. He then soothed disgruntled delegates by moving a resolution saying that admitting Stanton did not commit the NLU to endorsing her organization's objective. At the next congress the antifeminist hostility was aimed at Anthony, and a move to oust her was led by the typographical union, which charged her with supplying scabs to struck printing houses. Faced with the ultimatum that if she did not leave the congress the prestigious printers' union would, a majority of delegates voted to evict Anthony.

Sylvis was then dead. Whether he could have prevented the second confrontation (as Anthony believed), one can only speculate. Nevertheless, his efforts on behalf of women's participation in the movement had not been in vain. Strong support had been expressed for Anthony in 1869 by representatives of Massachusetts' shoe workers and especially by Martha Wallbridge, a shoe worker who had been the only other woman at the congress. Wallbridge returned to the 1870 congress as first grand directress of the Daughters of St. Crispin, the country's largest union of female workers. She had won its leadership during the previous spring because of her vigorous support for woman's suffrage. Her antisuffrage predecessor, the current second grand directress Mrs. Emma Lane, was also a delegate to the congress, as was Mrs. E. O. G. Willard of the Chicago Sewing Girls' Union, who was elected the NLU's second vice-president. During the same year Augusta Lewis, a pioneer organizer of women printers, was elected corresponding secretary of the International Typographical Union.

In short, by the time of Sylvis's death, a first small group of working-class women was making its appearance in the leading councils of the labor movement. Simultaneously and, perhaps more significantly, despite the intensity of the controversies the suffrage question provoked among women activists, outspoken foes of women's social and political subjugation were becoming increasingly prominent in their ranks.

Sylvis had lived through a creative epoch in the history of American workers. Out of the profound social revolution that destroyed slavery, reshaped the federal Union, and secured the grip of an industrializing elite on the machinery of national government, workers in many occupations had perceived a need to create new organizations and to cultivate a mutualistic code of ethics in defense of their own interests. They believed that in a society in which most people earned their livelihoods by creating wealth for others, citizenship and collective self-organization were inseparable. It was Sylvis's special talent to describe that connection in a way many people could grasp and to rally their efforts around precisely designed programatic objectives. His powers of concentration produced a single-mindedness that often alienated others, especially after he had fixed on the goal of currency reform. Even then, however, he worked effectively to reach out to other social groups and bring them into the orbit of the labor movement.

Shortly after his election to the presidency of the NLU, Sylvis met with Augusta Lewis and her sister printers, who had been brought together by Susan B. Anthony for the purpose of getting them into the International Typographical Union. He explained to the gathering why labor's struggles had necessarily begun with trade unions. Unions had gathered workers in a common cause and through their strikes and struggles had provided "a good schooling." It was only because of the unions that workers enjoyed "our present success in cooperation." With cooperatives and with political struggle, he continued, working people could now "abolish the wages system." Universal liberty and universal suffrage went hand-in-hand with "universal labor and co-operation." This vision of labor reform was to inform the workers' movement for the next twenty years and to be most distinctly embodied in the Knights of Labor.

Bibliographic Notes

The record of Sylvis's life was carefully assembled by his brother, James C. Sylvis, in *The Life, Speeches, Labors and Essays of William H. Sylvis* (1872). Archives of the Iron Moulders' union are now housed in the Sylvis Library in Cincinnati, Ohio. That collection and the Labor Collections of the State Historical

Society of Wisconsin provide the best holdings of labor records from the 1860s. Valuable documents have been reproduced in John R. Commons et al., *Documentary History of American Industrial Society*, 10 vols. (1910–11), and in Foreign Languages Publishing House, *Documents of the First International* (1964). The most informative newspapers of the epoch are the Chicago *Workingman's Advocate*, the Boston *Daily Evening Voice*, the Philadelphia *Molders' Journal*, the Philadelphia *Fincher's Traders Review*, and the New York *Revolution*.

Insightful nineteenth-century accounts of the National Labor Union and its epoch may be found in Friedrich A. Sorge, *Labor Movement in the United States*, translated and edited by Philip S. Foner and Brewster Chamberlin (1977); [Obadiah Hicks], *Life of Richard T. Trevellick* (1896); and George E. McNeill, *The Labor Movement: The Problem of Today* (1887).

Three biographies of Sylvis are available: Jonathan Grossman, *William Sylvis: Pioneer of American Labor* (1945); Reed C. Richardson, *Labor Leader, 1860s* (1961); and Charlotte Todes, *William Sylvis and the National Labor Union* (1942). Of the three, Grossman's is by far the most thorough and reliable account. The history of the National Labor Union is recounted at some length in four larger historical works: John R. Commons et al., *History of Labour in the United States*, vol. 2 (1921); Philip S. Foner, *History of the Labor Movement in the United States*, vol. 1 (1947); Norman J. Ware, *Labor Movement in the United States, 1860–1895* (1929); and Gerald N. Grob, *Workers and Utopia* (1961).

The political and social context of Sylvis's activity is analyzed in my own *Beyond Equality: Labor and the Radical Republicans, 1862–1872* (1967). Two accounts of the iron molders are indispensible: James E. Cebula, *Glory and Despair of Challenge and Change* (1976), and Henry E. Hoagland, "Rise of the Iron Molders' International Union," *Iron Molders' Journal* 49 (June 1913): 295–313. Black workers of this epoch are analyzed well in Charles H. Wesley, *Negro Labor in the United States, 1850–1925* (1927), and Peter J. Rachleff, "Black, White, and Grey: Working Class Activism in Richmond, Virginia, 1865–1890" (unpublished Ph.D. dissertation, University of Pittsburgh, 1981). My interpretation of the relationship of the woman's suffrage movement to the NLU has been strongly influenced by Ellen Carol DuBois, *Feminism and Suffrage: The Emergence of an Independent Women's Movement in America, 1848–1869* (1978).

Terence Powderly, The Knights of Labor, and Artisanal Republicanism

2

Richard Oestreicher

For fourteen years, from 1879 to 1893, Terence Powderly led the Knights of Labor, the largest organization of American workers in the nineteenth century. He was the first labor leader in American history to become a media superstar. No other worker in these years, not even his rival Samuel Gompers, captured as much attention from reporters, from politicians, or from industrialists. To his contemporaries Powderly *was* the Knights of Labor, and the Knights of Labor were a symbol of the central dilemma of a new industrial age: "the labor question."

The Knights argued that while industrialization offered great promise of social progress, its control by "aggregated wealth" was an "alarming development" that, if unchecked, would "lead to the pauperization and hopeless degradation of the toiling masses." Such degradation not only raised the specter of unjustifiable poverty in the midst of growing plenty but also threatened the basis of the American republic: an independent citizenry whose patriotism and virtue were guaranteed by the knowledge that equal rights and equal opportunities were available to all.

Various events in the post–Civil War era suggested that such fears were not unduly alarmist. In 1877 the entire country had been paralyzed by a great railroad strike, the largest strike anywhere in the world in the nineteenth century. In Chicago, St. Louis, Baltimore, Reading, and dozens of smaller railroad towns, tens of thousands of people had joined striking railroad workers who blocked railroad tracks and confronted state militias. In Pittsburgh nearly two miles of Pennsylvania Railroad tracks, depots, offices, and warehouses lay in smoldering ruins along with 104 locomotives and 2,152 railroad cars. The Knights were not responsible for these outbursts. Indeed, in many cities their leaders had tried to restrain angry crowds. But that anger was the raw material that helped to swell the

Knights to three quarters of a million members by 1886, and the Knights were quick to suggest that while they opposed violence, prolonged injustice could only lead to dire consequences.

Industrial conflict continued. The Knights, however, did not last. By the turn of the century only scattered vestiges (about twenty thousand members) remained, and Powderly had long since left the labor movement for a career as a government bureaucrat. In retrospect, both to many contemporaries and to later historians, the rise of the Knights of Labor appeared as a transitory outburst, and Powderly seemed less a genuine labor leader than a man on the make—a middle-class reformer, a pious windbag, a crank whose years in the Knights were a temporary interlude. And like those observers who had equated him with the entire organization, they saw the Knights as a mirror image of their leader: a collection of cranks motivated by frustrated petty bourgeois ambitions and nostalgic visions of a nonexistent preindustrial utopia. Such losers, they argued, had shown themselves unable to adjust to progress and change and had earned a well-deserved oblivion. The Knights were historically important only for the contrast between their fuzzy-minded reformism and the hard-headed pragmatism of their successors in the American Federation of Labor (AFL).

The thesis of this essay will be nearly the reverse: The Knights should be remembered not for alleged lessons to be drawn from their extinction but for their capacity to bring workers of different backgrounds and experiences together at a critical moment in American history. The Knights cannot be understood simply by reducing them to a reflection of their leader. Powderly was *not* the Knights of Labor, but he led the order at a time when, more than any other organization in nineteenth-century America, the Knights helped to focus a national debate about how the egalitarian vision of America's revolutionary tradition could be reconciled with the realities of concentrated wealth and power in an emerging corporate society.

Artisanal Republicanism

Terence Powderly was born in 1849 in Carbondale, Pennsylvania, a small mining and industrial community astride the rich anthracite coal deposits of northeastern Pennsylvania. His parents, Margery and Terrence Sr., had left Ireland in 1827, landing in Montreal the day after the birth of their first child. According to Powderly's autobiography, they arrived shortly thereafter in Ogdensberg, New York, with "one English shilling," but his father found work with a local farmer. After a couple of years they migrated 200 miles south to Carbondale.

It is likely that this account of early poverty is exaggerated. Throughout his career Powderly was never one to let the facts stand in the way of improving a story, and when he wrote his autobiography (just before 1920) he was already aware that scholars had begun to challenge the authenticity of his working-class credentials. At least by 1849 the family was fairly prosperous. His father, after fifteen years as a coal miner, had opened his own mine in 1845 and was on his way to becoming a respected member of the community. In 1851 he was elected to Carbondale's first city council. One of the main roads into town was named after him. The family lived in a six-room frame house. Like his brothers, young Terence remained in school until the age of thirteen before he went to work.

Small mines like his father's were precarious enterprises. By 1858 increasing competition in the anthracite industry had driven the elder Powderly out of business, but he found work as a mechanic in the Delaware and Hudson (D & H) Railroad shops. His business failure does not seem to have lowered his status in the community; he was still acquainted with some of the valley's most important businessmen, ties he was able to exploit to place his sons in good jobs. Young Terence, for example, began work on the D & H as a switch tender, progressing quickly to car examiner, car repairer, and brakeman before his father apprenticed him in 1866 to James P. Dickson, master mechanic of the D & H and father of Thomas Dickson, future president of the D & H and cofounder of the Dickson Manufacturing Company, the second largest employer in nearby Scranton.

Like his father, young Terence Powderly had ambitions. "I had higher aspirations," he admitted later, but serving as James Dickson's apprentice "would do for a starter." In an expanding industrial area like the anthracite region, craft skills could lead, he believed, to industrial entrepreneurship, just as they had done for the Dickson family. Powderly's brothers had similar hopes. At various times Huge and Joseph, as well as young Terence, tried running grocery and dry goods stores as well as small industrial firms. Hugh, like his father, became a Carbondale city councilman, while Terence would one day be mayor of Scranton.

As the mobility studies of social historians demonstrate, the seemingly erratic careers of both generations of Powderlys—from miner to mine owner and back to railroad mechanic, from apprentice to artisan to store owner and back again—were not especially unusual. The Powderly work histories, their political careers, and their access to prominent local families tell us something very important about the culture and relatively fluid social structures of Carbondale, Scranton, and other small northeastern industrial communities like them.

In such communities the dominant culture in the antebellum years was

Ohio Historical Society

neither proletarian nor really middle class. It was a world of homeowners, workers, and small businessmen who made their livings working with their hands, producing goods or serving those who did, and the social boundaries between classes were indistinct. Personal proprietorships and small enterprises were not beyond the hopes of an industrious artisan. But small firms faced tough competition and fluctuating demand; many failed. Still, failures did not discourage others, and towns like Carbondale and Scranton had many small mines, little metal shops, and tiny factories producing consumer goods like clothing or cigars, or corner groceries and neighborhood saloons that served the working population. Self-employed artisans or former coal miners who ran such businesses worked alongside their employees and lived amidst wage-earning neighbors who were their clientele. Miner and small mine boss patronized the same barber shop, prayed in the same church, and read the same newspaper.

Artisans and small businessmen were not the whole community. Below them was a large floating pool of unskilled workers: the mine laborers in the large mines, trackhands and ditch diggers who laid the rails and dug the canals, helpers and hands in the big ironworks and railroad shops. At the top, the small group of truly wealthy were beginning to distance themselves more clearly from the rest of the community. The artisans themselves were far from homogenous; they were Irish, Welsh, German, and American born, Catholic and Protestant. Yet despite these differences most of the community subscribed to a similar set of republican values, priding themselves in citizenship in a land unique in the extent to which virtue and industry, not privilege and inheritance, were the sources of status and reward. They filtered this republican ideology through their own experiences and through different ethnic and religious traditions. Republicanism did not mean the same thing to a mine laborer or a successful entrepreneur. And as industrial communities like Carbondale and Scranton changed dramatically in the next generation, these differences sharpened. Yet even when people in the community divided in bitter industrial conflict, they fought their ideological battles on the same terrain using the same set of intellectual categories.

The intellectual foundations of the community's republicanism were moral and religious; political and economic prescriptions rested on moral assumptions. As Terence Powderly said in 1879, God "in the beginning of creation . . . ordained that all things tangible should have certain qualities . . . [and] these qualities determine their fitness for the use of man." God had also given human beings the capacities to use these things "to produce the materials that promote the happiness of all." To do so, to produce, was "the highest and noblest duty of man to himself, to his fellow man and to his Creator." Work, human labor, was thus not only the source of all human happiness and all human progress but also a moral imperative. Labor was noble and holy. Through labor human beings produced all goods of value to themselves and society, but equally important they fulfilled the creative capacities that made them human.

Arguments for republican government and social equality flowed from this moral vision. The laborer deserved the fruits of his toil. Those who labored hardest most deserved reward; those whose thrift and investment increased the capacity to labor, to produce, and to satisfy human needs practiced the highest virtue. But only where all had an equal chance to labor, where all had an equal voice in determining the rules that governed their behavior, would labor be respected and virtue be rewarded. In a just society each human being must have the opportunity to labor, to prove his or her capacities, to have virtue rewarded. Each must have an equal chance to become unequal. Such inequality of rewards, prosperity justly earned as the product of hard work and thrift, was the natural outcome of a republican order. Capital that was the legitimate result of past labor was virtue embodied. Hence there could be no fundamental conflict between productive capital and labor so long as each respected the virtue and hard work of the other and accorded to each his or her just rewards. A republican society guaranteed the equal opportunity to labor, guaranteed to each the fruits of his or her toil, ensured that no arbitrary social distinctions offered special privileges to some, and gave equal rights to all.

Upon this sanctity of labor rested the other republican virtues. Respect for labor would generate a productive and energetic populace, the basis of a commonwealth in which individual efforts would reinforce a united quest for the public good. A productive citizenry would be an independent citizenry, free from intimidation and from the threat of political manipulation that leads to corruption. But protection of these virtues demanded constant vigilance. Americans lived in a world of aristocratic privilege; nor was their own society safe. Where privileges did emerge, so would the power to oppress, and the oppressed were dependent. From these twin evils, privilege and dependence, flowed all the social ills that accompanied political corruption.

To artisans in Carbondale in the 1860s, like the aspiring machinist Terence Powderly, this ideology both reflected much of their actual experience and sustained them when life did not match the ideal. For Powderly, for example, his father's rise from immigrant miner to city councilman confirmed the possibility of opportunity. His own apprenticeship contract offered only the most meager wages, and it must already have been evident that the metal trades were changing in ways that would make the all-around

35

machinist like master Dickson obsolete. Yet James Dickson's instructions in the "arts and mysteries of the machinist trade" instilled a fierce craft pride along with technical skills. Dickson carefully nurtured this pride and the republican values implicit in it, and when Powderly completed his apprenticeship, Dickson presented him with a set of tools that symbolized the deeper meaning both men gave to their labor. Dickson had served his apprenticeship under George Stephenson, the inventor and builder of the world's first practical locomotive, and Stephenson had given him a set of tools upon the completion of his training. These he gave to Terence Powderly. "Through the hands of James Dickson they passed from George Stephenson to me," Powderly wrote, "so you needn't wonder that I prize them highly." We need not wonder also why Powderly, throughout his life, could never fully comprehend doctrines of class conflict. It would have been difficult for him to feel injustice at the hands of an employer like James Dickson. "A kinder man or better mechanic I never met than James Dickson."

Changing Times

The ideology of artisanal republicans like Terence Powderly asserted the dignity of their labor and their right to social equality. It told them they would rise if they were virtuous, feeding ambitions fueled not so much by acquisitiveness—their culture's emphasis on thrift suggests asceticism more than conspicuous consumption—as by immigrant backgrounds and hard lives. While enough of them moved up a bit to give their dreams some substance, for most people daily life revolved not around advancement but around maintaining their precarious footholds on respectability. Perhaps their assertions of the dignity of labor, their insistent claims for respect, would not have been quite so insistent if the realities of it had been more secure.

Already in the generation before the Civil War in many American cities and towns the consequences of the railroad and canal booms, the beginnings of a modern banking system, the reorganization of industries, and the emergence of national markets had aroused widespread anxieties about the futures of artisanal republicans. To entrepreneurs or successful master craftsmen the dramatic acceleration of industrial and commercial activity that these changes made possible fulfilled their vision of the limitless possibilities of a republican society. But artisans whose skills were based on earlier modes of craft production now found themselves competing against machines or unskilled and underpaid "slop" workers who repetitively performed a single step in a subdivided process that the artisans had once carefully executed from start to finish. To such artisans, the merchant capitalists who bought the machines or the masters who hired "slop" workers were a new form of aristocrat whose wealth and power were built on oppression and whose greed not only undermined the craftmen's status but also threatened the republic. As early as the 1830s such conflicting reactions to economic development had fractured the republican consensus along class lines, leading to strikes and widespread protest in mill towns and large cities like New York, Philadelphia, and Boston.

Until the late 1850s the geographic isolation of the anthracite region had insulated Carbondale's workers from the full impact of these changes, but in the decade after the Civil War, the basic structures of the coal industry and the entire local economy were fundamentally altered in ways that threatened their security. Even the self-employed found their prospects increasingly depended on distant economic forces beyond their control. Everything in the region seemed to rise and fall with the national market price for coal. The anthracite coal fields had developed slowly beginning in the late 1820s. Carbondale had been one of the few anthracite mining communities with effective transportation outside the region. But in 1856 the Delware, Lackawanna, and Western (D, L & W) Railroad linked Scranton with New York. The Delaware and Hudson, the earlier line through Carbondale, began systematically acquiring coal lands in self-defense, and the D, L & W followed suit. Scranton soon dwarfed nearby Carbondale as it swelled from a small village, to a town of 9,000 in 1860, to a city of 35,000 in 1870. Terence Powderly moved there in 1869 after he was laid off by the D & H in Carbondale. By the early 1870s the two railroads controlled over half the coal lands in the northern anthracite coal field around Scranton and Carbondale. Concentration of ownership did not proceed quite as rapidly in the other anthracite fields south of Scranton, but several large corporations there, most notably the Reading Railroad, were also buying up coal lands. Overall, six major firms had emerged in the region.

Concentration of ownership had several consequences. Large-scale purchasing of coal lands, building longer rail lines, and sinking deeper mine shafts all demanded initial capital outlays far beyond the capacity of even the largest local entrepreneurs. Virtually all of the key mining, manufacturing, and transportation firms in the area came under the control of New York and Philadelphia financiers, and local industrialists like William Scranton and Thomas Dickson became hired managers for distant investors. Having invested heavily in coal deposits and transportation systems, these firms had to expand rapidly in order to cover their investments, but ownership was not sufficiently concentrated to facilitate effective price control.

The onset of depression following the financial panic of 1873 worsened conditions in the anthracite region. Major coal operators who had cut wages by as much as thirty percent in 1870, cut ten percent more in 1875, another ten percent in 1876, and a further fifteen percent in 1877. Everyone in Scranton and Carbondale suffered along with the miners. The small stores who depended on working-class customers could not sell to their unemployed or underpaid neighbors. The railroads, which depended on coal shipments for revenue, laid off workers and cut the wages of those they kept on. The industrial firms who catered to the mines and railroads responded in the same way. The D, L & W, for example, sharply cut wages for its shop hands and machinists; their machinists wages fell fifty-eight percent in the year 1876 alone.

Led by skilled miners and by machinists, one of the few crafts with an effective national union, miners, railroad workers, and metalworkers throughout the anthracite region tried to organize to resist the downward drift. At first they stressed the conservative and defensive nature of their goals. The Workingmen's Benevolent Association (WBA), the union of anthracite miners, attempted to portray itself as the regulator of an industry in which mine owners as well as miners suffered from the consequences of an erratic and capricious market. This posture reflected both strategic considerations—the desire to enlist community support to sustain miners through strikes and to diminish the likelihood of legal suppression—and the republican ideological heritage that depicted mineowners and miners as coproducers now victimized by distant investors who reaped the fruits of the producers' toil in the form of unearned speculative profits. The machinists similarly asserted their desire "to harmonize . . . the interests of society. . . . Capital is as dependent on Labor as Labor [is] on Capital."

The WBA was never able to overcome the rivalries between operators in the various anthracite fields and the cultural and ethnic divisions among miners. Welsh and Irish even confronted each other violently from opposite sides of the picket line. Nearly all of the many miners' strikes between 1868 and 1871 ended in defeat. The remnants of the WBA were extinguished in the Long Strike of 1875, and when Irish miners attempted clandestine resistance through their fraternal society, the Ancient Order of Hibernians, Franklin Gowen, president of the Reading Railroad, hired Pinkerton detectives to infiltrate their ranks. Nineteen so-called Molly Maguires, alleged Irish terrorists, were hung between 1877 and 1879 after trials in which Gowen himself had served as prosecutor. Miners, railroad workers, and machinists in the Scranton area fared little better. Miners' strikes in 1871 and 1877 ended in death and defeat, as did railroad and machine shop strikes in 1876 and 1877.

Amidst this cycle of declining wages, periodic unemployment, violent picket line battles, and defeated strikes, workers turned to political action. While many small businessmen had supported workers in these struggles, the key business leaders in Scranton had remained intransigent, categorically refusing to entertain the WBA's proposal for market regulation and personally leading armed vigilantes to break picket lines at mines and railroad shops in 1871 and 1877. William Scranton was twice arrested, at the insistence of local union leaders, for his role in these activities, but was twice acquitted. Local officials repeatedly acceded to business demands to request state militia to break strikes. Yet strikers, who had proclaimed their orderly and conservative goals all along, believed that they were doing no more than exercising their constitutional rights of assembly, claiming their republican birthright. Why should they suffer at the hands of state and local officials who had allegedly been elected to serve them? A republic that turned on its citizens, that gave a deaf ear to the suffering of the unemployed while it did the bidding of monopolists and speculative idlers was no longer true to its heritage of equal rights for all and special privileges for none. Workers took to the ballot box as they had taken to the picket line to assert their continuing loyalty to that republican heritage as well as to protect their own interests. A series of independent labor candidates in Scranton between 1872 and 1878 expressed these convictions.

An analysis of the choices of candidates, their programs, and their shifting base of electoral support shows that the experiences of the 1870s had angered a large portion of Scranton's workers but had not altered their thinking fundamentally. On the one hand, their manifestos had a provocative ring. The 1877 labor party county convention declared that "the wage worker has no hope of redress through either of the old parties." In the 1878 Scranton city elections, Terence Powderly, the party's mayoral candidate, proposed municipal public works projects, financed through low interest government loans, to provide work for the unemployed. The conservative *Scranton Republican* greeted Powderly's candidacy and proposals with horror, titling its columns on the activities of the Knights of Labor and the Greenback-Labor party with the large headline "COMMUNISM."

Yet a careful study of these campaigns shows that most of the programs of the labor candidates between 1872 and 1878 differed only in minor details from their major party rivals. In office, successful candidates behaved more like contemporary middle-class clean government reformers than like social activists. They appear to have been elected not to implement any major agenda of social change but as a protest against the antistrike policies of their predecessors.

This was clearest in 1872 when the labor candidate for Scranton's mayoralty, a veteran GOP politician and incumbent alderman, was chosen to appeal to the normally Republican Welsh miners, who had been the chief victims in the previous year's strike. Ebeneazer Leach placed second in the three-way race, receiving thirty-eight percent of the vote but carrying the Welsh miners' wards. By the fall, as strike memories faded and normal partisan loyalties asserted themselves in a national election, these wards returned to the GOP fold. Strike memories were still strong enough, however, to defeat a state militia officer as a Republican county judicial candidate in 1874, when the Welsh miners again crossed normal party lines to support the Democrat. But an attempt at another county labor ticket in 1875 fell flat, receiving less than eight percent of the county vote. Only after the 1877 strikes did the local labor party reassert itself, carrying most of the county offices in the fall 1877 elections and leading to Powderly's mayoral victory in February 1878 with nearly fifty-five percent of the city vote.

Historians have argued extensively whether labor politicians of this era, like Powderly, and the organizations that spawned them, especially the Knights of Labor, were fundamentally backward looking or progressive, basically conservative or implicitly class conscious. I believe that they were both.

Workers in Scranton and much of industrial America had come into the 1870s with an underlying but often unarticulated loyalty to republican values. The conflicts of the late 1860s and 1870s stimulated many of them to think explicitly about what those values meant to them and how their understanding of republican principles must be different from that of their employers and their political leaders, who seemed to profess the same ideals yet cut their wages and called out troops to break their strikes. Not surprisingly, their responses suggest convention and tradition, but recognizing such continuities in their thought should not lead us to miss how important the process of articulation itself was. Only as workers began to express their beliefs could they start to act together to shape a new industrial order. The presence of class politics, even for limited goals, even with erratic support, reflects workers whose thinking was in transition and not mired in the past.

Scranton's labor mayor was a case in point. Powderly was eminently respectable, a family man, a teetotaler, in many ways a cultural conservative. He assured those who worried that he was loyal to law and order and that he respected the sanctity of private property—good traditional republicanism. His conduct during his six years as mayor did little to lead local businessmen or conservatives to doubt that loyalty and respect. Yet during those same years Powderly was also a national official in the Clan Na Gael, an Irish-American secret society pledged to liberate Ireland through armed struggle, a secret member of the Socialist Labor party from 1880 to 1882, and the national leader of a labor organization pledged to the destruction of the wage system, the Knights of Labor.

From Journeyman to Grand Master Workman

The seemingly contradictory ideological loyalties of Scranton's new labor major reflected his mixed reactions to the changes in his community. In many respects Powderly's thinking was still shaped by the world of his boyhood and by his continuing desire for personal success, yet his associations with radical Irish nationalists, monetary reformers, and socialists exposed him to new doctrines. The labor mayor still thought in the ideological categories of his past but not in the same ways that journeyman machinist Powderly would have only nine years before.

He completed his apprenticeship in the summer of 1869 and was promptly laid off as the D & H cut back operations in response to the WBA's first industrywide strike. Not until the end of the year did he find regular employment as a machinist for the D, L & W in Scranton. He worked there for four years with occasional layoffs.

Powderly later claimed that the 1869 miners' strike first stimulated his interest in the labor question. He was distressed, he said, when he realized that "there was . . . so little sympathy . . . [among] workingmen generally for the striking miners." His fellow machinists and shopmen blamed the miners for their layoffs. When John Siney, the WBA organizer, spoke in nearby Avondale after a terrible mine disaster, Powderly alleges that he traveled there to hear Siney and express his sympathy. "I caught inspiration from his words and realized . . . for the first time that day . . . a call to the living to neglect no duty to fellow man."

An examination of Powderly's diary suggests no such sympathy. He did not travel to Avondale that day, although many of his shopmates did. He did not join the machinists union until the end of 1871 and did not participate in the 1871 labor conflicts in Scranton. Indeed, given the nature of his community and his later career, he seemed remarkably uninterested in labor affairs before 1872. He read avidly, mostly literature, probably seeking inspiration for his efforts to become a professional writer, an avocation that consumed much of his spare time in those years.

Exactly why he became active in the local machinist's union in 1872 is unclear. Perhaps he recognized a possible outlet for his talents and ambi-

41

tions. Once he did become active, his skills as a writer, speaker, and organizer quickly impressed his union brothers. He was elected local president in February 1873 and corresponding secretary later that year. His tendency to gravitate toward the more bureaucratic union tasks, a tendency no doubt welcomed by less-educated associates who felt unsuited for these functions, reveals something basic about his personality, his relationships with fellow workers, and his approach as a labor leader. Throughout his life he felt uncomfortable with the earthier side of male working-class camaraderie, and all through his career he was more enthusiastic about keeping records, answering letters, drafting constitutions, or writing pronouncements than about addressing crowds or socializing with his supporters. Such preferences and skills help to explain his rapid rise in the labor movement and also some of his eventual failings. It is hard to detect in his private writings any of the intense emotion or deep empathy for working-class suffering that seem to have fired many other labor leaders of his era.

His role as a local union official quickly brought him into contact with a wider circle of sophisticated labor activists. Such contacts both provided avenues for advancement and a clearer rationale for his activities. The national leaders of the machinists were in the forefront of trade unionists who were trying to rethink the meaning of republican ideology. Inspired by the democratic idealism of the Reconstruction era as well as his analysis of the changing structure of industry, Ira Steward, their leading theoretician, compared the plight of wage and chattel slaves, asserting the need to republicanize labor just as Radical Republicans in Congress were trying to republicanize the formerly slave South. "The anti-slavery idea," Steward wrote, "was that every man had the right to come and go at will. The labor movement asks how much this abstract right is actually worth without the power to exercise it." Although workers were nominally free, they had to work to survive, and in industries dominated by large corporations or requiring considerable capital investment for entrance, the opportunities for work were controlled by capitalists who set terms that made workers into wage slaves little better off than the black slaves so recently freed. As Steward's associate George McNeill explained, theoretical freedom of contract was no freedom at all for the wage worker. "The laborer's commodity perishes every day beyond possibility of recovery. He must sell today's labor today or never. . . . An empty stomach can make no contracts. . . . [Workers] *assent* but they do not consent, they submit but they do not agree." "The answer," union president John Fehrenbatch declared to the machinist's 1874 national convention, "looms before us: to be freed from the slavery of the *wages system.*"

42

To Steward, McNeill, Fehrenbatch, and their supporters like Terence Powderly, the demand for abolition of the wage system did not mean an abandonment of their earlier republican concepts or a call for socialist revolution. To them property was not theft but stored up labor. In part such rhetoric was designed to capture the imagination of audiences who had just witnessed the abolition of slavery after a great civil war and to wrap themselves in the mantle of the abolitionists who had also seemed like a visionary minority but had lived to see their vision realized.

It also indicated how interpretations of republicanism were fracturing along class lines. For such artisans hard work, honest labor, self-denial, and virtuous behavior did not seem to be leading to just rewards but to pay cuts, lost strikes, and unemployment. To them earlier formulas no longer rang true. Wealth, not virtue, was becoming the measure of individual worth. Workers, they believed, now had to organize not only for their own protection but also to recapture the republic from monopolistic plunderers and to protect their republican birthright for themselves and their posterity.

Only a minority of working-class activists in the 1870s, however, were prepared to follow the implications of these arguments toward a full-scale confrontation between wage earners and employers. In part this reluctance reflected the continuing hold of interpretations of republicanism that emphasized the harmony of interests between journeymen and small manufacturers, themselves former journeymen, who had struggled to proprietorship and now found themselves victimized along with their employees by the cutthroat competitiveness of aristocratic monopolists and unproductive speculators. In part it also reflected their awareness of the precarious weakness of most labor organizations and their desire for sympathetic allies. Such allies were to be found in the ranks of a variety of other contemporary movements: greenbackers and monetary reformers, land reformers, and Irish nationalists. Greenbackism, as a movement of small manufacturers, farmers, and workers, embodied the producerist alliance of traditional republican theory. It also provided an explanation of why financial speculation oppressed producers and how the monetary system could be regulated to increase opportunities for all industrious citizens. Land reform offered an alternative to wage labor, an alternative reinforced by the arguments of Irish nationalists, who drew parallels between the land struggles of Irish peasants and the struggles of American farmers and workers.

That labor activists grounded their critique of postwar industrial America in the moral assumptions of traditional republicanism does not mean that they nostalgically sought to recapture the past. Nor was their analysis a middle-class outlook divorced from the experiences of ordinary workers.

They were workers, and what they proposed on the basis of their own experiences was a program designed to adapt republican morality to a new industrial order: worker-owned firms or producer cooperatives, monetary reform to make cheap credit available to workers, a shorter work day without a cut in pay to allow workers the time for education and self-improvement, and increased government regulation of the economy to ensure genuine equality of opportunity. It did not take Powderly long to absorb most of these ideas, and he did so at a time when he first experienced protracted unemployment, severe economic hardship, and victimization for his union activities. These personal experiences sensitized him to the plight of other workers and made him receptive to the quest for solutions to workers' problems.

In October 1873, within weeks of the national financial panic, the D, L & W discharged Powderly along with a large number of his fellow workers. Over the next two years he was repeatedly unemployed for several months at a time. He was blacklisted and forced to accept prolonged separation from his wife and family when he had to leave Scranton in search of work. He became depressed, doubted himself. Not until November 1875 was he again able to find steady work in Scranton, and the following year his wages were sharply cut. Finally, in May 1877 he was discharged once more. He never did work as a machinist again.

By then he was already nationally known in labor reform circles. He had attended national conventions of the machinists' union, had become a protégé of Fehrenbatch and a rival for top union leadership, had been active in the Industrial Brotherhood (a national federation of trade union leaders and labor reformers designed to supplant the defunct National Labor Union), had been a chief organizer for the local Greenback-Labor party for more than a year and a district officer of the burgeoning Knights of Labor. After his firing he became a full-time organizer for the Scranton district of the Knights, which had virtually taken over the Greenback-Labor party in the region. As he entered local politics more seriously, he became active in Irish fraternal associations both because his exposure to Irish radicalism in the labor movement had kindled a deeper awareness of his own heritage and because he recognized that political success demanded a wider political base than the labor movement alone could provide. With this ethnic base as well as his labor credentials, his nomination as the Greenback-Labor mayoral candidate in 1878 was no surprise, nor was his election the following year as grand master workman of the national organization of the Knights of Labor after Uriah S. Stephens, the founder and first master workman, resigned.

The Knights of Labor

The Knights of Labor began in Philadelphia in 1869 as a secret society founded by Stephens and other former members of the Philadelphia Garment Cutters Association, a local craft union of skilled clothing workers. At first the motives of the majority seem to have been craft related: to keep "loose-mouthed members" from revealing union plans to employers, to prevent persecution of union activists, and to stem the influx of "incompetent workmen" that was exerting downward pressure on the wages of skilled workers. For the first year the majority rejected proposals that they accept as members workers from other trades.

Stephens, however, had loftier goals. He was convinced that industrial development had rendered isolated craft unions obsolete. Union efforts at negotiations and strikes, at best temporary expedients, usually failed. Such unions were inherently incapable of resisting the superior power of unjust employers. More importantly, they did not address the cause of the degradation of labor: "the present arrangement of labor and capital . . . capital dictating, labor submitting; capital superior, labor inferior."

Equally important, many workers, in his experience, absorbed with the daily struggle for survival and divided by ethnic and religious prejudices, competed with each other in a spirit of greed and narrow self-interest hardly different from that of unscrupulous employers. Only if workers could come together, amalgamate in a "great brotherhood" pledged to mutual aid and cooperation, could they understand that "an injury to one is the concern of all." Only then could they hope to abolish wage slavery and emancipate the wage earner.

In these same years, federations of union leaders like the National Labor Union and the Industrial Brotherhood were seeking to organize labor more broadly, but they failed to inspire a widespread sense of solidarity among rank-and-file workers. Stephens had another model. He had been a Mason, an Odd Fellow, and a Knight of Pythias. Such fraternal organizations impressed him with their organizational stability, large following, and capacity to command intense loyalty. Here was a tradition with existing roots in the popular culture of the working classes. At one time Stephens had also trained to be a Baptist minister. He recognized that although workers were divided into many religious denominations, the underlying tenets of Christian theology common to all—individual moral responsibility and human brotherhood—seemed to provide a basis for inspiring solidarity.

The Knights of Labor, Stephens hoped, would amalgamate labor by individually educating workers, pledging each to mutual aid, cooperation, and brotherhood. Such a labor fraternity could grow into a grand labor army far more effective in defending workers' immediate interests than any narrowly based union and capable of laying the foundation of the Cooperative Commonwealth that would liberate workers from wage slavery. Many of those who had first joined Stephens in the Knights were motivated by similar concerns. They convinced the others that their organization had to go beyond the garment cutters' craft by seeking out worthy artisans from other trades who could be taught the principles and ritual and who could then serve as missionaries, carrying the message to fellow workers in their trades who would join together in assemblies like their own.

Little of either the basic ideas or the organizational style of the Knights was original to Stephens and his friends. His analysis of labor's dilemma, his devotion to mutualism and to the Cooperative Commonwealth, mirrored the concerns of other trade unionists, such as the machinists. His emphasis on more broadly define solidarity was the essence of all the attempted labor federations of the decade. Many trade unions adopted secret rituals for the same reasons as the Knights. Across the country dozens of similar societies sprang up in the decade after the Civil War. We know less of the internal details and early histories of the others because none were as successful as the Knights, but their proliferation suggests that what the Knights preached found a large and ready audience.

Perhaps the Knights succeeded because their particular mix of labor republicanism and fraternalism overlaid with Christian phraseology was somewhat different, and also perhaps because Stephens and the other early leaders were particularly able organizers and propagandists. Equally important, they were situated close to the two most important coal mining regions in the country—the anthracite region of northeastern Pennsylvania and the bituminous region around Pittsburgh—at a time when other miners' unions were being decimated. After honeycombing the Philadelphia area with local assemblies in the early 1870s, the order spread quickly through the coal regions in the mid–1870s. When Terence Powderly took over national leadership in 1879, at least half of their 9,300 members were coal miners and almost fifty-four percent of the local assemblies were miners' locals.

Between 1879 and 1882 the Knights spread beyond this regional base, increasing their following among coal miners, establishing beachheads in most major metropolitan areas, recruiting a substantial cadre of energetic trade union leaders, creating craft organizations within the order for window glass workers and telegraphers, and absorbing the remnants of the Knights of St. Crispin, the national shoemakers' union. In early 1882 they relaxed their secrecy in order to publicize the organization and make recruiting easier. Membership, which had already reached 40,000 in 1882, topped 100,000 by the summer of 1885.

The Knights had accomplished something no one else before had been able to do in American history: they built a genuine labor federation from the ground up. They had supporters in nearly every city and town in the United States with a population over 8,000. Their leaders, recognized as national labor spokesmen, had been called to testify before congressional committees and investigations. Their members wrote and edited most of the rapidly expanding labor press. Hundreds of Knights had been elected mayors, public officials, and state legislators. Within their ranks were workers of virtually every race and nationality, nearly every major industrial occupation.

And then something even more remarkable happened. Since 1883 the Knights had led an increasing succession of large strikes. In most cases only small fractions of the strikers were members of the Knights, and usually the Knights national leaders tried to discourage local organizers from undertaking the strikes. Yet as the recognized spokesman for labor, local and district leaders of the Knights were repeatedly brought in to lead strikes and serve as negotiators, directing great publicity to the order and reaping the organizational credit for the Knights. In the summer of 1885 the Knights won the most dramatic strike so far—a general strike on Jay Gould's Southwestern rail system—probably the greatest strike victory up to that time in the United States. Gould was the most well known example of a Wall Street tycoon, the Southwestern was the largest rail system in the country, and the contract signed by railroad officials and Knights of Labor officers was one of the first written contracts between a major American corporation and a national labor organization. The Gould victory further accelerated a national strike wave, unleashing one of the largest groundswells of popular protest in American history, stimulated even more the next spring by an audacious attempt to institute the eight-hour work day all across the country at once by means of a national general strike. Powderly disavowed the eight-hour day strike, but perhaps a half million workers participated, and local Knights of Labor leaders were its main instigators; that spring workers flocked into the Knights. In a single year the Knights membership increased sevenfold, reaching 700,000 by July 1886.

This was far more than an organizational triumph. Everywhere the Knights seemed capable of mobilizing wider audiences than their own ranks. In Rhode Island textile mill centers, southern cities, midwestern rail junctions, and manufacturing metropolises the Knights organized torch-light parades, mass demonstrations, and monster rallies denouncing their oppressors. They entered local politics, overnight creating local labor parties in more than two hundred cities and towns. And everywhere they built on older traditions of mutualism, ethnic and craft fraternalism, and neighborhood identity to organize a vibrant movement culture incorporating drama and singing clubs, picnics and social events, militia companies and marching bands, newspapers and debating societies. For millions of workers they had kindled the hope that republican dreams were not yet dead. As a Rhode Island labor editor wrote that spring "labor breathes freer . . . than ever before. The time was, and not so long ago, when an artisan in the presence of his employer or overseer scarcely dared say that his soul was his own, or speak above a whisper; but the Order of the Knights of Labor has changed all this. There is an atmosphere of independence on all sides. It is felt in the workshop, the mill, the cars, on the street; even the boys and girls show a spirit that they lacked before."

The labor question became the number one political topic of the day. Independent labor candidates for mayor in New York and in Chicago, the two largest cities in the country, although defeated, each received nearly a third of the votes in elections that winter, while labor candidates were successful in Milwaukee, Rutland (Vermont), and many smaller towns. That year a larger percentage of American workers organized, struck and boycotted, marched and rallied, voted for labor candidates, and supported a vast array of movement cultural activities than would do so again for more than a generation.

The Knights stood at the center of this activity and helped to make it possible, first because their rhetoric had inspired workers coming from diverse backgrounds and experiences to believe that their problems were related, and second, because their organizational structure made it possible to bring all of the major trends within the labor movement under a single umbrella. The order's ideology was ambiguous, perhaps purposely so, an ambiguity that both explains why subsequent scholars could disagree so basically about the organization's character and why activists with quite different objectives could use it as a vehicle. Slogans like "abolition of the wage system" could be interpreted by radicals as euphemisms for socialist revolution, whereas to artisanal republicans like Powderly and Stephens these slogans evoked a much more modest call for evolutionary reform. To working-class politicians and political reformers, the Knights offered a ready-made political base. To unionists in isolated or tactically weak crafts, it offered potentially vast organizational resources and an unmatchable capacity for mutual assistance. To moralists, it was the embodiment of Christian brotherhood and a source of moral uplift. To feminists, it was one of the few predominantly male organizations that allowed full participation by women. To demoralized artisans undergoing skill dilution and loss of status, it offered the hope of escape. To workers suffering through long hours of hard work at low pay, its growth and success were an antidote to fatalism, living proof that working people could organize and change the world.

That the Knights could offer solutions to such a wide range of needs tells us as much about the American working class and American industry in the 1880s as it does about the Knights. The United States was an extraordinarily large country in which modern mass production technology coexisted with cottage industries. Such contrasts could be found not only by moving from region to region or industry to industry but also in nearly every large city by moving from one side of town to the other. These differences in industrial scale, technology, and organization meshed with equally dramatic variations in the cultures and backgrounds of the workforce. Black tobacco workers in Richmond, German furniture workers in Chicago, native railroadmen in Iowa, or second generation Irish machinists in Scranton's railroad shops brought different memories and traditions into different work settings. Yet in the years in which the Knights flourished, all were finding it difficult to meet their needs alone. The Knights ultimately represented an historical moment of mutual recognition.

But such varied people still had different understandings of just what the Knights were. The order's ritual, structure, and rhetoric tried to produce a spirit that could overcome craft, ethnic, regional, and ideological differences. In fundamental ways the appearance of unity that common symbols and ritual provided was artificial. The Knights had not overcome the basic fragmentation of the American working class, but had provided organizational forms that could partially supercede it. None of the basic tactical or ideological disagreements between labor activists were worked out. Quite the opposite. They made common cause, buoyed by the élan of an expanding movement, each perhaps convinced that their vision would win out in the end.

Until 1885 most of the order's activities were directed by local and district organizers, and apparent centralization was illusory. Powderly and other national officers conceived of themselves mainly as propagandists (they called it "education"), not administrators. Powderly treated his office as a part-time job until 1884, as did most of the other national officers. The full-time national office staff was smaller than that of a medium-sized twentieth-century local union. Before the upheaval of the mid–1880s, most potentially divisive strategic decisions by national officers could be avoided.

Factionalism

After the great upheaval of 1886, however, Powderly and other leaders could no longer avoid difficult decisions for at least three reasons. First, the Knights were subjected to a furious counterattack by employers. Except for the eight-hour day strike, most of the largest strikes of the year were lockouts; often renunciation of Knights of Labor or union membership were preconditions for reemployment. Powderly found himself overwhelmed by an increasing number of pleas for help from members whom the order was morally bound to assist. The survival of the organization seemed to be at stake. Some action by national officers and, more importantly, an unambiguous national strike policy could no longer be avoided.

Second, by elevating the labor question to the center of national consciousness and debate, the events of the mid–1880s threatened many other groups besides the immediate participants. In the polarized climate, as workers were generally more assertive, all employers were nervous. Some tried to be conciliatory, but others became more determined to resist any invasion of their authority. Moreover, craft unionists, especially those in stronger and more stable crafts, who had maintained harmony with the Knights in the early 1880s, sometimes even wholeheartedly supporting them, now began to change their minds. They were afraid that anxious employers might be unwilling to respect the craft prerogatives that they would normally concede, prerogatives that some Knights of Labor officials also seemed inclined to ignore. Equally important, many trade union leaders found entire locals deserting them for the Knights; their organizations might be threatened by this popular enthusiasm for the Knights. Likewise, politicians recognized that the Knights' capacity to inject class loyalties into local politics might reshape the political balance in virtually every major city and industrial town in the country. Such political realignment potentially threatened everyone with a stake in urban politics, from real estate developers and building contractors to saloon keepers and ward heelers.

Finally, the Haymarket bombing in Chicago on May 4, 1886, provoked the country's first major Red Scare. When eight Chicago radicals were convicted of the bombing that summer, no evidence had been uncovered directly connecting any of them with the act, but to the judge and prosecutors, to the jurors, to most newspaper editors, and to middle-class conservatives, the eight men symbolized what they perceived to be a growing threat to property and public order. The defendants had to be punished in order to send a message to the labor movement and to the working class in general. To many labor activists that message was no more than an order to cease and desist in their efforts to end working-class oppression. The defendants were comrades and fellow workers whose only crime had been to speak out against injustice. If they could be convicted on such flimsy grounds, no labor organizer would be safe. How would the Knights respond? Would they stand with those who feared disruption of order or would they send back another message of defiance by defending the men as victims of unjustified judicial attack?

Powderly and the other national leaders of the Knights faced five strategic issues: strike policy, political tactics, craft prerogatives, the Haymarket defendants, and internal authority. Would they urge strikers to hold out, mobilizing financial support and publicity in their behalf? Or would they pressure strikers to settle wherever even a semblance of compromise was possible? Would they endorse the proliferation of labor candidates and commit the organization's resources to political campaigns? Would they soothe the ruffled feathers of craft unionists and skilled workers within the order, surrendering autonomy over immediate craft issues as both groups had begun to demand? Would they denounce the Haymarket defendants, thus freeing themselves from the taint of guilt by association? or would they join the national campaign to support the defendants' appeals and urge the governor of Illinois to commute the death sentences? Finally would they force on the ranks whatever decisions they reached, attempting to exert an internal discipline where none had existed before?

Powderly's answers to each of these questions reflected a series of related assumptions. Only systemic reform, he believed, could alter the status of workers or fundamentally improve their basic conditions. Whatever short-term gains were won through strikes and other forms of direct action, they were at best only marginal improvements that did not affect the basic wage relationship. But systemic change would only come about after a long period of agitation. In the meantime, confrontation was counterproductive. Strikers and their families lost wages, he believed, they were unlikely to regain; they were the victims of picket line violence. Needless disruptions of production also harmed innocent bystanders, such as shopkeepers or workers in industries dependent on those on strike. Employers as well as workers had to be taught the wisdom of reform, but confrontation made employers less receptive to reasoned persuasion. The Knights could play a critical role in the educational process that would be a prerequisite to any meaningful change. It was, therefore, his responsibility to follow policies that would ensure the order's stability and survival.

Translated into practice, these assumptions led Powderly to actively oppose strikes and to evaluate political campaigns cautiously. He tolerated craft prerogatives only as an unfortunate necessity. He denounced the Haymarket defendants and relentlessly fought any attempt to swing the organization behind the clemency campaign. Finally, he tried to purge those within the Knights' hierarchy who opposed his policies.

Powderly had always expressed skepticism about the value of strikes. At first this was a practical judgment as much as an ideological one, the result of witnessing the dismal record of defeats in the anthracite region during his years of political maturation. This opinion was not far out of step with most other labor leaders of his generation, and it was consistent with republican morality, which shunned social strife and activities that would polarize classes. Only the revolutionary Left, who believed that strikes educated workers about the brutalities of capitalism, unequivocally encouraged strikes. Most nonrevolutionary labor leaders were more cautious, trying to restrain rank-and-file enthusiasm for strikes, convinced that only carefully planned and limited struggles had a reasonable hope of success. One of the primary objectives of emerging union bureaucracies was to create formal mechanisms to control strike initiatives.

Yet in the crisis that the upheaval of 1886 had unleashed, Powderly went far beyond this conventional wisdom, resisting support for nearly all strikes, apparently unwilling to recognize that strikes had often been forced on workers. Even cautious trade union leaders who tried to dissuade workers from striking usually acknowledged a responsibility to defend strikers once a strike had started, yet Powderly seemed increasingly indifferent to the plight of striking members, even those who had been locked out. This attitude provoked astonishment and then outrage among strikers and even among some of Powderly's closest associates. A Mississippi local wondered why their letters went unanswered. They were being forced to strike, yet their letters asking for advice had gone unanswered. "Must we do just what the factory men say, if so, it was of no use of Organizing a lodge of K. of L. . . . We had better disband and not Pay our monthly dues . . . and forward our charter from whence it came." As Tom Barry, Powderly's chief critic and opponent on the Knight's general executive board, argued in 1887, locked-out textile workers in his native Cohoes, New York, who were refused financial aid by the executive board "were freezing and starving to death." Local Knights of Labor leaders whom he visited in Clifton, South Carolina, the following year had been locked out and evicted from company houses "because of their allegiance to the K. of L.," and Barry found them sharing "their last pound of corn meal" with fellow workers. They too found their request for $500 denied. But Powderly was convinced that too many strikes threatened the order's survival, setting it up as an unjustified target for employers, and he was willing to go to any lengths to make his point. He not only opposed virtually all appeals for strike assistance but also publically denounced strikers in the heat of battle. To Barry's disgust, Powderly ordered 20,000 Chicago stockyard strikers back to work in November 1886, on penalty of expulsion if they disobeyed, just when Barry, the negotiator, believed he was on the verge of reaching an agreement with packers. Not surprisingly, Knights of Labor membership in the yards dwindled rapidly thereafter.

Although Powderly was himself a veteran labor politician who had repeatedly lamented the failure of most workers to vote according to their interests, his reaction to the local labor party movement of 1886–87, like his reaction to the strike wave, was cautious and unenthusiastic. The order's objectives were political, he admitted, but partisan politics threatened the organization's survival. Most workers had intense partisan loyalties conditioned by political cultures in which party labels were highly charged symbols of ethnic and religious identity. For that reason, Powderly had repeatedly forbidden local assemblies to discuss candidates or parties in the assembly room for fear that such discussion would provoke disruptive hostilities. Locals were urged to consider political questions in the abstract and then leave political action to individual choice. Intense lobbying efforts in behalf of various bills in the early 1880s, however, led many of the Knights' officials, including Powderly on occasion, toward a more activist version of this political nonpartisanship, as they hoped to increase the number of "friends of labor" in state legislatures and in Congress through "reward your friends" campaigns similar to those later pursued by the AFL. Many of his associates viewed the labor party movement in that light.

But Powderly worried that, in the political climate of 1886, attempts to oust incumbent urban political machines would appear as confrontations much like mass strikes and invite similar counterattacks against the order. Thus while he continued to issue lengthy theoretical promulgations on such issues as monetary or land reform, which he urged members to remember on election day, he opposed formal participation by the Knights in labor parties or direct commitment of their resources. Such a posture satisfied neither those who were even more skeptical than Powderly about political action nor those who felt that his failure to act more energetically was cowardly and even traitorous. When most of these labor parties faded badly by late 1887, Powderly felt vindicated, but his growing array of opponents held him at leastly partly responsible.

By that time the anger of craft unionists, who felt increasingly embittered by the Knights alleged disregard of craft interests, provided ammunition for factional opponents alienated by Powderly's other decisions. In this role within the factional struggle inside the Knights much more than through the rivalry of their new union federation, the AFL, the craft unionists helped to seal the order's doom. Powderly's critics had generally welcomed, not feared, the unrest and confrontations of the mid–1880s. By 1887 they had become convinced that Powderly was sabotaging the movement. His policies, they believed, were largely responsible for the sharp decline in the Knights' membership already visible by July 1887. His denunciations of the Haymarket defendants, still facing the gallows in November, seemed like a fundamental moral breach of the Knights' code of solidarity, and as Powderly counterattacked by suggesting that his critics were really all anarchists bent on destruction of the organization, they accused him of dictatorially attempting to squash dissent.

Led by dissenting executive board member Tom Barry, critics coalesced into an anti-Powderly faction and began mobilizing all of the groups alienated by Powderly's policies in hotly contested district elections for delegates to the upcoming 1887 Minneapolis general assembly. Yet in an atmosphere of organizational crisis, even delegates doubtful about many of Powderly's policies feared that open opposition at such a nationally publicized event could only further harm the order. As the general assembly convened in October, opening credential fights over several contested delegations quickly revealed that Powderly retained firm control over the organization's administrative apparatus. On two key votes over resolutions censuring Powderly's conduct in the packinghouse strike and urging support for the Haymarket clemency appeal, while opponents mustered a third of the votes, Powderly was sustained. General Secretary Charles Litchman privately cautioned Powderly that control was still in doubt. "It would need but little to turn against us many who were on our side at Minneapolis. . . . Many who voted with us were only luke warm in their fidelity," motivated more by loyalty to the order than by agreement with Powderly's policies. But the opponents were so alienated that they abandoned further debate and stormed from the hall after the final roll call on the Haymarket resolution.

About thirty-five delegates, one quarter of the general assembly, met in Chicago on their way home to form a provisional committee to continue their campaign against Powderly or to lead a secession from the Knights. But Powderly's opponents were bitterly divided among themselves, as craft unionists, German Marxists, and native and Irish non-Marxist radicals had quite different bases of opposition. Perhaps as a result the opposition did not seem, even to some of Powderly's most bitter critics, like a credible alternative. None of the provisional leaders, even Barry, the most well known among them, approached Powderly's national stature. Whereas dissatisfied locals were ready to question Powderly's policies, they did not want to threaten the continued existence of the organization "that is the only hope of the working man." John Ehmann, a Wheeling, West Virginia, delegate who had attended the Chicago provisional meeting, explained to another of the provisional leaders that his "position as a kicker is approved but not as a seceder." His local refused to endorse the provisional committee. Equally important, by the time Powderly's opponents had begun to organize openly against him, the enthusiasm and hopes that had propelled the Knights the year before had already been shattered. Rank and filers discouraged by strike defeats or disillusioned with national policies were far more likely to quietly withdraw from their assemblies than join a fight for control of the organization. Still, for the next six months the organization was consumed with a bitter factional struggle as districts debated often wildly conflicting general assembly delegate reports and fought out contests for district officers. Barry toured the country openly denouncing Powderly and the other national officers, but it was clearly a losing battle. Powderly supporters in many districts began expelling critics, a process culminating in October in Barry's expulsion from the Knights by Powderly's order. Barry contested the order at the 1888 general assembly, on constitutional grounds—only locals were authorized to expel individuals—but the general assembly overwhelmingly endorsed Powderly's action.

Powderly appeared to have won every round in the factional war, but his victories were pyrrhic: he had regained supremacy in an organization that was melting away around him. By the fall of 1889 membership was back to where it had been before the great upheaval of the mid–1880s. Its 120,000 members still made the Knights a substantial organization, but now they were faced with a rival trade union federation, the AFL, which had already topped 200,000 members. The Knights most energetic organizers, people who had built the order in the late 1870s and early 1880s, were deserting in disgust. Even Powderly's factional victory was only temporary. The same issues reemerged, and in 1893 a coalition of ideological critics joined forces with a group of personal rivals centered around a former Powderly ally, General Secretary Treasurer John W. Hayes, to drive Powderly from office.

The Knights, trading on their name perhaps, still attracted small groups of new adherents throughout the 1890s, but few believed any longer that they were harbingers of the Cooperative Commonwealth. With their decline went most of the impressive array of working-class political, cultural, and educational institutions that had flourished in the 1880s. The Knights had provided a critical institutional glue that made it possible for an ethnically and sectorally divided working class to come together in such activities. The AFL, with only 300,000 members as late as 1898, neither captured more than a fraction of the former Knights nor attempted to maintain most of the subsidiary movement activities that the Knights had directed.

Powderly's later career was anticlimatic. After a surprisingly half-hearted attempt to rally friends and supporters to regain his position in the Knights, he abandoned the labor movement completely. Although still sought after by reporters and editors for his opinions on labor questions, it became increasingly difficult for him even to exercise the honorific role as labor statesman and speaker to which his earlier credentials and reputation should have entitled him. Labeled as an "enemy of labor" both by AFL leaders and by many former Knights, he was often subjected to organized heckling when he did speak, and he found labor opposition one of the main obstacles when he sought appointments to government jobs.

He faced a brief financial crisis after he left the Knights. He tried to find work as a machinist but no one would hire him, considered going into business but had no capital, and decided to return to legal studies he had abandoned before he joined the Knights in the 1870s. An ironic choice, given the Knights opposition to lawyers as parasites (only lawyers, bankers, liquor dealers, and gamblers had been prohibited from initiation into the Knights), it fit his bureaucratic talents. Accepted into the Pennsylvania bar in September 1894 he successfully practiced law in Scranton and entered local Republican politics. After campaigning actively for McKinley in 1896, he was rewarded the following year with an appointment as Commissioner General of Immigration. He was removed by Teddy Roosevelt in 1902 after a dispute over his firing of corrupt officials at Ellis Island. Between 1902 and 1907 he participated in several business ventures as well as continuing his legal career, while he struggled to exonerate himself from the charges that had been brought against him. Finally in 1907 President Roosevelt appointed him to another post in the Bureau of Immigration, and he continued there, and later in the Department of Labor, until his death in 1924.

Historical Judgement

Powderly had hoped to steer the Knights of Labor through the crisis of the 1880s and preserve the organization for its great mission, yet he failed. While the circumstances that the Knights confronted—the diverse and conflicting backgrounds and needs of American workers, the depth of opposition, and the stability of American capitalism—would have ensured rough going for the Knights in any case, Powderly's leadership during the Great Upheaval made the situation worse.

Yet Powderly had been an energetic and capable organizer, who had risen quickly in the labor movement and won widespread acclaim early in his career. By the mid–1880s hundreds of thousands of Knights admired him. They carried his picture on their parade banners, named their local assemblies after him, and wrote him letters asking for advice because they saw in him someone who had also suffered from the consequences of industrialization, someone who expressed their fears and kindled their hopes. Powderly was an able exponent of the ideas he had learned from other activists and reformers in the 1870s, ideas that reinterpreted the republican symbols most Americans accepted in ways that helped to explain the reasons for workers' distress. His intense desire for respectability can also not have seemed out of place to working-class republicans whose nightmare was the destruction of artisanship and the descent into wage dependence. His analysis of their problem captured their imagination; his prescriptions for its solution looked forward, as well as back, to a new era in which technological progress would blossom, solving age-old problems of poverty and want, but in ways that would reward traditional values of hard work, thrift, and individual morality. Why then did he do so poorly at the critical moment? By 1886, although Powderly still had sufficient support among the artisanal reformers in the Knights local and national leadership to keep control of the organization, he seemed increasingly out of touch with the immediate practical needs of craftsmen, strikers, and local activists.

Powderly's own accounts of the Knights' demise and the end of his career as a labor leader provide no explanation. In *Thirty Years of Labor*, published in 1889, he belittled the order's dwindling membership totals claiming that peak figures had been exaggerated (in fact they had probably undercounted the number of participants), he denounced all of his critics as anarchists or fools, and he predicted a rosy future for the organization. His autobiography, written shortly before 1920, although less belligerent and self-confident, is equally uninstructive. It is full of rationalizations for his most controversial decisions, repeats his earlier accusations that his opponents had been anarchists bent on destroying the organization, and asserts that all "true knights" had always supported him.

Perhaps the transparent self-justification of these laments does suggest one explanation for his ultimate failings as a leader: ambition and vanity. Powderly's diaries, private correspondence, and public statements reveal a self-centered and self-glorifying personality, convinced that extraordinary talents destined him to greatness and obsessed with his success and personal advancement. Throughout his early years, one of his biographers argues, Powderly never made decisions without considering their impact on his career. In the mid–1880s, when he earned a salary of $5,000 a year (plus generous expense allowances) as general master workman, an amount that was at least ten times the annual income of an average worker, he constantly complained of the great financial sacrifices he was making in behalf of an ungrateful membership. He was flattered by the attentions of industrialists, senators, and big city newspaper reporters, impressed with the politeness and civility of even such bitter antagonists of the Knights as Jay Gould. Seen in that light, his cautious anticonfrontation policies may have been influenced by a desire to maintain approval among the powerful people he came to refer to as "the best men."

Yet certainly an equally crucial source of Powderly's mistakes was the limitation of the artisanal republicanism that had inspired his early success. While he may have drifted from real empathy with his members, his ideas were not out of touch with working-class culture and traditions. They were, nonetheless, wrong. Most importantly, artisanal republicanism attempted to straddle two divergent interpretations of republican assumptions. On the one hand, the labor theory of value and the insistence on the sanctity of labor led to an increasingly sharp critique of acquisitive individualism and unbridled accumulation of wealth; on the other hand, the insistence that property was the fruit of toil and that its use should therefore be free and unrestricted, undercut much of that critique. On this basis, however, artisanal republicans continued to insist on a doctrine of class harmony that seemed unrealistic in a world not of small workshops but of large corporations and mass strikes.

The apocalyptic predictions of the consequences of industrial development proved equally misguided. While the work settings and authority of most skilled workers were fundamentally altered over the next generation, given the enormous expansion of industry, the absolute demand for skilled labor increased. Nor did industrial development, as Powderly had believed, make workers' struggles over immediate demands hopeless or obsolete. Quite the contrary, industrialization created new opportunities for struggle and improvement at the same time that it wiped out old ones. Wage and shop floor control struggles would continue to be at the heart of all working-class movements, even the most visionary, for the next half century. Nor were the efforts of skilled workers to maintain the prerogatives of their crafts necessarily an elitist anachronism. Many trades effectively defended their prerogatives, successfully adjusting even to fundamental changes from hand to machine production, and such struggles would produce rebels as well as labor aristocrats for some time to come. Powderly was also wrong in his hope that moral appeals to middle-class good will would lead in the short run to systematic arbitration of labor disputes and in the long run to widespread recognition of the necessity for alternatives to the wage system.

Yet none of these ideas were as idiosyncratic as Powderly's harshest historical critics suggest. The debate over immediate demands versus ultimate goals was, and continued to be, one of the staple questions for labor and the Left. The belief that capitalist development, left unchecked, would quickly proletarianize the entire working population, wiping out distinctions of skill and craft, was as fundamental to Second International Marxism as it was to Powderly's artisanal republicanism. Powderly's appeals to good will or his distinctions between good and bad capitalists are not so different from Gompers' defense of the National Civic Federation. The difference, perhaps, was that in each case Powderly let theory carry him beyond the point at which good judgment might have restrained others with similar ideas.

Ultimately, however, explanations based both on personality and ideology must be tempered by the reality of the difficulties that anyone would have faced who tried to alter the basic character of a society that was becoming the pacesetter and bulwark of twentieth-century world capitalism. Quite simply, no one else did much better than Powderly or the Knights over the next forty years. As Norman Ware perceptively summed it up more than fifty years ago, for all their failures the Knights "put the labor movement on the map." They popularized the code of solidarity that made all future activity possible. They trained the next generation of activists. We need only consult the many labor organizers' autobiographies—Haywood, Abraham Bisno, and Oscar Ameringer come to mind first—that credit the Knights with first kindling their sense of justice and solidarity in order to appreciate the order's legacy. Unless we take the position that any attempt to remake the world is a priori misguided, Powderly and the Knights must be viewed with admiration and respect as well as with the wisdom of critical hindsight.

Bibliographic Notes

The Powderly and Hayes papers housed at the Catholic University of America, but widely available on microfilm in major university libraries, include Powderly's diaries and personal correspondence, the Knights' incoming correspondence files for the years he was master workman, general assembly proceedings, and some district proceedings. The labor press of the era is also an indispensable source of information on the Knights, especially because national sources give such a poor picture of the local nature of the organization. Among the papers I have read most extensively are the Knights' own *Journal of United Labor*, *John Swinton's Paper*, the Denver and later Chicago *Labor Enquirer*, the Chicago *Knights of Labor*, and the Detroit *Labor Leaf*. The Labadie Collection at the University of Michigan includes many letters, newspaper clippings, and pamphlets collected by one of Powderly's most vigorous critics. Michigan also owns (in the Michigan Historical Collections) a microfilm copy of Tom Barry's scrapbooks (originals still in the possession of his descendants).

Powderly tells his own story and defends his decisions in his two books, *Thirty Years of Labor* (1889) and *The Path I Trod* (1940). Both, in addition to presenting his point of view, include information on his background and on the early history of the Knights available nowhere else, but both should be used with extreme caution. Many statements in each are inaccurate or untrue.

Jonathan Garlock's "Knights of Labor Data Bank" (available through the Inter-University Consortium for Political Research) and unpublished Ph.D. dissertation, "A Structural Analysis of the Knights of Labor" (University of Rochester, 1974), allow us to describe and analyze the organizational development of the Knights more accurately than before. Some of the key assertions in earlier accounts of the Knights can be effectively disposed of by means of Garlock's quantitative analysis.

The best overall descriptive account of the Knights is still Norman J. Ware's *Labor Movement in the United States, 1860–1895* (1929). Ware did not have access to Powderly's papers; his book includes many minor factual inaccuracies. Moreover, it suffers from the tendency prevalent in all of the early studies of the Knights to generalize about a widely dispersed and extremely heterogeneous organization on the basis of a few national leaders and events. Yet Ware comes as close as anyone to grasping the essential nature of the Knights and appreciating their historical significance. No student of late nineteenth-century labor history can afford to ignore this book.

The most influential exponents of the point of view that describes the Knights as retrogressive and middle class are Selig Perlman and Gerald Grob. Perlman's narrative history of the Knights in John R. Commons' *History of Labor in the United States*, vol. 2 (1918) is less pejorative to the Knights than his more analytical *A Theory of the Labor Movement* (1928). Gerald N. Grob's *Workers and Utopia* (1961) develops Perlman's argument in greater detail.

Beginning in the late 1960s, many scholars have reexamined the Knights from a point of view similar to the one in this essay. David Montgomery's *Beyond Equality: Labor and the Radical Republicans, 1862–1872* (1967) helped to stimulate this reinterpretation. These works include Paul Buhle, "The Knights of Labor in Rhode Island," *Radical History Review*, Spring 1978; James Lazerow, "'The Workingman's Hour': The 1886 Labor Uprising in Boston," *Labor History*, Spring 1980; Gregory Kealey and Bryan Palmer, *Dreaming of What Might Be, The Knights of Labor in Ontario, 1880–1900* (1982); Leon Fink, *Workingmen's Democracy: The Knights of Labor and American Politics* (1983); and my own, *Solidarity and Fragmentation: Working People and Class Consciousness in Detroit, 1875–1900* (1986).

Powderly still awaits a competent biographer. Vincent Falzone's *Terence V. Powderly: Middle Class Reformer* (1978) is a weak narrative account that uncritically accepts the Perlman-Grob analysis and seems completely unaware of the methodological and historiographical revolution in labor history during the last twenty years. Samuel Walker's dissertation, "Terence V. Powderly, 'Labor Mayor': Workingmen's Politics in Scranton, Pennsylvania, 1870–1884" (Ohio State University, 1973), is much better, and I have depended on it for part of this essay, but only small parts are available in print. His article "Terence V. Powderly, Machinist: 1866–1877" in *Labor History*, Spring 1978, effectively argues for Powderly's genuine working-class background. Other sections of the dissertation provide additional understanding of Powderly's background and milieu, although Walker unwittingly accepts part of the Perlman-Grob argument that he otherwise criticizes when he fails to recognize how Powderly's republicanism diverged from earlier middle-class versions of similar ideas.

Samuel Gompers and the Rise of American Business Unionism

3

John H. M. Laslett

No figure has been more important in the development of the American labor movement than Samuel Gompers. Beginning in obscurity, he rose to become a confidant of presidents, politicians, and businessmen. More than any other leader, he was responsible for bringing organized labor out of the shadows of obscurity to a place near the center of American political and economic life. He did this by articulating the singular trade union philosophy of the American Federation of Labor (AFL), which he helped found and of which he remained president almost continuously from 1886 to 1924. This philosophy eschewed the socialism and independent labor politics of most European labor movements. Instead, it upheld a form of "pure and simple" or business unionism that concerned itself primarily with advancing the immediate economic interests of workers in terms of wages, hours, and conditions of work.

By 1913 Gompers was influential enough internationally to propose the establishment of an International Federation of Trade Unions. Simultaneously, he exerted considerable influence over the labor movements in both Puerto Rico and Mexico, and during the First World War he became a crucial figure in mobilizing working people behind President Wilson's policies. In 1919 the AFL, which had begun with less than three hundred thousand members, reached almost 3 million. When Gompers died a self-proclaimed patriot in San Antonio, Texas, on December 3, 1924, his casket was drawn to the railroad station on a flag-draped military caisson furnished by the U.S. War Department.

But aside from his obvious role in union building, there is surprisingly little agreement among Samuel Gompers' biographers as to the precise nature of his achievement. Almost universally, commentators have expressed either unstinting praise or barely concealed contempt. To his research assistant, Florence Thorne, Gompers was an "American statesman" of the first rank; to labor historian John R. Commons, he was an intellectual innovator to be put alongside Karl Marx; and to sociologist Daniel Bell, he was a man who "with driving force, created the American labor movement in his own stubborn and pragmatic image."

Perhaps the most important of Gompers' detractors is Bernard Mandel, who has written the most comprehensive biography. Yet his approach, like that of Gompers' admirers, is essentially ideological. Impatiently rejecting the idea that Gompers' leadership may have been, at least in part, an accurate reflection of the interests of the skilled workers who made up the AFL, Mandel condemns Gompers for his ambition, for his hostility towards socialism and industrial unionism, and for the exclusive, aristocratic brand of labor unionism that he allegedly foisted upon the AFL. Stuart Kaufman, the most thoughtful analyst of Gompers' early life, recognizes the radicalism of his youth. Yet by ending his study in 1896, Kaufman provides us with no effective means of explaining Gompers' transition to conservatism. Philip S. Foner notes the transition but dismisses Gompers as a labor bureaucrat and a cynical opportunist who abandoned his radical opinions when they no longer advanced his career. According to Foner, Gompers spent most of his years as AFL president practicing "class collaboration on behalf of the bourgeoisie."

Seen in the overall context of the American labor tradition, these negative evaluations contain more truth than the eulogistic ones. Both the Knights of Labor, which preceded the AFL, and the Congress of Industrial Organizations (CIO), which broke away from it, reflected a broader and in many ways more accurate conception of American labor militancy than did the AFL. Yet to attribute its dominance, even though it was only temporary, to the self-conscious manipulation of one man, or even a group of men, strains credulity. For one thing, such a mechanistic approach ignores the personality of Gompers himself. It is true that Gompers was ambitious—what pioneering leader is not?—as well as being self-righteous, bigoted, and increasingly rigid in his later years. Yet he was also scrupulously honest, willing to drive himself to exhaustion in the cause of trade unionism as he saw it, and capable of great personal courage when a principle he believed in was at stake.

For many years, also, the personal rewards to be gained from high union office were rarely sufficient to tempt large numbers of skilled workers to leave the workbench simply for the purpose of self-aggrandizement. At the beginning, Gompers ran the central office of the AFL from his own New York apartment, at a salary considerably less than he had been earning as a skilled cigarmaker. In the mid–1880s, too, the Knights of Labor was considerably larger than the Federation of Organized Trades and Labor Unions (FOTLU), the AFL's immediate predecessor. It, not Gompers' organization, seemed to be the wave of the future. In fact, it was not until after 1896 that the future of the AFL was assured; and it was not until after the First World War that Gompers could afford to purchase a home of his own. None of this squares with the modern picture of the business unionist as a bloated bureaucrat living off the earnings of a hard-working union membership.

Daniel Bell's assertion that Gompers "created the labor movement in his own stubborn and pragmatic image" is misleading not only because it ignores the role played by the great mass of rank-and-file workers in building the labor movement, both in the AFL and outside it, whose views were often at variance with those of the Old Man, as Gompers came to be called; it also exaggerates the extent of his personal power. It does this because at the time of its founding, as well as for much of its subsequent career, the AFL was a federation of previously established trade unions such as the Carpenters, Iron Moulders, Cigarmakers, and Printers, who were jealous of their sovereignty, and which the executive council could do little to control. At the turn of the century, for example, Gompers lost a thirteen-year-old struggle to establish a separate strike fund that the AFL could use to aid its striking members. Thus attacks on him for refusing to commit the AFL to a sympathy strike in support of Eugene Debs's American Railway Union at the time of the Pullman strike in 1894, or for failing to make a success of the 1919 steel strike, must be tempered with the knowledge that for much of its early history the federation was too small and vulnerable to have decisively affected the outcome of these events.

My purpose in this essay, therefore, is neither to pillory nor to eulogize Gompers further, a preoccupation that can only serve to further distort his place in history. Instead I shall attempt to explore, and perhaps to reconcile, some of the conflicting views about Gompers' leadership by placing the development of his opinions in the political and economic environment in which he grew to maturity. I shall also try to judge his behavior in terms of the influences to which he was subject and in terms of the choices that were realistically open to him, not in terms of some preconceived political standard.

During Samuel Gompers' earliest years, both in London and New York, he was forced to struggle with genuine poverty; and he worked in a trade that was even more subject to the vagaries of technological innovation and international capitalist development than most other skilled occupations of

AFL-CIO

the mid-Victorian era. Gompers was born on January 26, 1850, to Dutch-Jewish immigrant parents, in a crowded cigarmakers' tenement building in London's East End. At age ten young Sam was forced to leave school to help supplement the family's income, first as a shoemaker's apprentice and then in a cigarmaker's shop in Bishopgate Street. As he sat at the worktable cutting and rolling the tobacco, Gompers sang such popular songs as "The Slave Ship," which expressed sympathy for American blacks, and "To the West," which according to his autobiography created his "feeling for America" and "his desire to go there."

Economic deprivation soon turned this desire into a reality. In 1862 the United States levied duties on European tobacco products, severely depressing the London cigar trade and rendering Solomon Gompers' income inadequate to support his rapidly growing family. The Cigarmakers' Society of England, like other British trade unions of the time, established an emigration fund, and in June 1863 the Gompers family left for New York. They arrived during the course of the racially motivated, Civil War anti-draft riots that spread near the docks; young Samuel remembered his father shaking hands with a black seaman as they left the ship, causing a crowd of angry onlookers to threaten him with a lynching. For approximately the next twenty years Gompers continued to work at his trade, moving from one cigar shop to another, engaging in trade union activities, and living at the margin of poverty even after he married Sophia Julian, also a London-born émigré who worked in his shop stripping tobacco leaves.

The world of work that the young Samuel Gompers entered was a cut beneath the relatively safe, respectable existence that still characterized such skilled occupations as printing, iron molding, or carpentry in both England and America. All of his life, Gompers remained proud of his ability to roll a cigar, even though in the London home of his parents we catch occasional glimpses of the petty bourgeois lifestyle that some of his more affluent relatives had known in Holland. Although a desire for further education was clearly present in Samuel's attendance at night classes at New York's Cooper Union, in his personal life he manifested few of the other attributes of the self-improving artisan. He was not religious; he drank quite heavily; and he put little money away in the form of savings for the future. In fact, if anything, when he arrived in the United States both his own family and the trade that he practiced were downwardly, rather than upwardly, mobile. In the early 1870s the sweated, tenement system of cigar production was introduced on an even larger scale in New York than it had been in London. By 1877 half of the New York trade's production came out of seventy large units. This was a small proportion of the approximately 1,400 cigar firms in the city, the great bulk of which were family-style tenement shops. The evils of the tenement system made a deep impression on Gompers, and one of his first political aims was to abolish it.

Two further developments exacerbated the situation. One was the arrival of large numbers of unskilled Bohemian workers in the trade, who mostly worked in the tenements and who by virtue of their peasant background had different values from the skilled German, Dutch, and English immigrants who had hitherto dominated cigarmaking. The other was the introduction of the cigar mold, a mechanical press that enabled manufacturers to break down the skilled craft into two distinct stages, bunch-making and rolling, and to employ unskilled immigrants at lower wages. As a child in London, Gompers had already witnessed the human impact of mechanization on the neighboring Spitalsfields silk workers. One of his "most vivid early recollections" was the tramp of unemployed men walking the streets for work. Now he was faced with a similar problem in his own trade. The 1870 Cigarmakers International Union (CMIU) convention prohibited union members from working with bunch-makers, and in the early 1870s many cigarmakers struck unsuccessfully against the introduction of the cigar mold into their shops. Though some Bohemian cigarmakers later organized Local 90 of the CMIU, most were at first ineligible to join the International because of their system of work.

The initial effect of these experiences was to radicalize the young Gompers. His early poverty caused him to sympathize with the toiling masses long after he had left the cigarmaker's bench; the mechanization of his trade laid the foundations for his life-long preoccupation with defending the skills of the hand craftsman; his family's enforced migration, coupled with working alongside Bohemians, Germans, and other immigrants at the cigarmaker's bench, stirred his early internationalism; and his father's evident pro-abolitionist stand when the family first came to America suggested an initial sympathy for the America Negro that remained with him throughout his first years as an AFL leader. Gompers' formal acquaintance with socialist ideas came in the years just after 1873, when he began working in the cigar shop of David Hirsch, a political immigrant from Hamburg, Germany. Here, Gompers later wrote, he read "all the German economic literature that I could lay hands on—Marx, Engels, Lassalle, and the others." Soon he was attracted to the ideas of the First Marxist International.

Although he claimed in his autobiography that he never joined the First International or any other socialist organization, the attraction was in many ways a natural one. The First International had been founded in his native city of London, in 1864, to strengthen trade unionism, restrict the international migration of contract labor, and express sympathy and support for oppressed peoples everywhere—all causes with which he could identify. In David Hirsch's shop, and in the Economic and Sociological Club that met in a room above a nearby saloon, Gompers was influenced by a number of leading socialist émigrés who had been active in the different national branches of the First International in Europe and whose views commanded respect. Among them were Hirsch himself; J. P. McDonnell, an Irish Fenian who had worked beside Marx in London as secretary of the First International; and Gompers' fellow cigarmaker Ferdinand Laurell, who had served as secretary of the Scandinavian section of the First International until he was forced into exile in the United States.

Ferdinand Laurell was Gompers' particular tutor, translating a copy of the *Communist Manifesto* for him and interpreting it "paragraph by paragraph." But Gompers was influenced also through such pamphlets as *Praktische Emanzipationswinke* by Carl Hillman, a socialist from Saxony who, unlike the Lassallean school of German socialism that emphasized political action, laid particular stress on the trade unions' role in the emancipation of the working class. Hillman argued that working-class organizations, established on a bedrock of sound financial benefits, strong trade union journals, and the pursuit of ameliorative legislation, could become the instruments of the workers' education and power. These ideas became the common stock of the Marxist trade union wing of the First International in New York, and they were incorporated into Gompers' own philosophy.

Other incidents also occurred in these early years that appeared to strengthen Gompers' commitment not simply to radical ideas but also to the kind of broadly based, inclusive unionism that he was later to reject. In the summer of 1872 Adolph Strasser, the Hungarian bunch-maker who was later to head the CMIU, established the independent United Cigarmakers as a vehicle for organizing the unskilled German and Bohemian mold- and bunch-makers who were not yet permitted into the International. Its membership was open to all "regardless of sex, method, or place of work, or nationality"; thus it accepted female as well as male immigrant workers. In November 1875 Gompers engineered the acceptance of the United Cigarmakers into the CMIU as Local 144, which for many years remained his own local union. In October 1877, partially as a response to the great railroad strike that swept the country in the summer of that year, over ten thousand New York cigarmakers came out in a general cessation of work. Gompers did not oppose this shutdown, as he was later to do in the Pullman and other mass strikes. On the contrary, in order to provide employment for evicted cigarmakers, as well as to raise strike funds, he resigned his job at Hirsch's, became superintendent of a union-operated cigar factory, and was blacklisted for four months when the strike failed.

Hence it is not surprising to find that at this point in his life Gompers, unlike Powderly and the leaders of the Knights of Labor, who did not accept a class conflict model of the labor movement, fully endorsed the Marxist concept of class struggle. "From my earliest understanding of the conditions that prevail in the industrial world," he wrote later, "I have been convinced and I have asserted that the economic interests of the employing class and those of the working-class are not harmonious. . . . There are times when for temporary purposes, interest are reconciliable; but they are temporary only."

That this belief—as well as an early willingness to accept the need for a broadly based, industrywide form of trade unionism—was not an abberation can be seen in Gompers' support for the call, put out by the FOTLU, to urge a general strike of workers in behalf of the eight-hour day to take place no later than May 1, 1886. It can also be seen in his 1888 recommendation, as president of the fledgling AFL, that the federation remodel itself on the basis of industrial divisions that would hold their own conventions, legislate on subjects of interest to their own trades and industries, and be represented by a proportionate number of delegates to the AFL. This proposal was rejected by the more conservative leaders of the craft unions, suggesting once again the exaggerated nature of Daniel Bell's claim that Gompers created the labor movement in his own image. Up until the later 1880s, his radicalism even appeared to extend into politics. In the 1876 and 1880 presidential elections, Gompers voted for the candidates of the Greenback-Labor party, and although he resisted committing the AFL to independent labor politics, in the fall of 1886 he campaigned on behalf of the Single-Taxer Henry George in his bid to become mayor of New York.

But at the same time that his early experiences were propelling Samuel Gompers towards a radical interpretation of the role of the labor movement and of the workers' position under capitalism, other pressures that pulled him in the opposite direction were at work on him. Seen from this perspective the issue becomes not, as Philip Foner and Stuart Kaufman define it, whether there was a difference between the radical Gompers of the pre–1890 years and the conservative Gompers of the later period. The important issue is to establish what were the influences that drew him away from the radicalism of his youth, and why in the end these influences predominated.

Paradoxically, part of the answer lies in the narrow and historically dated view of Marxism held by the European émigré socialists in the Cigarmakers International Union, in the First International, and in the New York labor movement with whom Gompers associated in the 1870s and the 1880s. These men had little knowledge of, and even less sympathy with, the indigenous traditions of American political reform represented by greenbackism, by land and currency reform, and by the ideals of cooperation. Brought up with the proletarian orientation of classical Marxism, which saw the factory working-class as the only one capable of presenting a fundamental challenge to industrial capitalism, Friedrich A. Sorge and the other German leaders of the First International in New York considered the demands of the native-born American reformers to be middle-class nostrums that interfered with the organization of workers at the workplace. It was this that should be the primary, if not the exclusive, function of the labor movement. In 1872 Sorge expelled the largely native-born Section 12 from the First International. Its members included third-party-oriented Victoria Woodhull and Tennessee Claflin, two ardent women suffragists and preachers of free love, as well as elements of the New Democracy or Political Commonwealth, a group of intellectuals who believed that socialism could be legislated politically by the simple device of a popular referendum. These people, Sorge stated, had improperly intruded themselves into the labor movement "either for intellectual purposes or for advancing some hobbies of their own," instead of advancing the interests of the urban working-class.

Gompers agreed with this analysis. "The labor movement holds it as a self-evident maxim," he wrote some years later, "that the emancipation of the working-class must be achieved by the working-classes themselves. There is no doubt that men with the best of intentions outside of the ranks of labor can aid the movement. We court their . . . sympathy . . . but cannot give into their hands the direction of the affairs which rightfully belong and must be exercised by the wage workers." In such statements we find much of the basis for Gompers' subsequent hostility towards the Knights of Labor and towards populism and other agrarian movements, as well as the seeds of his anti-intellectualism. One of his most persistent criticisms of the Knights of Labor was that its concept of the producing classes permitted it to include agricultural laborers, petty bourgeois shopkeepers, and even small businessmen as part of the labor movement. Similarly, he attacked the People's party of the mid-1890s and attempted to prevent political support being given to it by rank-and-file trade unionists—despite the widespread participation of those who rejected his views—because it did not consist of urban wage workers. "Composed, as the People's Party is," he wrote in July 1892, "mainly of employing farmers without any regard to the interests of the . . . mechanics and laborers of the industrial centres, there must of necessity be a divergence of purposes, methods, and interests."

But Gompers had expressed similar opinions many years before this. Some of them, in fact, were formulated as early as 1874. In the winter of that year the severity of unemployment due to the industrial depression led a Committee on Public Safety formed by First International leaders in New York to plan a mass demonstration of protest in Tompkins Square. At the last minute the city authorities, fearing a mass uprising of the sort that had occurred three years earlier in the Paris Commune, cancelled permission for the meeting. The more radical members of the committee, however, refused to call it off, with the result that on January 13 mounted police charged into the crowd, inflicting many injuries. Gompers, who was present only as a bystander, was dismayed by the results. "I saw the dangers of entangling alliances with intellectuals who did not understand that to experiment with the labor movement was to experiment with human life," he later wrote. "I saw that leadership in the labor movement could be safely entrusted only to those into whose hearts and minds had been woven the experiences of earning their bread by daily labor."

Not long after this, Gompers and his associates in the Economic and Sociological Club identified the shorter working day as the first essential step in bettering industrial conditions. Later on, this formed the basis of the eight-hour day campaign, which reached its peak in 1886 and was intimately connected with the founding of the AFL. Gompers felt that the eight-hour day could only be achieved by trade union rather than by legislative action. Hence in discussing this issue, as well as other practical steps that could be taken to improve the lot of New York's workingmen, Gompers and Adolph Strasser of the Cigarmakers Union, as well as Peter McGuire of the Carpenters, found themselves increasingly at odds with the more politically-oriented radicals, most of them outside the First International, which wished to subordinate the economic activities of trade unions to socialist party activism. In July 1876, a few days after delegates attended what turned out to be the last convention of the First International held in America, a unity conference of disparate socialist groups met in Philadelphia and formed the Workingmen's party of the United States (WPUS), known as of 1877 as the Socialist Labor party (SLP). Although active on the fringes of the New York, American (i.e., English-speaking) section of the WPUS, Gompers and his associates came more and more to reject "Socialist partyism" as the instrument of change, identifying instead "trade unions, amalgamated trade unions, and national or international amalgamation of all labor unions," as the road to the future.

In the mid-1870s Gompers and Strasser also began advocating the introduction of benefit systems and tighter administrative control into their unions. They were first introduced into CMIU Local 144, then later in the national Cigarmakers' organization. The benefit idea, which was henceforth mandatory on all Cigarmakers' locals throughout the country, was begun in 1880 with the creation of separate strike and death funds. It was extended five years later with the addition of a strike benefit. Later, a pension fund was added. An "equalization of funds" system was also adopted. This made possible the transfer of funds from a prosperous local to one in distress, thereby increasing the availability of funds to organize new workers. And finally, as a result of a constitutional admendment passed in 1885, the CMIU placed much of the power to call strikes in the hands of the international executive board.

In all of these activities, which lasted from approximately 1873 into the 1880s and 1890s, Gompers and his fellow trade unionists believed themselves to be both innovators and followers of the precepts of Karl Marx. In establishing the high-dues, high-benefits form of trade unionism in Local 144 of the CMIU in the mid–1870s, Gompers and Strasser saw themselves elaborating "a new movement," which was being "born out of the experience of the old." At the same time, by asserting the primacy of trade union action and by rejecting the attempt of theoretically inclined radicals to dominate the labor movement, Gompers believed himself to be acting according to Marx's own precepts. In a limited tactical sense, he had some justification for this view. Gompers' statements about the need for the working-class to emancipate itself accorded with classical Marxist doctrine; the General Council of the First International in London, which was dominated by Marx's circle, had endorsed Sorge's ousting of the politically-oriented Section 12 in New York; and as late as 1891 Friedrich Engels upheld Gompers' refusal to permit the American Marxist SLP to secure indirect representation in the AFL via its association with the Central Labor Federation of New York.

In reality, however, Gompers' claims on both these points were somewhat specious. At best they reflected a rather superficial and relatively fleeting moment in the development of Marxism in the 1860s. This was a period when the revolutionary tide that had flowed so strongly in 1848 had temporarily ebbed, when the "new model" craft unions had come to dominate the British labor movement, and when the passage of the Ten Hours Act and the agitation for parliamentary reform in England dictated that pressure group tactics, rather than the immediate establishment of an independent working-class political party, constituted the best strategy.

But this was a tactical road only. That Marx had not given his approval to the English "new model" unionism as the optimal type of labor organization was demonstrated clearly in 1867 when he criticized them for seeking to prove their respectability before the British Royal Commission on Trade Unions, saying they had "offered up the principle of Trade Unionism on the altar of middle-class legitimisation." Throughout, Marx and most European members of the First International continued to believe in a further and more important role for trade unions. This was to educate workers into a revolutionary mentality in such a way that they would be willing and able to commit themselves to overthrowing the capitalist system as a whole.

Gompers' claim to have acted as an innovator in introducing the high-dues, high-benefit system into Local 144 of the CMIU—and which John R. Commons evidently believed Gompers to have elucidated for the first time—also had little substance. For in practice the "new movement" he advocated represented little more than the reproduction on the American continent of the mid-Victorian "new model" form of English trade unionism that had first been introduced at the national level in 1851 by the Amalgamated Society of Engineers. This form of unionism involved amalgamating into one organization the collective bargaining and "friendly benefit" features of trade unionism that in Britain had hitherto been kept largely separate, under a system of tight administrative control. Gompers himself was even explicit about the derivative nature of his reforms. In his own autobiography he revealed that he had "gathered all the information I could get on the benefits provided by the British trade unions" and discussed them with fellow members of Local 144 before actually introducing them. Strasser was skeptical at first, but then he too, as president of the CMIU after 1877, turned to the British model, examining in particular the benefit features of the Amalgamated Society of Carpenters and Joiners. He became "convinced that their Protective and benevolent . . . character" was the "secret of the growth and power of trade unions in England."

Just how did Gompers' growing anti-intellectualism, coupled with his espousal of English-style "new model" unionism, propel him toward a more conservative position? The answer to the first half of the question is not difficult to find. Virtually all successful socialist movements have been built around an alliance of some kind between trade unionists and intellectuals, in a format that by the end of the 1890s Gompers was increasingly unwilling to countenance. Thus in deliberately cutting himself off, and—insofar as he was capable of doing—cutting the AFL itself off, from the advice and counsel of theoretically inclined persons both inside the labor movement and outside of it, Gompers was dissociating the trade unions from socialists and others who advocated independent labor politics. Later on, this distrust was extended to welfare workers and research experts, although this particular prejudice was softened somewhat during and after the First World War when Gompers came into closer contact with such persons, particularly those who because of the war and the Russian Revolution had become antisocialist. Nevertheless, throughout the latter part of his life he characteristically expressed doubts concerning the sincerity of anyone who did not work with their hands, calling them "careerists," "faddists," or "professional friends of labor." "Intellectuals usually suspend their labor programs from sky hooks," he wrote in the *American Federationist* in May 1918. "Their practical efforts are confined to criticizing the achievement and methods of workingmen. They can find nothing good in the practical structure of labor organizations which workers have built upon solid foundations upon the ground where labor problems exist."

The answer to the second half of the question is more difficult. It must be remembered that the English system of high dues and high benefits, and the increased amount of authority that was accorded to the officials who were introduced to administer them, was first established in order to provide Local 144, and later the CMIU as a whole, with sufficient discipline and financial strength to survive the depression of 1873–77, which decimated most other trade unions. Seen from this point of view, these reforms unquestionably paid off. The CMIU's national membership, which in 1877 had fallen to as little as 1,016, had by 1901 reached a total of more than 30,000. Its benefit system and large treasury were admired by other craft unions and were used widely as a model of what by then had become publicly known as business unionism. Nor did there appear to be anything inherently conservatizing in the adoption of benefit systems as such. Indeed, it might be argued that such systems could just as readily be used to fund large, class-based trade unions as they could be to defend the interests of small groups.

But the effect, if not the intention, of these changes was conservatizing in several aspects. In the first place, by explicitly making financial advantage rather than social idealism the basis for trade union loyalty, it reinforced those tendencies toward respectability and material success that were already present among many of the skilled artisans with whom Gompers habitually associated. Secondly, the act of leaving the workman's bench to become a paid official, the need for a hierarchical system of authority that the centralized system of administering AFL unions necessitated, and the sense of caution that preserving significant financial reserves induced, all tended to undermine the proletarian outlook with which many trade union leaders began their careers and encouraged them to identify with each other rather than with the workmates they had left behind.

Gompers was even more subject to such pressures than were most other AFL leaders, because he was responsible for administering a much larger bureaucracy than most of his colleagues, as well as for spending a greater proportion of his time in the company of businessmen and politicians, a fact that inevitably affected his outlook. The presence of rabbis, merchants, and even inventors and poets among his forebears also suggests that Gompers' eagerness to collaborate, as president of the AFL, with statesmen and business leaders may have reflected at some level a desire to retrieve the fortunes of a family that had earlier been declassé. Whatever truth there may be in this, there seems to be little doubt that Gompers' own sense of militancy, his willingness to take risks in supporting large-scale strikes, and his willingness, also, to put the financial resources of the AFL at the disposal of those who sought to organize the great mass of unskilled and semiskilled workers were significantly diminished by the way of life he came to adopt when he turned from a labor agitator into a labor administrator.

This last point brings up the third, and by far the most serious, consequence of the high-dues, high-benefit system that by 1900 had become characteristic of most unions in the AFL. This was the fact that the payment of high dues, which in the case of the cigarmakers had by 1896 reached the sum of thirty cents per month, was beyond the reach of the majority of the American work force, even if they could qualify for the apprenticeship system that many unions helped introduce into their trades. Significant additional payments were also made necessary by special levies and by high initiation fees. These high dues were not, in themselves, inappropriate, because employer opposition often made major expenditures necessary in order to protect the immediate, and legitimate, self-interests of skilled craftsmen. Nor were they by any means confined to the United States. But the logic implied by the American version of the English "new model" unionism, which Gompers and Strasser initially introduced, in the words of the one historian, was to close the trade unions "to all but the thriftier and better-paid artisans."

The preceding section has provided a basis for understanding Samuel Gompers' pragmatism, his anti-intellectualism, and his determination, stemming initially from his own misconceptions about the nature of Marxism, to keep the AFL free from the kind of entangling alliances with other elements in society that would have been necessary if it was to develop into a broad-ranging social movement. But by itself, this analysis does not fully explain the conservatism of Gompers' later years. In particular, it does not take into account Gompers' nativist attitudes towards the new, peasant immigrants who by 1885 were pouring into the United States; his espousal of the doctrine of political voluntarism; his growing preoccupation with trade autonomy in opposition to industrial unionism; or the bitter hostility (as opposed to personal disassociation) that he displayed towards socialists and other radicals in the period after 1900. Nor does Gompers' early development enable us to explain why, after the turn of the century, he showed a willingness to cooperate with the National Civic Federation and with other elements of the business community. This was a course that during the 1877 cigarmakers' general strike he would undoubtedly have shunned. On the other hand, some elements of his later conservatism were consistent with his earlier opinions. For example, he remained skeptical about the desirability of abolishing large-scale trusts on the ground that they were part of the logic of the development of capitalism. This was very similar to the position taken by moderate socialists in both Germany and Great Britain after the turn of the century.

But by no means did all of Gompers' other attitudes display such consistency. In his earliest years as a labor leader, for example, Gompers had shown more than the sentimental attachment to the plight of minorities that was then common among British and German immigrant artisans. By engineering the acceptance of the United Cigarmakers into the CMIU as Local 144, he had taken a practical interest in organizing both the poor, Bohemian cigarmakers in his own industry, as well as the women who worked in the trade. The early AFL also refused to charter international unions that excluded black workers; Gompers commissioned several black organizers to work in the South, subsequently praising their worth; and he gave strong support to the November 1892 interracial general strike that for a time shut down most industries in New Orleans. "If we fail to organize and recognize the colored wage-workers," wrote Gompers to H. M. Ives on November 10, 1892, "we cannot blame them if they accept our challenge of enmity and do all they can to frustrate our purposes. If we fail to make friends of them, the employing class won't be so shortsighted and [will] play them against us. Thus if common humanity will not prompt us to have their cooperation, an enlightened self-interest should."

To some extent, liberal attitudes also marked Gompers' early attitudes towards the organization of recent European immigrant workers, although not towards the Chinese, who were almost universally excoriated by white artisans. Yet by 1896 or thereabouts Gompers had agreed to admit into the AFL unions that retained the color line, had abandoned much of his earlier support for female workers, and was expressing both racist and nativist sentiments freely. New peasant immigrants (Italians, Bohemians, Hungarians, Poles, Lithuanians, and Russians, for example) were, unlike northern Europeans, "a heterogeneous stew of divergent and discordant customs, languages, institutions; and they were impossible to organize." And the failure to enroll blacks in large numbers was now attributed not to any inadequacy on the part of the labor movement, but to the alleged tendency of Afro-American workers to offer themselves spontaneously as strikebreakers.

What explains this reversal of outlook? On this point, perhaps more than on any other, it is difficult to ascertain the personal motivation that lay behind Gompers' change of mind. On the question of organizing blacks and recent immigrants, for example, it might be argued that the period of the 1880s and 1890s was a time of rising Negro-phobia and of nativist sentiment throughout the country, and that in accepting unions that excluded new immigrants and blacks Gompers was simply reflecting the prevailing cultural biases of the white, north European or native American, skilled workers who predominated in the AFL. In the mid-1890s for example, he was frequently criticized for attempting to organize poor black workers alongside of whites in the South, on the grounds that he would thereby alienate the much more important category of white southern artisans.

But such an argument not only ignores the fact that a few years earlier the Knights of Labor—and a few years later, the Industrial Workers of the World (IWW)—succeeded in organizing significant numbers of poor black as well as poor peasant immigrant workers alongside each other in racially integrated unions. It also ignores the point that Gompers' own letter to Ives of November 1892 made plain, that he was aware that the interests of the labor movement would themselves be damaged if he gave in to such narrow, exclusionary policies. The employers would, and did, take full advantage of the AFL's racism and nativism by deliberately exploiting the racist and nativist sentiments present in many white workers. The best that can be said about Gompers' personal views on these matters is that he appears to have been one of those English and German immigrants of the Civil War period, of whom there were many in both of the main political parties, who sincerely believed in the abolition of slavery and in other aspects of political reform, but who continued to regard both blacks and peasant immigrants as intellectually inferior to skilled white workers and as incapable of participating in the benefits of trade unionism. Indeed, he said as much regarding blacks after the turn of the century when he responded to criticism from Booker T. Washington that he had, in a recent speech, "read the Negro out of the labor movement." Not so, replied Gompers. What he had said was that it was difficult to organize Negro workers because they "did not have the same conception of their rights and duties as did the white workers, and were unprepared to fully exercise and enjoy the possibilities existing in trade unionism."

As for the AFL's own exclusionary policies, which Gompers exercised a crucial influence in developing, they were in a sense a logical extension of the high-dues, high-benefit systems that he and Strasser had earlier introduced into the CMIU. For since most women workers, as well as most peasant immigrants and blacks, toiled either in domestic work or in such heavy, unskilled occupations as steel, coal mining, meat packing and common laboring, they were by definition ineligible for admission into the AFL's skilled unions. Thus Gompers managed to avoid confronting the issue directly by pointing to the rationale that lay behind the form of unionism that he did so much to develop. That such a rationale was an extremely slim excuse upon which to depend, however, was amply demonstrated later when the AFL was itself challenged successfully by the Congress of Industrial Organizations (CIO), which managed to incorporate precisely those workers whom Gompers believed were impossible to organize.

A similar retrograde pattern can be seen at work in Gompers' growing preoccupation with trade autonomy and in his opposition to industrial unionism, which became almost an obsession in his later years. Beginning with the Building Trades Department in 1907, the AFL did establish consultative departments within the federation in such industries as railroads and mining to adjudicate jurisdictional disputes between unions. In 1901, in the Scranton Declaration (and with Gompers playing a leading role in the debate), the AFL even conceded to the United Mine Workers the right to organize all workers "in and around the mines," irrespective of their levels of skill. But for the most part it hewed rigidly to the doctrine of trade—which in most instances meant craft—autonomy, despite the fact that technological changes in industry were rendering many distinctions based upon hand skills obsolete. On this issue, as on a number of others in his later years, Gompers' early pragmatism was transformed into blind obstinacy.

The origins of this rigidity can largely be found in the years of instability and trauma that were visited upon the labor movement generally, and upon Gompers personally, by the prolonged period of rivalry for the loyalties of the cigarmakers, which occurred between the late 1870s and the year 1886 when the Cigarmakers International Union finally emerged triumphant in his own trade. In turn, this rivalry involved the far more momentous issue of who would emerge victorious in the struggle between the trades unions and the Knights of Labor for the control of the labor movement, a struggle that was to determine the shape of the entire labor movement until the rise of the CIO. As the Knights' strength grew in the mid-1880s, jurisdictional disputes occurred with increasing frequency between the Knights and a wide range of craft unions, which complained that the Knights failed to respect their picket lines, urged trade union members to desert their organization for Knights of Labor assemblies, and undermined their strength generally. The reverse also occurred, of course.

But it was the bitter dispute that erupted in 1886 between the CMIU, on the one hand, and the Cigarmakers Progressive Union backed by powerful District Assembly 49 of the Knights of Labor in New York, on the other, that ended any apparent prospect of collaboration between the two movements; it also initiated Gompers' life-long hatred of dual or rival unionism and his preoccupation with the sanctity of craft autonomy. In January 1886 the United Cigar Manufacturers Association of New York locked out approximately fifteen thousand workers in one of the largest disputes in the city's history. In February the association revoked its earlier agreement with the CMIU. Instead, it signed a contract with the Progressives, as well as with District Assembly 49 of the Knights, thereby recognizing the Knight's white union label instead of the CMIU's blue one. Recognition of the union label was a crucial tool in boycotts and organizing work. Seriously alarmed, Gompers was dispatched on a nationwide speaking tour to dramatize the cigarmakers' grievances against the Knights for supporting the Progressives in their challenge to the CMIU's jurisdiction.

A prolonged struggle for control of the American labor movement then followed. It was most acute in New York, where the fight was between District Assembly 49 of the Knights of Labor, the largest in the order, on the one hand, and national unions such as the CMIU, backed by the Printers, the Carpenters, the Iron Moulders, and the Granite Cutters, on the other. Despite efforts at reconciliation, the Knights of Labor General Assembly backed District Assembly 49 against the CMIU. Terence V. Powderly added insult to injury by accusing Gompers of being a drunkard with whom it was impossible to do business. Stung, Gompers replied that Powderly and other leaders of the Knights floated "like scum on the top of a part of the labor movement, continually seeking to divert it to their own ends." Although the CMIU eventually won, it was this conflict more than anything else that led to the final break between the craft unions and the Knights, and to the establishment of the AFL in December 1886.

It would be going too far to say that this dispute alone determined all of Gompers' subsequent attitudes toward trade autonomy and established his hostility towards industrial or broadly based forms of trade unionism that would attempt to incorporate unskilled or semiskilled elements of the labor force. Nevertheless, it was to this 1886 conflict between the craft unions and the Knights of Labor that he repeatedly referred in later years when he sought to justify the principle of craft autonomy and when he excoriated alternative bodies that he considered to be threats to the AFL. What probably clinched the matter for Gompers was the fact that the Progressive Cigarmakers had been influenced by the Lassallean wing of the New York socialist movement. It was as a result of this dispute that the triple evils of dual unionism, jurisdictional poaching, and socialist politics became permanently linked in his mind.

This first came apparent in 1896, when Gompers reacted angrily to the establishment by Daniel DeLeon and other leftist SLP elements of the Socialist Trades and Labor Alliance (STLA). The STLA was set up in December 1895 as a rival body to the AFL to organize workers on a more radical basis than the AFL had been willing to do. The now weakened District Assembly 49 of the Knights of Labor backed the new organization, a fact that infuriated Gompers. But it was the dual unionist or competitive character of the STLA and the support that was given to it by the DeLeonite wing of the SLP that he focused on in his criticisms. A number of local unions attached to the AFL had been "rent asunder," he reported to the December 1896 convention of the federation, "and brother workmen have been organized into hostile camps, to the destruction of their own interests and to the delight of the enemies of labor." Earlier in the year he had condemned the "union wrecking" that, he said, had been "taken up by a wing of the so-called socialist party of New York." Such men as DeLeon, Hugo Vogt, and Lucian Saniel, the chief architects of the STLA, "should be pilloried as the enemies of labor, and held, now and forever, in the contempt they should so justly deserve." This kind of language was henceforth to characterize most of Gompers' references to labor radicals.

Gompers' reaction to the IWW, which was established in 1905 by the Western Federation of Miners, by the followers of Eugene Debs, by disaffected AFL elements, and by what remained of the STLA, was almost identical. It can be questioned whether the IWW was in fact a dual union in the same sense that the STLA had been. Its main aim was to organize the unorganized workers that the AFL had ignored. But by this time Gompers had become so fanatical in his devotion to the idea of trade autonomy that he was unwilling to make the necessary distinction. He denied that industrial unionism was the real purpose of the organization, ordered all AFL affiliates to expel IWW members, and even sanctioned the breaking of IWW strikes. The real and only purpose of the new body was "to divert, pervert, and disrupt the labor movement" in order to promote socialism, he later wrote. The whole venture simply proved that "the trade-union smashers and rammers from without and the 'borers from within' are again joining hands."

By extension, this distrust of SLP support for such bodies as the STLA spilled over into an overall repudiation of independent labor politics, even though the Socialist party of America, which was founded in 1901, specifically rejected the dual unionist policies followed by DeLeon and by the IWW, and sought instead to cultivate the friendship of the existing trade unions. Hence when, after the turn of the century, a conservative Congress refused to adopt legislation favorable to the interests of workers, Gompers and the AFL leadership turned, not to the Socialist party as most European trade union movements would have done, but to the nonpartisan "reward-your-friends, punish-your-enemies" political policy that was henceforth to be the hallmark of the federation's approach. In March 1906 the AFL issued its celebrated Bill of Grievances, demanding among other things an effective eight-hour work law for federal employees, enforcement of the exclusion law against Chinese immigrants, an anti-injunction bill, and protection against the low prices charged for the products of convict labor. In the November 1906 congressional elections, the AFL spent considerable sums of money attempting to defeat Republican Charles E. Littlefield of Maine, a sworn enemy of labor; and in 1908 it presented the same demands to both the Republican and Democratic national conventions. The more favorable response that it received from the Democrats started the labor movement towards de facto support for the Democratic party.

Of course, many other factors besides Gompers' personal predilections account for this swing towards the Democrats. Among them were the traditional support that working-class immigrants had given to the party and the body of favorable labor and social legislation that was enacted by President Woodrow Wilson's first administration between 1912 and 1916. But although the relationship between the AFL and the Democratic party continued to deepen, as far as the AFL was concerned—unlike the later CIO—it was always accompanied by extreme caution about the dangers of the labor movement becoming overly dependent upon the political largesse of the state. This was another reason for Gompers' hostility towards the socialists. The political principle that lay behind this attitude was voluntarism. It derived, in turn, from the antimercantilist tradition that was present, to a greater or lesser degree, in other Anglo-Saxon labor movements as well as in that of the United States. Thus the general idea that informed Gompers' attitude toward political action after 1906 was that the trades unions should only seek "to secure by legislation at the hands of government what they could [not] accomplish by their own initiative and activities."

Hence Gompers supported federal legislation to limit or control immigration from China and later from Europe, women's suffrage, inspection of factory working conditions, and prohibitions on the sale of convict-made goods. All of these were objectives that the AFL itself could not either initiate or enforce. However, even at the height of the Progressive movement just before the First World War, the AFL consistently opposed the enactment of legislation fixing the hours of male workers in private industry, minimum wage legislation, and anything that smacked of compulsory arbitration. All of these things were better left to the independent power of the trades unions.

Gompers' distrust of state power can also be linked to his post–1900 willingness to collaborate with elements of the business community in ways that he would never have contemplated in his early years. The connection resulted from the fusing of two new developments that by the turn of the century had transformed the workplace environment that Gompers had known as a young man. These were the growth that took place in the size and scale of business corporations and the increasingly successful use that was made by employers of court injunctions to break strikes on the ground that they interfered with interstate commerce or with the operation of free trade. Companies like Standard Oil of New Jersey, U.S. Steel, as well as numerous railroad, coal, and other industrial manufacturers, were now giant corporations with immense financial resources, which could invoke the power of the state to defeat the trades unions. Their political influence was such that they could secure court injunctions forcing union members to desist from striking and summon state and federal troops to protect their property rights and to back up the power of the law.

During this period Gompers did press for legislation that would exempt unions from prosecution under the Sherman Anti-Trust Act. This was successfully achieved, even if only temporarily, with the passage of the 1914 Clayton Act. But the general lesson that Gompers drew from the defeats that labor had suffered in the Homestead, Pullman, and Cripple Creek strikes, defeats that resulted from state or federal intervention on the side of the employers, was not that labor should challenge the corporations in the political field; it was that some kind of accomodation should be made with them at the workplace. The large, trustified industries, in particular, were too powerful to be challenged directly. They would only tolerate trade unionism, Gompers came to believe, if it was confined mainly to the skilled trades, if it rejected militancy and radicalism, and if it was in general reasonable in its demands. The agency that was to carry out this new policy was the National Civic Federation (NCF), a voluntary association established in 1900 by representatives of labor, capital, and the general public whose purpose was to mediate industrial disputes.

A good example of Gompers' new policy was his handling of the summer 1901 steel strike. This took place in a relatively new, modern industry employing almost 150,000 unskilled and semiskilled Slavic, Italian, and Polish workers in which the Amalgamated Association of Iron, Steel and Tin Workers—the old union of skilled Anglo workers—had only a toe-hold, but which it was imperative to unionize on a larger scale if the AFL were to grow beyond its narrow constituency of skilled craftsmen.

The strike began when the union attempted to secure union contracts in several of the subsidiary companies of the recently established United States Steel Corporation, which was now the largest single business organization in the United States. At two conferences held between Amalgamated leaders and banking magnate J. P. Morgan and Charles Schwab, who between them controlled U.S. Steel, the steel executives agreed to grant the union wage in the plants already organized, but specified that the Amalgamated was not to organize the nonunion mills. Morgan assured President Shaffer that he was not hostile to organized labor and that he would be willing to sign a contract with the Amalgamated for all of the mills within two years but could not do so just then.

Once its offer had been rejected, however, U.S. Steel began importing strikebreakers to start up the mills. The Amalgamated replied by appealing to Gompers to make the steel strike the central fight for unionism and to call for a conference of the leaders of the appropriate international unions in Pittsburgh. Gompers would not do so, and he refused even to call a meeting of the AFL Executive Council to consider tactics. A compromise was then proposed by the National Civic Federation under which the union scale would be signed for the steel mills that had been organized the previous year, union wages would be paid in the additional mills on strike, and no worker would lose his job because of striking. President John Mitchell also appears to have promised to bring out the United Mine Workers, which had the ability to cut off the fuel supply for steel, on sympathy strike if the employers rejected the offer.

U.S. Steel did reject this compromise offer, the United Mine Workers failed to come out in sympathy, and on September 14, 1901, the Amalgamated was forced to concede defeat. The overall result weakened the Amalgamated even further in the skilled sections of the trade and ended all efforts to organize the great mass of unskilled Slav and other immigrant workers in the industry until 1919. Gompers' conduct in this strike was in some ways understandable. He had warned President Shaffer ahead of time of the dangers of taking on the largest company in the United States without adequate preparation, and he had no power to force the United Mine Workers to come out on sympathy strike.

Yet it is also clear that in his refusal to make the steel strike the central concern of the AFL, in his unwillingness to put even the slightest pressure on John Mitchell to bring out the miners in support, and in his willingness to rely on the National Civic Federation as a genuinely neutral body that could alone bring about a compromise result, Gompers did far less than he could have done to unionize the steel industry. There is even a suggestion in the evidence that under pressure from Mark Hanna, NCF president, Gompers moderated his support for President Shaffer of the Amalgamated because he had favored the establishment of an industrial union in the trade.

There is also little doubt that Gompers' position was based on several underlying considerations that he did not bring into the open during the controversy: his fear of the steel trust and his readiness, if not eagerness, to accept the professions of the officials of the corporation at face value. Gompers and Mitchell, one historian notes, "prizing union recognition by the leaders of finance and business as their greatest possible achievement, were anxious for a speedy ending of a situation that put labor in an unfavorable light." Gompers was even impressed by J. P. Morgan's avowal of friendship for organized labor in ways that suggest a degree of naiveté more than a little odd for a man of his experience. Ten years later, the investigation of the Stanley congressional committee revealed the true value of such friendship when it published the text of a resolution that had been adopted by U.S. Steel at a directors' meeting just prior to the 1901 strike: "We are unalterably opposed to the extension of labor organization," it read, "and advise subsidiaries to take firm positions [against it] when these questions come up."

Thus by the time of the First World War, if not before, Samuel Gompers had in many ways come full circle. Beginning in the 1870s as a socialist sympathizer, a believer in the class struggle, and an avowed student of Karl Marx, in the 1890s he insisted that he was not antagonistic to socialism but attacked individual socialists who were hostile to trade unionism as he saw it, or who antagonized it by forming dual unions. By 1903 he had dropped his belief in the class struggle, telling the socialist delegates to the AFL convention of that year: "Economically, you are unsound; socially you are wrong; industrially, you are an impossibility." In 1913 Gompers openly confessed that he was no longer an opponent of the capitalist system in any way, shape, or form. He told a House investigating committee that he had come to the conclusion that "it is our duty to live out our lives as workers in the society in which we live and not work for the downfall or the destruction or the overthrow of that society, but for its fuller development and evolution." In the reference to living out our lives "as workers," there is a faint echo of the Marxist beliefs he once held. But Gompers' insistent disavowal of even the slightest interest in fundamental social change pointed far more insistently towards the narrow, red-baiting, self-righteous patriot who lay upon the flag-draped caisson in San Antonio, Texas, in December 1924, than it did towards the idealistic young radical that he had been in his early years.

Yet there was an alternative to the narrow, craft union policies that Gompers pursued so exclusively in his later years: organization of the mass production industries on the basis of an open, socially progressive, and inclusive form of trade unionism that would have accepted unskilled and semiskilled workers of all races, and of both sexes, into its ranks. It is not difficult, if one accepts the logic of business unionism and focuses upon the policies of a narrow group of trade union leaders, both to find justifications for much of what Gompers stood for and to accept the intellectual rationale that lay behind the Commons-Perlman school of labor writers, who based many of their own ideas on Gompers' achievements. But, as more recent historians have shown, to accept these assumptions is to ignore the opinions of many among the great mass of American workers, both organized and unorganized, who did not share Gompers' opinions. It is also, in an important sense, to misinterpret the American labor tradition itself.

This is so partly because, as I pointed out earlier, the supposed "uniquely American" form of trade unionism that Gompers thought he had discovered in reforming the structure of the Cigarmakers International Union was, in fact, an import from Great Britain. In the second place, the native American tradition of labor reform, which the First International and the group of men among whom Gompers came to maturity so curtly dismissed, did not consist simply of "middle class nostrums." As represented by the National Labor Union, by the Knights of Labor, and by other organizations, it encompassed a wide range of policies, social groups, and methods of labor organizing—ranging from republican idealism, the mixed trade assembly, and communal resistance to the inequalities created by post–Civil War industry—that were far more "uniquely American" than the alternative model that Gompers himself espoused.

To say this is not to deny the achievements of the American Federation of Labor or of Gompers himself. As the representative of skilled craftsmen, the AFL did much that was indispensable. But with the passage of time, its narrowness of vision became increasingly unrepresentative of the interests of the great mass of unskilled workers, minorities, and factory labor. This becomes particularly clear if we examine the fortunes of the AFL in the period between 1919 and 1924, the last years of Gompers' own life. During the course of the First World War the trade union movement grew dramatically, Gompers became a member of the National War Labor Board, and he was a frequent and influential visitor at the White House. But the years 1919 and 1920 were to represent the high point of the AFL's growth until the late 1930s. By 1921 union membership had fallen from 3,120,000 to just under 3 million. In 1924, the year of Gompers' death, the figure was 2,724,000.

The reasons for this decline were, of course, complex. Some of them, like the Red Scare movement of 1919, which at its height was directed as much against staid craft unionists as it was against supposed Bolsheviks, can in no way be laid at Gompers' feet. Collectively, however, as the most recent commentator on Gompers' life has pointed out, they called into question several of his most cherished principles. As employers all across the country, both large and small, sought to roll back labor's wartime gains, his long-sought policy of seeking acceptance from the corporate community seemed dubious, at best. One result of this, as Gompers pointed out in his own autobiography, was that he was unable to secure even a response to a letter from one of his erstwhile allies in the National Civic Federation, Judge Gary, during the course of the great 1919 steel strike. By 1920 the open shop campaign that business pursued had turned into a frontal attack on the very concept of unionism, against which all of Gompers' pleas for moderation and behind-the-scenes negotiation were powerless.

Much the same thing happened on the political field. With the ending of the First World War and President Wilson's increasing preoccupation with the Versailles peace treaty and his ensuing illness, the AFL lost its most influential Democratic ally. Until 1924 Gompers still received a polite hearing in Democratic party councils. But in that year the party not only nominated a highly conservative presidential candidate, John W. Davis, but it also disregarded virtually all of labor's legislative requests. As a result Gompers belatedly committed his support, and that of organized labor generally, to the independent presidential campaign of the aging Wisconsin senator Robert M. LaFollette. Few people seriously thought that the candidate of the Conference for Progressive Political Action would win, of course. But it was disconcerting that so few urban workers, nationwide, cast their ballots for a candidate who clearly stood for labor's interests.

It is less easy to be critical of Gompers' political policy of "reward-your-friends, punish-your-enemies" than it is of his trade union policies. In the New Deal period, this willingness to support labor's supporters within the Democratic party was probably more advantageous than commitment to an independent party of the working-class would have been. Yet in the latter part of his life both Gompers' industrial and his political policies, not unlike those pursued by Booker T. Washington on behalf of American blacks, betrayed an unfortunate tendency to place too much trust in those leaders of society whom he considered to be labor's friends and not enough trust in the broad masses of the working-class where his own roots lay. In his search for acceptance on behalf of a relatively small—and hence relatively weak—segment of the labor force, he jettisoned the vision of working-class unity that had motivated him in the 1870s and 1880s. Gompers did this not out of any deliberate attempt to practice class collaboration but because he sincerely believed his policies to be in labor's best interests. But in doing so he not only neglected the interests of a large proportion of the American working-class, he also jeopardized much of its as well his own birthright.

Acknowledgments. The author wishes to thank members of the Los Angeles Study Group in Social History for their comments on an earlier draft of this essay.

Bibliographic Notes

I have been helped in writing this essay by having prepublication access to Stuart B. Kaufman (ed.), *The Samuel Gompers Papers*, Vol. 1: *The Making of a Union Leader, 1849–1886*, which is forthcoming from the University of Illinois Press. Aside from this, I have relied on the rather inadequate list of standard biographies, the best of which is Kaufman's own study of Gompers' early life, *Samuel Gompers and the Origins of the American Federation of Labor, 1848–1896* (1973). Among the others are Bernard Mandel, *Samuel Gompers, A Biography* (1963); Florence L. Thorne, *Samuel Gompers, American Statesman* (1957); and Harold C. Livesay, *Samuel Gompers and Organized Labor in America* (1978). Samuel Gompers' own two-volume autobiography, *Seventy Years of Life and Labor* (1925), is indispensable but must be used with care, because it was completed in old age and was largely ghost-written by Florence Thorne, Gompers' research assistant and an uncritical admirer.

References in the text to the opinions of Philip S. Foner, John R. Commons, and Daniel Bell can be found in Gerald E. Stearn (ed.), *Gompers* (1971). The reference at the end of the essay to the most recent commentator on Gompers' life is to the introduction by Nick Salvatore in his abridged edition of Gompers' autobiography, *Seventy Years of Life and Labor* (1984). Readers should also consult Louis S. Reed, *The Labor Philosophy of Samuel Gompers* (1930), and my own early article, "Reflections on the Failure of Socialism in the American Federation of Labor," for material on the early Cigarmakers Union. It was published in the

87

Mississippi Valley Historical Review 50, no. 4 (March 1964): 643–51. Useful material on Gompers' life can also be found in Warren Van Tine, *The Making of the Labor Bureaucrat: Union Leadership in the United States, 1870–1920* (1973); in the early chapters of Robert Christie, *Empire in Wood, A History of the Carpenters' Union* (1956); and in the multivolume history of American labor written by John R. Commons's research team, entitled *History of Labor in the United States* (1919–35). A partial list of Gompers' own writings can be found in the bibliography of Reed's book.

Eugene V. Debs: From Trade Unionist to Socialist

4

Nick Salvatore

On June 12, 1894, Eugene V. Debs walked to the podium of a noisy and crowded convention hall in Chicago, struck the gavel to call the assembled delegates to attention, and then made the keynote address at the first annual convention of the American Railway Union (ARU). Founded only a year earlier, the ARU sought to transform railroad workers' organization through the creation of an industrial union that would enroll workers regardless of their skill or craft position. Understandably, this effort encountered the intense hostility of the railroad brotherhoods, those older organizations of workers in the industry built upon craft lines. As Debs opened the convention, however, both he and the assembled delegates reflected a proud confidence from the events of the past spring. In its first serious test, the ARU withstood the opposition of a major railroad (James J. Hill's Great Northern) and the craft brotherhoods to achieve a decisive victory that both restored the wage cuts and emphasized the potent sense of solidarity and worker unity industrial unionism encouraged. Yet major difficulties loomed before the delegates and, as Debs concluded his enthusiastic account of the union's first strike, he addressed the basic issue before the convention in a far more somber tone.

The workers at George Pullman's railroad car shops just outside of Chicago had sent a delegation to ask the ARU to support their strike, then in its fifth week. As Debs explained the conditions in Pullman, the level of anger in the hall rose noticeably. Not only had these workers suffered wage cuts and worsened working conditions, but many of them were also forced to live in the town of Pullman. There George Pullman and his management executives set the rents for housing and the fees for water, gas, and sanitation service, established the library with its annual fee, banned saloons, built the churches, and hired the ministers and priests to staff them. Despite

Pullman's references to the community as a model for avoiding industrial strife, most workers experienced that company town as less a utopia than a further extension into their personal and family life of Pullman's assumed right to exploit their existence. Indeed, as Debs explained, George Pullman set the fees for these essential services to provide a steady six percent return on investment and never once cut those fees despite the wage cuts. Further, Debs stated in a taut angry tone, when a delegation of workers approached a company executive to protest the most recent wage cut on May 10, 1894, they were summarily fired the next day despite assurances they had gained that there would be no retribution for the simple act of presenting the petition. The strike began on May 11 as news of the firings spread throughout the plant, and these workers were now at the ARU convention requesting the full support of the new union.

In spite of the catalogue of horrors he had just recounted, Debs urged caution. Money, supplies, organizers, speakers—all this and more Debs gladly supported, but he warned against committing the ARU as an institution to the strike. The recent success against Hill's railroad notwithstanding, Debs knew that the ARU was organizationally weak. Since the conclusion of their first strike, new members had streamed into the ARU at an incredible rate of 2,000 a week. Impressive as this was, the figure also suggested the difficult task the ARU faced: its own membership was new, poorly organized on the local level, and inexperienced with a nationwide strike or boycott. As Debs's concluding words of caution faded from the auditorium, the representatives of the Pullman workers rose to appeal to the delegates for aid. The poignancy of their testimony, fused with the delegates' own enthusiasm over their recent victory, led the convention to overrule its president. The ARU, the convention decided, would support the Pullman workers with a nationwide boycott of any railroad company whose management refused to detach Pullman cars. The vote taken, Debs prepared to lead the union into battle.

After repeated failures to arbitrate the dispute (George Pullman refused even to meet with his workers), the ARU ordered the boycott of Pullman cars to begin on June 25. In the cities and towns west of Chicago, where the ARU strength was strongest and where management refused to separate the Pullman cars, workers of all levels of skill quit work in protest. Within a week the boycott proved successful, and even the appeals of the leaders of the craft brotherhoods went unheeded by their members. But Debs and other leaders of the ARU were not the only ones watching these developments. With far less pleasure major railroad executives across the country viewed the success of the boycott with great concern. They understood, as did Debs, that the issues involved in this struggle were central to the future

Archives of Labor and Urban Affairs, Wayne State University

development of America's industrial system. As the *New York Times* warned its readers, the Pullman strike was "in reality . . . a struggle between the greatest and most powerful railroad labor organization and the entire railroad capital. Success in the Pullman boycott," the *Times* continued, "means the permanent success of the one organization through which it is sought to unite all employees of railroads." If the ARU were successful, both sides agreed, this dispute would mark the beginning of a major redistribution of power between employer and worker that could eventually transform the face of industrial America: industrial unionism might be extended to other industries and with it would spread the workers' collective ability to check and counter traditional management prerogatives.

Precisely because the stakes were so high, railroad companies prepared a detailed counterattack. Through the General Managers Association, an organization of executives from the twenty-four railroads with terminals in Chicago, they created a series of committees to devise overall strategy, to implement day-to-day tactical decisions, to hire strikebreakers, and to coordinate these efforts with local, state, and federal authorities. Backed by seemingly unlimited resources, the association declared on June 25 that the announced boycott by the union was both "unjustifiable and unwarranted" and that any workers who participated in such activities were subject to immediate dismissal. Up to this point, the actions of the association did not differ significantly from earlier corporate responses to major threats to their autonomous control of production. Had they intended simply to defeat workers' efforts in this specific dispute, the battle would have been fought on these grounds until its conclusion. But the managers had a quite different purpose in mind. Although only the Pullman company was the target of the boycott, the association joined forces with Pullman for the purpose of eliminating the American Railway Union and, they hoped, eradicating all militant unionism from the industry. To achieve this goal they intended to secure the active involvement of the federal government.

On June 30, the fifth day of the strike, the association implemented the first step in its plan. Through the good offices of Attorney General Richard Olney, a former corporate lawyer for the industry who retained close ties with railroad leaders, the managers had Edwin Walker appointed as special government attorney to aid in the prosecution of the Pullman strikers. The fact that until a week before his appointment Walker had been counsel for the association caused the ARU lawyer, Clarence Darrow, to comment: "I did not regard this as fair." However, this was but the first step in a complex plan. Working closely with officials in Washington, the managers in Chicago first deputized some five thousand new U.S. marshalls that they themselves selected and had them fan out through Chicago with instructions to aggravate rather than ease potential trouble spots. Simultaneously, Olney decided to charge the strikers with obstruction of the U.S. mails and ordered his federal attorneys to prepare injunctions against Debs and other ARU leaders. On July 2 a disturbance at Blue Island, Illinois, on the outskirts of Chicago, largely instigated by the newly deputized marshalls, triggered the plan. Federal officials in Chicago wired Olney for assistance, and on July 3 two federal judges granted the injunction against the ARU that, among other provisions, prohibited Debs from any communication whatsoever with ARU locals or members. Olney also met with President Grover Cleveland, read him the telegrams from Blue Island, and pressed upon him the urgency of the situation in Chicago. On July 4, Independence Day, the final tactic in this joint corporate-governmental plan fell into place as the president ordered federal troops into Chicago over the expressed opposition of the city's mayor and the governor of Illinois. Lest anyone think that the troops were to be neutral peacekeepers, General Nelson Miles, commander of the soldiers, quickly dispelled such notions. As his troops occupied the city, Nelson gave a newspaper interview in which he expressed a bitter dislike of Debs and claimed that the ARU men were less strikers than rebels against government authority. He left the interview to hold the first of his many meetings with the association. Their goal achieved, the managers retired to watch the ensuing conflict: "It has now become a fight between the United States Government and the American Railway Union," a spokesman for the association commented on July 4, "and we shall leave them to fight it out."

Confronted by the direct power of the government, the successful strike of the ARU collapsed as members nationwide faced arrest and imprisonment. In Chicago, Debs and other leaders of the union were also arrested first on charges of conspiracy and then, a week later, for contempt of court for ignoring an earlier injunction. Although never convicted on the conspiracy charge, Debs was sentenced in the contempt case and served a six-month sentence in the Woodstock County jail. It was this jail experience, coupled with his triumphant address to a crowd of over one hundred thousand upon his release in Chicago, that established the central myth of Debs's career. The close alliance between the government and the business community had raised the Pullman strike to a level of dramatic national importance and focused enormous attention on Debs himself. Then, still in the glare of this fame, a little more than a year after his release from jail, Debs publicly announced that he had become a socialist. To many Americans, the relationship between the term in jail and his embrace of the socialist label seemed intimate, and many came to look on that jail term as the source and site of Eugene Debs's conversion. The most prominent promoter of this theme was Debs himself. Prior to the Pullman strike and his subsequent prison term, Debs wrote some years later, "I had heard but little of Socialism." But during that strike, "in the gleam of every bayonet and the flash of every rifle *the class struggle was revealed*." While in jail, Debs continued, he avidly read a series of books on social problems and when Victor Berger, Milwaukee's socialist leader, visited him, bearing as gifts the three volumes of Marx's *Das Kapital*, that experience set "the wires humming in my system." Drawing on the archetype of Saul on the road to Damascus, Debs and his followers suggested that, in a moment of blinding insight, he understood the systematic problems with capitalism and the promise of socialism, and he emerged from jail a changed and charged man.

The Woodstock incarceration is critical in any evaluation of Debs's life and career. It remains the portal through which one understands the meaning of socialism for him and other Americans in the decades to come. If that dramatic conversion did in fact occur, Debs's socialist activity then marked a sharp break with the concerns and ideas of his earlier career. Further, it places his socialist years outside the boundaries of traditional American political discourse and, therefore, outside the experience of most American working people. But a less mythic view of Debs's life suggests that, important as it was, the Pullman event was but one aspect of a complex development in the career of this preeminent American native son.

Eugene Debs was born in Terre Haute, Indiana, on November 5, 1855. The third of six children and the oldest male, there was little in his early life that foreshadowed his post-Pullman career. At the time of his birth, Debs's parents, Marguerite and Daniel, were quite poor, but by the end of his teen years these immigrants from Alsace, France, were the proprietors of a successful retail store that sold fine foods and liquors. Debs's own experience during these years reflected a similar tone. A student in the local public schools, he diligently absorbed the moral as well as the intellectual education provided there. After winning a spelling bee in the eighth grade, his teacher presented him with a Bible that she had inscribed with the admonition: "Read and Obey." There is no contemporary evidence to suggest he thought to do other than just that. Despite his scholastic record, the young Debs left school after the first year of high school to begin work as a paint scraper on the Vandalia Railroad. Motivated neither by family poverty nor poor grades, Debs simply seemed anxious to enter the bustling world of work.

Many in Terre Haute in 1870 felt that the community was poised on the edge of dramatic economic development, and the prospectuses of the business community and the editorials of the newspapers prophesized a time in the near future when the community would surpass even Pittsburgh as a center of iron production. Debs's early work experience seemed to affirm this optimism. Within a year he was promoted from his unskilled position into the ranks of the locomotive firemen, a group of workers generally considered to be in training for the premier skilled position in the industry, the locomotive engineer. By 1874, however, the serious depression that had begun a year earlier reached Terre Haute and Debs, along with many other workers, was laid off for the first time in his life. He traveled to St. Louis in search of work, encountered urban poverty on a large scale for the first time, and in a letter explained his motivation to his sister, Louise, back in Terre Haute: "I don't expect to stay away from home forever," the nineteen-year-old Debs wrote, "nor even for an unreasonable length of time; I only want to stay long enough and to prove that I can act manly when must be."

Debs did not find work in St. Louis but when he returned home his mother, fearful of the high fatality rate associated with railroad work, prevailed upon her son to wait for an upturn in the railroad industry. Through the intercession of his father, Debs instead obtained a clerk's position in Herman Hulman's wholesale grocery. A few months later, when Joshua Leach, founder of the Brotherhood of Locomotive Firemen, came to Terre Haute to organize a local, Debs became a charter member and was elected recording secretary of Vigo Lodge, No. 16. While the juxtaposition of Debs's actual work with his position in the new Brotherhood might appear odd to the modern eye, it did not strike his contemporaries in the same fashion. The Brotherhood at that time was less a trade union than a benovolent society, and the organization's basic concern was to provide accident and death benefits to members. The Brotherhood neither entered into negotiations with management nor saw in their organization an alternative to management's right to structure and direct the work force and the work day. Further, class lines were not understood to be as sharply drawn in the Terre Haute of the 1870s as they would be perceived in the decades to come. Employment as a clerk or as a soon-to-be skilled worker did not necessarily either exclude future social mobility or erect personal and society barriers between people in those occupations in this small, decentralized urban center. As a teenage friend of Debs's explained years later, recalling the Terre Haute of his youth, he and other friends in the 1870s foresaw the time "when Gene would reach an eminence in trade equal to Herman Hulman, or step into a Master Mechanics job in charge of all the engine men."

This perception of Terre Haute as a community free of permanent class distinctions and possessed of extensive opportunities for advancement was common in post–Civl War America. In marked contrast with such major urban centers as New York, small urban communities such as Terre Haute, with their lesser level of industrial development and their largely local business elite, appeared to maintain a sense of social cohesion and harmony even into the industrial age. The republican values associated with the tradition of the American Revolution, which stressed the primacy of citizenship and the duties and obligations inherent in the fulfillment of one's manhood, and which rejected as of primary importance economic differences among citizens, were considered still vital. Even when the social deference based on economic distinctions (the paint scraper and the railroad owner, despite their common citizenship, did not occupy the same social plateau) was recognized, it was seen less as a permanent barrier than as a positive asset even by many on its far side. Thus the success of others was often seen as essential for one's own eventual improvement. As Debs noted frequently in his later years, the Terre Haute of his youth was a community where "all were neighbors and all friends."

But in Terre Haute as across the nation the emergence of industrial capitalism, with its firmer class lines, demands for stricter work discipline, and renewed calls for a stronger hierarchical social structure, slowly altered the community. In Terre Haute, the first evidence of this change came during the great nationwide railroad strikes of 1877. The strike began in Martinsburg, West Virginia, on July 16 to protest a wage cut by the Baltimore and Ohio Railroad. As other roads announced the same wage cut in turn, the strike spread across the nation. Although the violence that dominated strike activity in cities such as Pittsburgh and Chicago did not occur in Terre Haute, the Vandalia Railroad workers did strike and occupy the railroad depot en masse. Despite this dramatic action, the motivation of the majority of these workers fell far short of the revolutionary fears then proclaimed in the nation's newspapers. They struck, the strike committee explained to the local paper, not so much to protest the wage cut announced by their owner but rather to protest the manner in which their owner was forced to cut wages in an attempt to stay competitive with the dominant railroad lines. There existed a community of interest between themselves and the Vandalia management, these strikers asserted, and they claimed that both workers and the local owner reeled under the pressure of the major monopolists. Thus, when the coal miners of adjoining Clay County telegrammed their offer to march on Terre Haute to institute a general strike in support of these workers, the strike committee flatly refused the suggestion. They were striking in defense of their community and its values, they asserted, and their employer was not the target. But the strikers' employer, William Riley McKeen, proved to have a quite different understanding of those values than did his workers. In private, unbeknownst to the strikers, McKeen and a number of local business associates requested from a federal judge in Indianapolis that a detachment of federal troops be sent to evict the men from the depot and break the strike. The troops did arrive and the strike was broken, even as McKeen continued to assert in public his own commitment to social harmony and to the values associated with American citizenship.

McKeen's private actions clearly revealed the limits of that concept of harmony, at least as interpreted by the business community. But most strikers were unaware of those actions and continued to present their strike activity as a defense of the basic values they presumed were shared by all Terre Hautians. Yet even a strike proclaimed for these ends proved too dramatic an action for the twenty-two-year-old Debs to endorse. During the events of that last week in July 1877, Debs took no known public role. The following September, however, at the annual convention of the Brotherhood of Locomotive Firemen, he made his feelings well known in a long speech to the delegates. Although he recognized the justice in the call by the strikers for a fair wage, Debs stridently rejected the strike as a tactic for working people. "Does the Brotherhood encourage strikers?" he asked, and then proceeded with his answer: "To this question we most emphatically answer, No, Brothers. To disregard the laws which govern the land? To destroy the last vestige of order? To stain our hands with the crimson blood of our fellow beings? We again say No, a thousand times No." It was not surprising that McKeen and other business leaders in Terre Haute vigorously applauded this speech; but the fact that it was also warmly received by the majority of delegates at the convention suggests something of the direction of the Brotherhood as well during these years. As did Debs, most delegates placed responsibility for social discord on the shoulders of working people and looked to their employers as both personal and social models for maintaining the qualities of manhood, harmony, and community.

Given this accord between Debs and the majority of delegates, it was not surprising that his 1877 speech also marked his rise within the Brotherhood. Elected grand marshall for the year following that speech, Debs became, within two years, first assistant editor and then editor of the Brotherhood's magazine, the *Locomotive Firemen's Magazine*. In 1880 he was named grand secretary-treasurer of the Brotherhood. In the Terre Haute local of the Brotherhood, Debs received similar rewards for the sentiments expressed at Indianapolis. Of the local men holding office in the lodge during the strike, all of whom except Debs had taken active roles during the strike, only Debs was returned to office, first as recording secretary and then as master of the lodge.

Based on the expression of social harmony, in which both railroad workers and their employer publicly applauded the position taken by the young Debs, it was only a matter of time before Debs and his supporters sought to capitalize on that accord in the political arena. Debs rejected efforts to create an independent working-class political party because he perceived it to be destructive of the community he sought; instead he ran as a Democrat for the office of city clerk in 1879. In a three-way race against Republican and labor candidates, Debs won a decisive victory and received more votes than the successful Democratic candidate for mayor. The nature of his electoral coalition in 1879 reinforced his belief in harmony. He received public support from both McKeen (a life-long Republican), Hulman, and other employers, and he carried the wards of railroad workers by decisive majorities. But the key to his success lay in the results from Terre Haute's second ward. Traditionally Republican, it housed the majority of the town's elite. In that three-way race, Debs attracted more than forty-five percent of these votes. A politician with a potent appeal to working people, Debs swamped the labor candidate by more than two to one citywide and by almost three to one in the railroad workers' wards. Simultaneously, he also did well in traditional Republican strongholds. As the local Republican newspaper ruefully admitted after the election, Debs was "the blue-eyed boy of destiny."

Debs's successful reelection campaign in 1881 revealed a similar pattern. By now a leader of both the local lodge and the national Brotherhood, Debs nonetheless retained the active support of employers such as McKeen and expanded his support among working people. In 1884 this cross-class support brought Debs first the Democratic nomination and then election to Indiana's state assembly. The nature of his own political consciousness and the foundation of his appeal to employers and workers alike can best be gauged by a brief examination of Debs's participation in the debates over two bills in the assembly in 1885. The first, concerning the responsibility of railroad corporations to their workers, Debs sponsored himself. It sought to end the common law assumption that injury or fatality were either the worker's individual fault or the result of other workers' mistakes—in either case, the employer had traditionally been deemed to be without legal responsibility. Although this bill passed the assembly, the state senate emasculated the bill and even Debs refused to vote for the final version. If this bill indicates why many workers supported Debs, it was also only a part of his response to the growing system of industrial capitalism. In that same session of the assembly, Debs was one of a minority of Democrats who joined ranks with the Republicans to vote for the establishment of a state militia. The debate on this bill was both intense and pointed. As one opponent of the bill argued, it was simply an antilabor measure, "a direct blow at wage laborers, and if they dare to raise their voices to oppression this militia is to declare a riot and charge upon the laborers." But for Debs, still seeking harmony and community amid increasing factionalism, his understanding of the lessons of the 1877 strike remained uppermost in his consciousness. Further, he argued, although he now publicly claimed that he represented worker' interests in the assembly, never could he approve an action on behalf of one group that might violate his understanding of broader community interests. Thus the failure of his bill to enforce responsible action by railroad corporations did not release working people from their obligations to the larger community.

Debs's identification as a worker's representative by the early 1880s was no idle boast, nor simply a ruse to catapult himself into an easy position in politics or the Brotherhood. He was deeply engaged in organizing workers both in Terre Haute, where with P. J. McGuire he helped start the first carpenter's local, and across the country. On his trips for the Firemen, Debs also aided railroad workers of every job description to organize, and he was also responsible for the unionization of workers in other industries as well. Although he was no *pie card*—a worker's term for labor officials interested primarily in their own salary and prerogatives—Debs did hold a quite particular idea of his role at this time. He argued consistently in his editorials in the *Firemen's* magazine that the concept of manhood, with its attributes of personal honor, industry, and responsibility to one's duties, was the essential foundation of American citizenship. Fulfillment of these duties, he held, was incumbent upon all regardless of economic station. While this emphasis could lead to a strong union consciousness, Debs did not develop it in this fashion during the early 1880s. For even as he urged all to rise to the responsibilities of their manhood, Debs remained highly suspicious of working people's ability to do just that by themselves. In a central way his incessant organizing trips reflected this concern. If left to themselves, Debs felt, workers might easily repeat the anarchy of 1877. But if brought into an organization such as the Firemen, whose aim, Debs explained, was to "instill the love of sobriety into the putrid mind of debauchery, and create industry out of idleness," then workers would find the necessary encouragement to fulfill their duties. For in that organization they would benefit from the example of men like Debs who, in turn, themselves had the respect of such community leaders as McKeen and Hulman.

With the work force so organized, and with the Brotherhood cleansed "of all worthless material," success was assured, for then "we will be beckoned onward and upward by those who have the power to assist us."

Debs persisted in these attitudes despite the increased tension evident nationwide between employers and workers. He essentially ignored the founding of the Federation of Organized Trades and Labor Unions in 1881 and remained publicly silent when that group emerged in 1886 as the American Federation of Labor. Similarly, Debs had little positive to say about the Knights of Labor prior to 1888, despite the attraction of that organization for many firemen. Indeed, during the Knight's major strike against the Gould railroads in 1886, Debs, along with other Brotherhood officials, actually urged their members not to honor the strike. Privately, however, Debs began to question his premises even as he, for the moment, maintained a consistent pattern in public. At the core of his thought was a commitment to the idea of the independent citizen living within a community of relative equals. His understanding allowed for economic differences between men but asserted that the bonds of common citizenship would prevent the emergence of permanent divisions within society. Debs still held to that understanding, but in the mid–1880s, he began to question, at first quite hesitantly, whether employers as a group were acting in a similar fashion. The year-long strike of the Brotherhood against the Chicago, Burlington, and Quincy Railroad in 1888 forced him to clarify his thinking and marked the beginning of a central transformation in his life.

The immediate causes of the Burlington strike were relatively simple. The engineers and firemen who worked for the railroad demanded an end to the classification system (by which they received apprentice pay for the first three years, although they performed the full job) and the establishment of a uniform pay scale based upon actual mileage traveled. Led by President Charles E. Perkins, Burlington officials refused to negotiate these demands, and a joint strike of engineers and firemen began on February 27, 1888. That the strike began with the official support of the two brotherhoods suggested a potential new development for workers in the railroad industry. Not only had the two brotherhoods been extremely cautious in authorizing strike activity in the past, but they had rarely worked together in any capacity before. Tension had long existed between them over jurisdictional disputes (the Firemen, for example, allowed members promoted to the engineer's position to retain membership in their brotherhood), and recently these feelings had intensified due to the bitter public criticisms of each other expressed by Debs and the Engineer's chief, P. M. Arthur. But in the initial days of the strike, this show of harmony appeared to foreshadow ultimate success. Where company officials had privately estimated that forty percent of the workers would refuse to honor the strike call, fully ninety-seven percent walked out, although only sixty-six percent belonged to either brotherhood. When a week later, on March 5, a joint meeting of the grievance chairmen of both brotherhoods endorsed a boycott of all Burlington freight cars hauled by other railroads until the company and the men settled, it seemed as if success was assured.

But success proved elusive for these workers in 1888, and in the complex reasons for the strike's failure lay many of the lessons Debs himself would take from this experience. To begin with, the Burlington officials were adamantly opposed to considering the strikers' demands. Instead, their aim was the elimination of all unionized workers in their employ. As Charles Perkins had noted, union workers "owe allegiance to somebody else, and not to the railroad company that employs them." To achieve employee loyalty in 1888, the Burlington management successfully sought an injunction before a sympathetic federal judge to end the boycott and to impose penalities on managers of other roads and brotherhood officials if they continued to refuse to handle Burlington cars. This injunction led the two chiefs of the brotherhoods, P. M. Arthur and Frank P. Sargent of the Firemen, to call off the boycott. Second, divisions within the ranks of labor strengthened management's hand even before the injunction was granted. Both brotherhoods had a history of breaking the strikes of the Knights of Labor in the industry, and as the Burlington strike began, Chicago-based officials of the railroad received telegrams from Knights of Labor organizers offering their members as replacements. Finally, the promising show of unity between the two brotherhoods itself did not last the duration of the strike. Following the injunction that March, Arthur cooled noticeably in his support of the strike and that fall, at the Engineer's annual convention, he had his members withdraw from the strike without prior consultation with the Firemen. The firm opposition of management and the basic lack of unity within labor turned the strike's promising beginning into total defeat. In the aftermath, neither the Engineers nor the Firemen were able to reestablish lodges on the Burlington road until the twentieth century.

As complete as the defeat was, the Burlington strike nonetheless proved to be of major importance in Debs's life. The uncompromising position of the Burlington officials and the expressions of support they received in major newspapers across the country forced Debs to reexamine his belief in the concepts of manhood and community. These traditional values existed in a social structure, Debs had held, where at a minimum all could agree that "a fair day's work demanded a fair day's pay." But the position of the Burlington officials led Debs to question whether that tacit agreement still retained its social force. The system of industrial capitalism,

101

with its structured hierarchy, firmer class divisions, and extended control over daily work life, challenged the foundation of Debs's traditional value system. As Debs mulled over these thoughts, he came to reinterpret his earlier ideas while remaining firmly within a broad democratic tradition. Where his earlier expressions had emphasized the opportunities available to Americans and looked to successful men such as William Riley McKeen as models, his new perceptions questioned whether men such as McKeen used their success to inhibit the success of others; and he now stressed the examples of Thomas Paine, John Brown, and Abraham Lincoln as models for his audience. The democratic tradition, he now suggested, had to address the class realities of a maturing industrial society. Debs's view of the world of labor also changed in the aftermath of the Burlington strike. The fratricidal conduct of the various unions before and during that strike led him first to suggest and then to advocate the industrial organization of all workers in the industry. To create an organization of railroad workers that transcended divisions among workers based on level of skill, or ethnic and religious differences, became for Debs a consuming passion. "The spirit of fraternity [is] abroad in the land," Debs wrote in 1890, and this conviction led him to help establish the American Railway Union a few years later. For Debs, as for other railway workers, the Burlington strike had taught critical new lessons.

The Pullman strike of 1894 sharpened the lessons Debs and others had learned during 1888. The close working relationship between the federal government and major railroad corporations led Debs and many other workers to acknowledge more clearly the presence and permanence of class divisions in American society. The simpler affirmations of an earlier period, oblivious of the growing concentration of economic power, and the real expectation by local and national elites that working people defer to their judgment no longer explained present experience. As Debs moved toward a firmer class awareness, however, and ultimately toward public identification as a socialist in 1897, he did not therefore discard the democratic political ideology that had so informed his earlier career. As his dramatic speech before a crowd of over one hundred thousand people in Chicago upon his release from Woodstock County jail in November 1895 indicated, Debs sought instead to integrate his new awareness of class with his still deeply held democratic beliefs. He appealed to no European theorist but rather argued that his new awareness was actually consistent with the best of that earlier American tradition. "Manifestly," he began, "the spirit of '76 still survives. The fires of liberty and noble aspirations are not yet extinguished." Addressing his audience as "lovers of liberty and despisers of despotism," Debs focused on the growing threat industrial capitalism presented to those traditional values. In the present day, he declared, "corporations [know] the price of judges, legislators and public officials as certainly as Armour knows the price of pork and mutton." The corporation reigned for the moment, but Debs saw in a self-conscious and aggressive American working class hope for the future: "They are not hereditary bondsmen. Their fathers were born free—their sovereignty none denied and their children yet have the ballot." In that speech Eugene Debs established the major themes that would occupy him, and attract millions of Americans, over the next thirty years. In the context of industrial capitalism, Debs told audiences time and again, commitment to class struggle was neither unpatriotic nor a negation of earlier beliefs. Given the revolutionary transformation of society and politics engineered by the corporations, he argued, a socialist commitment, informed by the democratic tradition, was indeed the fulfillment of the basic promise of American life and the values of manhood, duty, and citizenship that sprang from it. In an odd way Debs did not see himself as a revolutionary but held that he sought both to conserve from the past and reinterpret for his generation the best of American experience. In the years after the Pullman strike, he dedicated himself to this task first in the Populist party and, when that movement splintered after the election of 1896, in the Socialist party of America. Debs's jail term, then, did not reflect a dramatic conversion. His turn toward socialism emerged from the events of the past twenty years in his community, its political arena, and most importantly, in his experience as a leader of the Firemen. The slow circuitous path he traveled from the 1877 strike to public identification as a socialist—a path he traveled by touch and feel rather than through discussions of theory—accounts in part for his less than orthodox interpretation of socialism. Simultaneously, that same path explains much about the appeal of this native son to Americans of his generation.

Eugene Debs's career as a socialist proved to be a long and at times tumultuous one, with the numerous moments of exhilaration ultimately offset by recognition of the persistent resistance by the majority of American workers to join the Socialist party of America. Never comfortable with theoretical discourse, Debs found his relations with certain comrades (perhaps especially Victor L. Berger of Milwaukee and Morris Hillquit of New York) particularly strained. These allies were often aghast at Debs's unorthodox formulations of socialism and frequently angry at Debs's reluctance to take a firm public position on a series of debates within the party. Yet at the same time Berger, Hillquit, and other party leaders were fundamentally dependent upon Debs. When Americans of varied political persuasions mentioned socialism, inevitably Debs came to mind. The leader of the Pullman strike had become the titular leader of the socialist movement, its national symbol and spokesperson, and had emerged as the single most important vehicle through which the party might reach the American working class. Recognizing this, even his opponents acceded to Debs's nomination as the party's presidential candidate in five of the six national elections between 1900 and 1920. He was, for Americans of all political faiths, the embodiment of that movement.

From the perspective of his almost twenty year involvement with the Brotherhood of Locomotive Firemen, however, his socialist career contained a certain paradox. Debs achieved national fame and acclaim at precisely the time he relinquished daily intimate contact with working people and their institutions. From 1875 until his painful last appearance before a Firemen's national convention in 1894 (where, in the aftermath of the Pullman strike, a significant portion of the delegates voted *not* to grant him speaking privileges), Debs's daily life had revolved around the needs of railroad workers. While his understanding of how best to meet those needs changed substantially, he nonetheless remained firmly rooted within the world of work. Following the Pullman strike, however, the context of his agitation altered. As he sought to impress upon his fellow citizens the necessity of applying their democratic political traditions to an economic system that increasingly determined large aspects of daily life, Debs of necessity moved beyond the world of the trade union. He did not dismiss the trade union as irrelevant but rather came to insist that, to be effective even in the arena of wages and work conditions, the trade union had to broaden its perspectives. This position brought Debs into conflict with certain trade union leaders such as the chiefs of the brotherhoods and Samuel Gompers, president of the American Federation of Labor (AFL). It also demanded that he enter more fully the world of socialist debate and. disputation, and for most of his career that world remained uncomfortable and even alien to him. Thus the leadership he provided the socialist movement was often erratic: from the podium he could be powerfully effective in moving Americans to view their society from a different perspective; in inner party councils, he was most often either silent or tentative, even contradictory, in his positions. Not surprisingly, then, Debs came to glory in his role as a public leader and increasingly shunned the more bruising world of party meetings and debates.

Oddly, what turned Debs in this direction involved an issue of fundamental importance to the trade union movement. In developing the ARU with its industrial union organization, Debs alienated leaders of the craft unions. But as he saw in the industrial union a more effective economic and political institution to meet working people's needs, this advocacy pushed him beyond the familiar dimensions of his pre–1894 world. From the coal fields of West Virginia to the steel mills of Pittsburgh, from the textile mills of Lawrence to the railroad junction towns of Kansas, the socialist Debs preached industrial unionism. It would eliminate caste divisions within labor, he told his working-class audiences, and from that unity which transcended level of skill or ethnic background on the job would emerge, he insisted, a more unified political consciousness that could sweep the working class into power. Not surprisingly, when the Western Federation of Miners in 1898 sponsored the Western Labor Union built on industrial union principles, Debs was present to applaud the decision. Four years later, the Western Labor Union claimed a national jurisdiction and directly challenged the American Federation of Labor in creating the American Labor Union. Once again, Debs attended that convention and relished the opportunity to follow Gompers' emissary to the podium with a slashing attack on the AFL's exclusionary craft policies. In 1905, when that group reorganized as the Industrial Workers of the World (IWW), Debs again was a delegate and publicly endorsed the new movement.

Ironically, however, Debs's involvement in the industrial union movement also brought him into further conflict with other socialist leaders. Men like Berger and Hillquit held that the proper position was to work within a Gompers-led federation with the aim of slowly changing it over time. Debs fundamentally disagreed and argued that the federation would never significantly broaden its craft base to include the immense numbers of unorganized, unskilled immigrant workers then staffing America's mass-production factories. Although he made this point in public, he still avoided participation in the inner party debate to determine policy. After 1908, moreover, his own position changed. While he remained committed to industrial unionism, he allowed his membership in the Industrial Workers of the World quietly to lapse. The withdrawal of the Western Federation of Miners in 1906 had eliminated the one strong union force in the IWW, Debs felt, and the continued bickering among the various caucuses rendered the organization ineffective. Further, as one deeply committed to political action as well as economic organizing, Debs strongly opposed the increasing rhetorical emphasis on sabotoge and direct action by workers on the job by such IWW leaders as William "Big Bill" Haywood. In a long and acerbic response to a Haywood speech in 1912, Debs termed the measures Haywood advocated as "reactionary, not revolutionary," understandable only as "the tactics of anarchist individuals and not of Socialist collectivist." Within the year that followed, Debs assisted in the recall of

Haywood from the Socialist party's national executive committee on the grounds that the latter opposed political action and favored violence. By 1913 Debs had completely dismissed the IWW and actually warned workers to avoid the group, for they would be "most basely betrayed, sold out and treacherously delivered to their enemies by the IWW Judases." It is paradoxical that one of the few internal party debates Debs entered found him aligned with Berger and Hillquit.

Although Debs continued to advocate industrial unionism, it was not until two decades later that that concept was transformed into an effective organizing tool for mass-production workers. But Debs's role as a socialist political leader had a broader success in his own time. In the 1900 presidential election Debs, the candidate of a young and inexperienced Socialist party, received just under one hundred thousand votes. Four years later, Debs's total was more than four times that figure. Simultaneously, in a growing number of communities, voters elected Socialists to the mayor's office, the city council, and the state legislature. Expectations for 1908 ran high, and the Socialist party leased a special railroad train, immediately dubbed the "Red Special," to carry Debs and his entourage into thirty-three states. The final vote was, however, depressing as it barely topped the 1904 total. The belief in inevitable progress was momentarily fractured, and Socialists sought to explain the results by pointing to the profusion of reform platforms and candidates within the major parties. In time reform would run its course, they suggested, and those voters would then turn to socialism. The off-year elections in 1910 encouraged this interpretation, as Victor Berger was elected to the United States Congress from Milwaukee and nearly one hundred Socialists won election to state and local office. Nominated again in 1912 for the fourth consecutive time, Debs led an invigorated party to the polls. The results that November were gratifying, as Debs received nearly one million ballots in the race against the winner Woodrow Wilson, the incumbent William Howard Taft, and former president Theodore Roosevelt. State and local Socialist candidates also did well and in the Southwest, especially Texas and Oklahoma, the party's electoral strength grew astronomically.

As encouraging as the results were, they ultimately represented the high point of Socialist party strength. Following 1912, an electoral decline ensued that did not end until, in the 1920s, there were but a handful of elected Socialist officials nationwide. In part elections themselves proved to be a faulty barometer of socialist consciousness. In the drive to build the vote, socialist principles often gave way to pragmatic political compromise, and party members might ignore the long-term educational value of electoral campaigns in developing a worker self-consciousness. As Debs himself had warned in 1911, "Voting for socialism is not socialism any more than a menu is a meal." Where elected, Socialist officials often found themselves bound by the expectations of their own supporters to lower taxes. As the young Walter Lippmann pointed out in 1913, after serving a two-year term as secretary to the Socialist mayor of Schenectady, New York, such a tax policy prevented fundamental restructuring of "the returns on privilege. . . . And because of that, [Socialist] political action in Schenectady must be ineffective." But there was no simple alternative course. If reform politics did not inevitably lead to future Socialist strength, a "purer" revolutionary platform repelled all but a few of the faithful. Ultimately, Debs had to confront the painful realization that, despite the tumultuous crowds that often applauded his talks, the majority of American workers, native and immigrant alike, affirmed their allegiance to the dominant political parties each November. As one Socialist coal miner lamented decades later, remembering his hero: "Poor old Debs! . . . The people wouldn't vote for him the way they should have. He told people the truth, but they went on voting Democrat and Republican."

Debs did not run for the presidency in 1916. In the years since 1912, he had suffered two serious physical collapses and was incapable of sustaining a national campaign. The party nominated Allan Benson in his place, but Debs did run a less demanding campaign that fall. The party ran him as a candidate in Indiana's Fifth Congressional District, which included Terre Haute and its vicinity. The campaign possessed an odd personal tone for the sixty-one-year-old Socialist leader, as he appealed for votes in the same political district that, some thirty years earlier, had applauded him for his more regular political analysis. Debs campaigned hard and finished a distant second to the Republican candidate. Through 1917 and the first half of 1918, Debs was mostly sick, confined in bed or recuperating in a sanitarium. From his sickbed he watched as America entered the First World War and as, under the guise of a national emergency, agents of the state and federal governments arrested Socialists, IWW members, unionists, and dissidents. The Bolshevik Revolution in November 1917 broke like a thunder clap on a generally depressed and defensive American socialist movement. If the Russians were successful in a society barely a step from feudalism, many socialists suggested, all that might stand between the dark American present and the future could be hard work and the application of proper tactics. As Debs himself wrote early in 1918, the Russian Revolution is "the soul of the new-born world," and he declared: "We stand or fall by Russia and the revolution—the whole program clear-cut from start to finish."

In this mood, Debs rose from his sickbed in June 1918 to undertake a series of antiwar speeches. In Canton, Ohio, Debs delivered a stirring speech in which he warned of the dangers to the basic idea of citizenship that the war hysteria encouraged: corporate leaders, he noted, "are today wrapped in the American flag [and] shout their claim from the housetops that they are the only patriots." To counter this debased view of citizenship, Debs raised the memory of earlier American dissenters and reminded the audience they did not stand alone in the current struggle to enable working people to control their "own jobs . . . own labor and be free men instead of industrial slaves." Socialists, Debs concluded, have a "duty to build the new nation and the free republic. We need industrial and social builders. . . . We are pledged to do our part. We are inviting—aye challenging you in the name of your own manhood and womanhood to join us and do your part . . . [to] proclaim the emancipation of the working class and the brotherhood of all mankind."

Two weeks after that speech, Debs was arrested and charged with violating the Espionage Act of 1917 for giving it. Following a trial that September in federal court in Cleveland, the jury found Debs guilty and the judge sentenced him to ten years in federal prison. Appeals delayed his incarceration until the next April, when Debs surrendered and was sent to a prison in Moundsville, West Virginia. That June he was transferred to the Atlanta Federal Penitentiary, where the climate and stricter prison regime took a toll on the aging Debs. Political affairs also weighed heavily on him. The repression of dissidents of every political persuasion continued throughout 1919, and the Socialist party was in disarray. Already reeling from the arrests, the party confronted another attack from the Left in the form of newly founded American Communist party. The Communists dismissed the Socialist party as lacking proper revolutionary ardor. They attacked their former comrades unstintingly and insisted that they had, in their adherence to the Bolshevik model, the proper tactics and strategy for the American movement. Both Socialists and Communists, moreover, constantly badgered Debs in prison to declare for their side. By 1920, Debs begged off and told both sides that neither his health nor prison regulations (which seriously limited his correspondence) allowed him to enter the debate with full knowledge. That fall, however, federal prisoner 9653 did conduct his fifth and last campaign for the presidency from his jail cell in Atlanta. Debs received nearly one million votes, even as the movement he sought to rejuvenate lay in tatters across the nation.

The Republican, Warren G. Harding, won that 1920 election, and in an unexpected move just before Christmas in 1921, Harding ordered the release of Debs and twenty-three other political prisoners. Debs was elated but found he had little energy for politics. Most of 1922 he spent close to home, frequently in bed, attempting to restore his body and mind. He was now sixty-seven, and the prison years had taken a severe toll. He did issue a press release affirming his membership in the Socialist party, and toward the end of that year he began to speak in public again. But only on occasion did even flashes of his earlier power and effectiveness appear. It was not just that he was frail—he was—but also that the prewar movement as he knew it no longer existed. The government repression had wreaked havoc on the party, and the more recent nationwide open shop drive, designed to eliminate even the trade union, far more accurately reflected the dominant political tone than did the Communist party's claims for a revolutionary moment. Debs remained weak during these years, and he periodically entered sanitariums in attempts to restore his health. On September 20, 1926, he entered the Lindlahr sanitarium just outside Chicago. He left but one time, bundled in heavy blankets against the sharp October air, for a short drive in the sun. On October 20, after lying unconscious for five days from a massive heart attack, Eugene Victor Debs died.

Debs's record of commitment to working people over more than forty years remains impressive. The evolution of his understanding of the proper structure for unionists was credible and instructive in his own era, although the fruits of that idea appeared more clearly in the 1930s, a decade after he died. Equally impressive was Debs's understanding of the need to reclaim a democratic political tradition from elite domination. His insistence on the intimate interdependence between political ideas and economic life remains his most potent legacy to American society. Despite the resistance to many of his specific programs from many Americans, Debs was a powerful public leaders who could evoke the best from his fellow citizens. As one friend wrote the week after he died: "His real moment lives in the hearts that beat with saddened cadence this week; hearts which dared hope because our 'Gene raised their eyes to the sun."

Bibliographic Notes

The most important manuscript source on Eugene Debs is the collection at the Cunningham Library, Indiana State University, Terre Haute. Recent accessions have increased this collection's value, and the entire collection is now available in a microfilm edition. The Debs Foundation and the Fairbanks Memorial Library, both in Terre Haute, also contain important material. The Indiana State Library and the Indiana Historical Society, both in Indianapolis, and the Lilly Library at Indiana University, Bloomington, house important Debs material as well as archives relating to Debs's contemporaries in the state.

The most complete biography of Debs is Nick Salvatore's *Eugene V. Debs: Citizen and Socialist* (1982). Earlier biographies still of interest include Ray Ginger, *The Bending Cross* (1949), and McAlister Coleman, *Eugene V. Debs: A Man Unafraid* (1930). The context of Debs's pre-Socialist labor activities are explored in Robert V. Bruce, *1877: Year of Violence* (1959); Ruth A. Allen, *The Great Southwest Strike* (1942); Donald L. McMurry, *The Great Burlington Strike of 1888: A Case History in Labor Relations* (1956); and Almont Lindsey, *The Pullman Strike* (1942). The two best surveys of American socialism remain Howard H. Quint, *The Forging of American Socialism: Origins of the Modern Movement* (1952), and David A. Shannon, *The Socialist Party of America, A History* (1955). Recently, a number of more specific works have appeared that have greatly expanded our knowledge of American radicalism. They include Melvyn Dubofsky, *We Shall Be All: A History of the IWW* (1969); James R. Green, *Grass-Roots Socialism: Radical Movements in the Southwest, 1895–1943* (1978); Lawrence Goodwyn, *Democratic Promise: The Populist Movement in America* (1976); Sally M. Miller, *Victor Berger and the Promise of Constructive Socialism, 1910–1920* (1973); and James Weinstein, *The Decline of Socialism in America, 1912–1925* (1967). Sharply negative assessment of American socialism's meaning and achievements can be found in Daniel Bell, *Marxian Socialism in the United States* (1967), and Aileen S. Kraditor, *The Radical Persuasion, 1890–1917: Aspects of the Intellectual History and the Historiography of Three American Radical Organizations* (1981). The volume edited by John M. Laslett and Seymour Martin Lipset, *Failure of a Dream? Essays in the History of American Socialism* (1974), provides the best introduction to the debate over American socialism's promise and performance.

William D. "Big Bill" Haywood: The Westerner As Labor Radical

5

Joseph R. Conlin

Early on the morning of March 31, 1921, a shambling man wearing a monocle and carrying a single trunk climbed the gangplank to a transatlantic passenger liner tied up in Hoboken, New Jersey. He was subdued as he cleared his papers for Stockholm—weary, ill, perhaps melancholy—and retired immediately, by his account, to the steerage. There is no evidence that anyone but the big man himself thought twice about the episode.

The ship, the SS *Oscar*, had a rather interesting history for a second-rate vessel in the Atlantic and Baltic passenger trade. In November 1915 the automobile magnate Henry Ford had chartered the *Oscar* for a party of prominent pacifists. They set sail for Europe, then beginning its second year of savage warfare. Henry Ford believed that the wealth and prestige of many of the passengers, and the goodwill of all, would restore calm to a distracted continent. But Ford knew little about the powerful historical forces at work in the world.

In 1915 he also knew little about journalists. Rather than reflecting admiration for the mission of the *Oscar* and the ideals of its passengers, they dispatched sometimes ribald accounts to New York and London that depicted a ship of cranks. The voyage was such a fiasco that the mortified pacifists began to disembark at the first port the Peace Ship touched. Ford himself returned quietly to the United States to make automobiles. After the United States entered the war in the spring of 1917, he satisfied numerous government contracts for submarine chasers, airplanes, tanks, and ambulances.

The man who boarded the *Oscar* in March 1921 knew more about sensationalist journalism than Ford had. And he had greater respect for the forces of history, however deficient his understanding of them. He was no pacifist but, like Ford, he had been appalled at the European slaughter.

111

Unlike Ford, however, he had counted not on the eminent but on the ordinary working people of Europe to stop it. He was a prominent union leader and radical, a former member of the Socialist party's national executive committee and an American delegate to the Congress of the Second International. In the words of *Outlook Magazine*, he believed in ordinary people "not as you and I believe in them, but fervently, uncompromisingly, with an obstinate faith in the universal good will and constancy of the workers worthy of a religious leader. That is what makes him supremely dangerous."

He had expected his European comrades to live up to their pledge that in the event their capitalist masters tried to send them into battle against one another, the workers would refuse to fight and instead turn to a general strike. When, instead, the workers of Europe took up arms for king and country, he shook his head in dismay and reconsecrated himself to the revolutionary industrial union he had come to personify, the Industrial Workers of the World (IWW)—the famous "Wobblies." He and the Wobblies determined that at least Americans would not be sucked into the fight. They thus added a militant antiwar campaign to their efforts to organize the unskilled workers of the United States into "One Big Union." One of the scathing lyrics in the most famous Wobbly document, the *Little Red Songbook*, was a parody of the hymn "Onward Christian Soldiers," John Kendrick's "Christians at War":

> Onward Christian Soldiers! Duty's way is plain;
> Slay your Christian neighbors, or by them be slain.
> Pulpiteers are spouting effervescent swill,
> God above is calling you to rob and rape and kill.
> All your acts are sanctified by the Lamb on high;
> If you love the Holy Ghost, go murder, pray, and die.

And yet, William Dudley "Big Bill" Haywood and the IWW began to profit from the Great War even before Henry Ford did. During 1915 and 1916, before the United States entered the conflict, European purchases fostered a boom in the grain belt that made it possible for the IWW to sign up and successfully represent a substantial proportion of the "hobos," the casual migrant laborers who followed the wheat harvests from Minnesota to Oklahoma, from the Mississippi to the Rockies and beyond into eastern Washington and Oregon.

Remarkable as this development seemed to many, it should not have surprised Haywood. Big Bill had been a specialist in organizing into unions workers that Samuel Gompers' American Federation of Labor

(AFL) shunned as unorganizable: hard rock miners, who were still half frontiersmen; unskilled immigrants who were bewildered by American ways and divided among themselves by language and culture; and now the despised casual workers of the West. By 1917 it looked as if he had succeeded. He was what his closest friend, Ralph Chaplin, called a "revolutionary tycoon," head of an organization that had grown from a few thousand members in 1914, when Haywood took over as secretary-treasurer, to over one hundred thousand by mid–1917. In 1916 alone, 20,000 harvest hands took out "Little Red Cards," most with enthusiasm, some because possession of one was a man's free ticket to ride the freights from one job to another. After the United States declared war in the spring of 1917, the Wobblies began to sign up thousands of workers in two other western industries critical to the war effort, copper and lumber. The union was particularly strong in the Sitka Spruce forests of the Pacific Northwest, where the light, strong lumber essential to aircraft construction was harvested. The union was also growing in the copper mines of Montana and Arizona. The Wobblies, like many American workers in 1917 and 1918, struck not to impede the war effort but to remedy often execrable conditions. The employers "could have paid workmen $10 a day and then made fat profits," Haywood told newspaperman Carl Sandburg. "The IWW has been fighting and will keep on fighting for higher wages to pay for a higher cost of living."

The IWW's success in organizing workers willing to strike during wartime regardless of purpose accounted for Haywood's presence on the *Oscar*, and it was the IWW's revolutionary image that made it easy for his enemies to prosecute him and crush the union. Despite the fact that Haywood toned down the union's opposition to the war to mere statement— deleted "Christians at War" from the songbook, leashed the most strident antiwar Wobbly leaders like Frank Little, and refused to let the organization actively obstruct the draft—the federal government, at the behest of business interests and western governors, indicted Haywood and nearly two hundred other IWW leaders for violation of the Espionage Act. A jury found most of them guilty of obstructing the war effort, and a judge fined Haywood $20,000 and sentenced him to twenty years confinement in the federal penitentiary at Leavenworth, Kansas.

It looked like a life sentence for the fifty-year-old and none-too-healthy Haywood. After losing a series of appeals, and before the Supreme Court handed down a final decision in April 1921, he decided not to submit. Along with several other prominent Wobblies, he had been invited to the Soviet Union to join in building the workers' state. On the evening before he shipped out, Haywood attended an IWW dance in New York City. Sophie Cohen, a pretty young silk weaver from Paterson, New Jersey, where Big Bill had helped lead a strike eight years earlier, remembered dancing with him. When she started back to rejoin her husband, Haywood said poignantly, "Stick with me. Don't leave me."

Sophie Cohen's recollection sums up one historical image of William Dudley Haywood and the struggle to build an anticapitalist labor union movement in the United States: plaintive, beaten, despairing, hopeless. It is by no means the image that has been most popular in radical hagiography, nor among people who have merely been disappointed by the alacrity with which the organized labor movement has accepted its role as but one contender among many for a larger piece of the American pie. There has been a powerful impulse among us to remember Haywood's life as larger than that of mere mortals, "like a melodrama of the old west" in another historian's phrase. Even in flight from a fate that, however unjust, was partly a consequence of his own doing and represented a betrayal of friends and comrades, he has been remembered as defiant, pugnacious, a rough-neck revolutionary. In his autobiography, *Bill Haywood's Book*, Haywood encouraged this legend when he wrote that he remained below in the steerage of the SS *Oscar* until he knew the ship was nearly clear of New York harbor. Then he climbed up to the deck to look at the Statue of Liberty. "Saluting the old hag with her uplifted torch, I said: 'Good-by. You've had your back turned on me too long. I am now going to the land of freedom.'"

William D. Haywood was born in Salt Lake City on February 4, 1869. He was the son of gold rush westerners, his mother a South African by birth, his father a midwesterner whose ancestry was "so American it would probably run to the Puritan bigots or the cavalier pirates." The senior Haywood became a miner and died when Bill was just a boy, compelling him to work at a variety of jobs on the broad avenues of the Mormon Zion. His formal education amounted to only a few years in Roman Catholic and public schools.

For a while after his mother married another miner, William Carruthers, he lived in Ophir, Utah, a short-lived boomtown, but returned to Salt Lake in early adolescence. In 1884, at the age of fifteen, he left home for good to work at a small mine in northern Nevada, a marginal venture that paid a profit when the price of precious metals was up but closed when the market shivered. Haywood claimed that while conditions were good at the mine, where about a dozen men worked, he was initiated into the lore of the labor movement there by Pat Reynolds, a co-worker who was a fierce partisan of the Knights of Labor and who had recently assaulted a miner owner for hiring Chinese workers. In dated newspapers they followed the prosecution and execution of the Haymarket anarchists, and Haywood said, the infamous miscarriage of justice in Chicago confirmed him in his commitment to radicalism and the union movement.

Perhaps. But there was no union at the little Ohio Mine and Milling Company. What Haywood undeniably got a taste of there were the values of the vanishing mining frontier from which, rather than from the Marxist tomes he read, his version of what America should be was formed. There was a bit of William F. Cody humbug in the way, later in life before wide-eyed eastern audiences, Haywood exploited his reputation as a son of the wild cayuses. Mormon Salt Lake City, for example, was no Roaring Camp. But if not a dime-novel character, he *was* a real westerner who had plowed a first-generation farm; worked cattle from horseback on the open range; married the daughter of a rancher, Nevada Jane Minor, and delivered one of their daughters without help. He had ridden the rails in search of work and briefly traveled with Kelley's Army. He tried to homestead at an abandoned army installation at Fort McDermitt, Nevada, and he prospected for gold in a camp where he went to bed and awoke to find "that four houses had been put up on the road overnight." Haywood lived through the industrialization and urbanization of the mining frontier.

The search for gold that began in 1849 and ended only with the collapse of the last of the wide-open boomtowns in Goldfield, Nevada, early in the twentieth century, instilled in western miners both a sense of independence and a tradition of egalitarian cooperation that carried over even when they became wage workers for highly capitalized and integrated industrial enterprises. Looking for gold, a man worked alone. To mine it efficiently, however, whether from a placer (creek gravel deposit) or from a lode, the lucky discoverer had to take partners. Not employees—few would work for wages in a world where a man could dream of a glory hole of his own—but partners whose share in the take was usually equal to the finder's. Because the size of a claim was limited (at first by the miners themselves, later by law), the typical mining camp in California or in the early days of any strike in Nevada, Colorado, Idaho, Montana, South Dakota, or wherever, was in effect a confederation of such partnerships that wrote its own rules, administered rough justice, and guaranteed the rights and property of its constituents.

Property was gold in a sack, not real estate. The frontier miners established "claims" on public land, not fee simple title to the land itself. When impelled to move on by exhaustion of the metal, news of richer diggings elsewhere, or whim from a whiskey bottle, they moved without further thought of the ground they had occupied. In the meantime, possession of a claim depended on occupation and the actual working of it. One of the most captivating illustrations of this organic version of the labor theory of value was the custom that a miner who had to be absent from his claim for a short time left a tool at the site—a pick or a shovel, a symbol of toil— to show that the claim was still active. One of the signs of change was recorded by Haywood, who returned to his cabin, traditionally left unlocked in mining country, to discover that the code of hospitality had been violated by burglary.

In such a world, the idea of an absentee owner was preposterous, its principle of capitalism rather different from that espoused by mining moguls like the Guggenheims and Hearsts. And so, when the easy diggings played out and mining gold and silver came to require great capital administered by hired trained engineers and superintendents, the miners at first refused to accept their employers' financial combinations, centered in San Francisco, New York, or London, as quite legitimate. "The barbarous gold barons," Haywood wrote, "they did not find the gold, they did not mine the gold, they did not mill the gold, but by some wierd alchemy all the gold belonged to them." When miners occupied several properties during a strike in 1901, a reporter quizzed Haywood about the rights of "the men who have invested their money in these properties." He replied, "If we follow your question to its logical conclusion, you'd have to tell me where the owners got money to invest in the mines. Who has a better right to be in peaceful possession than the miners?"

In order to understand Big Bill Haywood's place in the history of the American labor movement, his vision of what a union should be, and what he and the IWW called "revolutionary industrial unionism"—unions including all workers, unskilled as well as skilled, women as well as men, black and oriental as well as white; unions militant and dedicated to fighting employers at the point of production rather than primarily on the political field; and unions committed to the ultimate replacement of capitalism by a system in which the actual workers in an industry ran that industry— it is not necessary to refer to the formal syndicalist ideology propounded by Georges Sorel, Antonio Labriola, Emile Pouget, and the young William Z. Foster. Instead we should look to the world from which Haywood came. If his radicalism must be labeled, it might better be called strains of populism rather than Marxism, a latter-day Jacksonian producers' radicalism rather than syndicalism.

For example, he and other miners drew a distinction between mines owned and operated by former miners and those owned by corporations. They may have been deluding themselves when they claimed conditions were always better in the former, but their opinion reflected actual experiences. Ed Boyce, the head of the Western Federation of Miners (WFM) and Haywood's patron, who condemned the AFL as an organization of effete easterners and committed the WFM to socialism, retired from the union when a mine in which he owned a share struck it rich. Vincent St. John, Haywood's predecessor as head of the IWW and correctly considered more militant than Haywood, quit union work to go back to prospecting, looking for El Dorado. In *Hard Rock Miners*, Richard Lingenfelter has pointed out that the men on the Comstock Lode speculated in stocks as avidly as they wagered on roulette. While there is no evidence that Haywood gambled on the exchanges, he prospected, held a mining claim, considered dabbling in real estate, and remembered his unsuccessful homesteading experience with a wistful nostalgia, as if having a place of his own might have been a satisfactory alternative to living in the Soviet republic from which he wrote his memoirs. There is a sense of dispossession of legitimate private property about Haywood's and the miner's radicalism that is more vivid than proletarianism as defined in *Das Kapital* precisely because it happened to them not as an "historical process" but personally and very quickly indeed. Marx recognized this when, in 1880, he wrote to Friedrich Sorge asking for something "meaty" on economic conditions in California. The mining frontier was "very important" for him "because nowhere else has the upheaval shamelessly caused by capitalist centralization taken place with such speed." Such historians as Melvyn Dubofsky have fastened on the rapidity of industrialization in the mining camps as the fact of central significance in the origins of western working-class radicalism.

In a way, the miners' unions were the forty-niners' partnerships transformed in order to function in the industrialized, capitalist West. Where the unions were strong, as in Virginia City and Gold Hill, wages stayed high and relations with employers peaceful and orderly. Where the unions were weak, however, or where they faced a single or a few powerful and united companies bent on destroying them, as in Cripple Creek and Telluride, Colorado, the miners fought back with eye-gouging ferocity. Both sides in these battles were ruthless. The mine owners imported scabs, hired thugs, and in the last resort called in state militia and federal troops. The workers used the guns most still owned and the dynamite with which they worked daily.

Ironically, for he would be associated with violence throughout his career, Haywood learned his unionism in a place more like Virginia City than Cripple Creek. In 1894, the homestead gone and Nevada Jane ill with a rheumatoid arthritis that cursed her entire life, Haywood went to work underground in Silver City, Idaho. In August 1896 the camp was organized easily by Ed Boyce, head of the Western Federation of Miners. Partly because he was out of work with a mangled hand and partly because of his obvious intelligence and willingness to work long hours in the cause, Haywood rose quickly to the head of the local and to membership on the WFM's national executive board. Even in his twenties, Haywood was an excellent administrator, the type of union functionary so offensive to those who insist their revolutionaries be reckless or bohemian. He ran a nononsense organization in Silver City. Haywood maintained one hundred percent membership, perhaps in part owing to strong-arm methods. He collected the dues of a thousand members and negotiated in a businesslike manner with management, maintaining top-of-scale wages and the WFM policy that workers doing mucking and surface jobs (into which the skilled miners were bumped in times of contraction) were paid the same wages as miners. And he administered a medical plan and built and ran a hospital.

When Ed Boyce resigned as president of the WFM in 1901 to be succeeded by Charles Moyer, Haywood moved to Denver as secretary-treasurer of the union. His duties included putting out the monthly *Miner's Magazine*. He was a good if inelegant writer, and he performed editorial work ably. But the WFM was entering a period of crisis. Although there were still a few silver and gold discoveries to come, most notably at Tonopah and Goldfield, Nevada, the mining frontier was closing. The change was expressed in unsigned words Haywood may himself have penned for the magazine in 1900: "The conditions that confront the miner today are entirely different than the conditions of a quarter of a century ago, when the mines of the West were owned largely by individuals who were not too proud or arrogant to live in the same community with their employees." The industry was being consolidated to include practically every paying hole, dramatically so in Colorado, and the owners were engaged in a campaign of union destruction inspired by the newly founded National Association of Manufacturers. Although the WFM had fought bloody battles before—the union was born in an ugly fight in the Coeur D'Alenes district of the Idaho panhandle in 1891—none were so bitter as those that broke out again in the Coeur D'Alenes in 1899 (which Haywood helped coordinate); among the Colorado City smelter workers in 1902, which in turn led to the infamous Cripple Creek strike the next year; and in Telluride, Colorado, in 1904.

At Cripple Creek, mine property and a railroad depot where strikebreakers were waiting for a train were dynamited. Miners took to the hills, where they fought small arms battles with company goons and militiamen. An unpopular superintendent in Telluride was shot through his kitchen window. State troops under General Sherman Bell, who explicitly an-

119

nounced that his job was "to do up this damned anarchistic Federation," abused people they took as union sympathizers, abetted vigilantes who wrecked the offices of a pro-WFM newspaper, and routinely routed strikers from their homes, "deporting" them across the state line.

On his trips from Denver to the strike-torn camps to organize relief funds, to found union stores, and to shore up morale, Haywood took to carrying a sidearm. He was involved in fistfights and was arrested several times, once for desecrating the flag on a broadside he prepared. On one occasion he used his revolver, wounding a deputy marshal. (No charges were filed; Haywood was on his knees being brutally pummeled when he fired.) Because WFM president Moyer was in jail more often than Haywood, chief responsibility for leading the violent strikes fell to Big Bill, and he bore the brunt of the blame when, one by one, they failed. The WFM was still a formidable presence in the West at the end of 1905, thanks to sturdy, stable locals like No. 66 in Silver City and No. 1 in Butte. But it was battered and in retreat before the Mine Owner's Protective Association and its allies in state government. An analyst of battlefield tactics might be excused for calling the situation ripe for either a knockout blow by the anti-union forces or an act of desperation by the leadership of the WFM.

On December 30, 1905, Frank Steunenberg, a former governor of Idaho who had helped crush the Coeur D'Alenes strike of 1899, was killed when he opened the gate to his home, tripped a detonator, and was dynamited. The assassin was arrested almost immediately. A Canadian ne'er-do-well, Albert Horsley, who went by the name Harry Orchard, was found in his hotel room with abundant evidence to implicate him in the murder. An unsavory character by his own admission (he took to religion in jail), Orchard had a plausible personal motive for killing Steunenberg. When the governor's actions had forced him to leave the Coeur D'Alenes in 1899, he lost interest in a mine that later paid off.

But Orchard also had connections with the leaders of the WFM. Bill Haywood dispatched a WFM lawyer to Idaho to defend him, later saying this was standard procedure when a member was arrested, and he admitted having met Orchard. In any case, neither the legal nor Haywood's other services were wanted in the penitentiary in Boise. After shrewd questioning and masterful psychological manipulation by the same Pinkerton detective, James J. McParland, who three decades earlier had broken the Molly Maguires in the Pennsylvania coalfields, Orchard confessed to a multitude of murders and other acts of violence, claiming he was employed for that purpose by the "inner circle" of the federation—Moyer, Haywood, and George Pettibone, a blacklisted union activist become small business-man. The murder of Steunenberg was planned in Denver both as revenge for the victim's anti-union actions and as a warning to others who thought to resist the WFM in the future. Orchard's confession was kept secret. Because normal extradition procedures were risky, McParland and the governors of both Idaho and Colorado connived in the virtual kidnapping of Moyer, Haywood, and Pettibone, spiriting them off to Idaho in a sealed train that took on water and coal only at isolated stations. For a year the three remained in the Ada County jail while their suit against illegal extradition made its way to the Supreme Court. Finally, the court held itself powerless in the matter because the defendants were presently in custody in Idaho. About the same time, President Theodore Roosevelt joined what seemed to be the unanimous determination of government to be rid of the "inner circle" by calling Haywood "an undesirable citizen."

Haywood was the first to be tried. McParland had learned of disagreements between Big Bill and Moyer and may have hoped to enlist the WFM president in the prosecution's case against the union leader regarded as the most dangerous. If so, the tactic failed. Moyer remained silent and Haywood was ably defended by Clarence Darrow who, in effect, prosecuted Orchard, on whose testimony and character alone the charges rested. In one of his most eloquent summations, the Attorney for the Damned told the jury that the working people Haywood fought for were the real defendants. On July 28, 1907, Big Bill was acquitted. Not only did he leave Idaho as a free man, Haywood left as a celebrity. He was deluged with offers for lecture tours, some from vaudeville circuits, and became overnight a hero of the Socialist party. Eugene V. Debs had written a famous editorial in the *Appeal to Reason* during the trial declaring that: "If they attempt to murder Moyer, Haywood, and their brothers, a million revolutionists will meet them with guns," and the Socialist party nominated Haywood (in 1908) for governor of Colorado.

Haywood enjoyed the adulation and soon developed a national reputation as a powerful speaker. Curiously, his effectiveness, which all acknowledged, owed little to the theatrical oratorical style associated with the age or to his often overstated height. Haywood was undramatic and simple in his message and delivery. "The platform from which he speaks never becomes a stage," Andre Tridon wrote, "and when he speaks from a stage that stage becomes a platform." Nor was Big Bill exceptionally tall, just five feet eleven inches. But he weighed nearly 220 pounds and more on occasion. (In spells he drank heavily and suffered from diabetes.) Even in photographs one senses the *presence* of the man under the broad-brimmed

Stetson, the defiant scowl, and the dead and vaguely sinister-looking right eye (blinded in a boyhood accident) that aroused audiences from Malmo, Sweden to Paterson, New Jersey. The overworked but appropriate word is *charisma*. Hutchins Hapgood was saying this when he wrote of "the real marriage there is between Haywood's feeling and his active life. His is not a complex or split-up personality. His thought and action go together." It is difficult to explain the hold he retains on the American radical imagination to this day in any other way.

Haywood's Socialist following came from among the left "revolutionist" wing of the party (the Socialist party in America), which elected him to the SPA's national executive committee and, in 1910, as a delegate to the Congress of the Second International in Copenhagen. The revolutionists scorned the reformist wing of the party, which staked everything on coming to power through winning elections and appealed for votes by espousing an immediate program of progressive reforms. The revolutionists found Haywood's elemental bluntness vastly preferable to what they took to be the compromising slickness of politicians like New Yorker Morris Hillquit, Chicagoan Algie Simons, and head of the successful Social Democratic Federation of Milwaukee, Victor Berger.

It was also his simple forthrightness that won Haywood the acquaintance of eastern intellectual radicals, especially those who gathered in Greenwich Village around the bohemian socialite Mabel Dodge. Irreconcilably alienated from his wife and daughters by now—they lived in Denver—Big Bill exploited the romantic awe in which young women in the circle held him. But those who came to Mrs. Dodge's radical "evenings" to hear wisdom from the lips of the "one-eyed colossus" discovered that Haywood had no gift or real interest in theory or intellectual discourse. "He talked as though he were wading blindfold in sand," Walter Lippman wrote of the days in Greenwich Village. Lippmann echoed Ramsay MacDonald's observations of Haywood at the Congress of the Second International in Copenhagen, where Haywood was "useless in debate." In fact, while Haywood enjoyed his retreats into bohemia whenever he was near New York, he was never at home there. Nor, it turned out, was there a home for the union man in either the WFM or the Socialist party.

The quarrel between Haywood and Moyer in Idaho had been real. Whatever their possible involvement in the Steunenberg affair had been, Haywood was, as the prosecution's decision to try him first demonstrated, closely identified with the WFM's reputation for violence, a reputation Moyer was determined to shed. Haywood continued to draw a salary from the WFM after his release but never resumed his administrative duties in

Denver. Moyer's allies had taken control of the union and were not disappointed to see Big Bill off regaling audiences in the East. In April 1908, with Moyer out of jail and back in personal control, the *Miner's Magazine* ran a tiny notice at the bottom of a page: "To whom it may concern: This is to inform you that the Executive Board of the Western Federation of Miners has decided to terminate the services of William D. Haywood as a representative to the field."

As for the so-called reformist socialists, who were the majority of the party, they likewise disapproved of the constant pairing of Comrade Haywood's name with violent action. His party offices were gained in spite of Berger, Hillquit, and the others. His speaking tours were sponsored not by the party, which they controlled, but by the *International Socialist Review*, a magazine of the left wing from which Simons had been fired. But the most aggravating sticking point between Haywood and the reformists was his support of the industrial union he helped to found in 1905, calling it "the continental congress of the working class."

Between 1905 and 1908 the IWW had been, except for the nominal support of the WFM for little more than a year, a paper organization. Then, following a series of colorful Free Speech Fights on the skid rows of the western cities where casual laborers spent their winters, beginning in Spokane in 1909, and strikes by unskilled immigrant workers in the East, the first in McKee's Rocks, Pennsylvania, in 1909, the IWW began to grow. Through its association with Haywood, the IWW was thought of by many as an organization committed to violence. While individual members did, no doubt, set fire to wheat fields and drive nails into logs to be rolled into buzz-saws, the organization denied advocating violence, and in fact, no Wobbly was ever found guilty of an overt violent act performed under the auspices of the organization.

The union was also criticized for opposing political action—electoral campaigning—and somewhat unjustly. While the IWW under Vincent St. John officially disdained political action as an organizational instrument, many Wobblies were also loyal SPA voters. They believed it was important to elect sympathetic Socialist officials both because of the educational value of campaigns and because Socialist officials could help working people in times of crisis, as Congressman Victor Berger helped Wobbly strikers in Lawrence, Massachusetts, in 1912 by calling for a House investigation of conditions in that city. What they did not believe was that socialism could be "voted in." The postcapitalist commonwealth could be established only by the workers through economic action "at the point of production"—through the general strike.

Haywood was the most prominent spokesman for this point of view. "It is decidedly better in my opinion to elect the superintendent of some branch of industry," he said repeatedly, "than to elect some congressman to the United States Congress." During the same period, however, one of his favorite platform conceits was to drawl, "I'm a two-gun man from the West, you know," and to pull his IWW and SPA membership cards from his jacket pockets. And when pressed on his position, he espoused joining the Socialist party and voting for its candidates.

This was not enough for Berger, Hillquit, and the other reformist socialists. After 1909 they were thinking in terms of capturing the American Federation of Labor from the antisocialist Samuel Gompers. As the Socialist vote surged in the elections of 1910 and 1912, the reformists thought in terms of major party status—if only they could appeal to more reform-minded voters whom, they believed, were frightened away from the SPA by the party's apparently unofficial partnership with the IWW. Haywood was the most obvious link between the Socialist party and the IWW, between socialism and violence. Haywood had become a living legend by hastening about the country and taking charge of such tumultuous strikes as the immense and successful battle in the woolens industry of Lawrence in 1912.

The reformist socialists moved against Haywood in 1913 by adopting an amendment to the party constitution that barred from membership anyone who advocated the doctrine of sabotage. The IWW, devoted to fighting capitalism at the point of production, defended sabotage as one weapon in labor's arsenal. But what was sabotage? To the reformists and in the popular mind, it was violence. To Haywood and the IWW leadership, it was "striking on the job," working to rule, and the "conscious withdrawal of efficiency." In the debate that followed the proposed amendment to the party constitution, Wobblies admitted that sabotage could mean violence, but Haywood and other IWW leaders explicitly rejected that aspect of sabotage. "I for one have given up on violence," Haywood said. The most violent thing a working man could do was to keep his hands in his pockets.

In truth, Haywood seems to have been as frightened as Charles Moyer by the close scrape in Boise. Once, after speaking to turpentine woods workers in Louisiana and learning several days later that violence had broken out at the scene, he exploded spontaneously in a completely candid statement, "Why is this sort of thing always following me around?" By 1913, however, Haywood appears to have been deeply committed to the belief that merely by striking peacefully the workers could both win immediate goals and ultimately topple capitalism.

To no avail. In the SPA referendum, Haywood was recalled from his position on the national executive committee. He was not expelled from the party. Nor was anyone else. But, further disillusioned with "sewer socialists," Haywood apparently allowed—albeit quietly, with no manifestos—his membership to lapse. So did thousands of others. The reformists had guessed wrong. Progressive voters remained loyal to the Democratic administration of President Woodrow Wilson or, in some states like Berger's Wisconsin, to the Progressive party, while many Socialists who had approved of Haywood and the IWW simply dropped out. From a membership high of 135,000 in May 1912, before the adoption of the anti-IWW Section 6 of the party constitution, the SPA declined to 80,000 after Haywood's recall. A majority of the more than three hundred public offices the party had won between 1910 and 1912 were lost in 1913 and 1914. The vote for presidential candidate Eugene V. Debs was just shy of a million in 1912 and probably more than that had every local count been honest. In 1916, anti-Haywood Socialist presidential candidate Allen Benson won only 585,000 votes. SPA newspapers and magazines folded by the dozen and merged by the score. A friend of Haywood, Frank Bohn, asserted that the party's peak strength between 1910 and 1913 flowed from its informal association with the IWW as personified by Haywood. Perhaps he was right.

The IWW also suffered. In 1913 a strike among silk weavers in Paterson, New Jersey, fizzled and failed. Haywood, the IWW, and the Paterson workers had the support of the bohemian radicals of New York during the strike, including Mabel Dodge and John Reed. They helped put on a grand pageant in Madison Square Garden. What the Paterson Wobblies lacked was the support of an active and significant Socialist party. It may be that, almost alone among SPA analysts of the time, Frank Bohn was perfectly correct in understanding what underlay the golden age of American socialism: the tacit cooperation of a union and a party committed independently to displacing the capitalist order.

At the IWW's annual convention in 1914, Big Bill Haywood returned to doing what he did best, running a union. Vincent St. John resigned as secretary-treasurer (the position from which effective power derived in the organization that claimed "we have no leaders!"), and Haywood succeeded him. Although he continued to travel as much as any drummer, Haywood spent longer and longer periods at his desk at IWW headquarters in Chicago. There was plenty of work to be done there. Not only did the European war soon bring prosperity to the grain belt, providing an opportunity to sign up casual workers in agriculture, but the IWW also adopted, with Haywood's support, a new technique for organizing such a dispersed work force. Instead of attracting attention when they were laying over between force. Instead of attracting attention when they were laying over between jobs on the skid rows of western cities, active committed Wobblies, commissioned as "job delegates," signed up the men on the job. If discovered and fired, they moved on to a new bunkhouse and started over. The system depended on a large corps of devoted members but such spirit was the IWW's forte and the making of the Wobbly legend. Big Bill Haywood found the job delegate system appealing not only because the increased dues made it possible for the expansion of the IWW's central apparatus in Chicago, but also because through it his union worked at the point of production where, he believed, a working-class organization belonged.

This same insistence that working people seize their own fate and concern themselves with the concrete realities of their lives dictated Haywood's position on the war. Between the time of the first hostilities in Europe in August 1914 and the American intervention in April 1917, Haywood and the IWW avidly condemned the conflict and opposed every suggestion that the United States join in. His reasons were the time-honored reasons of the anticapitalist for opposing wars between nations—the Great War was a war for the benefit of the rich but the working people fought and died in it—and Wobbly rhetoric, coming from an embittered and exploited section of the working class, was sometimes more pungent and sardonic than the pleas of pacifists, members of the Socialist party, isolationist progressives, and others who were disgusted by the fall of Europe's "Proud Tower." Haywood and the IWW were, moreover, in tune with the vast majority of Americans through at least the first year of the war and with a substantial part of the population at the time of United States intervention.

Indeed, even after the United States intervened, Haywood impressed on the IWW a policy that can only be described as "quiet." The IWW did not rush into emergency convention and issue an antiwar manifesto as the Socialists did. The organization did not, like the Progressive senators LaFollette, George Norris, and their allies, noisily resist the declaration until it passed Congress, nor even then fight conscription. Nor did the IWW take the absolutist position of noncooperation espoused by some religious groups, radical sects, and thousands of individuals. The IWW did not even require members who enlisted or were drafted to let their membership lapse, as did the prowar American Federation of Labor.

On the contrary, Haywood alternately pressured and cajoled militant antiwar Wobblies like Frank Little into muting their statements. He cancelled the circulation of antiwar tracts and took a sharp editorial knife to Wobbly publications like the *Little Red Songbook*, excising lyrics that were likely to arouse patriotic hysteria. The IWW never took a position on conscription, Haywood arguing that to submit or not to submit to the draft was an individual's prerogative.

Haywood never changed his own opinion of the war. Privately and officially but "quietly," he continued to condemn it as a catastrophe for both the Western world and especially the working people. But he deduced that the IWW was powerless to stop or even hinder the carnage, and he was frankly frightened of repression in the name of patriotism. Long-standing enemies began condemning the IWW's willingness to strike as treasonous even before the United States entered the war. A congressman from Arizona stated that the initials IWW stood for "Imperial Wilhelm's Warriors." Too few people laughed. As it turned out, Haywood failed to appreciate the lengths to which patriotism could be used against radicals and dissenters. Yet his anxiety about the survival of the IWW, the One Big Union of All the Workers that was the culmination of his life's work, underlay his caution concerning the war.

The IWW's wartime goal was to survive. "Keep a cool head; do not talk," he wrote to the fiery Frank Little. "A good many feel as you do but the world war is of small importance compared to the great class war." To Wobblies in Detroit he wrote: "Keep cool and confine our agitation to job control. . . . Now is the time for cool heads, sane judgment and earnest work. There is no need of going on record for or against any movement that arises from other sources." To those who accused him of accommodating a revolutionary organization to the workings of the established order, Haywood replied that the workers' chief business was at the point of production in providing a decent life for themselves, and he supported every Wobbly strike during the period.

Herein lies the significance of William Dudley Haywood in American labor history. He was the consummate union man, a person who exalted the working people and their indigenous organization to the level of a religious faith transcending and taking priority over all else, whether electoral politics, defense of the Bill of Rights, or global war. William H. Sylvis thought of unions in this way. So had many of the Knights of Labor in the 1880s, and so would both organizers and grass-roots members of the Congress of Industrial Organizations during the 1930s. Haywood was a link in this tradition. The union was more than a pressure group. It was a symbol and a faith, to be nurtured and protected.

The first irony of Bill Haywood's career is that so little of the IWW's destiny turned out to be in Wobbly hands. His accommodations to wartime fervor did not work. In Bisbee, Arizona, on July 12, 1917, two thousand vigilantes led by the sheriff roused from bed almost twelve hundred striking IWW copper miners, sympathizers, and suspected sympathizers, herded them on a train, and dumped them in the desert across the New Mexico state line. When Haywood telegraphed President Wilson to protest this gross maltreatment, he was not favored with a reply. At three o'clock in the morning on August 1, Frank Little, with a cast on a broken leg, was kidnapped from a boarding house in Butte, Montana, possibly by policemen in disguise, and hanged from a railroad trestle outside the city. Again neither state nor federal government took an interest in the incident. By this time, the Justice Department had posted increasingly obvious surveillants around Wobbly headquarters in major cities. Haywood communicated with both Washington and federal agents in Chicago that IWW files were open to them at any time. When there was no response, he and his chief aide and closest friend, Ralph Chaplin, concluded that the government was going to raid them for the dramatic effect it would have.

The first Wobbly raid came on September 5, 1917, when federal agents stormed not only into central headquarters in Chicago but also, on the instant, into regional centers in towns as small as Astoria, Oregon. They spent three days hauling out everything from files to furniture and a death mask of Frank Little. Their take weighed five tons, and even then, the agents returned in another ballyhooed sweep on September 28. This time they confiscated what little wreckage was left and arrested those of 168 indicted Wobbly leaders they could find.

The charges against the arrested Wobblies were based on the Espionage Act of 1917. In five counts the Justice Department accused the IWW—the organization—of hindering the execution of the declaration of war; conspiring to intimidate those who supplied the government with war material; conspiring to obstruct the draft; conspiring to cause insubordination and refusal of duty in the armed forces; and conspiring to violate the postal laws by using the mail to further these goals. The prosecution did not cite a single illegal action such as Haywood had been meticulous in avoiding. Every "overt act" cited in the indictment was an expression of opinion, two of them, curiously, Haywood's telegrams to President Wilson protesting the vigilante action in Bisbee.

It also appeared to be a sloppy piece of legal work, as the Espionage Act (and Sedition Act of 1918) were sloppy pieces of legislation. Because every one of some two hundred indictees were accused, as members of the organization, of every crime, the counts totaled 10,000. This overkill heartened Haywood and encouraged him to make a fatal error. He knew the IWW was not guilty of the offenses charged as an organization; he had had his way with its policies. Therefore, any attempt to find the hundred individual Wobblies who were to be tried in Chicago guilty of conspiring to commit them was absurd. He instructed all those who were named in the indictment to surrender to authorities. Attacked as an organization, the IWW would fight as an organization in one great Wobbly trial.

All but a few of the indicted Wobblies complied. Several fled—to the Soviet Union or to new identities. Elizabeth Gurley Flynn, later a Communist party workhorse, and Joe Ettor, a Wobbly organizer, insisted that they be tried as individuals.

So strident and effective had been the propaganda campaign against Big Bill, so intimately was he identified with the unpopular IWW in the public eye—its incarnation—that his case alone would have been a cause célèbre. And a cause célèbre was what the government wanted, a circus in which through rousing hatred of the IWW a guilty verdict could be gotten. In uniting the hundred cases in Chicago, therefore, Haywood played into prosecution hands. There is no evidence that in reducing the charges to the absurd, which is what a trial of a hundred conspirators was, Haywood was trying to protect himself by hiding amidst second- and third-rank Wobbly leaders who, obviously, did not make organization policy. More likely Haywood was motivated by the Wobbly credo of solidarity. Or, in hoping to dispose of the charges in one fell swoop (and he did expect the IWW to win), the union could that much more quickly be back at its proper business. He may have been remembering the Free Speech Fights of 1913 when Wobblies arrested for street oratory demanded separate trials, attempting to clog the courts. The IWW had abandoned the Free Speech Fight tactic because it was not proletarian.

The story of the Chicago trial has been told many times and well; it is one of the few episodes in IWW history and Haywood's career that is well documented. Defense Attorney George Vanderveer shared Haywood's optimism "about our ability to make the position which the government has outlined look ridiculous." Judge Kenesaw Mountain Landis, soon to be named the first commissioner of baseball, promoted this optimism by a cool impartiality such as Wobblies were not accustomed to in court. In the Cook County jail during recesses, the Wobblies published a handwritten newspaper, the *Can-Opener*, organized themselves so that supervision was hardly necessary, sat quietly during long sessions, and in some cases, like Haywood's, acquitted themselves admirably on the witness stand. The trial lasted four months.

But the verdict had little to do with the merits of the case. The nation was feeling the frustrations of a war that created more problems than it resolved. By August 17, 1918, when the case went to jury, the United States was only a few months from the hysteria of the Red Scare and the repressions of 1919. There were three surprises on that day. First, Vanderveer delivered no summation. He was confident to the end. Second, Judge Landis, theretofore apparently determined to try the case according to strict legal procedure, told the jury that proof of overt acts was not essential to finding the defendants guilty. "You do not need to decide whether a conspiracy was completely successful. . . . It is not necessary that anyone has been induced to refuse to register, that anyone has been made impotent to furnish supplies, or that any other ultimate act has been accomplished. It is enough to show that a conspiracy was formed and that some of the defendants committed one of the overt acts." Landis had effectively ruled that if some Wobblies were guilty of what the government alleged to be illegal, all of the defendants, by virtue of their membership in the union, were guilty of conspiracy in violation of the Espionage Act.

Despite this ill omen, Haywood and the Wobblies were stunned by the day's third surprise. With 10,000 crimes to consider and four months of testimony before them, the jury returned a verdict in only a few hours. The defendants were guilty as charged. Two weeks later, Landis stunned them again. With the exception of two defendants who received sentences of ten days in jail, Landis handed down fines ranging from $20,000 to $30,000 and prison terms of from a year and a day to twenty years. Haywood's sentence, along with fourteen others, was a fine of $20,000 and twenty years in Leavenworth. The government had determined to crush the IWW. A jury of the Wobblies' peers had obliged them, and Judge Landis finished the job. For Haywood, whose health was not good, the sentence meant he would die in prison.

It could not have been easy for Haywood to trust to the appellate courts after the mockery of the jury trial. He had no difficulty in appreciating the venality of a state that, throughout his career, had indeed seemed the steering committee of the capitalist class. Because of his faith in people, a confidence that had seemed merited by the verdict in the Steunenberg trial, it was the jury verdict in the great Wobbly trial that crushed him. Out on bail raised in part by Clarence Darrow and millionaire socialist William Bross Lloyd, and in part by a loyal, unmonied friend, Mary Marcy, who mortgaged her home, he spoke at dozens of fundraising functions through 1919 and 1920. But he was, by the testimony of his associates during those two years, not the same man.

Nor was the IWW the same organization. To the extent that the federal government had set out to destroy a labor union that threatened the hegemony of employers in agriculture, copper, and lumber, it succeeded. No matter what happened in the appellate courts, the IWW had already been transformed from a functioning union into a fundraising defense organization. The Wobblies' resources and energies were exhausted in an expensive legal battle to protect the liberty of its leaders.

The union did not die. Many timber workers remained loyal to it, as did harvest hands. In fact, the IWW actually led more workers out on strike during the 1920s than in the previous decade. During the construction of Boulder Dam, early Wobbly successes in organizing the workers under the hellish conditions provided in the Nevada-Arizona desert panicked project supervisors and contributed to rapid improvement (but no IWW representation). As late as the early 1960s, an IWW local was the recognized bargaining agent in a Cleveland machine shop. But the conclusion is inescapable: so identified had Haywood and the Wobblies become—to the public as well as to members—that the IWW's history after March 1921 was anticlimactic, a *coda*.

It is not known just when Haywood was invited to flee to the Soviet Union. The invitation may have dated from 1918. In deciding to do so, however, he violated the all-for-one and one-for-all solidarity to which he had appealed in September 1918. He also betrayed close personal friends who went to prison and particularly Mary Marcy, who lost the home she had mortgaged to raise his bail and committed suicide. Any number of explanations for Haywood's action were bandied about. The Soviets apparently promised Haywood they would recompense those who had posted bail; the money was actually dispatched but was lost or stolen. The fact remains that Haywood refused to face the consequences that, from his position of authority, even idolization, he had urged others less eminent to chance.

Nevertheless, so compelling a personality was he that except for a few muted grumblings from the IWW, which soon soured on Soviet communism because the Comintern ordered Wobblies to join the AFL, he remained and has remained a hero to American radicals. Indeed, the variety of radicals (and antiradicals) who insisted on Haywood as their own is no less than astonishing. With the exception of the ever-waspish anarchist Emma Goldman, admiration of Big Bill was practically unanimous among the Left.

The Communists claimed him, of course, and his presence in Moscow supported their case. However, most Wobblies also continued to look to him as a leader, claiming that he soon soured on communism but was prevented from returning to the United States. Ralph Chaplin, Haywood's good friend who went to prison and later espoused technocracy and became a devout Roman Catholic, refused to describe Big Bill as other than a great man. Benjamin Gitlow, a communist turned militant anticommunist superpatriot, informer, and probably fabricator of lies, claimed that Haywood felt the same way in his later years. Walter Durant, *New York Times* Moscow correspondent during the 1920s, became a friend who described Haywood sympathetically in his dispatches and memoirs.

Durant and almost everyone who visited Haywood in the Soviet Union said he was unhappy there. There is the hint of this in the letters of his last years to American friends, particularly to Elizabeth Serviss, his personal secretary when he was the IWW's "revolutionary tycoon." But he did not return. After an unsuccessful stint as a supervisor at a steel factory run by foreign workers in the Kuznets region of the Urals, Haywood returned to Moscow. He was allotted a small apartment and pension, became figure-head director of the International Labor Defense, and was trundled out now and then as platform bunting at revolutionary ceremonials. He married a Russian woman—Nevada Jane died in 1920—but little is known of her save her likeness as she sat by Haywood's bier and the fact that she spoke no English, and Haywood little Russian. On March 16, 1928, at the age of fifty-nine, he was paralyzed by a stroke. After three weeks in the hospital he returned to his apartment but was felled again on May 18. He died within hours and was buried in the Kremlin Wall.

Bibliographic Notes

The fragments of Haywood's correspondence that survive and other primary source material that shed light on his life are scattered in two dozen archives from the Idaho State Historical Society to the Tamiment Institute, now part of New York University. The most important of these are the Labor History Archives at the Reuther Library at Wayne State University, Detroit, and various files of the Justice Department itself in the National Archives. For others, see the bibliography prepared by Dione Miles for Joseph R. Conlin, *At the Point of Production: The Local History of the IWW* (1981).

The principal source of information about Haywood's pre-Wobbly days remains his autobiography, *Bill Haywood's Book* (1929), although some historians have expressed their doubts concerning its reliability.

Almost everyone who knew Haywood and wrote a memoir devotes some number of pages to him. See, for example, Ralph Chaplin, *Wobbly* (1949); Clarence Darrow, *The Story of My Life* (1934); Elizabeth Gurley Flynn, *I Speak My Own Piece: The Autobiography of the Rebel Girl* (1955); Emma Goldman, *Living My Life* (1931); Hutchins Hapgood, *A Victorian in the Modern World* (1939); Mabel Dodge Luhan, *Movers and Shakers* (1935); and for mentions, almost any reminiscence from his circle and era.

Carl E. Hein made the first attempt at an objective historical biography in Harvey Goldberg (ed.), *American Radicals: Some Problems and Personalities*

William D. "Big Bill" Haywood

(1957). A more thorough analysis is ventured in Melvyn Dubofsky's "The Radicalism of the Dispossessed: William Haywood and the IWW," in Alfred E. Young (ed.), *Dissent: Explorations in the History of American Radicalism* (1968). Focusing on the Wobbly trial is the essay in Frederick C. Giffin, *Six Who Protested: Radical Opposition to the First World War* (1977).

There are two full-length biographical studies of Haywood. My own *Big Bill Haywood and the Radical Union Movement* (1969) suffered from the same paucity of primary sources as the shorter sketches just mentioned and, indeed, the one in this volume. Peter Carlson, *Roughneck: The Life and Times of Big Bill Haywood* (1983), is a graceful, readable biography, although the book is marred by some misconceptions about the nature of western mining, by romanticization, and by some sequences that seem more in the realm of imagination than history. Nevertheless, *Roughneck* is especially valuable in illuminating Haywood's character, personal life, and his years in the Soviet Union, which, because of limited space, I have neglected here. Heretofore unknown information on Haywood's early years may be found in Guy Louis Rocha, "Big Bill Haywood and Humboldt County," *Humboldt Historian*, Spring-Summer 1985.

On western miners, see Vernon Jensen, *Heritage of Conflict* (1950); Richard Lingenfelter, *Hard Rock Miners* (1975); Mark Wyman, *Hard Rock Epic* (1979); and Ronald C. Brown, *The Hard Rock Miners* (1980). The most important single essay for understanding Haywood's kind of radicalism, however, was written well before these: Melvyn Dubofsky, "The Origins of Western Working Class Radicalism," *Labor History*, Spring 1966: 131–54.

Also by Melvyn Dubofsky, *We Shall Be All: A History of the IWW* (1969) is the definitive work on the IWW. For a more popular book on the subject, see Patrick Renshaw, *The Wobblies: The Story of Syndicalism in America* (1964), or the very perusable collection of IWW documents and miscellanea by Joyce Kornbluh, *Rebel Voices* (1964). My own *Bread and Roses Too: Essays on the Wobblies* (1969) includes detail on several interpretations of the IWW that I have hastened through in the present essay.

Among the Russian language material on William Haywood, T. K. Gladkov's *Zhizn Bolshovo Billa* (1960) is little more than a reprise of *Bill Haywood's Book*; it is not available in English. An article in the *Soviet Encyclopedia* for 1929 by B. Reinshteyn includes some credible information in Haywood's Soviet years but nothing that is not presented in my *Big Bill Haywood* or Peter Carlson's *Roughneck*.

William Green and the Ideal of Christian Cooperation

6

Craig Phelan

In the textile mills that dominated the economic life of southern Appalachia, during the year 1929 there took place a dress rehearsal of the militant labor uprising that would occur across the United States in the 1930s. Sixty-hour work weeks, subsistence wages, and oppressive working conditions had long been the predicament of southern textile operatives. When mill owners further intensified the work rate, the operatives resisted with a vengeance. Beginning in 1929, a series of spontaneous strikes rocked the mill towns of Tennessee and North and South Carolina. Battle lines hardened throughout Appalachia as contestants on both sides prepared for an aggressive struggle.

For the first time since William Green had assumed the American Federation of Labor (AFL) presidency in 1924, the federation had an opportunity to organize large numbers of hitherto nonunionized workers. Unlike the auto workers whom the AFL was also attempting to organize in 1929, the textile operatives could not be accused of indifference to unionism. Nor were the craft unionists apathetic to their plight. Delegates to the 1929 AFL convention exhibited, in the words of one observer, "a pitch of enthusiasm not seen in labor gatherings since the spring tide of the Knights of Labor." Indeed, they unanimously agreed to launch a massive campaign, involving all international affiliates, to organize southern workers.

On January 6, 1930, the AFL opened its drive with a conference at Charlotte, North Carolina. Although delegates from the South urged militancy, Green, in a two-hour speech, explained that while he sincerely desired to unionize southern workers, he would not countenance force or violence. In fact, he devoted much of his speech to contrasting the methods of the Communists (who were also organizing mill workers) with the peaceful, constructive, and Christian mission of the AFL. The AFL would achieve better results, Green suggested, if it set out not to antagonize, but to convince employers and the public of the social and economic benefits of trade unionism. "There is no sword in our scabbard," he declared. "There is no weapon in our hand. We come not with the mailed fist but with the open hand to the employers of the South appealing to them to give us the opportunity, to try us out and see whether we can help this industrial situation in the South."

Green formulated a tripartite strategy for the drive: organizers would try to interest workers in the AFL; an industrial engineer, Geoffrey Brown, would attempt to persuade employers of the merits of trade unionism; and Green himself would sell the idea of unionism to the southern public. Green made two extensive speaking tours through the South in the early months of 1930. He mustered all the charm and eloquence at his command as he appealed to college gatherings, chambers of commerce, Rotary and Kiwanis clubs, three state legislatures, and four governors. Green assured the South that the AFL was not composed of godless radicals and troublemakers. Rather, he explained, the AFL is "paralleling the work of the Church." AFL members fully believed that, in resolving differences between employers and employees, "the law of righteousness, religion and morality must control if settlements arrived at are to be just and fair to all." Above all, he declared that the AFL was not a violent, destructive force. Its ultimate purpose was to create "a healthy environment, a favorable psychological condition in the homes and communities where workers dwell so that the seeds of Gospel Truth may not fall upon stony ground."

Although the southern public responded favorably to Green and his message, the AFL organizers and Geoffrey Brown met only resistance. Green had instructed organizers to counsel against spontaneous strikes in the hope that employers would recognize the AFL's peaceful mission. But such advice alienated the operatives, who sought tangible support in their struggles. Only three employers, all of them located in Columbus, Georgia, agreed to allow the AFL to organize their workers. The combined work force at the three firms—a syrup factory, a food packing plant, and a hosiery mill—was at most eighty-two workers. Not a single textile employer expressed interest in working with the federation.

The climax of the southern campaign occurred at Danville, Virginia, home of the Dan River and Riverside cotton mills, the largest in the South. Confronted with a ten percent wage cut imposed in early 1930, employees asked the United Textile Workers (UTW) to help them form a union. UTW vice-president Francis Gorman took personal charge of organizing activities, while Geoffrey Brown and Green tried to sell the AFL to the mill's management. In response, Dan River began to fire all operatives suspected

135

of union affiliation. By September two thousand workers had been dismissed. Thus the AFL had little choice but to override Green's protests and support the workers in a strike that lasted four months. The management of the mills resorted to injunctions, evictions, and the state militia. In the end, the strike failed, and with it died the hope of a peaceful campaign to introduce unionism to the South.

Several factors accounted for the defeat of the southern organizing campaign: AFL affiliates proved unwilling and sometimes unable to provide the necessary financial support for a large-scale campaign; and the South had a large pool of unskilled workers willing to break strikes, a pool made larger by the onset of the Great Depression. Added to these factors was Green's adamant refusal to sanction militant rank-and-file action to secure union recognition and collective bargaining rights. All that southern workers received from the federation were warnings against ill-advised strikes. Oppressed mill workers found no relief in Green's religious commitment to industrial peace and cooperation between labor and capital.

Strange as Green's preachment of a Christian cooperative ideal may seem in the face of southern realities, it was nonetheless explicable. Green was among the last heirs of a strain of labor thought that can be traced well back into the nineteenth century. Religious idealism had been a major component of the Knights of Labor ideology in the 1870s and 1880s, and Green's own union, the United Mine Workers, was particularly suffused with social gospel thought in its early years. Moreover, in the Progressive Era, as Green rose to power in both the AFL and the UMW, the federation sought to establish close ties with churchs through such activities as "Labor Sunday" and association with groups such as the Federal Council of Churches of Christ in America. A surprising number of labor officials joined Father Peter Dietz in the Militia of Christ for Social Service, and from 1912 to 1916 the AFL launched an organizing drive, the Labor Forward movement, that borrowed the methods of evangelism and the ideals of the social gospel. Thus, as Green matured, he was only one of many trade union officials who embraced a religiously inspired dream of labor-management cooperation.

By the 1920s and 1930s, however, as industrial relations became increasingly complex and depersonalized and as society became more secular, the ideal of Christian cooperation waned. Yet Green was so strongly wedded to those values that he proved incapable of abandoning them even after years of failure. His became an increasingly estranged and isolated voice for Christian fellowship in industrial relations. Under his guidance the evangelical-labor tradition, while still upholding the virtue and humanity of labor, became, as we shall see, a hindrance to working-class orga-

Ohio Historical Society

nization, a handmaiden to craft unionists, and a contributor to the division of the labor movement.

William Green was born in a miner's shack in Coshocton, Ohio, on March 3, 1870, the first child of Hugh and Jane Oram Green. His parents had recently moved to the United States as part of the large migration of English, Welsh, and Scottish miners in the 1860s, inspired to some extent by the British miners' leader Alexander McDonald, who urged his followers to go to America where they might eventually acquire land and become farmers. Those immigrants who settled in Coshocton were perhaps more fortunate than most, for while a few were able to escape the pits and become farmers, they nonetheless built a stable community of British miner families. This helped cushion the adjustment to life in a foreign land and also saved the Greens from the fate of so many immigrant miners, who were forced by economic necessity to move from town to town in search of steady work.

Life in a nineteenth-century mining town—in which the entire economy rested on the pits—created a communal solidarity born out of a common plight. A strike or a shutdown could spell disaster not just for the miners but also for the shopkeepers and professionals who were dependent on the miners' business. Green recalled that especially among the miners there was always "a sort of friendly, fraternal feeling. . . . The very nature of the work brings the men engaged in it into a close, friendly and sympathetic relationship." Another UMW official, John Brophy, remembered that feelings of solidarity bound the whole community: "Especially when the work became slack the whole community drew together. The boss was not so different than the rest of us; slack times were almost as hard on him as on the miners. And we were all the same breed of cats; we shared the burdens of the mine."

Green was twenty-five years old before he left Coshocton for the first time to attend a UMW district convention in nearby Columbus, and by then his character was well formed by this sense of community. Coshocton remained Green's home for his entire life, and even as AFL president he would try to return there twice each month to be with his family and friends. Throughout his life he remained an active participant in community affairs, a member not only of the local union but also of such fraternal societies as the Elks, Odd Fellows, and Masons.

One of the bonds holding Coshocton together was Protestantism. Green's parents were both devout Baptists who, like so many of their immigrant neighbors, clung tenaciously to their religious faith in the new land. Twice each day, at 6 A.M. and 6 P.M., the family would hold religious services in their home. Because neither his father nor mother were literate, it was up to William, the eldest of five children, to read from Scripture. In his youth, Green aspired to the Baptist ministry. But the paltry earnings of a coal miner denied him the requisite training for such a career. Later, as a local union official, Green conducted Sunday school classes for the local Baptist church, and as AFL president he pursued opportunities to address churches and religious organizations.

An intensely religious young man in a working-class community, Green was alive to the rising concern in late nineteenth-century Protestant churches over the suffering of workers. He became aware of Washington Gladden, a minister in Columbus, who was one of the leading proponents of the "social gospel." The principal message of Gladden and the social gospellers was that "the power of Christian love" was the only force strong enough "to smooth and sweeten all relations of capitalists and labor." In 1892 the Baptists, led by Walter Rauschenbusch, established the Brotherhood of the Kingdom, dedicating themselves to "obedience to the ethics of Jesus." The Brotherhood was a body of progressive churchmen who sought to apply the true meaning of the Kingdom of God to industrial society and "to assist in its practical realization in the world." While there is no evidence that Green was ever a member of the Brotherhood, he sympathized with its goals and, indeed, the ideas of the social gospel had a profound influence on Green's trade union philosophy.

At the age of seventeen Green began full-time work at the mines, where he remained for nineteen years. He continued to entertain hopes of pursuing the ministry, but finally abandoned this dream in 1892 when he married Jenny Mobley, the daughter of a local miner. In time he fathered five daughters and one son. As a matter of course, Green followed his own father into the local chapter of the Progressive Miners' Union in 1888. An eighth-grade education served him well, for he was one of the few men in his local of about sixty-five miners who was able to record the minutes of a meeting, compose a formal letter, or frame a resolution for subdistrict or district conventions. In 1891, one year after the Progressive Miners' Union merged with Knights of Labor District 35 to form the United Mine Workers, Green was elected secretary of his local.

Green threw himself wholeheartedly into union work and served his local in every capacity: as secretary, business agent, vice-president, on committees, and ultimately as president. The union movement became for him the "calling" he had once sought in the ministry. It offered a way to serve his fellow miners while at the same time receiving recognition, gaining status, and fulfilling his need to be useful.

Green's work at the local level in the UMW, combined with his interest in the social gospel, nurtured his belief in the necessity of Christian cooperation in labor relations. The early issues of the *United Mine Workers Journal* revealed that the union was steeped in Christian idealism and social gospel values. Religious treatises, sermons, and prayers can be found in most issues. Early UMW national conventions always began with a prayer, and even resolutions were sometimes drowned in religious rhetoric. As had often been noted, Chrisitan precepts could sanction militant as well as conservative trade union practices, but for a man such as Green, Christianity was more apt to justify a conservative, cooperationist approach.

In the last quarter of the nineteenth century, bituminous coal mining developed into a major industry, displacing wood as the principal fuel in homes and industries. By 1898 over 163 million tons of soft coal were produced per year by about 245,000 miners. The industry, however, was beset by ruinous competition and overproduction. Because a relatively small capital outlay was required to begin operations and because soft coal could be found in nearly every part of the country, the bituminous industry defied the rationalization common to other major industries at this time.

Overproduction and cutthroat competition created serious difficulties for labor as well as operators. Wage slashing, temporary layoffs, and unemployment were all too common. UMW officials and a few progressive employers recognized the need for rationalization—the establishment of uniform costs of production and the limitation of output. Indeed, in its early years the UMW tried to "sell" itself to operators by pointing out that a national union, by standardizing wage rates, could stabilize the industry.

Realizing that the traditional union goals of higher wages, shorter working hours, better working conditions, and job security could be gained only if the industry was stable, UMW officials led a massive and successful strike in 1897 that established the eight-hour day and a standard tonnage rate with local differentials in Pennsylvania, Ohio, Indiana, and Illinois. Equally important, the settlement of the strike created a Central Competitive Field, composed of the four above states, in which operators agreed to recognize the UMW and set up a system for resolving labor-management disputes that lasted into the 1920s. Through collective bargaining, operators and union officials hammered out contracts that allowed operators to plan their production and marketing and provided some assurance that competitors in the Central Competitive Field would face similar labor costs.

Leading economists, such as John R. Commons and W. J. Ashley, praised the sytem of labor-management cooperation in the soft coal industry. So, too, did William Green. His espousal of the union's approach, along with his energy and administrative talent, led to steady advancement. He was elected subdistrict president in 1900 and president of the entire Ohio district in 1906. As a frequent participant in the joint conferences and wage scale committees, Green had first-hand knowledge that when capital and labor were both well organized, they could work together for mutual benefit. He concluded that the interests of labor and capital, far from being irreconcilable, were in fact mutually dependent. The relationship was "an interdependence so fixed and irrevocable as to make complete success attainable only through understanding and cooperation." Cooperation would bring workers increased job security and stable wages, whereas employers would partly eliminate wasteful competition and strikes. The policies and practices of the infant UMW revealed that Green's Christian cooperationist views had a basis in economic reality.

His intense personal ambitions and commitment to labor cooperation led Green to run unsuccessfully for the UMW presidency in 1909, and for the post of secretary-treasurer in 1910. Having lost two elections in two years, Green's future seemed in doubt. He received several offers of employment from coal operators, but considered a career with management "distasteful." Counting on his popularity among local miners, Green abruptly decided to seek a seat in the Ohio State Senate as a Democrat in a largely Democratic district. He captured the nomination and won the election easily. In a rare achievement for a first-year senator, Green was elected president pro tem. His record proved worthy enough to merit reelection to the senate in 1912 and another term as president pro tem.

The Coshocton coal digger proved himself to be an adept Progressive politician. His election as president pro tem placed him in the position of mediator between contending political forces, the most powerful of which at this time were the Ohio Manufacturers' Association and the Ohio State Federation of Labor. As he had done in the UMW, Green pursued a course of mutual accomodation, hoping to improve capital-labor relations through the rationalization of industry. During his first term, Green authored and led the successful fight for passage of the 1911 Workmen's Compensation Act, which established a state insurance fund to be paid into by all employers with five or more workers who chose to participate. This act was rewritten with support from both employers and organized labor when the Ohio General Assembly unanimously approved the Green Compulsory Workmen's Compensation Act on February 26, 1913. By compelling employers to contribute, the new law rationalized production costs at the same time that it benefited workers. It proved so successful that it also served as model legislation for other states.

Another example of how Green pressed for labor advances by accommodating industry was his Ohio Mine Law, enacted in February 1914.

Miners were paid according to the weight of coal dug, but until this law passed, Ohio miners were not compensated for coal falling through the mine screen, the size of which often varied from mine to mine. The Mine Run Law rectified this situation, thereby increasing miners' wages and at the same time standardizing labor costs for operators.

Green also wrote and campaigned successfully for bills establishing a maximum nine-hour work day for women, a one percent income tax measure, the direct election of senators, and the nonpartisan election of judges. He labored fruitlessly for a minimum wage law and a state health insurance plan. By promoting legislation that advanced the interests of capital and labor through mutual accomodation, Green not only implemented his Christian cooperationist ideals but also became quite popular in state politics. Rumors circulated in Columbus that Green would become the next lieutenant governor. Yet just when his political career seemed most promising, Green returned to full-time work as a labor official.

The chief reason Green did not pursue a career in politics was the affinity he felt for miners and the UMW. Even while a state senator, Green considered himself to be first and foremost "the servant of the miners." More than politics, trade unionism offered him the opportunity to practice what he preached: voluntary Christian cooperation. Thus he was pleased when President White, who considered Green "one of the finest young men in the Organization," appointed him international statistician in 1911. He served so dutifully at this post in between senate sessions that, in August 1913, White named him secretary-treasurer.

Green was an unusually active secretary-treasurer, a champion of White's administration, and an advocate of progressive union reform based on religious ideal. He constantly reminded both operators and the rank and file that the Bible should serve as their guide in industrial relations. As he wrote in the 1911 Christmas issue of the miners' journal, "The teachings of the Master if obeyed and practiced would establish the Brotherhood of Man." The selfishness and greed of those employers who refused to cooperate with unions were responsible for much of the misery in the world, and it was up to union members to show recalcitrant employers the light, to make the UMW a "vital force for righteousness and social progress."

By no means was Green the sole advocate of religiously inspired unionism in the Progressive Era. He was only one of many labor officials who shared a vision of society perfected through trade unionism and Christianity. Indeed, the AFL in these years conducted organizing drives in 150 cities, which advertised labor's commitment to the social gospel and Christian cooperation. Green undoubtedly shared the desire of the editor of the

142

William Green

Amalgamated Sheet Metal Workers' journal, who wrote in 1912 that he hoped some day to see the rise of a "band of preacher-labor leaders" who would not be "bound by narrow creeds, but . . . will teach the intensely human Gospel which Christ Himself preached."

Yet another unexpected honor befell Green in 1913. The death of an AFL vice-president created a vacancy on the executive council, and AFL president Gompers offered the post to White because the powerful miners' union was unrepresented. White scorned the position of seventh vice-president as beneath his dignity, pointing out that the last UMW official to serve on the council, John Mitchell, had been second vice-president. Gompers, still eager to have the UMW represented, then offered the post to Green, who proudly joined the council.

In light of later events, it is ironic that before 1924 Green as a council member was a persistent critic of traditional AFL policy. His experiences as a Progressive politician and as an official of a progressive union led him to speak out against a number of established AFL practices, practices he would later have to enforce as AFL president. First, Green was the highest ranking spokesman for industrial unionism in the AFL. In 1912 and again during World War I, he introduced UMW resolutions to AFL conventions calling for the restructuring of the labor movement along industrial lines. He railed against the "selfishness, ill-feeling and obstinacy" of the craft organizations as they butted heads in jurisdictional disputes. When the UMW resolution lost in 1912, Green wrote in the miners' journal that "great reforms come slowly. Men are slow to change their views even in the labor movement. However, this progressive change will come—in fact, it is inevitable, because it is fundamentally right and ecnomically sound." Little did he imagine that by the 1920s he would be among those standing in the way of industrial unionism.

Second, Green rejected the AFL's opposition to labor legislation on behalf of working people. He struggled to secure the federation's endorsement for a government-sponsored health insurance plan. And, at the 1915 AFL convention, he spoke strongly in favor of eight-hour legislation for all workers. He made an eloquent, if unsuccessful, attempt to convince Gompers, the executive council, and the delegates that politics served to advance workers interests. "Is there anyone here," he asked, "who believes that the man who enjoys the benefit of the eight-hour day through the strength of his economic organization, appreciates and enjoys it more than the man who secured the eight-hour day through legislation?"

The rise to power of William Green in the labor movement was a matter of ambition, talent, and luck. But it also attested to the pervasiveness of the vision of cooperation in labor circles. His tremendous popularity

143

among the UMW rank and file would have been impossible had not his religious idealism struck a responsive chord. The failure of the Labor Forward movement, however, revealed that Christian cooperation resonated less among unorganized workers in mass-production industries, many of whom were immigrants less influenced by the social gospel movement. And the dramatic rise of John L. Lewis demonstrated that even in established industrial unions such as the UMW, hard-nosed, opportunistic union leadership was becoming increasingly common.

In the fall of 1917 John P. White resigned the presidency of the UMW to accept a position on the Federal Fuel Board and, in fulfillment of the union's constitution, Vice-President Frank Hayes automatically succeeded to the top post. Hayes and White together selected Lewis, at that time UMW statistician, for the vice-presidential slot. But when Hayes proved to be an alcoholic and an incapable administrator, Lewis literally took over. On January 1, 1920, Hayes's drinking problem forced him to resign the presidency, and Lewis replaced him.

Working for Lewis was a novel and not entirely pleasurable experience for Green. Between 1922 and 1924 Lewis authorized the expenditure of more than $12,000 in union funds to secure information or influence. When he told Green not to record these expenditures in the union's books, Green was aghast. He protested, but ultimately bowed to his boss's will. In 1923 and again in 1924, when Green performed his duties in accordance with the constitution and union precedent, Lewis upbraided him: "I would be very glad to have you accommodate your bookkeeping arrangements . . . so as to square with the President's office."

While the working relationship between the two men was hardly ideal, there is no evidence that Green ever defied Lewis or spoke out in opposition to him. On the contrary, Green praised his boss in public, as he did in 1921 when he nominated Lewis for the AFL presidency. A successful bid by Lewis would have closed Green's only avenue for advancement, yet he supported him. In 1924, when the AFL Executive Council chose Green to replace Gompers, Green accepted the position only after conferring with Lewis and receiving his approval. Green's actions as secretary-treasurer showed not timidity or an unwillingness to stand up for his convictions so much as implacable loyalty to his organization, a trait he would later exhibit as AFL president.

Gompers trounced Lewis in the 1921 election for the AFL presidency. The result was hardly a surprise because Gompers dominated the affairs of the federation. He had served as president for all but one of the thirty-eight years of the AFL's existence. Not only was he the founder, but many also considered him the federation's life blood and guiding spirit. Thus he death in December 1924 was such a profound blow that there was some concern over the AFL's ability to survive without him. Even the selection of a successor threatened to tear the AFL asunder.

Certainly Green seemed an unlikely choice for the vacant post. Other men wielded far more power in the labor movement, particularly John L. Lewis, the president of the largest affiliate, and Matthew Woll, considered Gompers' favorite and known as the "crown prince." Neither candidate, however, could command a majority. It was Lewis, in his determination to keep Woll out of office, who offered Green as the compromise candidate. Lewis used his influence to persuade council members to vote for his lieutenant. This proved an easy task, for although Green had been a critic of AFL policy, he had always upheld majority rule, was well liked by council members, and was not prone to aggrandize power. In the end, even Woll decided to vote for Green.

Becoming AFL president was a crowning distinction for Green, but the honor came at a time when the resources of the federation were in decline and the opposition to it most powerful. The membership of many of the most powerful affiliates was dwindling; the 1920s did not provide a climate favorably to union growth; and labor faced the hostility of both the judiciary and employers. In the early part of the decade, a great number of employers implemented the American Plan, a frontal assault on unions using every conceivable belligerent tactic. By the end of the decade a more subtle approach to the "labor problem," paternalistic welfare capitalism, grew in popularity, as employers consciously sought to supplant unions by directly providing employees' benefits.

Under Green the AFL reacted to these developments by changing strategy. The new strategy was simple—the AFL endeavored to "sell" itself to industry. In the hope that employers voluntarily would allow their workers to organize and bargain collectively, the AFL's high command abandoned whatever vestigial militancy it retained and advertised all the virtues of trade unionism. For most, if not all, executive council members, the shift in strategy was a calculated response to union weakness and employer hostility, a temporary maneuver that they would readily abandon when times grew more auspicious for union growth. But Green viewed the new approach as a secularized expression of the timeless ideal of Christian cooperation, a major step toward establishing an ethical basis for capital-labor relations. His role would be that of public relations director; he packaged and marketed the new AFL. And he took his product door-to-door to industrial associations, financial groups, patriotic organizations, college campuses, churches—in short to anyone willing to listen.

The most publicized expression of the AFL's campaign for respectability was union-management cooperation. In many ways similar to Green's religious vision of cooperation, union-management cooperation was a concrete plan to extend collective bargaining procedures. Once a union had been recognized, collective bargaining would determine wages, hours, and working conditions. Militancy would then give way to cooperation, and unions would join with management to make production more efficient. Green set out on a quixotic quest to persuade employers of the benefits of such a scheme. He described his ideal of union-management cooperation in May 1927: "I would like to see a condition established where the manufacturers, exercising their right to organization, would grant to the workers the exercise of the same right and then I would like to see their respective committees sit down around a conference table, at stated periods, and discuss together the common problems of industry. At these conferences, the workers . . . could point out to the management how waste could be eliminated, how duplication could be avoided, how economies could be introduced."

Green stressed the righteousness of union-management cooperation as much as the economic benefits that would accrue to industry. If only employers were guided by Christian precepts, he suggested, they would embrace the AFL's plan. Cooperation afforded employers the opportunity to atone for their selfishness and greed and simultaneously improve efficiency and increase output.

An essential corollary of union-management cooperation was the AFL's new wage policy. In order to stimulate rank-and-file interest in cooperation, the AFL leadership devised a wage policy that promised high wages and periodic wage increases based on labor's constructive contributions to efficient production. Thus employers were told that cooperation from unions carried a price tag. While other AFL leaders focused on the role of high wages in stimulating consumption and maintaining prosperity, Green stressed the moral virtue of paying high wages. He argued that "decency and justice require that workers share fully and equitably in all the blessings and benefits which flow from . . . ever-increasing production."

From Green's perspective, the AFL in the 1920s was not simply pursuing "more, more, now." Union-management cooperation promised a new era in industrial relations; it could improve workers' social as well as economic status. Under it, management might come to respect the opinions of workers. Employers would recognize that their employees were something more than an element in production costs, that they could contribute to the successful operation of industry. And if employers would also relieve employees from overwork, they would learn that employees could be active community leaders working for the common good. Green thus sought for workers a voice in decision making on the job, a rising standard of living, and the respect and status due productive and responsible citizens.

Green perceived himself not as a mere trade unionist pursuing higher wages, but as a missionary among the public and industry. He recognized, quite correctly, that if the AFL marketing campaign was to be successful, employers would have to experience something akin to a religious conversion. Green was calling for nothing less than a radical change in human behavior. Spiritual values must overcome material concerns, and the nature of industrial relations must be permanently altered. "Human welfare, spiritual values and social well-being," he wrote, "must be made paramount to industrial success. Industry must be made a contributing force to the advancement and promotion of all that is good and beautiful in life."

Despite his conviction that the AFL had a moral mission, Green was not a utopian visionary. He always held that human nature contained so many "contradictory characteristics" that perfection in industrial or human relations was unattainable. Yet he did believe that America had the resources—both natural and human—to create a cooperative and egalitarian society. Capitalist structure would be maintained, but the rights of each party to the production process would be guaranteed by mutual need and respect.

Green made many appeals to advance labor's interests. He courted middle-class support by pointing to the AFL's patriotism, its opposition to radicalism, particularly communism, and its commitment to free enterprise. But the moral dimension of industrial relations remained central to his approach, and religion always informed his thought and actions. He remained forever the Baptist preacher calling on sinners to repent.

Despite Green's enthusiasm, the AFL's new strategy failed. The package was attractive enough, but firms that already recognized AFL unions were unwilling to experiment with union-management cooperation, and nonunion employers proved unreceptive to trade unions. The serious deficiencies of the AFL strategy were most visible in the two organizing drives the federation conducted in the late 1920s. As we have seen, the militancy of southern mill operatives had stirred the fighting spirit of AFL members, many of whom urged an aggressive organizing campaign. Yet driven by the logic of cooperation, Green refused to support strike action. Southern workers, who expected financial aid and a commitment to militancy, quickly became disillusioned with the AFL.

In retrospect, the auto campaign (1926–29) was from the start a lost cause. First, the question of jurisdiction presented a serious obstacle. Green pressed for the organization of all workers into a single industrial

147

union, but the craft union leaders refused to waive their jurisdictional claims over potential union members. A compromise was reached at the Janaury 1927 session of the executive council, one that later would be applied to the organizing campaigns of the 1930s. All production workers were to be temporarily organized into federal labor unions (local unions chartered directly by the federation), and then later parcelled out among the various craft unions. Auto workers themselves vehemently opposed this policy and demanded in its place an industrial union.

Second, auto workers in the late 1920s lacked the militancy found among textile operatives in the South. The intense anti-unionism of employers, the large surplus of unskilled labor in Detroit and other auto centers, and dissatisfaction with federal labor unions all diluted militancy. The auto workers' relative quiescence reinforced the belief common among craft unionists that mass production workers were unorganizable.

Finally, Green's moralistic leadership killed whatever chance of success the AFL had. Applying his strategy of gentle persuasion, Green, on September 10, 1926, asked Max S. Hayes, editor of the *Cleveland Citizen*, to determine Ford's attitude toward union-management cooperation: "Could you learn if it would be possible for the American Federation of Labor to establish contractual relations with the Ford Motor Company along cooperative lines? . . . Could you find out if it might be possible to arrange a conference to be composed of responsible representatives of the American Federation of Labor and the Ford Motor Company where a frank, full, and free discusion might take place?" Several months later, Green unofficially launched the campaign by issuing a "challenge to Henry Ford" in the *American Federationist*: "We have brains as well as brawn, give us a chance to mobilize the creative ability of workers and cooperate with management." Green hoped that Ford would become a "manager of men, cooperating with them in a quest for better methods and better results." He issued a similar challenge to General Motors (GM).

Green honestly expected Ford and GM to respond. He did not even assign organizers to auto centers until June 1927, and even then he told them to counsel against strikes. A month later, the chief organizer, Paul Smith, wrote Green complaining that organizers were already discouraged because no progress had been made. Green then suggested that instead of concentrating on the recruitment of workers, organizers should devote their energies to persuading employers "to try collective bargaining."

Green could not comprehend the refusal of GM and Ford to confer with him. His belief that he could, through rational argument and moral suasion, convince these militantly anti-union companies "to try collective bargaining" revealed incredible naiveté. His faith in the public image campaign of the AFL clouded his understanding of reality. By the end of 1929 Green was virtually the only AFL representative trying to organize the industry, an effort fated to fail.

As long as wage rates for organized workers continued to rise, as long as a handful of experiments in union-management cooperation still existed, and as long as a few employers favored the shorter work week, Green could maintain that the AFL's cooperationist strategy was a success. He could deceive himself and try to convince others that a majority of employers were steadily moving toward the Christian cooperative ideal, that they were beginning to act in accordance with human values rather than naked self-interest, and that they were coming to recognize their long-range interest in bolstering mass purchasing power.

The depression shattered this illusion. Green was slow to realize it, but the depression proved clearly that AFL policies had failed and that employers did not regard their interests as being identical to labor's. Extensive wage cuts and layoffs revealed that self-interest, not morality, determined corporate policy. As the economic crisis deepened, Green continued to preach the gospel of cooperation. When at last his patience was exhausted, Green composed sermons predicting imminent class warfare and social revolution. He even made veiled threats about a general strike and a labor party. But militancy never suited Green. Not only was the AFL weak, but also militancy violated every precept Green held dear.

Green's dilemma was resolved by the AFL rank and file, who forced the executive council to turn to the federal government for assistance. As AFL membership rolls and wage rates plummeted, the rank and file grew increasingly disaffected with federation inactivity, particularly its voluntarist dogma. Discontent became powerful enough in 1932 to force AFL endorsement of federal unemployment insurance and shorter hour legislation. Green happily assumed his chores as leading lobbyist for organized labor. He had always regarded the state as a potential ally, and he viewed the Black bill, which would have established a maximum thirty-hour week, as a cure-all for depression and unemployment. Despite his zealous lobbying efforts, the Black bill never became law.

Green's hopes were never lower than in March 1933. A Democrat had at last been elected president, but Roosevelt, by selecting Frances Perkins over Teamster president Daniel Tobin as secretary of labor, seemed no friendlier to labor than Hoover had been. And the federation Green revered was crumbling under the weight of the depression. Membership continued to decline, union treasuries emptied, and the partial abandonment of voluntarism had yet to yield any tangible returns.

Within two months, however, he was more excited about AFL prospects than ever before. The difference was the National Industrial Recovery Act (NIRA). To Green, NIRA was a godsend. By guaranteeing labor's right to organize and by compelling labor and capital to agree on industrial codes, NIRA promised to establish by governmental decree the only basis for true prosperity—cooperation. For Green and for many others, NIRA rekindled hopes that the relations between workers and their employers could be established on a basis of morality and mutual respect.

NIRA stimulated a labor upheaval unparalleled in the twentieth century. The despair born of years of depression and the promise of Section 7a fostered a widespread and militant demand for unionism among workers. "We are witnessing a sight," Green told delegates to the 1933 AFL convention in an emotional speech, "that even the old, tried veterans of our movement never saw before." Workers were joining the AFL "because they realize there is a new deal," and nothing, he concluded, "is going to stop them from coming in." Green's remark was only half true. Workers were clamoring for unions, but very few of them joined and remained in the AFL.

Much like President Roosevelt, Green expected organizing under NIRA to be peaceful, lawful, and cooperative. He had neither the resources nor the stomach for militant campaigns. Success for the type of organizing Green envisioned depended on the cooperation of government, industry, organized labor, and the mass of workers. Government would have to implement NIRA fairly and honestly, aiding workers in their quest for organization and punishing recalcitrant employers. Employers would have to succumb to the dictates of federal law and allow the unionization of their work force. And Green expected the unorganized to be undaunted in their desire for unions yet peaceful in their approach.

Unfortunately, the campaigns were neither cooperative nor successful. First, the federal government often implemented Section 7a in such a way as to hinder organizing work. The early labor boards had little success with recalcitrant employers, and they subverted the original purpose of Section 7a by sanctioning company unions. Second, mass-production industries did not abandon their long-standing hostility to unions. Blacklisting of union leaders, industrial espionage, and company unions remained in use. Third, rather than devote its resources to organizing the unorganized, the AFL wasted precious energy on the issue of jurisdictional rights, a question that would subsequently split the federation. Finally, unorganized workers, growing impatient with the impediments to organization, committed the unpardonable sin (in Green's view) of militant action. The lack of cooperation among contending interests brought Green's campaigns in mass-production industries to a virtual standstill by early 1934.

One of the greatest impediments to successful organizing in these years was Green's refusal to support militant rank-and-file action to secure union recognition. His commitment to industrial peace alienated many mass-production workers who were willing to join the AFL but who did not share his social gospel approach. Green was always ambivalent about the use of economic power. In the first months of NIRA he applauded and even encouraged the fighting spirit of unorganized workers, but he soon became concerned about the number of strikes and their willingness to use force to achieve labor's goals. What pleased him about labor activity in the New Deal era was the widespread urge to take advantage of Section 7a and to join the AFL; what troubled him was workers' impatience when government and industry resisted their efforts. "I freely admit that I glory in the fighting spirit of the working people," Green declared in September 1933, "but it seems opportune to counsel conservation of effort and wisdom in all our efforts."

Green believed that NIRA made possible, theoretically at least, the resolution of all disputes between labor and capital at the conference table rather than on the strike field, something to which Green had been committed since his early days in the UMW. He dedicated his life to securing for American workers a middle-class lifestyle and middle-class respectability, and he firmly believed that this goal could not be achieved through militancy. Workers could improve their status only if industry freely accepted them as partners, at least junior partners, in the production process. Force and violence might secure economic gains, but not acceptance and respectability. Respectability rested on a moral relationship between labor and industry, and force meant the failure of morality. Time and again Green lectured that "the use of force in industrial relations is always a confession of failure."

His righteous opposition to labor militancy placed Green in a curious position. On the one hand, he was the highest ranking official in the largest, most established labor organization in the nation at a time when millions of workers sought the benefits of unionism; on the other hand, he was becoming increasingly alienated from rank-and-file sentiment. More and more he found himself acting not as a labor leader, but as a mediator between labor and capital. He tried to secure for workers the most favorable legislation from Congress; he reasoned with employers in the hope that they would compromise their anti-union position; and he devoted himself to restraining a restive working class.

Green's role as mediator proved untenable. It was based on the false premise that the interests of labor and capital were identical and that employers were susceptible to moral suasion. It could only be maintained by sacrificing the interests of workers, by failing to unionize mass-production workers, and ultimately by splitting the AFL itself. Green was a decent and moral man, but he did not realistically address the issues confronting organized labor in the 1930s.

The Toledo Auto-Lite strike of April–May 1934 best illustrated how Green found it necessary to oppose workers' interests in the name of industrial peace. The Toledo federal labor union (FLU) organized workers in all the city's auto plants, including the three largest parts plants. On February 23, 1934, FLU members staged a walkout after management refused to grant their demands for union recognition and a ten percent wage increase. Five days later, the strike ended when workers agreed to a vague management commitment to negotiate a new contract. In early April, however, Auto-Lite abrogated the agreement and ordered the FLU business agent off the premises. The union thereupon issued a strike call for April 12. Unlike the February walkout, only a minority of the workers responded, allowing Auto-Lite to maintain operations by hiring strike-breakers.

Green, of course, opposed the strike call. He offered no support to the strikers and later chastised the secretary of the Toledo Central Labor Union for failure "to prevent strike actions when conditions were unfavorable." Unable to obtain assistance from the AFL, the FLU turned to A. J. Muste's leftist American Workers' party (AWP), which proceeded to organize mass picketing and rally public support behind the strikers. By the middle of May, public sympathy was fully on the side of the strikers, and Green was worried about the possibility of a general strike. In a letter to the Central Labor Union, he expressed his fears that labor unrest would cause "great injury" to the labor movement and cautioned that a general strike was "a serious matter and should not be ordered."

In spite of Green's desire to contain the strike, public sympathy grew and the strike dragged on. Less than a week after Green mailed his letter, ten thousand people gathered in the streets of Toledo in a parade of solidarity. Police tried to maintain order, but when a deputy beat an unarmed elderly man in full view of the crowd, a pitched battle ensued. For three days the "Battle of Toledo" raged, pitting police and their tear gas and shotguns against strikers and their supporters. While naked, violent class conflict consumed Toledo, Green remained in Washington, silent and disapproving.

Green's position was both ludicrous and pathetic. By not supporting the

152

strikers, he had shown himself to be completely out of step with rank-and-file sentiment in unions directly under his control. In setting himself up as a mediator between labor and capital, Green had in effect deserted the strikers, who nevertheless won. Although not all of the strikers' demands were met, the FLU negotiated a contract that recognized its status as a collective bargaining unit in the three parts plants. For many FLU members and workers across the country, this was yet another example of Green and the AFL "selling them down the river."

Despite the widespread disaffection among workers, Green maintained his fruitless cooperationist strategy. Sixty-three years old in 1933 and rather set in his ways, he found it impossible, even in the face of repeated failure, to discard attitudes towards the labor movement that had been engrained for decades. Recalcitrant employers, who found nothing funny about trade unions, surely must have laughed when Green begged: "Masters, render unto your servants that which is just and equal, knowing that ye also have a Master in Heaven." Appeals such as this made to class-conscious employers had no effect. "If we are to go forward to a better world without a transition marked by class hatred, violence and bloodshed, progress must come through . . . the voluntary relinquishment of privilege and power by our priviledged classes." The mere asking of Ford, GM, Republic Steel, and other mass-production firms to relinquish voluntarily unilateral power revealed just how far removed Green was from the realities of the 1930s.

Green's failure to sanction worker militancy left the door wide open for radicals to win the confidence of workers. In the great strikes of 1934 workers followed radical leaders not because of a shared hostility to capitalism, but because radicals educated them in the use of militant tactics and gave them confidence in the power of collective economic action. The Toledo Auto-Lite strikers were certainly not all Musteites, but they welcomed the support of the AWP because this group showed them how to organize mass pickets and how to use the unemployed to help the employed. Wyndham Mortimer appealed to auto workers not because he was a communist, but because he understood their needs and respected their militant spirit. William Green did not have this confidence in the rank and file. He placed his faith in religious principles.

Largely because of the failure of Green and the AFL to establish strong unions in the mass-production industries, in the years between 1933 and 1935 there was a growing polarization of views within the AFL between craft-conscious labor officials and those favoring more militant tactics. John L. Lewis, Sidney Hillman, and other champions of industrial unionism made increasingly strident demands that the federation set aside juris-dictional disputes, pursue a more aggressive strategy, and create a labor movement with real political and economic power. In response, their craft union opponents, who dominated the executive council and controlled AFL conventions, banded even more closely together to protect their in-terests. No one in the AFL, it seemed, was willing to compromise on the grave questions facing organized labor. No one, that is, except William Green. Just as Green intended to mediate between labor and capital, he also sought a basis of accommodation within the labor movement. As he told the executive council: "I would grab at a straw to . . . preserve the solidarity of the American Federation of Labor. It has been my whole pol-icy in life to compose differences, to find a way out of a difference or dispute. I try to do that as President . . . because I fully appreciate in this great voluntary movement we are dealing with men holding different opin-ions, different views and the real problem . . . is to compose differences, hold men together, because as Mr. Gompers said years ago the Federation is a 'rope of sand.'" Composing differences between men holding such divergent views as to the future of the labor movement was the greatest challenge of Green's professional career. Yet he lacked the machinery, the leadership ability, and, above all, the values necessary to meet the chal-lenge.

There is little question as to where Green stood on the basic issue of industrial versus craft forms of organization. That he personally continued to believe in industrial unionism in the 1930s was well known. But Green did not crusade for industrial unionism as AFL president, for he sincerely believed that his principal duty was to maintain peace and unity within the labor movement. He continued to hope that the federation would adopt new forms of organization, but he was unwilling to sacrifice unity to achieve this goal.

Even though a primary function of the AFL presidency was the resolu-tion of disputes between affiliates, Gompers had never established formal machinery to do so. He had relied instead on an informal network of per-sonal relationships that aided him in maintaining relative peace. Green lacked Gompers' network, which had died along with the old man, and Green possessed neither the ability nor the vision to develop his own. Un-like Gompers, Green was never "one of the boys." He kept a formal dis-tance between himself and other executive council members, which restricted his ability to resolve disputes amicably and informally.

Failing to develop a personal following, Green relied almost exclusively on formal procedures to maintain harmony. He believed such legalisms guaranteed his own neutrality and assured a fair settlement of grievances, yet those formal procedures actually worked to the advantage of those already in control of federation policy. At several key junctures during convention debates, craft unionists were able to outmaneuver their industrial union opponents, and Green, in an attempt to remain an impartial mediator, unwittingly served the old guard.

An even more serious defect of Green's leadership, one that assured craft union victories, was his mechanistic view of majority rule. The primacy of the majority vote at conventions had always been a cardinal tenet of Green's trade union philosophy. He never questioned whether the majority vote at AFL conventions in fact reflected the majority sentiment of organized workers, let alone the entire working class. According to the AFL's constitution, international unions were allowed one vote for every hundred members. City centrals, state federations, and FLUs were given one vote each regardless of their size, and some were quite large. Thus these latter bodies were denied an adequate voice during conventions, and the sentiments of mass-production workers were never a factor in determining policy. Moreover, many unions had unit rules requiring all delegates to vote as a bloc, thus eliminating the view of delegates who may have sympathized with the industrial union outlook.

All in all, Green was a weak, unimaginative, and ineffectual peacemaker within the labor movement. His reluctance to shape policy, his dogmatic adherence to parliamentary rules of order, and his mechanistic view of majority rule—all of which he believed guaranteed his impartiality—functioned to maintain craft hegemony. Green did not, as some historians claim, bow to the will of craft unionists solely out of respect for their power within the federation. He was not so crude or self-serving. In this and most instances during his professional career, Green's actions were lofty in purpose, but his leadership was passive at a time when only dynamic leadership could have succeeded.

The defeat of the industrial union resolutions at the 1935 AFL convention and the subsequent rise of the Congress of Industrial Organizations (CIO) shaped the remainder of Green's career as a labor official. For the rest of his life his energies were consumed by a moralistic crusade against the rebel movement. And in the thousands of speeches and articles in which he damned the CIO, Green took further opportunity to extol the virtues of Christian cooperation between labor and capital.

Submission to majority rule had long been central to Green's trade union philosophy. Thus while Green labored ceaselessly to pacify Lewis and other CIO leaders, he demanded that labor unity be based on the prouncements of the AFL convention. And when it became obvious that the CIO had no intention of accepting the decision of the majority in 1935, Green allied with the enraged craft leaders first to suspend and then, in 1938, to expel the UMW and other unions connected with the CIO. The fact that Green went along with what he recognized as an "illegal" expulsion made clear that much more was involved that the issue of law and order.

An equally compelling reason for Green's opposition to the CIO was his personal antipathy to John L. Lewis. Lewis represented a radically different style of union leadership than Green. Lewis was unprincipled and opportunistically practiced the politics of conflict rather than consensus. He was obsessed with power and was willing to use any means at his disposal to wrest it from industry and government. What infuriated Green, however, was Lewis's role in founding an opposition movement within the federation. Green perceived the CIO as a Lewis plot to foist his brand of unionism on the entire labor movement and also to undermine the power and prestige of the AFL president. Lewis had outmaneuvered Green to capture the UMW presidency in 1919–20, and he was now making a bid to supersede Green as the leader of all organized labor. In his book *Labor And Democracy* (1939), Green expressed his disgust with Lewis and his methods: "Consumed with personal ambition, he gave the lie to the democratic process after it had rejected his leadership. He raised the voice of dual unionism and disunity, a voice which while pretending to unite sought to disrupt; a voice which while declaiming democratic ideals sought dictatorship."

The overriding factor behind Green's vindictive crusade against the CIO, however, was his disdain for worker militancy. His entire career rested on the notion that labor would gain only insofar as all parties to the production process promoted harmony and cooperation. He considered the CIO's approach barbaric, futile, and immoral. He referred to the sit-down strike as "sabotage beyond the wildest dreams of the I.W.W.," and he remained unwilling to admit that such tactics could ever be successful. Green's need to justify Christian cooperation led him to claim that even the contracts that CIO unions signed with GM and U.S. Steel were failures for organized labor.

The CIO's capacity to translate worker militancy into trade union gains, particularly in 1937, pointed out the fallacy of Green's approach. Cooperation had failed to secure a single signed contract with a major employer in any mass-production industry. The "immorality" of the CIO, not Green's cooperation, had brought millions of workers into the trade union fold and had made organized labor a force to be reckoned with in the nation's political and economic life.

After 1935, in his continuing effort to cultivate public acceptance of the

AFL, Green stressed the real or supposed differences between the rival labor federations. The picture he painted of the AFL was that of a responsible, patriotic organization committed to the free market and cooperation with management; the CIO, by contrast, was dictatorially controlled, a bastion of communists and other radicals, and a militant organization bent on class conflict and social strife. His speeches made him more popular among the middle class, but they bore little resemblance to reality. The AFL affiliates that successfully met the challenge of the CIO—the Machinists, the Carpenters, and the Teamsters—did so not by following Green's advice but by adopting the tactics of their CIO competitors.

Indeed, competition from the CIO invigorated rather than crippled AFL affiliates. Between 1935 and 1941, AFL membership jumped from 3.5 million to 5.2 million. Competition forced AFL unions to loosen jurisdictional boundaries and to conduct their own militant organizing drives, rather than to rely on union-management cooperation. The AFL's success coincided with the decline of Green's power and influence. In 1939 the executive council named George Meany secretary-treasurer of the AFL, and he immediately began to assume many of Green's administrative duties. In his declining years, Green served largely as a figurehead, devoting much of his energy to that which he did best—selling the AFL to the public.

The Second World War provided Green with another golden opportunity to stress accommodation between labor and capital. And during the war years management, government, and labor cooperated on an unprecedented scale in an effort to mobilize America's resources. Immediately after the declaration of war, Green proudly announced that the AFL would forgo voluntarily all strikes for the duration, a pledge the federation was remarkably successful in keeping. Yet it is ironic that despite the cooperation of labor in fighting the Axis powers, the war years gave rise to powerful anti-union sentiment among conservative congressmen and the general public. The Smith-Connelly Act and the Taft-Hartley Act revealed that significant political forces were still unwilling to accept the existence of a strong labor movement. Christian cooperation remained an elusive dream.

After the passage of the Taft-Hartley Act in 1947, Green began a campaign for its repeal, yet even here he battled for labor's rights with the outmoded weapon of moral suasion. He branded those who voted for the act as immoral, but he failed to mobilize adequately the federation's political resources. Labor's League for Political Education, which he established in 1947, did not depart from Gompers' nonpartisan policy, and in 1948 Green and the AFL balked at an official endorsement of Truman.

Only in 1952, when faced with the probable election of the Republican Eisenhower, did the federation endorse a presidential candidate, Adlai Stevenson. This break with tradition reflected the growing influence of a new generation of AFL officials who sought, among other things, greater political activism and unity with the CIO. Green's death on November 21, 1952, left a new generation of leaders in control of the AFL.

William Green's deficiencies as a labor official contributed to the failure of the AFL in the 1920s and 1930s to meet the needs of the millions of unskilled workers in mass-production industries. Under his leadership, the federation remained a weak and conservative organization of mostly skilled workers. The jurisdictional jealousies of craft unionists, the paucity of organizing funds, and the inherent weakness of the office of AFL president all exposed the limitations of the American labor movement. Green himself was not a narrow-minded craft unionist, but his inability to abandon the ideal of Christian cooperation, even after it had proved bankrupt as an organizing strategy, served the ends of exclusive unionism. This, as much as anything else, led to the collapse of the AFL's campaigns in the basic industries. Green's impotency came not from personal weakness, selfishness, or lack of effort. He was above all a decent, honorable, and even courageous man who recoiled at economic injustice and labored unsparingly to bring all workers into the union fold. His career reminds us that moral idealism in itself is a weak tool for the advancement of the working class. One cannot escape the conclusion that Green lacked a sophisticated understanding of the depth and breadth of economic injustice. Nor did he possess sufficient confidence in the power of working people themselves to improve the conditions of their existence.

Bibliographic Notes

Labor historians have paid less attention to Green than any other prominent labor official of the twentieth century. No full-length, scholarly biography exists, although I am presently at work on just such a study. Max Danish's *William Green: A Pictorial Biography* (1952) is uncritical and uninformative. Charles A. Madison, *American Labor Leaders* (1962), chapter 5, and Benjamin Stolberg, "Sitting Bill," *Saturday Evening Post*, October 18, 1941, are both useful essays but neither addresses the theme of labor evangelism. David Brody's short sketch in the *Dictionary of American Biography*, supplement 5 (John A. Garraty, ed., 1977) remains the single most informative account of Green's life. Readers who want to learn more are advised to consult Green's editorials and articles in the *American*

Federationist, his speeches and reports in the AFL's convention proceedings, and his book *Labor and Democracy* (1939).

Those interested in the evangelical tradition in the labor movement should begin with Herbert Gutman, "Protestantism and the American Labor Movement: The Christian Spirit in the Gilded Age," *American Historical Review* 72 (1966):74–101; Henry F. May, *Protestant Churches and Industrial America* (1949); and Warren R. Van Tine, *The Making of the Labor Bureaucrat: Union Leadership in the United States, 1870–1930* (1973). Marc Karson examines the role of Catholicism in shaping trade unionism in *American Labor Unions and Politics, 1900–1918* (1965), chapter 9. The careers of two social gospellers active in the labor movement are analyzed in John Aikens and James McDonnel, "Walter Rauschenbusch and Labor Reform: A Social Gospeller's Approach," *Labor History* 11 (1970): 131–50, and George H. Nash, "Charles Stelzle: Apostle to Labor," *Labor History* 11 (1970):151–74. Elizabeth and Kenneth Fones-Wolfe assess the Labor Forward movement in "Trade-Union Evangelism: Religion and the AFL in the Labor Forward Movement, 1912–1916," in Michael H. Frisch and Daniel J. Walkowitz (eds.), *Working-Class America: Essays on Labor, Community, and American Society* (1983).

For the AFL drives in mass-production industries in the 1920s and 1930s and the rise of the CIO, see Irving Bernstein, *The Lean Years* (1960) and *The Turbulent Years: A History of the American Worker, 1933–1941* (1970). Philip A. Taft, *The A.F. of L. from the Death of Gompers to the Merger* (1959) is a valuable source on Green's role. A landmark study of the schism in the AFL is David Brody's "The Emergence of Mass Production Unionism," in John Braeman et al. (eds.), *Change and Continuity in Twentieth Century America* (1964). Melvyn Dubofsky and Warren Van Tine, *John L. Lewis: A Biography* (1977) provides the most exhaustive and sophisticated treatment of the emergence of the CIO.

Rose Schneiderman and the Limits of Women's Trade Unionism

7

Alice Kessler-Harris

In April 1943, to celebrate the twenty-fifth anniversary of Rose Schneiderman's accession to the presidency of the New York branch of the Women's Trade Union League, Dorothy Canfield Fisher wrote in a brief biography: "by 29 [Schneiderman was] a figure of towering influence in the labor world, a terror to conscienceless employers, a pillar of light to underpaid women factory workers. . . . Here is a magnificent graphline of ascending power." Fisher's hyperbole did not stop there. This "little and red-headed warm-hearted" woman was described as "a valiant crusader . . . full of vitality, righteous wrath and hearty kindness, . . . magnetic" and with "great organizing ability." She achieved such recognition that "we as Americans feel almost as proud of her record, as we women are proud of the proof she gives that women are valuable citizens." Schneiderman, reading a draft of this tribute, objected only to the clause that described her as "a terror to conscienceless employers." "I have always," she wrote, "been a rather mild human being and have depended on my abilities to interpret and persuade people in order to get results."

The interchange offers an essential insight into Schneiderman's life-long devotion to improving the working conditions of women. She thought of herself not as a "terror" but as an arbitrator, not as one who waged war but as a peacemaker. In doing so, she accepted one reality of women's work situation. Like most people who thought about the issue at all in the early twentieth century, she believed that women joined the labor force as foot-soldiers—in transit between childhood and commitment to their own families. Wage-earning women, in Schneiderman's view, accepted this description of themselves and acquiesced in the relative powerlessness that followed from it. Any strategy for change had to accommodate to this essentially conventional self-perception.

160

But this set of assumptions created a dilemma for the woman labor leader. To improve women's work lives by this logic required the intervention of those with greater power and influence than working women themselves possessed. Soliciting such support required compromise. How and with whom proved to be less troublesome for Schneiderman than resolving the question of what such support would mean for working women themselves. The two sets of logical partners both posed problems. Reliance on union men meant adapting women's behavior to the world of working men, and reliance on benevolent women meant accepting the constraints of twentieth-century womanhood while battling to stretch the boundaries of women's lives. Either strategy required skill, patience, and flexibility in order not to alienate those with power. Together they demanded staunch allies among nonworking women, and a supportive atmosphere among working men.

Not all women labor leaders agreed with Schneiderman's assumptions. Other women of her generation (Julia O'Connor Parker, Dorothy Jacobs Bellanca, Fannia Cohn, and Agnes Nestor among them) chose to work inside the labor movement, where they attempted to represent women's interest as part of the working class. But there were many, including Elizabeth Christman, Leonora O'Reilly, and Mary Anderson, who like Schneiderman began their careers as wage-earners and union officers, only to decide that working women required the kind of help that could best be obtained by exercising leverage against an organized labor movement they supported but did not fully trust. Sooner or later, these women, often in the name of their commitment to organizing, sought either to circumvent or to work parallel to the established trade union movement. In doing so, they tried to encourage the labor movement to respond to too often neglected needs of women workers. Why and how these choices were posed, their implications for wage-earning women, and the insight they provide into gender differences around political strategy constitute some of the larger lessons of Schneiderman's life.

The poverty and struggle of Schneiderman's youth mirrors that of many of the young women whose cause she later championed. Born in Poland in 1882, she came to the United States at the age of eight with her parents and two younger brothers. Little more than a year after the family settled in New York's Jewish Lower East Side, her father, a tailor, died and her mother, pregnant and destitute, put first one child and then another into orphanages. Schneiderman spent about a year in an institution before her mother, her resources once more gathered, came to fetch her.

At first Rose cared for her younger sister, attending school only sporadically and yet completing nine grades in the space of four years. Then, at age thirteen, she found a job as a cash girl in a department store for the munificent sum of $2.16 per week. The sixteen cents was for laundering uniforms. It was not long before she became impatient with such low wages and over her mother's objections about its lack of gentility turned instead to factory work. By the time she was eighteen, she had found a relatively secure place sewing linings in a cap factory. With the help of a neighbor, she began to learn the skills of a sample-maker. As a more skilled worker, she would be less subject to layoffs and perhaps marginally better paid as well. Now she earned six dollars per week and instead of dutifully turning the whole sum over to her mother for household use, she kept a dollar a week for her own expenses. All this time she wore home-made or hand-me-down garments. It took Rose until she was twenty, by which time the family's economic situation had improved, before she retained enough of her slowly increasing pay to buy some ready-made clothing. Around the same time she became involved in the labor movement.

For her, as for many poor garment makers, that was a natural step, for the small unions that dotted New York's Lower East Side at the turn of the century were part of the landscape. There, where the major industry was in making one or another form of clothing, where the boss was almost always an immigrant like oneself, and where shops were small and vulnerable, unions sprang up and flowered or withered as their trade picked up and declined. Organized largely into an umbrella organization called the United Hebrew Trades, they reflected the weakness of a labor movement rooted in an industry of poorly paid workers and undercapitalized ventures. But in moments of crisis, unions benefited from being part of a community with a strong tradition of social justice. They shared at least the rough hewn socialism articulated by the Lower East Side's largest Yiddish language newspaper, the *Forverts*, and practiced in its early years by the International Ladies' Garment Workers' (ILGWU)—the union with which Schneiderman was in closest contact for most of her life. The Lower East Side was by no means entirely rebellious. But it did nurture a militant and diffuse radicalism that came from the desire to turn the American dream into reality. Where the peddler and the contractor were nourished by the prospect of social mobility, the socialist and trade unionist drew sustenance from the potential of a democracy that offered workers the capacity to change the world.

For Schneiderman, these experiences coalesced into a coherent desire to influence conditions around her during a fortuitous year that she spent in Montreal, where her mother moved to be near a sister. There Schneiderman became the protégé of a socialist family whose books and arguments

National Archives

confirmed her belief in the political promise of a socialist vision. She returned to New York, now twenty-one and open to the possibilities of trade union organization. In her autobiography, she recalls how she and three women friends, angry at such persistent injustices as paying for their own machines and thread and aware of the differences between their own treatment and that of the organized men in their shop, approached the United Cloth Hat and Cap Makers' Union in 1903 to seek help in organizing their co-workers. In the context of the Lower East Side, the success of this quartet in gathering the signatures of twenty-five women who agreed to join is remarkable only for the speed and·determination with which they accomplished the task. Within a few days, they were the proud recipients of the first charter for women in the union.

In this early period, the organization of workers seemed to Schneiderman to be the most effective way to raise wages and ameliorate working conditions. Like Samuel Gompers and the craft-oriented unions of the American Federation of Labor (AFL), she believed that workers had to rely on their united strength to achieve greater bargaining power with employers. So she threw herself into the struggle. She was rewarded with a meteoric rise. For three years, while she continued to earn her living in the factory as a capmaker and milliner, she organized for the capmakers. In 1904 she became a member of the union's general executive board, and in 1905 she played a leading role in the first successful industrywide strike of capmakers. It was then that she first encountered the Women's Trade Union League (WTUL).

Her efforts in the 1905 strike ran afoul of a series of problems commonly encountered by those who organized women. Their long hours of work and responsibility for some household chores as well made women's active participation in unions difficult. Marriage- and family-oriented, women believed their tenure in the labor force would be short and a commitment to unionization seemed unnecessary, as well as outside the context of their future lives. Because most women were only minimally skilled, their strikes could be easily broken. These problems were exacerbated by the reluctance of labor leaders, anxious to stretch limited resources, to invest in such poor candidates for organization. The success of the 1905 capmakers' strike was assured only when the Women's Trade Union League donated money and organizational skills to the effort. Hoping to find in their support better and faster ways of reaching women workers, Schneiderman joined the fledging organization in 1906.

The coalition of women trade unionists and affluent social reformers (called *allies*) who had founded the WTUL in 1903 shared with the AFL the conviction that organization would benefit women as much as men.

But whereas the federation talked about the expense of organizing the unskilled and the difficulty of appealing to women whose hearts were in leaving the labor force, the WTUL suggested that women workers would respond to tactics different from those used for men. The financial resources, political contacts, and public sympathy offered by the wealthy in conjunction with the skills and knowledge of men and women in the trade union movement could form a partnership that would enhance possibilities for organizing women. Traditional craft unions welcomed the WTUL's initiative as a solution to one pressing problem. Although reluctant to take on the task of organizing women, trade unionists nevertheless believed that their low pay and poor conditions mitigated against working women being good wives and future mothers. They also believed that women's low pay drove down the wages of less skilled men, leaving them without the resources to raise a family decently. Not because they cared so much about women's working conditions, but because they feared the negative impact of those conditions on the family, the American Federation of Labor and its affiliates welcomed the WTUL.

Schneiderman, who joined the New York branch, seemed to many WTUL activists a valuable asset. Already at twenty-four an experienced organizer, she could speak for the trade union movement whose cooperation the league so eagerly sought. And since Yiddish was her mother tongue, she felt utterly at home with that group of women workers who were among the league's major targets. While Schneiderman needed and wanted help in organizing women, she approached the league with some skepticism. Like her lifelong friend Pauline Newman, she wondered what "allies" understood of working women. Were they simply do-gooders in the progressive vein, quick to sympathize with the plight of the poor working girl but equally quick to impose their own solutions? Would they encourage trade union women to participate in making policy? Skepticism retreated a bit in 1907 when, only several months after she became a member, she was elected vice-president of the New York branch. It faded even further when a wealthy ally donated a year's wages to the league to enable Schneiderman to quit her factory job so that she could attend school and become a part-time organizer for the WTUL. She became a full-time organizer in 1909.

By now she was the essential liaison between the league and the intensive organizing activities of the Lower East Side. As a kind of roving agent, she led a successful white goods workers strike in 1909, organized the union that later became Local No. 22—the dressmakers local of the ILGWU—and participated in the famous shirtwaist-makers strike of 1909–10. To achieve some communication among the variety of groups active in enhancing the welfare of garment workers, she led the WTUL in developing a conference group to discuss industry policies. And she served as a troubleshooter, rushing home from a vacation in 1910 when the WTUL encountered a developing problem in the shirtwaist-makers union "which none of us can manage but you." Deftly she negotiated the difficult terrain that lay between skilled and organized male cutters and the semi-skilled female sewing machine operators who worked with them. When the cutters bargained for four paid holidays—which would leave operators without work or pay on those days—she persuaded the men to help organize the women in return.

Seeking new ways to bring women into unions, Schneiderman suggested a variety of techniques to appeal especially to women. We "have not considered seriously enough," she wrote in her organizer's report for 1908–9, "the joyless life of the working woman and that perhaps we have not done all that is necessary to give the labor organization a social as well as an economic attraction." The same year she proposed that the WTUL organize women into a separate federation rather than into trade unions led by men. The league, unwilling to offend the AFL, rejected the notion. Repeatedly she spoke in public and to allies about "the foreign girls," attempting to describe their culture and to discuss their conditions of work and need to organize. And always, as one of her correspondents wrote to her, she gave evidence of her "trade union class consciousness."

The years before 1911 exhibited a kind of unity that must have been very satisfying to Schneiderman. Working as an organizer in the garment trades for the New York branch of the WTUL, she was free to give herself to the cause she thought most important. At times, as in the waistmakers' strike of 1909–10, the ILGWU and the WTUL worked so closely together that her experience seemed of a piece. She remained a committed socialist, though she sometimes regretted her lack of activity in the Socialist party. Still, she wrote occasionally for the *Call*, attended party meetings, and consulted with members of the women's committee about appropriate speakers who were both good trade unionists and socialists. Briefly in 1911 she considered running for alderman on the Socialist party ticket. As if this were not enough, the women of the league introduced a new dimension into her life. The warm friends she made among the affluent women who still funded and guided the WTUL led her into feminism. She began speaking for suffrage in 1910. Not yet thirty, she had already earned recognition as a moving orator and an effective organizer. After listening to her appeal for votes for women, one observer commented: "No one has ever touched the hearts of the masses like Miss Rose Schneiderman. . . .

Strong men sat with the tears rolling down their cheeks. Her pathos and earnestness held the audiences spellbound."

But Schneiderman's attachment to the WTUL rested on its willingness to organize poor garment workers and when that commitment came into question in the winter of 1911–12, she began to differ with other league members. The dispute touched the heart of Schneiderman's commitment to the organization. In it crowning success to date, the WTUL had provided money, pickets, and publicity for the 1909–10 strike of more than twenty thousand young women waistmakers. ILGWU Local No. 25, the waistmakers' local, had entered the strike weak and with diminishing numbers. It emerged whole and hearty. In acknowledgment of their aid, the waistmakers offered the WTUL a seat on their executive board. This seat Schneiderman occupied. But shortly after the strike's end, membership began to decline once again, and the ILGWU and the WTUL blamed each other for the dwindling numbers. The union, happy to accept money and support at moments of crisis, wondered about the value of external advice on how to conduct its day-to-day affairs. For their part, Schneiderman and the WTUL proposed tactics addressed to women's specific needs that male local officers in the male-dominated union rejected out of hand. A shrinking membership merely confirmed their sense of women as ephemeral trade unionists.

Disquieted, the league leadership accepted what seemed a plausible explanation offered by one of its number. Melinda Scott, a league vice-president and a highly skilled and well-paid hat trimmer, persuaded the WTUL that more skilled and disciplined American-born women made better candidates for unionization. Membership loss, Scott argued, was the fault of the "Jewish girl," whom she described as too difficult to organize and as an unstable union member. She also pointedly questioned Schneiderman's organizing abilities and socialist politics.

In the spring of 1911, the league withdrew Schneiderman from the waistmakers' executive board, provoking a bitter split in the leadership of the New York branch that surfaced in the winter of 1911–12. One faction, led by Melinda Scott and supported by Executive Secretary Helen Marot, insisted that WTUL energy and funds should go to organizing American-born workers. Another, led by Schneiderman, aghast that the big victories of 1909–10 in New York and those that had followed in Philadelphia and Chicago should be so easily squandered, vehemently opposed abandoning foreign-born workers.

Torn by the debate and stung by the newly perceived notion that her socialism was a cause for alarm, Schneiderman gave up her job as an organizer and, as she describes it, offered her services to Anna Howard Shaw in the cause of women's suffrage. "I wasn't going to parade under false colors," she wrote in her autobiography, "so I told her that I was a socialist and a trade unionist who looked upon the ballot as a tool in the hands of working women with which through legislation, they would correct the terrible conditions existing in industry."

Now in her thirties, the unity of her life disrupted, Schneiderman weighed her commitments against each other. For nearly two years, she worked for the campaign for women's suffrage in Ohio and New York and between trips organized white goods workers. At the end of 1914, she withdrew from the league and went to work for the ILGWU as an organizer. She returned briefly to the suffrage campaign early in 1917 and, finally, in 1918 went back to the New York WTUL as its president and general organizer. In these years, the contrasting pushes and pulls of the suffrage and labor movements helped her to develop the approach that was to be the hallmark of her long life. She would be loyal to the labor movement but remain independent of it; she would support organization among women, although realism bade her not to count on it. And above all, she would commit herself to obtaining legislative relief for the most pressing problems of wage-earning women.

The suffrage campaign resolved whatever residual distrust she had of affluent women, for it provided evidence of the mutual dependence of wage-earning and more prosperous women on each other. In her early experience with the WTUL, she had had to rely on the good will of well-connected women whose money and influence sustained the organization and provided its political strength. The suffrage campaign, in contrast, taught her not only that women needed each other but that she could offer her better-off sisters something they desperately needed—access to working-class men. It enabled her, as well, to work out a position that assured her own importance in the battles that would follow a victory at the polls.

The National American Women's Suffrage Association (NAWSA) commonly argued that women ought to have the vote in order to bring to the electorate a sensibility different from that of men, and therefore more likely to induce morality and virtue in politics. Schneiderman, in contrast, harked back to the old Elizabeth Cady Stanton argument that women had a natural right to participate in government, derived from their common humanity, not from their special capacities. What differentiated her from more radical feminists organized in the Congressional Union is that, like NAWSA and unlike Stanton, she framed her arguments not on the ground of self-evident justice but on those of future ends. "Political democracy," Schneiderman argued, "will not do us much good unless we have industrial democracy, and industrial democracy can only come through intelligent workers participating in the business of which they are a part and working out the best methods for all." Her campaign speeches picked up themes on which she was later to act. The vote, she argued, would do even affluent women no good at all unless they understood and could develop a program to deal with the conditions under which most women lived and worked. Wage-earning women who daily encountered the abuses of the workplace had already begun to develop the capacity to deal with repeated affronts through their organizations. The middle class, which had so far been protected, would soon be left behind. For their own sake and so that they could vote intelligently when the time came, affluent women ought to recognize the "distinct contribution" of the organized worker and be ready "to stand by her in her heavily handicapped struggled to better her conditions." Without cross-class cooperation the women's vote would be, as she put it, "a blunt hammer." With it women could, together, humanize industry.

Optimistic possibilities inherent in women's suffrage contrasted sharply with Schneiderman's discouraging experiences with the trade union movement. Returning to the ILGWU as general organizer in late 1914, she encountered once again the difficulties women faced within this male-dominated organization. That is not to say she did not do useful work—participating in a strike settlement here or an organizing campaign there. Some of these settlements revealed the still primitive condition of women's work situations. In 1915, for example, a Springfield, Massachusetts, corset company agreed to a forty-eight-hour week, as well as to abolish payments for needles and ironing wax and to eliminate the scrubbing of floors by operatives. But frequently she felt undermined. The international moved her from place to place, pulling her out of difficult campaigns just as she had begun to make progress or assigning her to new areas for periods so short that she felt unable to do anything. One day before a planned strike of a Boston group with which she'd been working for months, the international sent a male who knew nothing of the situation to direct the strike. At the end of 1916, she submitted a letter of resignation. "For the last several months," she wrote, "I have been working in an atmosphere of . . . distrust which, to say the least, is not conducive to putting forth one's best efforts." Although these events show her weakened faith in the ILGWU, her loyalty to trade unionism in general remained untouched. She hoped, she said in her letter, to retain her "spirit and interest . . . for the sake of a cause which is bigger than any organization." When the ILGWU refused her resignation, she hung on in the hope of compromise for several more months, before she returned once again to become the chair of the 1917 women's suffrage party campaign in New York State.

169

Her experience with the ILGWU demonstrated, and later events affirmed, that the labor movement was not a reliable partner as far as women were concerned. Schneiderman never abandoned her sense of herself as a trade unionist. But she had already become impatient with the agonizingly slow path to change it offered to women. Coming at the same time as her positive experiences in the suffrage campaign, that recognition moved her towards the decision that labor legislation for women was the only way to assure that barbaric industrial conditions would not continue to exist.

In a sense she had already traveled some distance down this road before she realized where she was going. In the aftermath of the 1908 Supreme Court decision, in *Muller* vs. *Oregon*, that upheld a state's right to restrict working hours for women but not for men, many industrial states had moved to regulate women's working days. Agreeing with the famous Brandeis brief, the court held the state's interest in women as future mothers to outweigh women's own right to freedom of contract. Schneiderman and the New York branch of the WTUL fought unsuccessfully in 1910 for a bill limiting women's working hours to fifty-four in a week and ten in a day. They attributed their failure to women's lack of political power. Without the vote, legislators would not listen to them.

A year later the Triangle fire turned public interest toward such legislation as well as toward factory conditions in general. The Saturday afternoon in March 1911 that 146 burned bodies, mostly of women and young girls, ended their lives by plunging onto the sidewalks of lower Manhattan or crushing each other against locked exit doors, everyone's attention turned to state regulation. Schneiderman's bitter speech at the funeral service rejected attempts of "good people" to help. Workers, she insisted, would solve their own problems. But as social reformers used the tragedy of the fire to create commissions to investigate factory conditions and pressure for legislative action mounted, Schneiderman participated more and more in attempts to win such battles.

She committed herself once again to the fifty-four-hour bill, taking credit for fighting it through the New York Senate and Assembly in the spring of 1912; and she began to believe that if a senator "could be shown . . . that long hours and factory work [are] demoralizing to women and the race he would cast money and business to the winds and vote to benefit womankind." She testified before the commission formed to investigate the Triangle fire and to enact a new industrial code to abolish fire and health hazards in factories. And she worked closely with Pauline Goldmark's state committee on sanitation and comfort to establish standards of cleanliness for workrooms and factories, and for drinking water, washrooms, dressing rooms, and toilets. She insisted that achieving the ballot would enhance women's ability to win such legislation more easily. The effort moved her firmly, and this time permanently, into the ranks of social reformers committed to this goal. In 1918 she returned to the WTUL.

In some sense, Schneiderman had already made a choice about the future direction of her life. Yet the next few years were to solidify her assumptions about women and affirm the validity of the course she had chosen. Up to this point, she retained her radical vision, continuing to describe herself as a socialist until well after World War I. Early in the twenties, her vision narrowed as she accepted a more conventional portrait of women's sense of self. In public she began to talk and to write about women's own failures to unionize or to take on leadership positions. A mass-circulation newspaper quoted her on the difficulty of "prodding the working girl to a realization that she should be organized." She complained in a mid–1920s radio broadcast of women's failures to provide themselves with intelligent, informed leadership. The theme persisted for the rest of her career. It emerged, for example, in a 1935 speech in which she reproached the AFL for its failure to give adequate representation to women and then added, "one feels that a good deal of the blame lies with the women themselves." She repeated this idea twenty years later when, commenting that there was not a single woman on the executive councils of either the AFL or CIO, she wrote: "To be fair, however, I must say that a good deal of this is the fault of the women themselves."

This vision of women provided both justification and explanation for the direction into which she now moved. It explains how she could simultaneously berate the labor movement for its self-evident failures and yet remain loyal to it. It provides rationalization for the rigidity with which she held onto the idea of legislation even when it proved to be divisive. And it was affirmed by the recognition she received from important friends such as the Robins and the Roosevelts. In the aftermath of the victory over the ballot, she slowly abandoned her socialist dreams, turning instead to Democratic party politics that promised immediate, if more limited, results. Her move was sustained by the way in which the WTUL, the labor movement, and the women's movement intersected with each other in the 1920s.

After she became president of the New York WTUL in 1918, Schneiderman's strong antipathy towards upper class leadership created divisions that were exacerbated when she attempted to bring trade union women into positions of influence within the organization. "It is most important that the majority of our delegates be trade unionists," she wrote to East Coast members of the league before the 1922 convention. Simultaneously she altered the personnel of the league to ensure that its leading figures were products of trade union experience and the factory floor, rather than graduates of college. The strategy succeeded in enhancing the league's legitimacy as a representative of working women and it pushed the wealthy women who sustained its day-to-day activities into less active roles than they had previously occupied. Within four years she would use the support she got from the New York league to promote the candidacy of Maude Swartz, a trade unionist, for national president, and in 1926 when Swartz resigned the job, Schneiderman moved smoothly into leading the national organization and its strongest chapter as well.

The work of the WTUL as well as that of the New York WTUL now became largely routinized. Concerned with creating a generation of female leaders and still convinced that organization would enhance women's lives, Schneiderman supplemented the league's small training school by devoting effort and energy to the Bryn Mawr Summer School for women workers. An effective fund raiser, she successfully garnered enough money for the New York WTUL to purchase its own clubhouse in 1922. Once established, maintaining, organizing, and supervising the place as well as raising the money to keep it going occupied substantial chunks of her time. She had to "give the cafeteria a lot of time," she wrote to Mary Dreier in 1922. Repeatedly her secretary, apologizing for delays in answering letters, explained that "she is frightfully busy with the rummage sale."

Relative tranquility, however, was a product of having come to terms with the labor movement, not of being at peace with it. From the league's perspective, organized labor continued to evade its responsibilities towards wage-earning women. League offers of aid as well as requests for local unions to supports its work with financial assistance met only suspicion. In the city and state of New York, labor leaders objected to the potential of divided loyalty among their female members and disliked the two classes of members the WTUL created. So, the league's attempts to convince local unions to organize women often met with failure. Tensions grew in 1918 when the national president, Margaret Dreier Robins, tried to convince the AFL to persuade its affiliates to organize women. Gompers, not wanting to create friction, offered to place women who fell outside the jurisdiction of the craft unions into a federal or catch-all union. He refused to intervene on behalf of women who worked at jobs where the international affiliates that held jurisdiction simply did not wish to admit women to membership. Robins protested vigorously, to no avail.

Attempts to demonstrate loyalty to the AFL proved equally ineffective. The WTUL, which had sent Schneiderman as a delegate to the First International Conference of Working Women in Vienna and hosted a second conference in 1920 in Washington, D.C., withdrew from the International Federation of Working Women when the latter decided to affiliate with the existing International Federation of Trade Unions of which the AFL was not a member. Instead of acknowledging such loyalty, the AFL tried to undermine the WTUL further. In a sharp slap at the WTUL, which considered itself the federation's organizing arm for women, the AFL proposed in 1924 to create its own Women's Bureau. Had the measure passed, many feared that the new bureau would make the league redundant.

Although the national WTUL still continued to think of itself as a major force for organizing women, its activities languished. The league published a 1921 pamphlet called "Case for Trade Unions" and followed with a broadside letter that argued "We could not win political independence until women were organized for it and working women will never get equal pay for equal work and justice and fair play in industry if they are not organized as working men and as employers are organized." But its efforts to pressure the AFL into paying more attention to organizing women ended in stalemate. The AFL executive council did not deal with the question until 1924, and the increased organization of women it then called for produced virtually no response from its affiliates.

Schneiderman's problems in New York mirrored the national arena. The New York league attempted and failed to convince local unions to set up a joint organization council to "promote an intensive campaign among unorganized women." In the fall of 1921, Schneiderman sent a letter to all the upstate New York central bodies and unions offering the league's services in organizing women. Only one—a local of Binghamton machinists—responded. They would be delighted to have the WTUL's help in principle, they said, but in view of the depressed state of their industry, it would not be of much use just then. Still the league persisted. For a while it organized feather boa workers and fancy leather goods workers. By 1922 even these activities dwindled. Schneiderman refused to extend the leave of absence of a league organizer because she said, "for the past two years very little organization work has been called for." And not long after that, Schneiderman commented of the WTUL's services in support of a strike of milkmen: "It seems as though at this time there is nothing else to do but to organize the wives of strikers."

Still nominally a socialist, Schneiderman's residual radicalism seems to have exacerbated the tension. She ran afoul of James Holland, president of the New York Federation of Labor. Labelling her the "red rose of anarchy," he denounced her before New York State's Lusk committee called to investigate subversion. Ironically, Schneiderman had by now abandoned socialism as a political strategy. In the light of women's suffrage, she began to devote her attention to the kinds of lobbying that would achieve tangible results. But attempts at conciliation failed. In 1922 she resigned from New York City's Central Trade and Labor Council. She was, she said, "rather tired and disgusted with the machine and [I] have decided not to waste any more time on them." For the rest of the 1920s, the state Federation of Labor remained obstinately hostile.

Curiously, Schneiderman's commitment to labor legislation blinded her to the contemporary failures of the labor movement in regard to women. For while she viewed the strength wielded by organization as an important asset in winning legislation acceptable to working women, the legislative direction released her from dependence on organized labor. On this basis she appealed to the trade union movement for help in lobbying for legislation that unions often saw as less threatening than admitting women to membership. As one of several paths women could take, and as an instrument that would strengthen their hand, trade unions remained more than desirable in her eyes. But they were no longer absolutely necessary. Her relationship to the WTUL became clearer too. Less wedded to its organizing function, she acquiesced in the circumstances that de-emphasized this role, guiding the WTUL into educational activities and honing it into an effective lobbying organization on behalf of working women.

If the prevailing antipathy of organized labor to women members pushed Schneiderman and the WTUL toward protective labor legislation, the fervor with which the WTUL embraced that position created divisions among working women themselves. Many in the rank and file had benefited from the wartime (1917–18) opportunities for women and had hoped to hold on to their new jobs when the war ended. As a result, they chafed under provisions of New York State's six-day week and night work laws that had been passed in 1915 with the full support of the WTUL. Railway clerks, newspaper reporters, writers, and printers petitioned the state for exceptions. Although the legislature revoked restrictions on writers and reporters in 1919, and on printers in 1921, the WTUL vigorously opposed these petitions until 1921. Railway clerks whose unions opposed modifying the law on their behalf lost their jobs. The WTUL's rigidity alienated trade union women who found their individual rights restricted by protective legislation.

Such incidents alerted more militant feminists to the dangers of protective legislation and led them to begin discussions about an Equal Rights Amendment, which they introduced into Congress for the first time in 1923. Fearful that such an amendment, which they called the Blanket Amendment, would threaten the legislative gains of two decades, most social reform advocates vigorously opposed it.

174

Schneiderman took on the issue directly in October 1922 when Harriot Stanton Blatch, then an American Labor party candidate for the New York State Assembly, with whom she had worked closely for suffrage and whose opinion she very much trusted, made a speech opposing labor legislation. Shaken, Schneiderman wrote to the party asking for an explanation. She got little satisfaction. Julius Gerber, party chair, noted organized labor's shortcomings in regard to women and asked Schneiderman whether she didn't want to change her mind: "While Gompers and the AF of L are opposed to a minimum wage law or a law fixing the maximum hours in a day's work on the ground that it can be accomplished by the union, the AF of L favors these measures for women and children. Don't you see where the inconsistency comes in, and even you will object to being placed in the same class with children." Blatch pointed to the WTUL's lack of consistency on the issues. "You must not forget we saw the welfare workers bitterly fighting the women printers many sessions, at last admitting its mistake, allowing the amendment on night work to go through at Albany. If your long opposition was right, then your yielding was wrong, and if the final yielding was right, then the opposition was wrong."

The confrontation pushed Schneiderman into a weak defense but stiffened her spine. Like other WTUL leaders, she had always argued for protective legislation on economic and social grounds. Women's commitment to families, their lower skill levels, employers' eagerness to use them as replacements for male labor, their lesser bargaining power: these were the disadvantages that would be tempered or corrected either by unionization or by legislation. Legislation was simply faster. But in the face of the accusation of inconsistency she reverted to the argument used in the Brandeis brief and a favorite of women reformers. "We have got to see to it," she wrote to Blatch, that woman is "safeguarded from selling her labor at a starvation wage and that her hours of work are not to [*sic*] exhausting so that the child to come may inherit the strength and validity which is rightly due to it." If women were to be protected because they were the "mothers of the race," then the state had an interest in their well-being that transcended the individual rights of any woman. It was not merely their inability to compete effectively at the moment, a balancing of the scales of justice, that required legislative intervention, but women's ongoing biological and social roles.

An issue of equality had become one of morality; the concern with women's right to compete effectively in the labor force had become the concern with preserving her capacity to perform her present and future home-related tasks effectively. The labor movement had espoused the motherhood argument from the time it initially turned to labor legislation for women and children in the first two decades of the century. On the basis of this interpretation, Schneiderman and the WTUL reforged an uneasy alliance with the AFL. They could and did convince the Amalgamated Clothing Workers union to adopt a consistent anti-ERA stance. And they successfully persuaded the AFL and its constituent unions to adopt an anti-ERA position for three decades.

In the meantime, the league's lobbying activities intensified. Centered now on achieving legislation, Schneiderman organized efforts to achieve a forty-eight-hour week in New York, minimum wage legislation, state funded unemployment insurance, and old age pensions. The New York league housed a service to help women file claims under the state's accident compensation laws. It supported friendly legislators for reelection and worked to defeat those whose records it disliked. Schneiderman actively supported the national league's call to outlaw war as well as it campaign to ratify the federal child labor amendment.

It was into this policy-oriented, reform organization that Eleanor Roosevelt entered. Roosevelt first met Schneiderman and Maude Swartz at a tea in 1920 and was apparently quite taken with them. After 1922, when Roosevelt joined the league, the friendship developed rapidly. Eleanor invited Schneiderman and Swartz to visit her at Campobello and at Hyde Park. Increasingly she relied on them for advice about the labor movement and passed on what she learned to Franklin Delano Roosevelt. But it is hard to know who influenced whom more in the relationship between the Roosevelts and Rose Schneiderman, for Schneiderman was clearly taken with the Roosevelts as well. She bestowed on Eleanor an exuberant and affectionate gratitude for her contributions to the WTUL, addressing her in letters as "Dearest Eleanor" or "My dearest darling." Eleanor seems to have earned these accolades. In addition to her considerable financial contributions to the league, she sponsored an annual Christmas party contributing toys and clothing to poor children, and she could be counted upon to provide patrons for the league's benefit dinners and concerts, all this without intervening in the league's policy-making functions at all. By the time the Roosevelts entered the White House, Schneiderman had become a trusted friend subject to Eleanor's chiding if she failed to visit her on occasional trips to Washington. Trying to persuade Eleanor to follow the pattern of other presidents' wives and donate a portrait of herself to the nation, Schneiderman wrote to her, "Never before have we had a first lady who has been so genuinely interested in the public good. Never before has a wife of the president had the social vision and the desire to bring about a decent life for the majority of the people."

How much her feelings for the Roosevelts influenced her enthusistic response to New Deal policy is hard to say. By the late 1920s she had committed herself sufficiently to the necessity of legislation to welcome an administration that supported these goals. She had worked for FDR's election to the governorship, soliciting the support of labor leaders on his behalf and offering him legitmacy in labor's eyes. She worked again for his election to the presidency. And she was utterly delighted, if not completely surprised, when Secretary of Labor Frances Perkins suggested, and FDR approved, her appointment to the National Recovery Administration's (NRA) labor advisory board. It was a perfect job for her. Always a good administrator, she would be one of five labor representatives charged with supervising the NRA codes as they affected workers; she would have special responsibility for women. Then, as afterwards, she described it as the high point in her life. "Imagine setting standards for millions of women and girls," she wrote to Margaret Bondfield, Britain's minister of labor. "The codes are the Magna Charta of the working woman," she declared later, "a revolution . . . the most thrilling thing that has happened in my lifetime."

Eagerly she plunged into the job. She watched over codes in the textile and garment industries, paying special attention to the pleas of labor leaders and delighting at the role reversal involved in having men such as David Dubinsky look up to her. In the spring, she was sent to Puerto Rico on a special mission to investigate the extraordinarily low wages paid there and the impact of home work on those wages. Eleanor Roosevelt joined her briefly to add weight to the mission. Schneiderman counted the code she drew up there as one of the great achievements of her life. As she became a more public and political figure, she took on a series of regular radio programs in which she placed the great changes in the labor movement of the 1930s into the context of past struggles. She returned to New York when the NRA ended in 1935. But the fever had struck, and when, on Maude Swartz's death in 1937, the job of secretary to the New York State Department of Labor fell vacant, she snatched at the chance to move into public service once more. As the second ranking official in the state department of labor, she was in a good position to continue her efforts on behalf of women. Now she turned her attention to bringing household employees under minimum wage provisions and to including domestic workers in the workmen's compensation laws, as well as to enforcing a new wages and hours bill.

In her absence, the league floundered. She retained her job as president of both the national and New York State chapters during her tenure with the NRA and afterwards with the New York State Department of Labor.

Despite the resentment this caused, she turned over only the day-to-day administrative tasks to Elizabeth Christman, the national secretary. Schneiderman argued that her visibility spoke well for the league, bringing it into public view. But in her absence, and without alternative leadership, no new initiatives emerged. Her assertions that the most effective codes were those where the workers were organized and therefore well represented did not resonate in the league, which took little part in the rising tide of organization that marked the thirties. It was peripherally involved in campaigns to organize hotel chambermaids and laundry workers and supportive of department store workers, but its role was always on the sidelines. Instead the league lobbied for inclusion of household workers in new social security laws, for eight-hour days for all New York State employees, and against home work.

By 1941 Schneiderman had stopped defining the league in terms of its original aims. Rather, she described its "education" programs as its proudest accomplishment. The league, she wrote to Eleanor Roosevelt, gives to minimum wage boards, industrial committees, and legislative hearings, "a forthwright exposition by labor representatives of the economic and human factors in their industries." It equips women workers, she continued, with the capacity "to discuss their individual problems intelligently before public boards." Mrs. Roosevelt picked up the theme beautifully. "The basis of all good organizing," she wrote to Schneiderman, is "education, and I think the WTUL has contributed in a remarkable way to the increased knowledge of working women of today."

This approach enabled Schneiderman to handle the league's big challenge of the 1930s with equanimity. When the Committee for Industrial Organizations (CIO) split from the AFL, the WTUL confronted a dilemma. For all the tensions between the two organizations, the WTUL had remained loyal to the AFL for the twenty-three years of its existence. Yet the CIO's commitment to organizing plantwide and industrywide offered the promise of overcoming the WTUL's greatest frustration—its inability to convince the AFL to spend time and money organizing women into unions. Moreover, most of the constituent unions of the WTUL, because they represented women, were sympathetic to the CIO and some had moved into its ranks. At its 1937 meeting, the WTUL debated whether to stick by the AFL. The result was unambiguous. The executive board agreed that "the League must be true to its purpose and act accordingly to the principles it has always followed. . . . When the organization of women becomes impossible within the framework of the A.F. of L., . . . the local leagues are free to extend their activities and to aid in the organization of women workers wherever opportunity offers."

But Schneiderman dragged her feet, adopting a passive aggressive response to the CIO. She acceded to the AFL when its top leaders refused to attend a WTUL banquet in the presence of CIO leadership, invited AFL but not CIO leaders to conventions, and discouraged Eleanor from speaking to striking CIO women, while orchestrating appearances of the president's wife before members of AFL-affiliated unions. Several factors could account for this, none more compelling than Schneiderman's reluctance to challenge her own convictions about the strategy she had adopted early in the 1920s. For if women could and would organize in the CIO, then her characterizations of them as unwilling candidates for unionization came into question. And if women would willingly fight outside the bounds of propriety, then protecting them might have been less necessary. All this remained unspoken. Rather, Schneiderman expressed her discomfort with the CIO's radical leadership—discomfort exacerbated in the end of the thirties by John Lewis's outspoken criticism of the Roosevelt administration. She became something of Eleanor's conscience in this regard, advising her as to which organizations were safe and which were tainted by communist affiliation, and assuring her in 1941 that she had asked that her own name "be dropped from at least two organizations . . . because I find that the communists are using perfectly fine and public spirited people for their own ends." She was so offended when a political commentator, reviving the label that haunted her in the early 1920s, called her "the red rose of anarchy" that she threatened to sue for libel until he retracted.

These tactics contributed to the continuing decline of the WTUL, for their upshot was that the league removed itself even further from labor movement activism. Together the CIO and the AFL had nearly tripled union membership in the thirties, and of the new members, fully twenty percent were women. The unionization of the mass-production industries, which accounted for most of the increase, bypassed the league entirely. Its education activities dwindled, too, as the trade union movement, faced with a variety of regulatory agencies and new laws, developed its own training schools and institutes. More important, New Deal labor legislation blanketed nearly all workers with a protective coat, and although significant groups of women, including domestic workers and agricultural workers, were excluded, many felt it was only a matter of time before they would be covered too. And, in any event, the Women's Bureau continued to lobby for their protection. The league began to debate its future existence.

In an effort to rekindle labor support, Schneiderman once again turned her attention to the labor movement. Early in 1943, in one of the superb ironies of her long career, she persuaded Eleanor Roosevelt to send invitations out on her letterhead inviting leaders of forty trade unions to meet with her at the Cosmopolitan Club in New York City to consider the relationship between the WTUL and the labor movement. The meeting, nominally a success, prompted William Green to send a letter to AFL affiliates asking for financial help for the league. But it failed to spark any further interest among labor's leaders. Later that year, on the occasion of the league's fortieth anniversary, Schneiderman followed up with an address to the AFL annual meeting. Here she offered an incentive to the assembled leadership. "The League," she said, "has served the labor movement by interpretations of its principles and problems to the people outside our movement. . . . We hope to expand the work this year by undertaking an effective public relations job in the women's field designed to offset some of the untoward and downright false publicity directed against all labor." Nonbelligerent as ever, she thanked the AFL for encouragement and offered the league's services at the federation's pleasure.

Coming when it did, the address must have cost Schneiderman something, for by now she and other league officers understood that the WTUL was in serious trouble. As debts increased and as tensions mounted, Schneiderman's administrative assistant, Cora Cook, resigned in the spring of 1942 with a bitter letter in which she asked whether Schneiderman did not recognize that "the league may be coming to the end of its usefulness and must face the possibility of a gradual liquidation of its activities." Schneiderman acknowledged the reality "but before that time," she answered, "I want to make a last desperate attempt to revive it." A few months later, however, she asked Eleanor to give her a few minutes to discuss a decision she had made. "I have decided not to stand for reelection next Spring. I can no longer stand the strain and worry it takes to keep the League going and feel that we need new young blood."

But she did not resign—not for six years more. The best guess as to the cause of this delay comes from the role the league played in sustaining her self-image. The year 1943 marked the twenty-fifth anniversary of her accession to the presidency of the New York branch. In celebration, members chose to give a party for her, which Eleanor Roosevelt hosted at Hyde Park. The skit performed on that occasion reveals something of why Schneiderman could not yet leave. Read as a Greek chorus, with people speaking sometimes in unison and sometimes individually, it recalled the history of the WTUL and the great work it had done for working women over the years. At its center was Rose Schneiderman. Speakers began by recalling the ghosts of the past:

No light in the factories
No rest rooms
No water
Low wages
These were the evils which Rose dared to fight
In darkness of ignorance—in darkness of night
These were the death hands at working girls feasts
That wanted to turn them from humans to beasts.
But Rose dared to organize
And Rose dared to fight
Rose was so little
But Rose had great might.

They concluded, many tributes later, by proclaiming:

Rose, Rose, Rose, dearest president
Hail, Hail to you
Rose, Rose, you have been heaven sent
We honor you.

How was Rose Schneiderman, an orphaned, immigrant child of New York's Lower East Side, just resigned from her New York State Department of Labor job, to walk away from such adulation? And what does this remarkable expression of sentiment tell us about the WTUL, its leaders, and its members? It speaks to us of a community of women with boundless admiration and love for each other who stood together to oppose the forces of evil. No working-class identification here—only the ring of frail women bonding against elements that would deprive them of their humanity. The sentiments confirmed her sense of self as a tireless defender of the weak and the powerless. Not until 1949, aged sixty-seven and tired at last, did she decide to retire. Then she voted to dismantle the National Women's Trade Union League, while she turned over the presidency of the New York branch to a younger woman.

Looking back from retirement, Schneiderman re-created the connection between labor legislation and organizing in the following way: "We only began to stress legislative activities when we discovered, almost accidentally, a stepping stone cause and effect relationship in the American labor movement. If we organized even a handful of girls, and then managed to put through legislation which made into law the advantages they had gained, other girls would be more likely to join a union and reap further benefits for themselves." The memory here speaks less to what actually happened than to Schneiderman's wishes about what might have happened. But it does confirm one of Schneiderman's favorite theories: that strong organization would encourage effective legislative enforcement. And in that aspect, it resolves one of the basic dilemmas of the woman labor organizer in the years up to the New Deal. The discovery that for women legislation could provide many of the benefits of unionization, that it could be more efficiently achieved, and that it would touch wider numbers of women workers surely made it the more desirable alternative. And yet the labor leader that Schneiderman remained in her self-image had to reconcile the danger that Gompers and others in the early AFL most feared. Supporting legislation meant that the labor movement weakened its own appeal in the attempt to benefit unorganized workers. Absent such direct political influence as could be exerted by European labor parties, the American labor movement sought strength in service to its own members.

In urging legislation, Schneiderman came perilously close to having to acknowledge women's outsider position. She repeatedly and insistently affirmed her loyalty to the AFL in order to avoid that pitfall. So she claimed that organized women could most effectively influence the law's content, enforce its provisions, and ensure equity in its application. Those who were organized, she argued in her NRA years, profited more by the codes than "unorganized girls." Yet the dilemma persisted until the 1930s, at which time a new social compact affirmed labor's right to exist and a newly validated labor movement threw itself behind legislative restrictions for all workers. Not accidentally, the special role of legislation for women diminished as the new industrial unions offered the promise of membership to them. The WTUL's influence waned at the same moment.

But before this happened, the central concern of Schneiderman's life was how to obtain legislation for women without alienating them from the labor movement. The path to solving this problem broke down some of her class identifications, leaving her with a profound respect for the powers of the state and a growing dependence on its agencies for reform. It thus undermined her earlier radical analysis at the same time that it disengaged her from a labor movement that had proven itself so unwilling a partner. But it left her as dependent on the state as she had once been on the labor movement. Her life, then, represents one way in which a woman labor leader could serve her constituency. Freeing herself from the rigid and sometimes restrictive confines of a labor movement uncomfortable with female leadership, she nevertheless remained loyal to its principles and supportive of its goals. Eager to ease women's work lives and unable to conceive of them as a fighting force, she turned instead to the kind of protection the law could offer. And she salved her conscience by using the WTUL to educate the nation at large and women in particular as to labor's virtues. In the end, she was right when she denied that she was a terror to employers. For that would have violated the limits she imposed on her conception of womanhood.

Bibliographic Notes

Many of the manuscript sources for Rose Schneiderman are now available in the microfilm edition of the Papers of the Women's Trade Union League and its Principal Leaders. These include the papers of the New York Women's Trade Union League housed in the New York State Department of Labor Library in New York City; the papers of the National Women's Trade Union League located at the Library of Congress; the Rose Schneiderman collection from the Tamiment Library, New York University; and two useful collections from the Schlesinger Library: the papers of Leonora O'Reilly and Mary Anderson. The Eleanor Roosevelt papers at Hyde Park contain a number of Schneiderman letters, written mostly in the 1930s. At this writing the Pauline Newman papers, housed at the Schlesinger Library, remained closed to most researchers.

Although not a prolific writer, Schneiderman produced a number of pieces that capture her changing orientation. "A Cap Maker's Story," *The Independent* 58 (April 27, 1905):930–40, and "The Shirtwaist Makers' Strike," *Survey* 23 (Jan. 15, 1910):505–6, reflect the militance of her early years. "Is Woman Suffrage Failing?" *The Woman Citizen* 8 (March 22, 1924):730, reveals her continuing faith in women's political role; "Women's Role in Labor Legislation," *Industrial Bulletin* 25 (Jan. 1956):4–6, indicates that even at this late date she had not abandoned her interest in legislative solutions. Schneiderman's autobiography, written with Lucy Goldthwaite, *All for One* (1967), reduces many of her conflicts to platitudes.

The only full-length biography is Gary Edward Endelman, *Solidarity Forever: Rose Schneiderman and the Women's Trade Union League* (1982). Endelman sees Schneiderman as a social reformer committed to "the power of political action" and convinced that only big government could solve the problems of wage-earning women. In contrast Nancy Schrom Dye, *As Equals as Sisters: Feminism, Unionism and the Women's Trade Union League of New York* (1980), places Schneiderman within the context of women's collective action. See also Robin Miller Jacoby, "The Women's Trade Union League and American Feminism," *Feminist Studies* 3 (Fall 1975):126–40 for the feminist context. Ellen Lagemann, *A Generation of Women: Education in the Lives of Progressive Reformers* (1979), suggests that Schneiderman's life is best understood as an attempt to retrieve the educational opportunities she was denied as a child and to create them for other women. For the broader context of the WTUL see Allen F. Davis's still useful "The Women's Trade Union League: Origins and Organization," *Labor History* 5 (Winter 1964):3–17; and Gladys Boone, *The Women's Trade Union League in Great Britain and the United States of America* (1942). In the absence of a good critical history of the ILGWU, consult Louis Levine, *The Women's Garment Workers: A History of the International Ladies' Garment Workers' Union* (1924); and Benjamin Stolberg, *Tailor's Progress: The Story of a Famous Union and the Men Who Made It* (1944).

John L. Lewis and the Triumph of Mass-Production Unionism

8

Melvyn Dubofsky and Warren Van Tine

The 1930s were the most "turbulent years" in American labor history as millions of rank-and-file workers participated in a dramatic upsurge in trade unionism and exhibited unprecedented militancy and solidarity. In early 1933, fewer than 3 million workers belonged to trade unions, and most union members were then skilled craftspeople outside the basic, mass-production industries. They held membership in organizations affiliated to the American Federation of Labor (AFL), a national labor federation that had grown increasingly cautious in policy and practice ever since the early 1920s. In 1941, by contrast, total union membership had risen to nearly 10.5 million, union militants had established a new national labor center in the Congress of Industrial Organizations (CIO), and for the first time in American history millions of less skilled mass-production workers had embraced unionism.

The triumph of mass-production unionism won for American workers a new place and power in politics, economics, and society. No longer could giant corporations treat labor with disdain and assume employee passivity or trade union docility. No longer could politicians dismiss organized labor as a marginal bloc of potential voters; nor could they rely on partisan splits among labor barons to dilute working-class suffrage. To many contemporaries the transformation in labor's size and strength seemed unsettling and turned their conventional world upside down. Some journalists and pundits even predicted that the rise of mass-production unionism in the 1930s would herald a new day in American history, one in which class solidarity would dissolve ethnic and religious differences, radicalism would run riot, and working-class power would restructure the economy and society. Yet that new day never arrived.

Why a revitalized labor movement failed to transform the nation more fundamentally has been a question that has intrigued scholars and citizens since the Great Depression and the New Deal. For the most part, historians agree about the main contours of what happened to the American labor movement in the 1930s. In their narratives they stress the mass militancy of the year 1934, especially the Toledo Auto-Lite conflict, the Minneapolis teamsters' struggle, and the San Francisco general strike. So, too, do they emphasize the AFL's failure to organize the great mass of industrial workers and the consequent emergence of the CIO. Finally, historians focus on three events that solidified the triumph of the CIO and the establishment of mass-production unionism: first, the Roosevelt reelection landslide of 1936; second, the 1937 Flint sit-down strike and the United Autoworkers' victory over General Motors; and third, the Steel Workers Organizing Committee's (SWOC) agreement with United States Steel, signed in March 1937.

That, in bare outline, is a large part of what we know about labor in the 1930s. Few today would dispute the salience to labor history of the mass militancy of 1934 and 1937, the CIO's contribution to the triumph of mass-production unionism, and the impact of labor's new political activism. Yet the meaning of these developments, especially why mass-production unionism evolved precisely as it did, remains a far more contentious historical problem.

One clue to a fuller comprehension of the labor upheaval of the 1930s may lie in an examination of the role of John L. Lewis. Lewis's part in the "great upheaval" seems beyond dispute. To be sure, he did not by himself forge the CIO or precipitate the rise of mass-production unionism. He was, as are all great historical figures, as much a creature of the times as the creator of a new world of trade unionism. Lewis's contribution to the labor history of the 1930s was made possible by the hundreds of rank-and-file leaders who did the basic shop-floor organizing and by the millions of workers who walked off the job and onto the picket lines. His achievements owed much to the new political milieu for labor created by Franklin D. Roosevelt in the White House, by senators such as Robert Wagner and Robert LaFollette, Jr., in Congress, by governors such as Frank Murphy of Michigan, and by a host of friendly mayors scattered across the nation. Still, for most of the years between 1935 and 1940, workers, politicians, and the public-at-large recognized John L. Lewis as the personification of the CIO and labor's unprecedented militancy.

Understanding John L. Lewis's life and career is in large part an exercise in resolving contradictions. Len DeCaux, the founding editor of the *CIO News*, described the Lewis of 1932 as a "big-bellied, oldtime labor

Wide World Photos

leader. . . . An autocract, per capita counter, egotist, [and] power
seeker. . . . He was a man who had bowed the knee to capitalism, who
had been merciless against the red and the rebellious." The historian David
Brody has said that in 1933 Lewis seemed "merely a labor boss of the most
conventional kind, and a largely discredited one at that." Yet this "big-
bellied, conventional" labor leader decided to break with his cohorts in the
AFL hierarchy in order to gamble his power and future on the chance that
mass-production unionism would work. Initially, he tied his fortunes to
Franklin D. Roosevelt's political bandwagon but subsequently unabash-
edly challenged a president unprecedently popular among working-class
Americans.

What was there about Lewis—his character, his beliefs, his career—
that enabled a labor leader who appeared to many as unredeemably conventional in 1933 to play so extraordinary a role in American labor history
between 1935 and 1940? To begin with, Lewis brought to the 1930s values
and beliefs less conventional than many observers realized. Already fifty-
five years old in the year he created CIO, Lewis had lived a full and varied
life, one that had already experienced singular twists and turns.

John L. Lewis was born in the coal-mining hamlet of Cleveland, Iowa
(just beyond the larger coal town of Lucas), on February 12, 1880, a propitious birthdate for one who was to make great use of the Abraham Lincoln myth. Born to Welsh immigrant parents in a largely Welsh immigrant
community, the young John had little chance to absorb much Welsh culture
outside his immediate family. For, as was the case with many coal-mining
families, the Lewises moved frequently while John was still an infant and
youth. His childhood years and much else concerning his basic character
formation remain largely obscure. His father worked irregularly as a coal
miner and apparently also as a farm hand, and the family moved often from
one small central Iowa town to another. This persistent mobility makes it
extremely difficult to reconstruct Lewis's early life. But we do know that
at one point his father found steady work in the Des Moines area, which
enabled John to complete all but his last year of high school, no mean
achievement for a nineteenth-century coal miner's son. The family's migratory pattern and John's place as the eldest of eight children (two of
whom died in infancy) probably account for the protectiveness and bonding he exhibited toward his extended family throughout the remainder of
his life. It is also likely that some aspects of the "populist" Middle Western
culture and his mother's schismatic Mormonism shaped parts of Lewis's
personality. As a young adult, his character and behavior combined a peculiar amalgam of individualism, aggressiveness, and possessive materi-
alism balanced against forms of mutualism and social concern.

These traits became increasingly evident when he returned to Lucas at the age of twenty-six (1906) after a five-year sojourn in the Rocky Mountain West. For the next three years, Lewis unsuccessfully sought a career locally. Among other activities, he went back into the coal mines, became active in the United Mine Workers' (UMW) local and also in the town's most popular fraternal society, the Masons; Lewis dabbled in Lucas politics and business and in 1907 married advantageously to Myrta Bell, the daughter of a prominent and successful local doctor. In 1908 his fading prospects in Lucas and the more promising possibilities at the newly developed coal mines around Panama, Illinois, prompted Lewis to move his extended family (including his parents and siblings) to a new home in the Land of Lincoln, where the Lewis clan promptly built a power base in the town's UMW local.

By now Lewis had decided to fulfill his personal and social aspirations through a career in the labor movement. Combining hard work with opportunistic personal union alliances, Lewis by 1910 had become a full-time paid AFL organizer. He held this position for six years, using his ability to travel and his AFL connections to build a network of Lewis supporters within the UMW. Once again by cultivating the union leaders as much as the led, Lewis secured an appointment in 1917 as UMW statistician. He then climbed the Mine Workers' slippery hierarchy rapidly, each time by appointment, from business manager of the union's journal to vice-president. By 1919, only three years after returning to the UMW, Lewis was already serving as acting president. Then, by skillfully managing the 1919 coal strike and negating the appeal of his enemies inside the UMW, Lewis ensured his election in 1920 as president of the largest union in the country. Along the road to power, he had learned invaluable lessons—how to deal with a restive rank and file; how to cultivate other men of power; how to deal with opportunistic politicians; and how to use boldness, timing, and dramatic gestures to his own advantage.

The experiences of World War I and its immediate aftermath indelibly etched themselves on Lewis's mind. From those experiences he drew lessons about the relationship between the state and labor that he tried to follow for the remainder of his union career. As a loyal Wilsonian Democrat before and during World War I, Lewis saw how much positive assistance a friendly national government could extend to the labor movement. He learned firsthand from his participation in wartime Washington coal production conferences how state power might strip management of its anti-union weapons. He saw trade unions wax fat as a consequence of the war effort and a benevolent administration, the labor movement almost doubling in size between 1916 and 1919 and his own union penetrating the hitherto nonunion southern Appalachian coal fields. But in 1919 he learned quite different lessons about the uses of state power. He witnessed the Wilson administration withdraw its guardianship of trade unionism as the politics of inflation replaced the imperatives of reform in high Democratic councils. In consequence, the trade union advance of 1916–19 not only faltered, but it also retreated rapidly, losing its salients in steel, the packinghouses, railroad shopyards, and other industrial sectors. For Lewis such losses to the labor movement were dismaying but not decisive. What really troubled him was what happened to the UMW in 1919. Compelled to lead a coal miners' strike as a result of rank-and-file pressures, Lewis found himself fighting the federal government more than the mine operators. The president and his leading cabinet officers demanded that Lewis end the strike. A federal court injunction declared the miners' walkout illegal. Federal troops were ordered to patrol strike areas, and the attorney general tapped Lewis's phones. In the end Lewis had no choice but to call off the strike, declaring that "I will not fight my government, the greatest government on earth."

Thereafter the role of the state in the development of the labor movement remained central to Lewis's trade union career. He always remembered how state power could be used to promote and strengthen trade unionism. He also reflected about how suddenly the state could turn against its quondam allies and, in the process, threaten the independence and security of trade unions. Lewis thus simultaneously sought to use positive state action to promote trade unionism while just as persistently warning and guarding against the ability of the government to weaken trade union autonomy and create what he was to castigate as an American Leviathan. Above all, Lewis came away from his World War I experiences with an extreme distaste and distrust for politicians and public officials. For the remainder of his public career, he usually found it easier to deal with corporate executives than with high federal officials—and also more satisfying.

During the prosperity decade of the 1920s, neither John L. Lewis nor the United Mine Workers acted in a "conventional" manner when compared to the dominant elements within American trade unionism. In a labor universe marked by rigid jurisdictional boundaries and an artificial distinction between economic and political activities, the UMW organized all workers in and around the coal mines and linked its political and economic functions. In the early 1920s, in fact, John L. Lewis and his union acted as a part of the more militant wing of the AFL. In 1921, for example, only after two years as a prominent national labor leader, Lewis challenged the aging Samuel Gompers for the presidency of the AFL—and he did so as the "radicals'" candidate. Thus before Lewis became the scourge of "the red and the rebellious" and the best known labor Republican of the 1920s, he served an apprenticeship in the cause of union militants.

True, by the end of the decade, he seemed conservative and conventional. Yet Lewis's strategic shift to the trade union and political right must be understood in relation to the economics of coal mining, the realities of national politics, and the decline of UMW power. To comprehend why the apparently conventional Lewis of the late 1920s became the most innovative labor leader of the 1930s, we must first strip away many myths about his economic and political beliefs and practices.

For too long historians have assumed that Lewis was an orthodox Republican by conviction and a laissez-faire classicist by belief. Neither assumption has much basis in reality. From 1912 to 1919, as we suggested above, Lewis served as a loyal Wilsonian Democrat. As an AFL organizer, he had campaigned for Woodrow Wilson in the American Southwest in 1912 and later cleared potential judicial nominees for the administration. Lewis's rise to power in the UMW, moreover, was intimately connected to his activities inside the Democratic party and his union's influence in the Wilson administration. Finally, it is also significant that the Republican leader most closely associated with Lewis in the 1920s—Herbert Hoover—began his own political career as an ardent Wilsonian.

Lewis's relationship with Herbert Hoover provides clues to the labor leader's true economic beliefs. As secretary of commerce and then president, Hoover preached a doctrine of "cooperative capitalism," a system in which businessmen voluntarily joined to restrain cutthroat competition, practiced scientific management, stabilized wage rates, and bolstered mass purchasing power. Hoover's economic program flowed from what might be called an "underconsumptionist" perspective on the American economy. Unless workers obtained steady employment and earned high wages, they could not afford the cornucopia of consumer goods produced by the nation's mass-production economy. In Hoover's thinking, then, government functioned not to coerce or control private industry, but rather to induce businessmen to see the advantages of cooperative capitalism and high wages for a mass-production economy. After 1923, Hoover's program became Lewis's—and for good reason.

During the 1920s economic factors caused a rapid decline in the power of the UMW. The end of World War I left bituminous coal mining with an immense surplus capacity and the miners' union with many more members than employment opportunities. As labor productivity rose and demand for coal slackened, unemployment worsened and the UMW lost members and also the ability to use its most potent weapon—the strike. Worse yet, the

191

nonunion southern Appalachian coal fields rapidly increased their share of the market. Left untouched, the economics of coal mining in the 1920s threatened the ultimate collapse of the largely northern-based UMW.

Unable to use union power to protect wage rates or to organize nonunion mines, Lewis turned to the power of the state. Guided by the spirit of cooperative capitalism and Hooverian policies, in 1924 the UMW and the northern coal operators signed a new contract at Jacksonville, Florida, that stabilized existing wage rates and included a three-year no-strike pledge. More important, Commerce Secretary Hoover and President Coolidge both sanctioned the Jacksonville agreement. Without such direct federal intervention, neither the operators nor the union would have reached such a prompt and apparently amicable settlement to obdurate economic problems.

Almost as soon as the northern operators signed the Jacksonville agreement, however, they found themselves beset by declining demand for their coal and by nonunion southern competition. In order to survive, the northern operators began to violate their agreement with the UMW. Lewis responded to the employers' anti-union assault by publishing a book in 1923, *The Miner's Fight for American Standards.* By means of the book Lewis sought to carry public opinion to his union's side and to encourage Hoover and Coolidge to urge employers to honor the Jacksonville agreement. The laissez-faire principles and paeans to Americanism that Lewis's ghostwriters stuffed into the thin volume served only as rhetorical flourishes to the book's actual message: regardless of market conditions, wages must not be reduced (scarcely a principle of classical economics). Lewis, moreover, suggested that he and his union would gladly cooperate with Hoover's program to reorganize basic industry on scientific and efficient lines, provided that such a rationalized capitalism protected unionism and union wage rates. Unfortunately for Lewis and the UMW, Hoover's and Coolidge's conception of cooperative capitalism in practice differed substantially from Lewis's. The president and his Cabinet secretary offered wide scope for corporate cartelization but less space for independent trade unionism. Consequently, federal officials declined to intervene in private collective bargaining, and Lewis watching impotently as unionism collapsed in the northern coal fields and the welfare of coal miners everywhere suffered.

During the seven years from 1926 through 1932, Lewis persistently turned to the federal government to achieve for the UMW what it could not win for itself. But the same factors that weakened his union diluted Lewis's political influence. After 1925 the UMW lacked the economic muscle to cut off the supply of coal, thereby creating a national emergency; and its dwindling membership lacked the votes to swing state or national elections. Without economic power, labor lacked political influence, and in the world of American politics 1920s style, no officeholder would dare use state power to build union power.

What, then, was the heritage that Lewis brought to the Great Depression and the New Deal years? First, from his childhood he had developed a contradictory complex of values and beliefs that oscillated wildly between the poles of individualism and mutualism. Second, his Middle Western background, early trade-union experiences, and initial political entanglements produced an ideological amalgam that merged Wilsonian liberalism and Hoover republicanism with a latent left-wing populism. Third, from his contacts with federal officials before and particularly after the Jacksonville agreement of 1924, Lewis developed an abiding suspicion of politicians and the state. Yet he had also learned that union power required the support of a positive state. And, finally, the disastrous postwar experience of the UMW taught him that labor's success flowed from united, undiluted union power.

For most American labor leaders, the blight of the Great Depression and the coming of the New Deal represented no break with the immediate past; nor did it suggest any bright prospects for trade union innovations and triumphs. For John L. Lewis, however, Franklin D. Roosevelt's election in 1932 provided the opportunity that the labor leader had been seeking fruitlessly for almost a decade. When Roosevelt entered office in March 1933, Lewis and his personal economic adviser, W. Jett Lauck, knew what they wanted for labor and how to get it. Since the mid–1920s they had both urged Congress and the White House to enact a federal plan that would rationalize the coal industry by controlling production, allocating markets, fixing prices, and sanctioning the miners' union as a stabilizing force in the industry. They had failed in the past because the largest mining companies rejected government planning and collective bargaining and neither Coolidge nor Hoover had acted to implement the UMW's plan for survival.

Roosevelt's election now promised a real "new deal" for mine workers. The new president's advisers came from the same academic milieu as Lauck, and their proposals for national economic planning paralleled the UMW's designs for the coal industry. It was no wonder, then, that Lewis and Lauck were most responsible for the incorporation of Section 7a—the right to organize unions—into the 1933 National Industrial Recovery Act (NIRA), and that the coal industry adopted the first major code under the NIRA, which granted a substantial role to independent trade unionism.

With the passage of the NIRA and Section 7a, Lewis threw all his union's resources into a massive organizing campaign. In the process, he developed the strategy that would dominate the American labor movement for the remainder of the 1930s: a synthesis of economic and political action, of conservative syndicalism and radical parliamentarianism. Lewis freely resorted to state action to revitalize first a moribund UMW and later the larger labor movement. Yet unlike some AFL leaders, who expected government officials to organize workers for them, Lewis realized that workers must rely on their own militancy and strength. A benevolent state could take as well as give. Only after coal miners were fully and effectively unionized could they take maximum advantage of government and could Lewis exercise real political influence. John Brophy, the CIO's first director, later remember what Lewis would tell numerous workers' meetings: "We would be just as other people, as the man on the street, if it were not for the fact that back of us is the great force of the workers for whom we can speak. . . . The attention we get, the favorable attention . . . comes as a result of the fact that back of us is organization."

Those historians who stress Lewis's role as a restraining influence on rank-and-file militancy among coal miners in 1933 and among other workers later in the decade misunderstand his tactics and strategy. From bitter experience he knew that rank-and-file militants, however comprehensible and justifiable their activism might be, could grievously misread reality and force unions into inopportune conflicts. Yet the same experiences had also taught him that a labor organization without a militant rank and file deprived its leader of effective power. Thus nothing pleased Lewis more than the groundswell of militancy among coal miners that erupted in the summer of 1933. To achieve his union goals, Lewis had to split employers from public officials. On the one hand, he used the threat of mass rebellion and violence in the coal fields to coerce the president and the operators. On the other hand, he used his ability to restrain rank-and-file militancy to impress Roosevelt. During the complicated bituminous coal negotiations of 1933, as would be the case in subsequent labor disputes, the fact that workers appeared more militant than their leaders and frequently out of control served rather than hindered Lewis's strategy.

After 1933, political developments fused with the economic aspirations of American workers to lay the foundation for labor's great upheaval. As the labor journalist Edward Levinson observed, one force behind the workers' militancy "was personified, perhaps unwillingly, frequently with hesitation and backtracking by the Roosevelt administration; the other was represented by the dynamic leadership of John L. Lewis." From 1933 through 1937 Roosevelt and Lewis represented parallel currents flowing together in a merged economic and political stream. Both leaders focused on similar

194

enemies, used like images, and used the radio to great effect. Lewis, like Roosevelt, could be mellow as well as fiery, reassuringly concrete as well as scathingly demagogic.

Just as Roosevelt fastened responsibility for the Great Depression on Wall Street bankers and corporate Bourbons, Lewis blamed the plight of industrial workers on J. P. Morgan, the DuPonts, and reactionary corporate executives who obeyed their Wall Street masters. Just as Roosevelt promised to liberate the people from thralldom to the financiers, Lewis offered to deliver workers from industrial subservience. In speech after speech, Lewis reminded his audiences that the same people and interests who fought Roosevelt politically also opposed labor's right to organize. Early on Lewis grasped that the president wanted labor's political support for his reelection campaign; Lewis intended to turn Roosevelt's political need into an asset for labor. Above all else, Lewis perceived the inseparable connection between New Deal politics and the successful organizing of mass-production workers.

National politics, then, and not abstract disputes concerning the value of craft versus industrial unionism were decisive in the rift within the AFL and the emergence of the CIO. But it was never simply a question of labor Democrats versus trade-union Republicans. Rather it reflected a split between political realists and traditionalists. In 1935 and 1936 Lewis had no more bitter opponent within the AFL than the Teamsters' Union president Daniel Tobin, labor's representative on the Democratic National Committee. Tobin was pleased with the status his position conferred; that, for him, was the essence of labor politics nationally. Lewis, by contrast, dealt in real power, and power flowed not from representing a few thousand teamsters nor from claiming to speak for one wing of a politically divided and impotent labor federation, but from voicing the aspirations of millions of blue- and white-collar workers. Roosevelt's immediate and imperative electoral needs offered labor a critical opportunity. New Deal politics, as they evolved between 1933 and 1936, impelled Roosevelt to assist labor in organizing mass-production workers. And if unions indeed succeeded in organizing the mass-production workers, labor would win the political influence it had always sought. Twenty to thirty million unionized workers would make labor the balance wheel of American politics—hence an effective parliamentary force—and such extensive organization would enable labor simultaneously to defend its own workplace interests—hence a fighting syndicalist movement.

This was the challenge that Lewis presented to the AFL in 1934 and 1935 when he pleaded for industrial unionism at executive council meetings and on the convention floor. He called on his fellow labor barons to avoid arid disputes about jurisdiction and to seize the main chance. "That is the question, that is all of the question—whether our labor movement . . . can be modernized into an instrument capable of dealing with the modern problems that affect the workers of the land." Abstract principles concerning craft or industrial unionism meant little to Lewis; organizing the unorganized meant everything. "I am not concerned with history," Lewis wrote to AFL president William Green in 1936. "Rather I am concerned with the problems of today and tomorrow. . . . Candidly, I am temperamentally incapable of sitting with you in sackcloth and ashes, endlessly intoning *'O tempora' O mores.'*"

From 1933 to 1935, Lewis, to be sure, had abided by AFL precedents and rules. But he lost on that terrain, and he knew why. No matter how often craft unionists cited constitutional clauses in the long debate about industrial unionism and organizing the unorganized, Lewis realized that their rhetorical legalisms counted for naught. Lewis lost because the leaders of other large unions within the federation—A. P. Wharton of the Machinists, Bill Hutcheson of the Carpenters, and Dan Tobin of the Teamsters—all opposed him, and they were men who respected legality and precedent as little as the Mine Workers' chief.

Recognizing that power and not rhetoric counted, Lewis responded to the November 1935 AFL convention's failure to act on the industrial union issue by calling other like-minded labor leaders to his Washington office and launching a new vehicle for the organization of mass-production workers: the CIO. Over the next two years, Lewis refused to bog himself down in debates over the CIO's proper relationship to the AFL, and he remained undisturbed when the older house of labor expelled the member unions of the CIO. Just as Lewis subordinated constitutional labor issues to power realities, so too did he make the question of unity within the labor movement secondary to organizing the unorganized.

During the summer of 1936, Lewis devoted far more time, money, and energy to national politics than to bickering with the AFL leaders. In June, President Roosevelt assured Lewis that the administration would protect the UMW in every possible way until Congress passed a bill guaranteeing stability in the bituminous coal industry. He also promised the CIO leader that Washington would cooperate with the unionization drive in steel. Only a week later Lewis attended a conference at which plans were discussed to unite farmers and workers behind Roosevelt in 1936 and also to plan for a future farmer-labor political coalition. Lewis's speech on July 6 opening the CIO's organizing drive in steel specifically linked Roosevelt's recent denunciation of "economic dictatorship" to Wall Street's dominance of the steel industry. As the fall presidential election approached, both Roosevelt and Lewis championed industrial democracy. The UMW alone donated $600,000 to the Democratic presidential campaign, and in early October Lewis informed Roosevelt: "Command me any time I can be of service." In the late stages of the campaign, Roosevelt and Lewis appeared together in industrial and coal-mining towns. And in the event, the 1936 election results gave Roosevelt and Lewis all that they wanted.

Four days after Roosevelt's landslide reelection victory, Lewis told a CIO executive board meeting: "We . . . must capitalize on the election. The CIO was out fighting for Roosevelt, and every steel town showed a smashing victory for him. . . . We wanted a president who would hold the light for us while we went out and organized." Lewis viewed Roosevelt's reelection as providing the impetus for the CIO's organizing efforts in steel and autos. Quite early in Roosevelt's second term, Lewis won the rewards of his political strategy—CIO victories over General Motors and U.S. Steel. If the New Deal administration did not directly assist the CIO campaign among auto and steel workers, it did, in Lewis's phrase, "hold the light" while labor bargained with heretofore intransigent corporate officials.

Several factors must be borne in mind in analyzing industrial unionism's triumphs in 1937. First, one must recognize the role of a militant minority among the rank and file in the automobile industry, which served as the catalyst to activate anticompany sentiment among a more passive majority who became union sympathizers only after the start of the Flint sit-down strike. Second, one must respect the CIO's decision to expend all of its limited resources in a struggle against the largest, most powerful, and recalcitrant anti-union corporations, firms that in 1937 had tacit assistance from the AFL. Third, one has to appreciate the astuteness and perspicacity of Lewis as he negotiated with America's corporate elite.

Yet, in the final analysis, neither a militant rank and file, the firm CIO commitment, nor Lewis's bargaining genius would have prevailed had public officials chosen to enforce the law of property rights as then interpreted by the judiciary. The role of the state was the determining factor in the General Motors sit-down strike of 1937 and the rise of the CIO. Had Michigan governor Frank Murphy used the militia to enforce legal injunctions against the occupants of General Motors's property, or had President Roosevelt exercised his authority to drive out the sit-downers, the strike would likely have been broken. Aware of this, Lewis, during the winter months of 1937, constantly reminded Murphy and Roosevelt of their political debts to him, to the CIO, and to industrial workers. Only because public officials, on the one hand, kept their hands off the struggle in Flint and, on the other hand, coaxed corporate executives to bargain with labor did the United Auto Workers (UAW), on February 11, 1937, win a contract from General Motors.

The CIO's victory at Flint was the essential factor that prompted the U.S. Steel Corporation on March 2, 1937, to sign a contract with the Steel Workers Organizing Committee (SWOC) at a time when the union had only enrolled a minority of the company's employees. Myron Taylor, U.S. Steel's chief executive officer, knew Roosevelt well, admired him, and also understood the political imperatives of early 1937. He realized that Pennsylvania governor Earle and lieutenant governor Tom Kennedy (who was also the UMW's secretary treasurer) would offer U.S. Steel as little assistance in the event of a strike as Frank Murphy had provided General Motors. As Lewis lectured a CIO executive board session on March 9, 1937: "GM strike—sweeping effect on steel. CIO faced united financial front— GM settlement broke it."

Nineteen hundred thirty-seven was indeed the year of Lewis and the CIO. Everywhere—in the press, over the radio, in political circles, on factory floors—Americans debated the implications of the industrial union upsurge and Lewis's personal motives. His likeness, confronting them at the movie theater, on magazine covers, and in the daily papers' political cartoons, seemed to embody the spirit of the movement he led. His large frame, made to appear even more formidable by a carefully tailored wardrobe, communicated both his own and the CIO's power. His head, with its unruly hair, forestlike eyebrows, firmly set jaw, and ever-present scowl, suggested the anger, determination, and militancy of the workers for whom he spoke.

People wondered if Lewis had presidential ambitions. Unfriendly editorialists compared the CIO leader to Hitler, Stalin, and Mussolini. Experts pondered whether or not the CIO would transform the American social and economic order. For the first time in American history, many commentators suggested, class-conscious politics had entered the system and a labor administration in Washington seemed a real possibility. The CIO and Lewis, Lewis and the CIO!

In the spring of 1937, the CIO seemed the wave of the future; by midsummer of the same year it was beating a hasty retreat on all industrial fronts. The combination of economic power and political influence that Lewis had used so successfully in the negotiations with General Motors and U.S. Steel failed him in the spring and summer of 1937, especially during the bitter Little Steel strike. Why?

One cannot argue that the workers employed by the so-called Little Steel companies were any less militant than those in autos or big steel. Nor can one suggest that between March and July 1937 Lewis had lost his negotiating brilliance. What, in fact, failed Lewis and also the CIO was political influence. Earlier in the year 1937 Governor Murphy of Michigan and President Roosevelt had abetted the UAW's victory in Flint and thus motivated Myron Taylor of U.S. Steel to recognize SWOC. In May and June 1937, however, Governor Martin Davey of Ohio assisted Little Steel's management in strikebreaking, Governor Earle of Pennsylvania refused to protect union organizers against local vigilantes, and President Roosevelt, when implored by Lewis to defend his working-class allies in their battle against capital, declared "a plague on both your houses" (labor and capital).

Quite clearly, between the CIO's victory at Flint in February and its defeat during the Little Steel strike of May-July 1937, Roosevelt's political calculus had changed. This change portended ill for Lewis and the CIO. No longer did the president perceive political advantage in his support of Lewis. On the contrary, Roosevelt's advisers suggested that a strong popular reaction had arisen against the CIO and that the industrial union movement was a complicated situation "full of all kinds of dynamite, political as well as social." Moreover, by midsummer 1937 Roosevelt's interest in domestic reform had diminished. Beginning with his unsuccessful effort to restructure the Supreme Court along more liberal lines and on a variety of other domestic political issues, Roosevelt had lost ground to an emerging congressional coalition of conservative Democrats and Republicans. Simultaneously, the president's desire to balance the budget and congressional niggardliness precipitated an economic contraction, which began in late 1937 and lasted well into the following year, that can justly be labeled the "Roosevelt depression." Thwarted in Congress and baffled by economic failure, the president grew more interested and involved in foreign than in domestic affairs. Lewis's involvement in a progressive farmer-labor coalition thus seemed to promise Roosevelt fewer political gains in mid–1937 than it had in the summer of 1936. Rather than ally with Lewis in a domestic reform crusade, the president preferred to mollify the labor leader in the manner suggested by presidential adviser Rexford Tugwell: "Life for all of us will be so much easier if you will hold Lewis's hand once every three weeks regularly."

Holding hands proved to be no substitute for tangible assistance to the labor movement. Already weakened in pocketbook and image by the beating inflicted on it by the Little Steel companies, the CIO became one of the more notable victims of the "Roosevelt depression." As industrial production diminished and unemployment soared, the CIO lost momentum. Automobile and steel workers devoted more effort to defending their existing job rights than to advancing union claims. The great drive to organize the textile industry ground to a halt, and its failure was repeated on other industrial fronts. Both among the more successful of the new industrial unions and their less stable counterparts, paid-up membership declined. Never self-supporting even in its halcyon days of 1936 and early 1937, the CIO now faced grave financial problems, prompting Lewis to cut staff, salaries, and expenses for the national office. Equally frustrating to Lewis, the AFL, scarcely feeling the impact of the economic collapse, grew in size and strength. And as Lewis's political alliance with Roosevelt suffered successive shocks, the AFL gained friends among congressional conservatives and backdoor influence with the president.

Lewis never recovered fully from the dual blow of the CIO's defeat in the Little Steel strike and the rapid decline of industrial unionism during the economic downturn of 1937–38. Like Roosevelt, Lewis had no immediate remedy for the unexpected economic collapse. Unlike the president, the labor leader seemed to lose his certainty, assurance, and sometimes composure. Lewis's reaction to failure was to declare war on the Roosevelt administration.

The Little Steel strike and the economic depression were not alone in generating the rift between Lewis and Roosevelt. Another contentious source of conflict flowed from the two men's quite different conceptions of the United States' role in the world arena. From 1937 through 1941 the labor leader spoke for a tradition that dated back to Grover Cleveland, William Jennings Bryan, William Borah, George Norris, the LaFollettes, and Herbert Hoover, a tradition that perceived the world role of the United States as largely symbolic. The United States would serve the world best by domestic example, not foreign adventure. The president, on the contrary, represented the tradition of William Henry Seward, John Hay, Theodore Roosevelt, and Woodrow Wilson—a perspective that promoted a vigorous, sometimes adventurous, and even imperialistic foreign policy. Thus as the United States drew closer to involvement in a global war against militarist aggressors in Europe and Asia, Lewis and Roosevelt were fated to clash bitterly over American foreign policy.

After 1937, as Roosevelt increasing devoted himself to overseas affairs, he and Lewis fought repeatedly and bitterly. Lewis demanded ever more expansive and expensive domestic reforms. The president instead retreated on the domestic front as he sought the support of congressional conservatives and corporate executives for his foreign policy. While Roosevelt recruited Republican elites into his Cabinet in order to unite the nation in the event of war, Lewis discussed with Republican business elites how best to influence the president to ensure future peace with Hitler's Germany.

The quite real domestic and foreign policy disputes between the labor leader and the president were compounded by personality conflicts. Both men had colossal egos and refused to accept secondary status. In the luxurious new Washington headquarters of the UMW, no visitor could escape Lewis's visage. Every passageway, corridor, wall, and office bore a photograph of Lewis, usually full-face. Marquis Childs, the newspaper columnist, described a visit to Lewis's office this way. "You go to see him and he receives you almost like—I once went to Mussolini's office in the Palazzo Venezia and he gave somewhat the same impression. A great office and you waded through the rug a couple of miles and got over to the great man." Lewis himself told the following story: As he paused one day in front of his home in Alexandria to tie a shoelace, a bus full of tourists passed by. The bus stopped and all the occupants stared at the bent figure on the sidewalk. "Even the posterior of a great man," Lewis remarked, "is of interest." Lewis's immodesty led one hostile reporter to quip: "Lewis had come to believe that his own birthday should be celebrated instead of Christmas." Thus as Lewis's public reputation waned and the president's remained high, the labor leader grew increasingly restive.

By the summer of 1940 it should have been clear that Lewis would refuse to support the reelection of Roosevelt. As early as 1939 Lewis had used his influence in the labor movement and among independent left-wing political groups to scotch an incipient third-term movement. And at the January 1940 golden anniversary convention of the UMW, he was unsparing in his denunciations of Roosevelt. "Let no politician," the UMW president warned, "believe or dream that he is going to solve the unemployment question . . . by dragging America into war. . . . The formula of taking our young men and making cannon fodder out of them and covering the rest of the nation with grief and lamentations . . . that day is gone if my voice and strength can make any contribution to prevent it."

Just as Lewis's ultimate repudiation of Roosevelt should have occasioned no surprise, his decision to endorse the Republican Wendell L. Willkie should have been understood, at least by the labor leader's friends and associates. Yet many in the labor movement and in radical politics who applauded Lewis's opposition to the president were stunned by his support for Willkie, a former utilities executive whose foreign-policy outlook scarcely differed from Roosevelt's. Their shock was made the greater by the fact that from January through June 1940 Lewis had criticized Republicans as well as New Deal Democrats, and in several speeches he had

201

threatened also to lead a left-wing third party. Why, then, did Lewis in the event ask workers to vote Republican?

On one level Lewis's endorsement of Willkie can be easily explained. Always an opportunist, Lewis had read the 1938 and 1939 election returns carefully, and they suggested to him that republicanism was on the rise. Unable to gain what he wanted from the Democrats either in domestic or foreign policy, Lewis gambled on a Republican victory. Apparently Willkie personally assured him that labor would not suffer under a Republican administration. If Republicans would not actively promote industrial unionism, Willkie promised that at least they would not roll back labor's New Deal gains.

Even the political gamble involved in endorsing Willkie seemed minimal to Lewis. For Lewis, the defeat of Governor Murphy in the Michigan gubernatorial election of 1938 portended Roosevelt's fate in 1940. Lewis, moreover, honestly believed that the vast majority of American workers viewed the world overseas as he did and that they perceived Roosevelt as a warmonger. Finally, Lewis quite obviously considered himself indispensable to CIO members. That confidence led him in his radio network speech of October 25 endorsing Willkie to vow to resign as president of the CIO if Roosevelt won reelection. Given the apparent Republican resurgence and Lewis's egotistic conviction that he was indispensable to labor, he thought that in 1940 he had made a wise political choice.

As comprehensible on the surface as was Lewis's decision to back Willkie, at a deeper level it was more suggestive of the relationship at the end of the 1930s among the forces of class, union leadership, and politics. Lewis's repudiation of Roosevelt seemed a logical result of the class forces in operation. Since the 1937 Little Steel strike, the president had abandoned his full commitment to the CIO, and from the beginning of the New Deal he had neglected relatively small farmers, tenants, and sharecroppers. Moreover, as Roosevelt moved the nation towards war, he drew closer to the corporate-financial elite. It seemed only fitting in 1940, then, that labor militants and political radicals should form a farmer-labor party as both an alternative to Roosevelt and a continuation of the New Deal domestic reform tradition. And who better to lead such a third party than John L. Lewis? But Lewis chose republicanism.

Lewis's decision to support Republican bourgeois hegemony over class-based politics reveals much about this leader of American workers, and by implication, about the consciousness of his followers. At a time when Lewis seemed most dangerous to the established order, the radical journalist Louis Adamic grasped, as few others have, Lewis's essence. "Though an exceptional man," Adamic wrote in 1937,

Lewis is also a deeply ordinary one . . . he has a chauffeur in whipcords to drive him about in the twelve-cylinder automobile his union bought for him; which is what every ordinary American would like to have . . . there ride in that shiny car . . . vicariously—the four hundred thousand United Mine Workers of America, most of them ordinary men . . . full of the instinct and impulse to improve themselves, to get on, to acquire the material symbols of well-being, power, and progress that are the chief contemporary elements of the American "Dream." That fine machine and the snappy cap on the chauffeur's head are ordinary symbols, generally craved in America, though rarely attained, and which, incidentally, are apt to be an important source of Lewis's power in this country.

Occasionally Lewis himself openly revealed this aspect of his character. The same man who excoriated corporate and financial dictators and called workers to the class barricades lectured the 1938 UMW convention delegates as follows: This union "stands for the proposition that the heads of families shall have a sufficient income to educate these boys and girls and these sons and daughters of our people, and they go forth when given that opportunity. . . . They become scientists, great clergymen, . . . great lawyers, great statesmen. . . . Many of our former members are successful in great business enterprises." No coal miners in this lot. Nor even labor leaders. Rather, after almost ten years of depression, the gospel of individual success maintained its attraction for Lewis and for many UMW members.

Ten years later Lewis restated his belief in possessive individualism more bluntly. "You know," he said, "after all there are two great material tasks in life that affect the individual and affect great bodies of men. The first is to achieve or acquire something of value or something that is desirable, and then the second task is to prevent some scoundrel from taking it away from you." Upon the rock of possessiveness and the reef of individualism, as personified by Lewis, the class-based labor militancy and emerging working-class consciousness of the 1930s shipwrecked.

True to his word, two weeks after Roosevelt's reelection in 1940, Lewis stepped down as president of the CIO, to be replaced by his long-time lieutenant in the UMW, Philip Murray. For another year or so, Lewis tried to work within the labor organization he had done so much to create. Yet the CIO's increasing involvement and cooperation with the Roosevelt administration at a time of Lewis's growing estrangement from Roosevelt produced unbearable tensions. Finally, in late May 1942, Lewis brutally denounced Murray and ordered all UMW affiliates and officials to withdraw from the CIO.

As an independent actor in the labor movement after 1942, Lewis gained free reign for his hostility toward Roosevelt, and, more importantly, against the increasing power of the state in American life. Alone among major labor leaders, he spoke out against the class bias of government regulations during World War II and even led his coal miners in a series of months-long coal strikes in 1943 as part of an effort to smash government-imposed wage restrictions. His militant actions and battle against the wartime state—condemned by both the CIO and AFL—were applauded by millions of rank-and-file workers who themselves engaged in an unprecedented wave of unauthorized wildcat strikes in 1944 and 1945. Ironically, Lewis's struggle to liberate organized labor from state restraints actually did much to provoke further government control over unions, first through the War Labor Disputes Act of 1943 and then in peacetime through the Taft-Hartley Act of 1947.

In the immediate post–World War II era, Lewis continued to manipulate the state into advancing the welfare of his miners. By creating a national emergency in 1946, for example, Lewis forced the federal government to seize the mines and grant the union a welfare and retirement fund, a concession the private operators had adamantly refused to make. But for the most part Lewis's timeworn tactic of using coal miner militancy to compel government intervention now proved increasingly more injurious rather than beneficial. Following a series of long and bitter coal strikes in the late 1940s, in which the UMW's adversaries were more often federal officials than coal operators and in which Lewis and his union were legally punished for activities that had been permissable even in the midst of World War II, the elderly labor leader executed a surprising about-face in his labor relations strategy. After three decades during which coal strikes occurred as predictably as the seasons, a calm came over the coal fields.

With a certain irony, Lewis—one of the architects of the New Deal welfare state—became in the 1950s a more enthusiastic apostle of Herbert Hoover's cooperative capitalism than he had even been in the 1920s. As in the past, Lewis argued that the state should promote the health of the industry and the welfare of the miners, now through the coal purchase policies of the Tennessee Valley Authority and by promoting exports abroad. But unlike the 1920s, Lewis in the 1950s was far less eager for federal involvement in internal industry affairs, specifically labor-management relations. During the 1950s he even called for the repeal of the Wagner Act as well as the Taft-Hartley law.

More significantly, in the early 1950s Lewis allied with George Love, the guiding spirit behind the newly formed Bituminous Coal Operators' Association, to restructure collective bargaining in the coal industry. Their goal was to avoid the sort of confrontations that in the recent past had led to government intervention and to the settlement of disputes on a political basis or at the whim of a judge. Under this new system, negotiations were kept out of the public's view, the length of negotiated contracts grew more flexible to eliminate the crisis of approaching deadlines, and the actual settlements occurred in semisecrecy, without at times the union's rank and file even realizing that talks were under way.

Lewis's new collaboration with employers went beyond an effort to avert strikes and subsequent government intervention. Lewis, the champion of the coal miner, now strove to become an industrial statesman. He helped establish the National Coal Policy Conference to coordinate the activities of the various coal interests so that the industry could confront the government and the public with a united front. He invested UMW funds in the American Coal Shipping Company, which was organized to sell American coal in foreign markets. He even lent money from the UMW-controlled National Bank of Washington to coal firms in order to enable them to mechanize their properties, a policy that, while perhaps good for the industry's productivity, threw thousands of union members out of work.

John L. Lewis was a man of contradictory parts. More than any other labor leader, he had recognized the need to enlist state power in the drive to unionize mass-production workers and to assure an "American standard of living" for all citizens. Yet he always deeply distrusted the state, on the one hand for its probusiness bias and on the other hand for stifling private initiative. This man was a leading symbol of working-class power who simultaneously articulated the creed of possessive individualism and loved to socialize with the members of the power elite whom he publicly excoriated. And paradoxically, Lewis was a man whose life centered around attaining personal power. Yet when, in January 1960, he retired as president of the UMW, he stood alone among major American labor leaders as one who relinquished authority voluntarily. He lived for another nine years, dying on June 11, 1969, a man estranged from a labor movement and a welfare state that he had played such an essential role in creating.

Bibliographic Notes

Those interested in learning more about Lewis, the UMW, the founding of the CIO, and the labor movement's interaction with the state, should begin with our own *John L. Lewis: A Biography* (1977), which is acknowledged as the most extensive and accurate study available. The University of Illinois Press has published an abridged, less detailed edition (1986) more appealing to the general reader. A number of other biographies of Lewis may be consulted profitably, although they suffer from the repetition of myths and inaccuracies. The best and most popular of these is Saul Alinsky, *John L. Lewis: An Unauthorized Biography* (1949), which readers should approach with caution. For a readily accessible sample of Lewis's speeches and correspondence, readers should turn to past issues of the *United Mine Workers' Journal* and old UMW *Convention Proceedings*, where such documents are extensively reprinted.

There is no scholarly history of the UMW now in print, although specific episodes in its history have been fully studied. For a general synthesis of the union's past, therefore, readers must still rely on McAlister Coleman's journalistic and dated *Men and Coal* (1943). Likewise, a good history of the CIO is still needed, although readers can learn much from Art Preis, *Labor's Giant Step: Twenty Years of the CIO* (1964); Len DeCaux's autobiography, *Labor Radical: From the Wobblies to CIO* (1967); and sections of Matthew Josephson, *Sidney Hillman: Statesman of American Labor* (1952). For a general treatment of the labor movement during the 1920s readers should consult Irving Bernstein, *The Lean Years* (1960); and Robert H. Zieger, *Republicans and Labor, 1919–1929* (1969). Two excellent books on the 1930s are Irving Bernstein, *Turbulent Years: A History of the American Worker, 1933–1941* (1970); and Sidney Fine, *Sit-Down: The General Motors Strike of 1936–1937* (1969). Nelson Lichtenstein, *Labor's War at Home: The CIO in World War II* (1982), covers well the CIO during World War II. Finally, in *Workers in Industrial America: Essays on the Twentieth Century Struggle* (1980), David Brody offers some valuable interpretive insights into key aspects of twentieth-century labor history, including themes raised in this essay.

Sidney Hillman: Labor's Machiavelli

9

Steven Fraser

Years before he had reached the height of his power and influence in national politics, Sidney Hillman's reputation as a labor statesman was already well established. No one before or since has occupied quite the same position. While labor leaders have on occasion wielded considerably more actual power than Hillman, they have invariably done so on behalf of labor as an organized interest group. Sidney Hillman lived at a propitious moment and managed to become something more than a mere broker for organized labor's particular needs. During the final fifteen years of his life, he assumed a place in the Roosevelt administration, both through a series of official appointments and as a confidante of the president, and a power in the Democratic party that made him a participant in the shaping of domestic economic and social policy, including the country's various attempts to recover from the Great Depression and its subsequent econonic mobilization for the Second World War.

So it was that Hillman came to be known as a labor statesman. But it was a sobriquet with many shades of meaning. Thus it was always a debatable question as to whether Hillman represented the needs of labor within the councils of national power or, on the contrary, the viewpoint of an aggressive and self-aggrandizing state within the councils of the labor movement. Indeed the persistent political weakness of the American labor movement meant that Hillman served his people and nation on the sufferance of more powerful corporate, bureaucratic, and congressional elements.

The story of the rise of Sidney Hillman, in all its ambivalence, is therefore also a commentary on the political fortunes of American labor in the mid-twentieth century. To appreciate the tale entirely, however, it is necessary to note how improbable it was that Sidney Hillman should ever have become the country's first and, to date, its only labor statesman.

The "Half-Intellectual"

Sidney Hillman was the product of a clerical family and a secular education, of the provincial Russian Pale and cosmopolitan New York, of the Old World's socialism and the New World's social science. A Russian Jew, born in 1887 in Zagare, a small town in the Pale, he was raised in a family whose rabbinical traditions could be traced back several generations. Indeed, his family intended that Hillman would carry on that religious calling.

But the education of Sidney Hillman took a radically different direction. By the turn of the century even the smaller settlements in the Pale were exposed to the intellectual currents of the Jewish Enlightenment, or *Haskala*, and to the more recent spread of social democratic political thought. Against the wishes and threats of his pious father and the rules of the yeshiva, Hillman began to read in Russian translation the classics of Western social thought, including the work of Darwin, Marx, Mill, and Spencer. By 1902, he had joined the *Bund* (General Jewish Workers Union in Russia and Poland) for which he carried out a series of illegal but largely menial tasks while participating in secret cultural and trade union meetings, including his own attempts to organize the typesetters of Kovno.

The outbreak of the Russian Revolution in 1905 forever closed the door on Hillman's religious past. He was arrested when the *Bund* organized its first public demonstration and spent the next several months in the Kovno prison, where his secular education continued under the tutelage of veteran revolutionaries well-versed in the thought of Marx, Lassalle, Bebel, and Kropotkin. Jailed again following a *Bund*-organized insurrection in Zagare in 1906, he was forced to flee on a false passport to the home of his prosperous uncle in England.

A brief but formative experience, the *Bund* marked Hillman as a marginal man, in transit between very different cultures. Such unfinished scholars were so common in the Russian-Jewish social democratic movement that there was a special name to describe them—"half-intellectuals," those former yeshiva students abruptly uprooted from the world of the library and synagogue, who proved especially adept at transmitting the theoretical precepts of Marxism to the mass of the Jewish workers. These "half-intellectuals" distinguished themselves in practical work as expert organizers, agitators, and administrators and as mediators between the movement's intellectual elite and its less enlightened constituency. They

Amalgamated Clothing Workers of America

were doers, not thinkers, pragmatic in disposition, and organizationally creative, but without any vulgar hostility to ideas or worship of the narrowly practical. Throughout his subsequent career Sidney Hillman would remain a "half-intellectual," committed first of all to obtaining organized power, uninhibited by doctrinal beliefs should they obstruct his pursuit of power, but committed as well to the enlightenment's liberating message of reason, progress, and science. Indeed, he was eager to use the discoveries of Western social science to transform traditional cultures.

Hillman became the quintessential mediating figure whose notable later accomplishments depended on his ability to communicate across the often hostile borders of class and culture. But Hillman did not arrive in America in 1907 already possessed of the political sophistication and bureaucratic dexterity characteristic of his later career. Instead, he might have easily become a figure of strictly local, ethnic significance, the leader of a Jewish trade union in the Jewish needle trades with its heart and home in the peculiar self-enclosed world of New York City Jewish socialism and labor radicalism. That he was eventually invited to become part of a far wider universe of national influence had a great deal to do with his creativity and diligence in perfecting the arts of mediation during his first twenty years in the New World.

The Apprenticeship of Sidney Hillman

Sidney Hillman came of age in the world of urban progressive reform. In fact, he achieved his political adulthood under the direct care and tutelage of Jane Addams and the women of the Women's Trade Union League, as well as Clarence Darrow, Louis Brandeis, Felix Frankfurter, Walter Lippman, and other notable progressive jurists, politicians, and social scientists. It was a heady atmosphere for an obscure immigrant.

In 1910 Hillman was a lowly apprentice cutter (and a remarkably bad one at that) working in one of the Chicago plants of the largest clothing manufacturer in the country, Hart, Schaffner and Marx (HSM). In the fall of that year, seemingly without warning, there occurred a mass strike of all the company's workers, native and immigrant, skilled and unskilled, which had in fact been carefully planned by small groups of Jewish and Italian immigrant socialist and anarchist workers.

Sidney Hillman was not included within the original secret circle of strike organizers, but nevertheless he fathered the union that emerged from that strike. In the process, he displayed, at least in embryo, a flexibility of approach and a sensitivity to the broader political and social context of labor organization that later distinguished him as a labor statesman.

210

On the one hand, Hillman shared and helped mobilize the deep antagonism felt by the rank and file for the elitist presumptions, craft-minded parochialism, and nativist prejudices of the United Garment Workers (UGW, the American Federation of Labor's conservative affiliate in the men's clothing industry). In the middle of the four-month strike, the UGW tried to take advantage of the workers' sagging morale to conclude an agreement with the company that would have conceded nearly everything for which the strike had been fought. At a dramatic mass meeting, Hillman, unknown at that point, using a combination of broken English and Yiddish and with the help of an Italian translator, denounced the betrayal and reinvigorated the strike. The moment immediately transformed him into a popular leader, a commanding moral presence. On that basis he proceeded to work out an agreement, in close cooperation with Clarence Darrow and Jane Addams, acceptable to Joseph Schaffner, which arranged for the impartial arbitration of the workers' grievances. Because it too called for less than the strikers' originally demanded, it proved unacceptable to a militant minority. And so at a second critical juncture, in the course of an extremely tense strike meeting, Hillman was able to beat back the opposition to a settlement that was led by the Industrial Workers of the World (IWW). It was this act of diplomatic mediation that first persuaded Joseph Schaffner that Hillman was less a rebel than he was a man of "sweet reasonableness." More importantly, this remarkable piece of industrial statecraft inaugurated Hillman's alliance with the wider world of progressive reform.

If Hillman is rightly considered the father of the Amalgamated Clothing Workers of America (ACWA), then progressivism was certainly its godfather. There developed a marriage, born of expediency as well as idealism, between the mass of immigrant garment workers and segments of the progressive movement. Progressives entered into alliances with immigrant labor in part because they saw in independent unionism a way of taming the tendencies of laissez-faire capitalism to dissolve into economic anarchy and social catastrophe, of which garment manufacturing represented a particularly ugly example. The industry's glaring waste, inefficiency, and medieval labor and business practices particularly offended progressives committed to a rationalized and scientifically managed industrial and democratic order. It also troubled an elite segment of the industry itself— larger, modern companies like HSM, which because of their substantial capital investment and high-volume production sought to stabilize the production process, to standardize wages and hours, and thereby to eliminate the cutthroat competition characteristic of the business that caused chronic warfare on the shopfloor and disrupted production. They were joined in this quest for stability by mass retailers such as Macy's and Filene's who depended on the industry for a reliable supply of clothing at predictable prices to serve a rapidly growing mass market. These elite circles of business, political, and social welfare reform together recognized that only a union, and a powerful one at that, exercising constant surveillance over the industry's labor markets and shopfloor practices, could both civilize and rationalize garment manufacturing.

Hillman not only accepted aid from progressives, he made their ideology of industrial democracy and their organizational practice of scientific management his own, and in the process he created what was to be known, by the end of the First World War, as the "new unionism." A productive apparatus that ran according to scientific principles and with machinelike efficiency and was at the same time a model of social harmony enlisting the voluntary cooperation and participation of the lowliest industrial worker—such was the progressive vision of industrial democracy, a vision that seemed to offer a way of evading the intractable realities of power and coercive authority. Hillman subscribed to this vision, and even proved willing to embrace scientific management, but only so long as greater efficiency was accompanied and accomplished by mechanisms of democratic (i.e., union) control. The original agreement signed with HSM in 1911 established the sort of grievance machinery and the mechanisms for the impartial arbitration of outstanding disputes that Hillman felt could introduce the rule of law on the shopfloor, provide a constitutional basis, so to speak, for labor-management relations, and also introduce industrywide standards of production, scientifically determined and agreed to by all parties.

His vision grew more precise and sophisticated when, in 1914, Hillman moved to New York to administer, for the International Ladies' Garment Workers' Union, the Protocol of Peace, a system of arbitrating grievances essentially similar to the formal democratic procedures established by the HSM agreement. The job itself lasted but a few months. Hillman was soon drafted to become the first president of the new quasi-industrial union, the ACWA, born in 1914 when the rank and file of the men's clothing workers in Chicago, New York, and Baltimore revolted at the UGW's national convention in Nashville. But the move to New York was of lasting importance because it widened Hillman's professional and political associations.

He was, of course, exposed to the influence of Louis Brandeis, who had designed the protocols. In addition, Hillman developed a long-lasting relationship with the Filene brothers, Lincoln and Edward, founders of the retailing complex headquartered in Boston, and other noted business progressives. Through the Filenes he met Louis Kirstein, who managed the

Filene enterprises, and Kirstein in turn introduced Hillman to the liberal circles of scientific management and industrial labor relations. These men and women, including William Leiserson, Meyer Jacobstein, Otto and Clara Beyer, Mary Gilson, and above all Morris Cooke, became Hillman's advisers and collaborators. They widened his perspective immeasurably so that over the next five years of war, labor turmoil, and global revolution, Hillman became the principal spokesman and the ACWA the principal laboratory for experiments in industrial democracy.

Hillman's contacts extended beyond the strictly professional and business world into the political arena. This was mainly a result of American participation in World War I. The need for a reliable supply of military clothing, escalating rates of labor turnover, and the rising tide of labor unrest led the government to encourage collective bargaining in the garment industry, as it was doing in other industrial sectors. This cultivated the hot-house development of the ACWA so that its membership increased from 48,000 in 1916 to 138,000 by mid–1919. It also put Hillman in touch with progressives in government. Florence Kelley, secretary of the National Consumers League introduced Hillman to Walter Lippman and Felix Frankfurter, both then working for Secretary of War Newton Baker. Together they discussed the need for government action against sweatshop conditions if the ACWA were to honor its no-strike pledge. Thus began Hillman's relationship with Frankfurter, which was to last through the whole period of the New Deal.

A leading advocate of industrial democracy, Frankfurter pressed for the elimination of child labor, home work, and unsanitary facilities, for the eight-hour day, and for recognition of the legitimacy of the ACWA. In return Hillman justified the war against "German autocracy" as a struggle to defend labor's democratic rights, a position at odds with that of many of his associates in the socialist wing of the labor movement and most of the Jewish rank and file of the ACWA.

For Hillman the war was thus a formative and decisive political experience. It convinced him of the advantages of state intervention on labor's behalf and for the regulation of the economy more generally. It permanently established his relationship with urban progressives in both major political parties. And it furthered his acculturation into the cosmopolitan world of reform as he conferred regularly with political, industrial, and labor elites with larger designs for social harmony that wartime experiments with planning and industrial democracy had encouraged.

Quickly Hillman was coming of age, preparing himself to play a larger role in the country's affairs. The pages of the leading progressive journals like the *New Republic* and *Survey* were given over to praise of the ACWA union president's social prescience. Thus the *New Republic*, anxious about postwar industrial and political rebellion and aware that democracy was being subjected to "tests of unprecedented severity throughout the world," concluded that democracy's future "depends . . . upon the capacity of employers and workers to harmonize democratic ideals of freedom with the voluntary self-discipline essential to efficient production," and that "no group of men in America has a keener appreciation of this fact than Sidney Hillman and the ACWA."

Such praise was exhilarating for someone who less than ten years earlier had been struggling to master English and the rudiments of daily life in the New World. Less and less did Hillman share the sense of exclusion, radical disdain, and Talmudic-like doctrinal obsessiveness of the ghetto socialist he had once been. He was instead developing not only an instinct for power but also a taste for being close to those who wielded it.

Yet Hillman was far from being a cyncial man. Indeed, his sense of himself as a man of the *Haskala*, a messenger of reason, progress, and civilization, was never entirely effaced. The period of world war and revolution was a historical moment when it was possible to hold two divergent views of the future and not recognize or confront their irreconcilability. In such an unsettled time, full of possibilities, an older language of political messianism seemed once again appropriate. Thus, echoes of his revolutionary youth resonated in a letter to his small daughter written late in the war when the power of labor everywhere seemed irresistible: "Messiah is arriving. He may be with us any minute—one can hear the footsteps of the Deliverer—if only he listens intently, Labor will rule and the world will be free."

The messiah whose footsteps Hillman thought he heard appeared to be a cross between an Old Testament avenger of social injustice and a benevolent bureaucrat ready to apply the latest discoveries of social engineering. Hillman's ability to feel at home in both worlds, to translate the theories of one into the *lingua franca* of the other, was the secret of his remarkable rise, the reason he carried so much social weight in the world of respectable reform. Nowhere was this extraordinary ability to move freely across cultural borders more apparent and important than in Hillman's relationship with the ACWA rank and file.

Hillman realized that designing the apparatus of industrial democracy was a task of enormous psychological and social complexity. The ACWA was a polyglot ensemble of twenty-six nationalities whose sense of ethnic exclusiveness caused recurrent political, cultural, and organizational tension. Moreover, the "new unionism" confronted artisanal work groups who, while militant defenders of trade unionism, were also accustomed to regulating the pace and quantity of production informally and semiautonomously. But industrial democracy depended on the skilled workers' willingness to accept new work rules, technical innovations, standards of performance, disciplinary procedures, and new codes of shopfloor behavior. Designed first of all to maximize efficiency, the new system sometimes disrupted the internal hierarchies and moral codes of artisanal and ethnic solidarity. Not surprisingly, when the apparatus of industrial democracy was initially installed, it generated more antagonism than harmony. But it was Hillman's special organizational genius that he eventually managed to achieve an alliance between the informal traditions of workers' control from below and the rationalized, bureaucratic procedures of comanagement from above.

Hillman recognized that the combativeness and moral stamina of shopfloor militants were the union's greatest resources, and he never hesitated to conduct protracted and bitterly fought strikes, both before and after the war. Furthermore, he made sure that the creation of the ACWA reinforced and even institutionalized many traditional shopfloor prerogatives. At the same time, he transferred authority from shop chairmen to outside business agents and their superiors in the union hierarchy. Meanwhile, the union's elaborate educational and cultural programs and its attempts to dissolve separate foreign language and craft locals, to encourage members to take out citizenship papers, and to insist that English be spoken at union conventions helped transform the traditional artisanal and immigrant cultures of the membership into a new way of life better suited to industrial democracy. Traditional sentiments emphasizing the preservation of old world familial and communal values were reformulated to encourage and emphasize economic self-interest, contractual obligation, industrial equity, and purchasing power.

This period of great growth and unbounded optimism about the future (1916–19) crested and then receded along with the postwar wave of revolutionary enthusiasm. In the early 1920s, Hillman was part of a broader coalition of progressive trade unionists, including the miners, machinists, and railroad brotherhoods, that sought to convert the American Federation of Labor (AFL) to a program of public ownership of utilities, industrial unionism, and some form of workers' control. Cooperation proved possible but only briefly in the warm afterglow of the postwar strike wave. Before the thermidor that swept across the Western world froze all attempts at economic reform and political realignment, Hillman and the rest of the progressive trade union coalition joined with the Socialist party to organize the LaFollette presidential campaign of 1924. Even Gompers and the AFL, which had always considered Hillman the illegimate head of an outlaw dual union, lent their endorsement. Once LaFollette lost, however, the progressive coalition disintegrated.

The upward arc of Hillman's career might have ended there. Progressive reformers were relegated to the periphery of national affairs; Hillman could only pursue the possibilities of the "new unionism" in the provincial backwaters of the clothing industry. Here he was not lacking in new ideas and projects. During the twenties, the ACWA pioneered in the introduction of unemployment insurance, in the construction of low-cost cooperative housing, and in uniquely successful efforts at cooperative labor banking. Hillman did his best to broadcast these achievements nationally. But his was a solitary voice, calling for a socially conscious and politically active labor movement when that was perceived by some as hopelessly utopian and by others in the age of welfare capitalism as entirely unnecessary. In retrospect, of course, it is possible to see all these innovations in social welfare and collective bargaining as natural antecedents to the New Deal and the Congress of Industrial Organizations (CIO), as a kind of dress rehearsal on a small stage for Hillman's subsequent performance as America's first labor statesman. But as the twenties drew to a close and Hillman and his closest comrades in the ACWA struggled to keep the union alive, any talk of a national renaissance of labor and economic reform seemed wildly improbable.

In the Antechamber of Power

The Great Depression changed everything. It created a profound crisis of confidence in the old order. And by upsetting most prevailing political and economic institutions, it created a nearly unprecedented opportunity for the redistribution of political and economic power.

However much the depression discredited older established elites and political alliances, there remained the question of who and what was to replace them. The forging of new coalitions united by shared legislative goals for reform and recovery placed a premium on industrial and political statesmanship. Franklin Delano Roosevelt became the master of political coalition building in the national arena, while Hillman performed an analagous role within and for the labor movement. Together they realigned American politics and recast the economy. But before that could be accomplished a fierce struggle ensued between competing elites, interest groups, and classes, a struggle in which Hillman found himself deeply embroiled.

Hillman immediately realized that the future of the ACWA, of the large labor movement generally, and the national economy were hostage to developments in the sphere of national politics and depended on action by the federal government. Today we might describe his perspective as a cross between Keynesian and social democratic reform. Thus he identified the restoration of mass purchasing power as the critical element for economic revival. He called for national planning to guarantee industrial stability and argued that "if we are to avoid the cycles of depression . . . we must plan a more equitable distribution of our national income." During the early years of the depression, he campaigned for legislative proposals that included the shorter work week, countercyclical public works, unemployment insurance, and a national standard of hours and wages. More daringly, he called for some system of joint labor-management-government planning and proposed a tripartite labor board to regulate the conditions of labor.

It was one thing to propose and quite another to dispose, and there was no one more mindful of the question of power than Hillman. Entrenched business interests favored their own recovery programs diametrically opposed to the Keynesian-social democratic alternative represented by Hillman. Organizations like the U.S. Chamber of Commerce and the National Association of Manufacturers promoted various forms of industrial self-regulation in which the government would sanction the suspension of antitrust laws and allow the installation of a guildlike system of cartelization, production controls, the regulation of new entry into industry, price fixing, and the cooperative division of the remaining market—all in the interests of protecting the oligopolistic position of established industrial and financial concerns.

Hillman spent much energy denouncing these corporatist proposals, accusing businessmen of focusing on the fraudulent problem of overproduction, of fostering economic stagnation and artificial scarcity, and of deliberately ignoring the economic needs and political rights of labor. But corporatist spokesman like Bernard Baruch carried enormous weight in the Roosevelt administration. Hillman knew he needed help, but also realized he could not expect much from a paralyzed national labor movement. He looked instead to the multiple circles of progressive reformers in and outside of government. Progressive senators like LaFollette, Norris, and Wagner, liberal members of the Taylor Society like Harlow Person and Morris Cooke, and Keynesians and state planners in the policy-making circles collecting around Roosevelt, like Frankfurter and Tugwell and Perkins, were old friends. And they were offering their own proposals for wage and hour legislation, unemployment insurance, public works, and national planning.

At the same time Hillman cultivated relations with certain segments of industry and commerce. A newer network of manufacturing, retailing, real estate, and financial elites, whose interests were more directly tied to mass consumption, appeared more amenable to Keynesian approaches to generating aggregate demand than were the corporatists of heavy industry. They also adopted a decidedly less authoritarian approach to labor relations, and some like the Filene brothers, Henry Bruere of the Bowery Savings Bank, as well as innovative manufacturers like Henry Dennison, Morris Leeds, and Henry Kendall, were professional and political acquaintances of Hillman's.

Strategically, what Hillman thus envisioned was a cross-class alliance that would link restive elements of the labor movement with reform-minded technocrats and bureaucrats and likeminded elements of business. Together they would experiment with using the machinery of government to expand mass purchasing power, to plan for economic growth, and to systematically regulate business. It was a promising alliance, but in the beginning it failed.

The final draft of the new administration's National Industrial Recovery Act (NIRA) clearly represented a partial triumph for Baruch and the corporatists. Nevertheless Hillman defended the bill in public (while remaining privately skeptical), in part because of its public works section and in part because of its concession on behalf of collective bargaining as represented by clause 7a. But perhaps even more compelling was the fact that in the course of the maneuverings leading to the passage of the bill, Hillman had come close to the center of power and meant to get even closer.

For Roosevelt had appointed Hillman to the National Recovery Administration's (NRA) Labor Advisory Board. Not naive, he did not entirely depend on the new recovery act nor on his own influence within the government. He called for an industrywide campaign of labor organization to counterbalance the incentive to business domination the law provided. At the time, this double-edged tactic of pursuing his objectives within and outside of official channels seemed prudent, even shrewd. In the event, however, Hillman's proximity to the centers of power and his actual elevation to a government position made him overly sanguine about the possibilities of the NIRA. This was the first time, but it would not be the last, when he allowed his fascination with power and his ambition to succeed to cloud his usually acute political judgment.

The NRA did become a useable instrument of labor organizing for the ACWA, and in effect helped save the ILGWU from extinction. Its clothing codes, moreover, prevented the industry from devouring itself in internecine competition. A handful of other unions, including the United Mine Workers, were similarly benefited. So far as most of the labor movement was concerned, however, the NRA amounted to the "national run-around."

Nor did the situation improve substantially when, in September 1934, the president promoted Hillman to the new National Industrial Recovery Board (NIRB), the body charged with running the NRA. Hillman carried on a kind of underground resistance to the corporatist and antilabor impulses of the NRA, but did so from the standpoint of the loyal opposition, never willing to seriously endanger his first official position as a labor statesmen. As the NIRB ensnared him more securely in a web of bureacratic propriety and responsibility, he used his strategms to hold together an otherwise hopeless political and administrative undertaking. He became the NRA's strong man, and he defended it even against populist attacks from his one-time mentor, Clarence Darrow. He campaigned feverishly for its legislative extention in 1935. For Hillman it remained the only available channel through which to promote government planning and a Keynesian fiscal policy. It also constituted the last official bulwark standing in the way of wage-cutting and anti-union activity by "the Tories of industry."

Thus committed, he lost all patience with his critics: "Of course the liberals and the left-wingers could have told us—well wait till the revolution—but we might have to wait a hell of a long time: and in the meantime we would have destroyed what we had built up throughout the years." He claimed that "if the NRA continues; and if we have a labor movement vital and moving, we will make more progress than the dreamers can look to." It was the "half-intellectual" talking, the doer with his eye on the practical and the possible, wounded by the accusation that perhaps he had wandered from the mainstream of the movement.

In May 1935 the Supreme Court left him without a cause to defend when it declared the NRA unconstitutional. Hillman had seriously miscalculated. The NRA was a mésalliance from the outset with only the remotest chance of working in labor's interests. He was not, however, one to unduly lament the past. Once the NRA was killed, he turned to new strategic alternatives that would leave him less completely at the mercy of bureaucratic in-fighting or on having friend in high places. He reminded a Madison Square Garden rally that "it was my privilege, when just a boy of 16 to go to jail fighting against tyranny in Czarist Russia." The death of the NRA seemed to be offering him a chance to recapture a lost, more daring youth.

The Compleat New Dealer

Almost immediately following the Supreme Court decision, Hillman laid out the road ahead, a less traveled one to be sure: "Perhaps there is going to be a new law, fixing minimum wages and maximum hours, but we are not going to wait for it, we are not going to take a chance on it. We are going to forget about it and go ahead on our own." This did not mean he was preparing to abandon politics. On the contrary, he was more than ever convinced that all hope for labor and for economic recovery and reform depended ultimately on the realignment of national politics. But the failure of the NRA persuaded him that the labor movement would have to increase its independent organizational strength substantially if it was to influence government policy, that it was therefore necessary for labor to pursue its industrial and political objectives in tandem.

Even before there was such a thing as the CIO, Hillman conceived of industrial unionism as the pursuit of labor politics by other means. This is not to minimize his role in the sphere of industrial organization proper. Together with John L. Lewis he founded the CIO, became its vice-president, and was intimately involved in formulating its industrial strategy. He poured ACWA money and cadres into the principal CIO campaigns, pursued quiet, behind-the-scenes negotiations with friendly industrialists like Walter Chrysler and Gerard Swope, and drew on his considerable experience to resolve internal factional quarrels that threatened to tear apart fledgling unions like the United Auto Workers. And he masterminded an ambitious although unsuccessful effort to organize the textile industry.

Indeed, as chairman of the Textile Workers Organizing Committee (TWOC), established early in 1937, Hillman brought to bear all his talents at mass organization, his business connections, his political acumen and contacts, and his bureaucratic finesse. The TWOC, however, failed to penetrate the cotton-textile South, thanks first of all to the deep recession of 1937, but also due to the frailty of southern liberalism, the impact of rural fundamentalism, paternalism, and racism, and the implacable antagonism of the South's cotton manufacturers, whose closely-held familial firms and communal structures made them impervious to outside pressure. Against such odds, Hillman's artfulness as a mediator between cultures and classes was simply not enough.

The TWOC was a deep disappointment but only reinforced Hillman's political commitments so that he approached each and every problem confronting the CIO from the standpoint of how its solution might affect and be affected by relations with Roosevelt and the Democratic party. He was the compleat New Dealer and actively supported every major and minor piece of reform and social welfare legislation, including the controversial court reform bill. He was the principal lobbyist for the Fair Labor Standards Act (the last best hope for improving labor standards in the southern textile industry) and became a familiar face in the halls of Congress and in the backrooms of the Democratic party. And he was absolutely loyal to the president, prepared to defend even Roosevelt's most unpopular initiatives and flattered by his blossoming reputation as Roosevelt's confidante in the labor movement. In turn, the president rewarded Hillman with numerous substantive and honorary appointments to New Deal agencies and commissions.

At first there seemed to be no contradiction between his personal ambitions and his role as founder and vice-president of the CIO. But when the alliance between the "second" New Deal and industrial unionism grew tense under the pressure of the 1937 recession and the accompanying anti-Roosevelt political reaction, Hillman's role as matchmaker between the administration and the CIO became exceedingly more difficult. The seeds of discord were sewn earlier, however.

In 1936 Hillman played a critical role in founding Labor's Non-Partisan League (LNPL), the CIO's bid to influence presidential politics. In so doing, he had to justify a controversial departure from what constituted a cherished tradition of independent and socialist politics on the part of the ACWA rank and file. This he was entirely prepared to do, as by the mid 1930s Hillman had few reservations left regarding the principle of labor's political independence, especially when he sensed the opportunity to consolidate the CIO's developing alliance with Roosevelt. In fact he viewed the creation of LNPL, at least in part, as a way of circumventing third-party movements that might dissipate the strength of the reform coalition then in power in Washington. But he was shrewd and statesmanlike enough not to acknowledge openly that strategic purpose and instead to keep alive, especially early in 1936 when third-party prospects proliferated, the prospect that LNPL might someday become the vehicle of a truly independent American labor party.

Thus Hillman made vague allusions to the future realignment of American politics in which LNPL would play a critical role, and he told the ACWA membership he had not lost his "faith in a labor party." His language was deliberately loose; political realignment sometimes seemed to suggest a labor or third party, but at other times merely the capturing of the Democratic party by "progressive liberalism." Given the unsettled conditions and growing power of the CIO in the first half of 1937, both Lewis and Hillman found it useful to use the threat of independent political action while simultaneously swearing fealty to Roosevelt. It was possible to execute such verbal gymnastics so long as the forward momentum of the New Deal continued.

The delicate balance of forces shifted decisively, however, with the onset of the 1937 recession, the accumulating discontent with the New Deal, and the growing timidity of the Roosevelt administration in responding to its political opposition. As the administration's commitment to further social and economic reform withered, as it opted instead for a policy of compensatory deficit financing that avoided addressing those more politically sensitive issues concerning the structure of the economy and direct government regulation, and as Roosevelt distanced himself from the CIO, Hillman found it increasingly difficult to keep everyone happy. Without hesitation, Hillman tied his fate to Roosevelt and the Democratic party, and with equal resolve Lewis marched in the opposite direction.

Signs of what was to become by 1940 an irreconcilable conflict between Hillman and Lewis and an open fight for control of the CIO were already apparent late in 1937. Above all, two issues made the split irreparable. The first had to do with the future relationship of the CIO to the AFL. The second was the coming of World War II. Together they made Hillman into America's first labor statesman, but at a heavy price.

Hillman at War with Himself

While never quite as unyielding as Lewis in his attitude toward peace talks with the AFL, Hillman had nevertheless also turned aside feelers and proposals that even hinted at compromising the integrity of the industrial unions created by the CIO. But his attitude shifted when the president himself became the champion of immediate labor unity as a way of strengthening his campaign for a third term. While Lewis's relations with Roosevelt deteriorated, Hillman openly promoted the idea of peace negotiations with the AFL in part as a way of furthering his unique friendship with the president.

Labor unity was a lofty ideal everybody, even Lewis, subscribed to for reasons far less exalted. Thus Roosevelt sought to be reelected, while Hillman wanted to be annointed. It was all symptomatic of the end of an era of reform. By 1940 Hillman was convinced that there were no options for labor outside the Democratic party. He was willing to trust the fate of labor to Roosevelt, to in effect become his campaign manager within the CIO, precisely because both the CIO and the New Deal had lost the initiative.

Nowhere was this convergence of objectives clearer than at the 1940 CIO convention. There the Roosevelt administration collaborated directly if surreptitiously with Hillman to undermine Lewis and to transform industrial unionism into a device of party and government policy. Despite accumulating evidence to the contrary, Hillman declared that "not only has the New Deal held fast to the gains of the first six years, but . . . we have continued to move forward." He urged a blanket endorsement of administration domestic and foreign policy, including a conciliatory stance regarding unity with the AFL. Neither side emerged completely victorious at the November convention. CIO delegates refused to applaud the administration's record and rejected Hillman's plea for unity with the AFL. But they also accepted Lewis's resignation as CIO president and replaced him with Philip Murray, a Roosevelt loyalist.

Hillman suffered from one glaring weakness. He was acutely vulnerable because of his official association with the administration's foreign policy and in particular its defense mobilization for war. The CIO not only opposed American military participation in the war, it was extremely suspicious that the defense program would exclude labor's participation and erode those rights and standards won over the past five years of struggle. It was this position that gave real strength to Lewis's position of labor independence.

Hillman, by virtue of his presidential appointment as the only labor member of the National Defense Advisory Commission (NDAC), was committed to an unconditional endorsement of the administration's defense program. The capstone of his whole career, the invitation to employ his labor statesmanship at the highest levels of government on behalf of the national defense, threatened to become his greatest liability, a disabling weakness that could erode his moral authority among his old comrades in the labor movement.

At first Hillman seemed to accomplish a great deal, and this despite the opposition of the industrialists on the NDAC and their allies representing the army and navy. By September 1940, thanks to Roosevelt's support and the threat of labor unrest, Hillman had persuaded the NDAC to announce a labor policy that insisted that all businesses receiving defense contracts obey all labor laws, that forty hours be recognized as the desired maximum work week, and that contracts be withdrawn from those companies found to be in violation.

Even this initial "victory," however, turned out to be more apparent than real. Never throughout Hillman's whole tenure in Washington did any of the agencies of defense mobilization on which he served use their considerable power over industrial priorities and the issuing of lucrative government contracts to systematically enforce social policy, especially labor policy. Thus at the 1940 CIO convention Hillman remained vulnerable to the charge that notorious violators of the labor laws, like Ford, continued to receive handsome government contracts.

Indeed, it is the underlying irony of this phase of his career that Hillman's actual power to influence public policy declined in inverse proportion to the rise in his official position and prestige. Roosevelt had invited him to become part of a government of national unity, bipartisan in composition, and in theory deaf to the pleadings of special interests. In reality, the agencies of economic mobilization were honeycombed by special interests, and as the defense crisis evolved the voice of corporate America drowned out all other contending parties. Hillman was caught between his commitment to Roosevelt and the "national interest" on the one side and his anxiety over the mounting attacks on labor and the Keynesian welfare state on the other. Criticized by the leadership of both the AFL and the CIO, undermined by fellow bureacrats in the defense apparatus and Department of Labor, sabotaged by army and navy directives running counter to ostensible government labor policy, targeted by business, besieged with strikes by a resentful rank and file, and vilified by congressional reactionaries seeking to cripple labor, Hillman found himself increasingly isolated and politically paralyzed.

Thus there was no more basic service Roosevelt expected Hillman to perform than to prevent or at least drastically reduce the actual interruption of production by strikes. Yet just at the moment when he was elevated to the highest government position he was ever to hold, as associate director of the Office of Production Management (OPM, which replaced the NDAC in December 1940), he discovered that his actual capacity to control labor turmoil was substantially reduced. The year 1941 experienced more strikes than any previous year except 1919 and 1937. This was practically inevitable as worker morale steadily deteriorated in the face of overwork, speed-up, and racial discrimination, while resentment accumulated over war profiteering. By the middle of the year, faced with strikes in shipyards, repair shops, aircraft plants, lumberyards, and elsewhere, Hillman was nearly beside himself. He declared that "these actions reflect adversely upon the integrity and patriotism of the American labor movement," and that he did "unqualifiedly condemn and denounce the foregoing strikes."

However much such rhetoric reassured those in higher authority, it diminished Hillman's stature and credibility within the labor movement. Of course, Hillman was by no means the only labor leader to condemn such strikes, but as a government official he was in the most exposed position to suffer the consequences. In the most notorious and damaging case, Hillman sided with the decision of Roosevelt and OPM director William Knudsen to use federal troops to break the wildcat United Auto Workers (UAW) strike against the North American Aviation Company in June of 1941. For this he was roundly condemned by the CIO, despite the fact that he struggled to avoid precisely this course of action and despite the fact that the strike itself was disavowed by the national leadership of the UAW and the CIO.

Hillman simply had no remedy for the problem of the "wildcat" strike. His own preferred solution, not surprisingly, was to arrange for a détente between the CIO and AFL and then more broadly between business and labor, which would provide the latter with the sense of security it required to discipline its own membership. He therefore established elaborate mediation procedures, which did manage to forestall numerous potential strikes and to arrange workable labor-management stabilization agreements in the construction and shipbuilding industries. But as the war economy increasingly became a businessman's economy, rank-and-file discontent and unauthorized strikes grew.

He was somewhat more successful in carrying out his second great responsibility: to ensure a reliable, varied, and plentiful supply of labor. In some respects the problem of the labor supply lent itself to those techniques of social engineering for which Hillman had become celebrated twenty years earlier. That is to say, it was possible to view the issue as a problem in social statistics: one could arrive at a rough numerical approximation of the demand for various kinds of skilled and semiskilled labor and match it against the available supply.

This Hillman did. He immediately realized that the depression had severely undermined the nation's ability to staff high-technology war industries with adequate amounts and kinds of skilled workers, including tool designers and makers, marine mechanics, ship's carpenters and electricians, to name but a few. The answer was to train a whole new generation of such labor out of the pool of unemployed. Working at an exhausting pace, Hillman, together with Owen Young of General Electric, designed a vast vocational education program. They drew on every government agency having anything to do with the supply or training of manpower as well as public and private vocational schools, and, most importantly, on the "training-within-industry" programs conducted by major corporations, which Hillman caused to be greatly expanded.

It was a daunting piece of administrative architecture and an exercise of labor statesmanship that in many respects bore fruit. But the fatal illusion of such social engineering had always been that one might overcome political and social antagonisms through the magic of objective "social science." The question of labor supply, however rigorously it might be defined by the geometry of supply and demand, was at bottom a profoundly contentious business. Indeed, it ultimately became a feature of what was perhaps the most fundamental social question of the era: Who was to control and direct the vast expansion of productive facilities occurring under government auspices and at government expense?

If industry, for example, were to have a free hand in the training, recruiting, positioning, and transfer of skilled and semiskilled labor, it would immediately threaten the elaborate set of procedures defining apprenticeship, the skill content of occupational categories, seniority, and a host of associated work rules that unions had built up and jealously guarded for many years. Similarly, the power to determine industrial priorities carried enormous social consequences. A decision by the priorities branch of the OPM could turn a thriving community or region into a ghost town or do the exact opposite; it could throw thousands out of work, at least temporarily, or put thousands previously unemployed back to work and drive up local wages; it could determine the availability of consumer goods, disrupt families, devastate union locals, and force people to live in quonset huts on the sites of industrial "parks." Responsibility for maintaining and regulating the labor supply, therefore, ought to have carried with it some influence over such related matters as industrial priorities, contract placement, housing construction, the ordered phasing out of consumer good production, and a host of other vital questions. But this was the nub of the problem: Hillman's actual authority never equaled his responsibilities.

He was thereby doubly incapacitated. On the one hand, he was reluctant to make an open fight for greater labor participation in key economic decisions for fear of jeopardizing his bureaucratic standing. On the other hand, by vacillating he further isolated himself from the organized labor movement. Thus he was criticized for not supporting the CIO's "Murray Plan," which called for the creation of joint labor-management industrial councils with authority to make critical decisions regarding labor supply, priorities, the deployment of plant and machinery, and related matters.

Hillman preferred instead to pursue labor participation and industrial democracy by other means, namely by defending and extending his own administrative reach. And for that purpose he sought allies not in the labor movement but in the bureaucratic labryinths of Washington among groups of fellow New Dealers and presumably sympathetic businessmen. Thus he placed labor representatives from his own Labor Division on critical priorities committees only to see them systematically ignored by the businessmen in charge. He promoted the idea of local labor-management production committees under his authority and then watched them become little more than public relations devices to inspire production and build morale without a scintilla of real power to control life on the shopfloor. Hillman found himself presiding over an administrative ghetto of diminishing power.

Finally he attempted to break out, but he did so within the ground rules of bureaucratic politics and at an inopportune time. Working under grueling pressure, he confessed to a close associate: "I must work harder. If I fail it will be the failure of the Jew Hillman." He gathered together the dwindling group of New Dealers and Keynesians still left in the administration, and they drafted a plan for a broad program of economic, social, and labor stabilization, including proposals for progressive taxation, a price freeze, a war profits tax, compulsory savings, equitable rationing of basic commodities, a national wage stabilization policy, union security, and "equality of sacrifice."

This was Hillman's attempt to come forward as the champion of the New Deal, the Keynesian fiscal revolution, and social democratic reform. But it was a bid for power that waited on the president's pleasure, and on April 18, 1942, Roosevelt made clear that Hillman had outlived his immediate usefulness. On that day, Roosevelt created the War Manpower Commission and appointed as its director not America's first labor statesman but the former governor of Indiana, Paul McNutt. No one who really counted, either from the labor movement or from among those businessmen and bureaucrats who had found Hillman's services so helpful in the past, fought to see him made labor czar. It was a crushing blow. Hillman resigned and almost immediately fell victim to his third heart attack. It was nearly six months before he reentered public life.

Clearing It with Sidney

Yet despite this profound rejection Hillman remained personally loyal to the president and politically committed to the Democratic party. Moreover, the next dramatic phase of his career was devoted to converting the enormous but latent political and electoral strength of the CIO into a mighty machine for the salvation of Roosevelt and the New Deal. At stake was not only the future political complexion of the Democratic party but also the shape of the postwar political economy both at home and abroad.

The 1942 congressional elections were a serious setback for Roosevelt, his party, and especially its New Deal wing, and cause for alarm among the leading circles in both the administration and the CIO. Hillman explained to a CIO convention that political action had become imperative because "workers can no longer work out even their most immediate day-to-day problems through negotiations with their employers. . . . Their wages, hours, and working conditions have become increasingly dependent upon policies adopted by Congress and the National Administration. . . . Labor must bring its full influence to bear in shaping these decisions." He lost no time putting together the machinery to make good on these intentions, and by mid–1943 was able to tell Roosevelt that the

CIO had created a Political Action Committee (PAC), which would provide the basis for united political action by labor on the president's behalf. As chairman of the new organization, Hillman made it unmistakeably clear that PAC would have absolutely nothing to do with plans for a third or labor party, that he had forever interred such visions as utterly utopian. "We have no desire to organize another political party. As a matter of fact, we are opposed to the organization of a third party . . . because it would divide the forces of the progressives throughout the nation."

He kept the committee's attention focused on the enormous tasks of economic, social, and political reconstruction that would follow the war. PAC announced its "Peoples' Program for 1944," an amalgam of Keynesian fiscal policy and social welfare reform, which in its essentials was to remain the platform of organized labor for the next thirty years. Its long-term plans called for full employment at fair wages, a national planning board with power to implement compensatory public works spending, a guaranteed annual wage, federal aid to education, the extention and improvement of social security coverage, active antitrust enforcement, and permanent status for the Fair Employment Practice Committee (FEPC). Immediately, it demanded financial aid for returning veterans, rigorous enforcement of price controls, and a significant role for the institutions of organized labor throughout the world in the anticipated creation and operation of the United Nations.

The "Peoples' Program for 1944" was not, however, the program of the Democratic party in 1944. Nor was it likely to become so then or in the future unless PAC and its allies managed to checkmate the coalition of Dixiecrats, machine bosses, and corporate lobbyists whose influence had increased steadily during the war. For this purpose, PAC established an elaborate electoral machine based on the CIO unions and cooperative independent and AFL unions. Then, in the summer of 1944, Hillman created the National Citizens Political Action Committee (NCPAC), a middle-class analog of PAC, to make highly visible the extensive nonlabor support for labor's political program. While both organization's mastered the nitty-gritty of local electioneering, Hillman sped around the country directing state campaigns, resolving internal factional disputes, and making innumerable speeches and radio appearances. For a first attempt at playing the game of conventional two-party politics, PAC and NCPAC had a notable success, especially as PAC measurably increased the Democratic party vote in areas of CIO strength compared to 1942.

By outperforming the party's urban machines at their own speciality, Hillman and his PACs had certainly placed the Roosevelt administration in their debt. But prospects for the "Peoples' Program" depended even more on directly challenging the program and power of the opposition. PAC's opponents insisted on a modest role for government in implementing countercyclical fiscal policy and relied instead on corporate-led economic growth to take care of the material needs of American workers. The corporate growth strategy consigned the labor movement and its allies to a subordinate role in national politics, excluding them from serious participation in the institutions of the state and industry. The battle to determine the fate of the Democratic party soon made Hillman's name a household word in American politics.

Nineteen hundred forty-four was the year the Republican party and its presidential candidate, Thomas Dewey, tried to discredit their opponents by suggesting that the Democratic party had become the political hostage of the CIO. The evidence amounted to a rumor, given initial credence by a *New York Times* report, that with regard to the Democrat's choice of a vice-presidential nominee, President Roosevelt had instructed party leaders to "Clear it with Sidney."

From the moment the story appeared, "Clear it with Sidney" became the leitmotiv of a political opéra bouffe, conducted by the Republican high command and designed to arouse every nativist, anti-Semitic, anticommunist, and antilabor instinct in the electorate. Editorials and campaign speeches repeatedly mentioned Hillman's foreign birth—"Sidney Hillman, Russian-born immigrant"—or struck an anti-Semitic note with insinuations about Hillman's "rabbinical education." The chairman of the Republican Central Campaign Committee suggested that "Hillman and Browder [the chairman of the American Communist party] want to rule America and enslave the American people." Republican billboards across the country asked: "It's your country—Why let Sidney Hillman run it?"

Actually, all the lurid rhetoric served to conceal rather than expose what was an important change in the chemistry of the Democratic party. If "Mr. Truman was cleared with Sidney," as Dewey claimed, it represented not the capturing of the Democratic party by the CIO but the further subordination of organized labor to the political and economic consensus that would soon come to define postwar America. There is no question that Hillman was consulted on the vice-presidency, seriously and often, and that he had a voice not so much in selecting Truman but in aborting the candidacy of James Byrnes, author of the "Little Steel formula" hated by the trade union movement. What is not entirely clear, but highly probable, is that Sidney Hillman had for months been secretly negotiating with top party leaders to collaborate in dumping the vice-president, Henry Wallace, who was otherwise the official choice of Phillip Murray and the CIO. Hillman may have played such a double game precisely because he realized the futility of the Wallace candidacy and thus how relatively weak the CIO had become, Republican hysterics notwithstanding.

The enduring significance of the Wallace imbroglio was the way it helped forge a consensus among northern and southern conservative Democrats more attracted to Henry Luce's vision of an "American Century" than to the prospect of a global New Deal evoked by Henry Wallace's "Century of the Common Man." Hillman would spend the final two years of his life caught between those two centuries.

Machiavelli at Bay

The struggle for control of the Democratic party continued after the election. In the summer of 1945 PAC led the fight against attempts to kill the FEPC and to eliminate price and rent controls prematurely. It also called for federal legislation to cushion the impact of unemployment during the period of reconversion. Hillman worked assiduously to revive the old concert of interests between labor, business, and government. As the strike-breaking proclivities of the administration emerged early in 1946, it became very difficult to maintain cordial relations between the Wallace and Truman wings of the party. This was true not only with regard to domestic policy, but even more so in foreign policy. Nonetheless, Hillman tried very hard to marry the "American Century" to the "Century of the Common Man." Shortly before his death, Sidney Hillman had one last chance to play the labor statesman, this time on the stage of world politics.

During the war, Hillman had established contact with the leadership of the trade union movements in the principal allied countries and with the underground remnants of the labor movement in both Axis and Axis-occupied nations, including France, Italy, and Germany. His purpose was not merely to extend fraternal assistance, but in so doing to determine the political complexion of organized labor in postwar Europe. He sought to nurture an independent labor movement, one both pro-Western and social democratic in orientation, without offending either Soviet-supported communist trade unions or far more conservative nationalist and religious movements.

As the war drew to a close, Hillman spied the opportunity to create a world labor organization committed to a global version of the New Deal and one powerful enough to make its voice count within the councils of Allied governments deciding the fate of the postwar world. Hillman and the CIO were eager to establish the new organization forthwith, but immediately ran into the opposition of the British Trades Union Congress

(TUC) led by Sir Walter Citrine. Citrine, like Churchill, was most concerned with minimizing potential Soviet and Communist party influence. An uneasy compromise between Hillman and Citrine led to the founding convention of the World Federation of Trade Unions (WFTU) in Paris in September 1945, but tension with Citrine continued. Hillman characteristically tried to mediate between the TUC and the Soviet delegation.

The WFTU issued a series of declarations that echoed the CIO PAC programs of 1944 and 1945. It wanted a voice in liquidating fascist regimes and in helping reconstitute the German trade union movement and educational system to ensure its thorough denazification. Economically, the organization demanded the breaking-up of national and international cartels, a full-employment policy, and comprehensive social security benefits. Most of all, however, the WFTU sought an official position in the international apparatus then being erected by the principal Allied powers for administering the postwar world. In particular, the WFTU demanded at least an advisory role with the Allied Control Commission for Germany and representation at the United Nations, especially a place on the Economic and Social Council.

If the CIO PAC faced a too powerful coalition of domestic enemies, the WFTU suffered even greater disadvantages. Not only did the same business and conservative political elements oppose the WFTU program, but the organization also faced the overt opposition of the AFL, the subtle delaying tactics of Citrine, and a growing resistance to any form of collaboration with the Soviet Union. In February 1946, Truman wrote to Hillman unequivocally ruling out any official position for the WFTU, even of an advisory kind, either at the United Nations or on the Allied Control Commission in either Germany or Japan.

Just a year earlier, Hillman had been positively exultant as he viewed the prospects for labor in the "Century of the Common Man." Now he confronted his final defeat in what was clearly turning out to be the "American Century." Thus the war had exacted its toll. While seemingly the occasion for his own personal triumph, it had become the medium of Hillman's political and professional failure. And finally, it had destroyed his health. On the morning of July 10, 1946, he suffered his fourth heart attack and died at the age of fifty-nine at his summer home on Long Island.

The underlying pathos of Hillman's career is that as he drew ever closer to the center of power, he tended to lose his birthright, his Yiddish sense of irony, and with it the ability to tell the difference between the role of the courtier and that of the labor statesman. The same illusions that induced him to exaggerate the significance of his unique relationship with Roosevelt also blinded him to whatever possibilities remained for enhancing the political independence of organized labor and thereby his own real source of strength as a labor statesman.

In a larger, historic sense, however, Hillman's nearsightedness mirrored the inability of organized labor to initiate fundamental social change in America. Over and over again, the CIO insisted that what it sought above all else, whether in negotiating contracts or in urging social welfare legislation, was security. It was a recurring motif in almost every major speech Hillman delivered between 1930 and 1946. Security meant primarily the protection of the individual and the private family from the viscisitudes of modern industrial society. It was an undertaking designed to stabilize and integrate the industrial and political order. It had no need for the millennarian enthusiasms and universalist yearnings of Hillman's youth.

Bibliographic Notes

The only complete biography of Sidney Hillman is Matthew Josephson's *Sidney Hillman: Statesman of American Labor* (1952). Josephson's study is thorough, but largely uncritical, both because the author was close to the ACWA leadership and because he wrote the book so soon after Hillman's death when it was still difficult to establish a certain critical detachment from the subject. There is another partial biography of Hillman: George Soule, progressive journalist and for many years a confidante of Hillman, authored *Sidney Hillman: Labor Statesman* (1939). Although it mainly treats the first half of Hillman's career, it carries the story through the TWOC campaigns and the creation of the Textile Workers Union of America in 1939. As one might expect given Soule's relationship to Hillman, the book is in many respects a celebration of the latter's rise to "labor statesmanship." However, it contains some particularly valuable information about Hillman's activities during the early years of the depression. Len DeCaux's autobiography, *Labor Radical: From the Wobblies to CIO* (1970) contains substantial material on Hillman's role in the CIO in the 1930s and his political activities in the 1940s. DeCaux is critical of Hillman's "class collaborationism," but he maintains a basic respect for his achievements as a labor leader and sincere social reformer.

There are three histories of the Amalgamated Clothing Workers of America that cover the pre-depression era, all of which to one degree or another extol the "new unionism." J. M. Budish and George Soule, *The New Unionism in the Clothing Industry* (1920); and Charles Elbert Zaretz, *The Amalgamated Clothing Workers of America: A Study in Progressive Trades Unionism* (1934), are particularly concerned with the broader reform activities of the union. *The Clothing Workers of Chicago, 1910–22* (1922), prepared and published by the Chicago Joint Board, looks more closely at the innovative collective bargaining procedures introduced by the ACWA. My own article, "Dress Rehearsal for the New Deal: Shop-Floor

Insurgents, Political Elites, and Industrial Democracy in the Amalgamated Clothing Workers," which appears in *Working-Class America: Essays on Labor, Community and American Society*, edited by Michael H. Frisch and Daniel J. Walkowitz (1983), also presents an interpretation of these first two formative decades in the life of the ACWA and in Hillman's career in America.

On the 1930s generally, and for the CIO particularly, readers may consult Walter Galenson's *CIO Challenge to the AFL: A History of the American Labor Movement, 1935–1941* (1960), especially chapter 7, "The Men's Clothing Industry" and chapter 9, "The Renascence of Textile Unionism," although references to Hillman's activities are naturally scattered throughout the book. Similar references occur throughout Irving Bernstein's *Turbulent Years: A History of the American Worker, 1933–1941* (1970), and readers may want to pay particular attention to chapter 12, "The CIO Drives On."

Unfortunately, aside from the relevant chapters in Josephson's biography, there are no other studies of the union's history during the depression and the Second World War. However, ever since its founding in 1914, the ACWA has itself published a biannual documentary record of its activities on the occasion of its biannual convention (the only exception is 1932 when, due to the depression, the union was forced to cancel its convention so that the relevant volume for this period covers the years 1930–34). These documentary histories are, together with the papers of Sidney Hillman, of Jacob Potofsky who succeeded to the ACWA presidency after Hillman's death, and of the ACWA, the most valuable primary sources of information on Hillman's career. These papers, along with the union's convention proceedings, are housed at the Labor-Management Documentation Center of the Martin P. Catherwood Library of the New York State School of Industrial and Labor Relations at Cornell University, Ithaca, New York.

Philip Murray and the Subordination of the Industrial Unions to the United States Government

10

Ronald W. Schatz

At 10:30 on Tuesday night, April 8, 1952, sixty-five-year-old Philip Murray, the president of both the United Steelworkers of America and the Congress of Industrial Organizations (CIO), switched on the radio in his suite at the Hotel Roosevelt in Manhattan to listen to an emergency announcement by the president of the United States. Since becoming a member of the international executive board of the United Mine Workers (UMW) forty years before, Murray had represented American workers many times in pressure-charged negotiations with the federal government. This battle was the ultimate test of his policies. Although the United States was at war in Korea, the steel corporations had refused to meet any of the union's demands and had also rejected the recommendations of the government's Wage Stabilization Board. After cooperating with the government for four months, the steelworkers were set to strike at midnight.

President Truman came on the radio. His tone was harsh. He blamed the steel companies for the five-month-long impasse. "The companies insist that they must have price increases that are out of line with the stabilization rules. The companies have said that unless they can get those increases they will not settle with the union. The companies have said, in short, that unless they can have what they want, the steel industry will shut down." The manufacturers' price demands were "outrageous," Truman asserted. "They not only want . . . to cover any wage increase; they want to double their money on the deal." Since the nation must have steel to wage war, the president announced that he was ordering the secretary of commerce to take over the operation of the steel mills for the government of the United States.

"Attaboy, Harry!" Philip Murray shouted, bringing his fist down into his palm. "Attaboy, Harry!" he yelled again and again. "For the first time since

Franklin Roosevelt's death, he was delighted with Harry Truman," remembered Murray's long-time aide, David McDonald, who was with Murray that night. The mills would have the same managers; terms of employment would not change; but the president of the United States had recognized the steelworkers' patriotism and lent his backing to their cause. The speech over, Murray dialed union headquarters in Pittsburgh and called off the strike.

Philip Murray's career as a labor leader coincided with the growth of the federal government's power over the whole arena of industrial and labor relations. During the nineteenth century, federal policy toward wage workers and employers had alternated between a laissez-faire approach and, on rare but important occasions, violent repression of unions and strikes. President Theodore Roosevelt's appointment of a commission to resolve the 1902 anthracite coal strike represented the beginning of a new approach—one that involved federal pressure on corporations to bargain with unions, the enlistment of labor leaders into the federal bureaucracy, and continuous regulation of union operations by the government.

Philip Murray arrived in the United States with his father on Christmas Day in 1902. Only sixteen years old, he was already a coal miner and union member. By the time of the 1952 steel labor dispute, he was Harry Truman's favorite labor leader, a high official in a labor movement dependent on the federal government for whatever success it enjoyed. Philip Murray helped bring about this change. Yet in the end even he was not fully happy with the results.

Philip Murray was born in 1886 in Scotland, in a Lanarkshire village called Blantyre, and retained a Scots' burr all his life. His parents were Irish Catholics who had migrated to Britain a few years before. The Murrays and the Laydens, his mother's family, were both religiously observant. They were also pugnacious but not necessarily on behalf of liberal causes. Murray's maternal grandfather, with whom he lived as a small boy, had gone to Italy in the early 1860s to take up arms in support of the pope against Garibaldi. Murray's mother, Rose Ann Layden, was a weaver in a cotton mill. His father, William, was a coal miner and secretary of his local union branch. Like Walter Reuther, Phil Murray received instruction from his father regarding social questions and went with him to union meetings. In fact, at the age of seven he collected food for the miners, who were on strike for seventeen weeks.

Rose Ann died when Phil was two and his sister was four. William remarried a few years later, this time to a Scottish woman who had a child of her own. The couple had eight more children. The oldest boy in a family of thirteen, Phil left school for the mines at the age of ten to help support

235

his brothers and sisters. At sixteen he journeyed to America with his father to help the family make a new start. Carrying international coal-union transfer cards, they arrived at the port of New York, boarded a train for Irwin, Pennsylvania, in the southwestern part of the state, then walked miles through a blizzard to the town of Madison, in Westmoreland County, where William's brother Philip had already settled. The two men found work in the pits and within a year had saved enough to bring over the whole family.

Not long after the family was reunited in America, Murray got into a fight that had a lasting impact on him. Evidently Murray, who as a miner at the face was paid by the ton for his work, felt that he was being "deprived of my own weight in amounts approximating 40 percent of the amount of coal loaded." He protested to the weigh boss and demanded a union checkweighman on the tipple to ensure that the miners were paid in full for the coal they dug. Murray and his boss argued, then fought. Murray was fired and an unsuccessful strike ensued. "The day after the strike," Murray later testified, "my father and his eight children, including myself, were thrown from their homes out into the street." A sympathetic tavern owner took the family in, but "as soon as they seen or heard of Murray, the dogs of war were after him," Philip's old friend Pat Fagan recalled. Forced to leave town, Murray decided to devote his life to the union movement. Only a union, he felt, could protect the miners against fraud. "A coal miner has no money," he explained years later. "He is alone. He has no organization to defend him. He has nowhere to go. . . . It is not inadequacy of the State law. The law is there, but the individual cannot protect himself because he has no organization. He has no one to go to."

Murray worked in various southwestern Pennsylvania pits and in 1905 was elected president of a United Mine Workers local in a village called Horning. As a local leader, he rubbed elbows with Pat Dolan, Francis Feehan, John McCartney, and Pat Fagan, all Irish Catholics and members of the Ancient Order of Hibernians, who were trying to build the UMW in Westmoreland County. Along with union work, Murray spent time in self-improvement, investing sixty dollars—nearly one-tenth of his annual earnings—in a math and science course offered by the Scranton Correspondence School. Studying after supper, he finished the year-and-a-half-long course in six months. He also met and wooed Liz Lavery, the daughter of a miner killed in a pit accident. They were married in 1910.

With UMW membership increasing from 231,000 in 1910 to 413,000 in 1918, there was room for young men to rise, particularly in western Pennsylvania, a previously nonunion region whose leadership was divided into two bitterly opposed factions. Murray impressed John White, the

Photograph in the collection of the author.

president of the UMW, and John L. Lewis, then an organizer in the Pittsburgh area for the American Federation of Labor (AFL), as a leader who could pull District 5 together. He was a slim, muscular, and attractive young man, who had an unusual talent for retaining facts and figures, was sincerely devoted to the miners' betterment, was not afraid to fight, and yet could usually get his way by speaking softly. John Brophy, the president of UMW District 2 in central Pennsylvania, first heard of Murray from his brother-in-law, a representative for the union. "He said that Murray was a very interesting chap. He said I ought to meet him sometime, that he was a Scotch-Irish fellow who was quite a soft-soaper, as he phrased it, and that he got along with people very well, because he was friendly and conciliatory rather than arbitrary. He was very likable, and he's probably on his way up in mine workers' affairs."

In 1912 John White appointed Murray to a vacancy on the UMW's international executive board. Three years later White and Lewis arranged for Murray to replace Van Bittner, another young comer in UMW affairs but more abrasive than Murray, as District 5 president. In 1917 John White left the UMW to join the Wilson administration. UMW vice-president Frank Hayes moved up to the presidency and John L. Lewis sought the vacant vice-presidential slot. Sensing a chance to repay Lewis for his help, Murray traveled to UMW headquarters in Indianapolis where, according to John Brophy, he "stepped out and assisted in getting the necessary majority on the national executive board to confirm Lewis's nomination." Two years later Murray backed Lewis's drive to push Hayes aside as union president, arguing, as Brophy recalled, "that Lewis was a strong, able man, that he would really make something out of the United Mine Workers and that Frank Hayes was a well-meaning incompetent." In January 1920 John L. Lewis became acting president of the mine union. One of his first acts was to appoint Murray vice-president. Thus, at the age of thirty-three, Murray became the second-ranking officer of the largest labor union in North America.

For the next twenty years Philip Murray was John L. Lewis's right-hand man, handling such major responsibilities as negotiations for the anthracite fields, presentation of the UMW's case before congressional committees, and negotiations with union dissidents. Always he demonstrated complete loyalty to Lewis and his policies. Only in the arena of national politics did Lewis and Murray disagree, and until 1940 their differences seemed insignificant.

That these men should have formed a team seems at first unlikely. Lewis was Iowa-born and a teetotaler; Murray, an immigrant and a social drinker. Lewis was irreligious; Murray attended mass frequently, had priests as advisors and friends, and spoke often of his belief in God, which in his mind was closely connected to his faith in unionism. Lewis hobnobbed with financiers and top political figures; after moving the UMW's headquarters to Washington in 1933, Lewis and his family lived in an antique-filled colonial house in Alexandria, Virginia. Murray's brick home in Pittsburgh, though much more substantial than anything a miner could afford, was located in an ordinary middle-class neighborhood. Although he publicly advocated union-management cooperation, Murray privately dismissed corporation executives as "capitalist lackeys." Unpretentious and ill-at-ease in elite circles, Murray declined invitations to the White House. He preferred to spend his leisure hours at the track, sometimes in the company of his friend, the Pittsburgh labor priest Rev. Charles Owen Rice, or with friends and family in the coal towns outside Pittsburgh, drinking beers and tossing horseshoes. Lewis was imperious and seemed to delight in humiliating his subordinates. Murray, by contrast, was considerate and generous; everyone called him Phil.

Given these differences, it is hardly surprising that Murray and Lewis seldom saw one another socially. Yet they chatted every day and, despite their differences, formed a close and effective partnership. Murray, too, was a shrewd, ambitious, and forceful labor leader. It was only next to the bullying Lewis that he seemed to shrink. With his talent for persuasion, his kindly, dignified appearance, and his qualities of understanding and honesty, Murray complemented Lewis perfectly. Moreover, Murray admired Lewis, loved him even, and he had a keen sense of loyalty. As Murray confessed in 1941, after Lewis had brusquely cast him aside, "If I have never amounted to any other thing in life, at least I have always had that requisite. It may have been a human frailty, but I have it and I have had it, and that is loyalty."

Quite early in his career Murray seems to have decided that the way ahead for the United Mine Workers—and, by implication, American labor generally—was to get the federal government to insist that all employers engage in collective bargaining. The *quid pro quo* for labor leaders who sought such help was to accept contract terms decided by federal authorities, discipline union members who disobeyed those pacts, and support federal policy in other areas, notably foreign policy.

As early as the First World War, when he served as a member of the National Bituminous Coal Production Committee and the Pennsylvania Regional War Labor Board, Murray was enmeshed in three-cornered negotiations among the UMW, coal operators, and the federal government. As chairman of the Committee on Officers' Reports at the January 1918 UMW convention, he was the leading spokesman on behalf of the Washington Agreement, a pact negotiated under federal pressure, which gave miners sizable wage increases but mandated fines for those who struck. "The representatives of the Federal government . . . asked for something to be done that would have a stabilizing effect upon the coal industry of America," Murray replied to Kansas district president Alex Howat, who had characterized the penalty clause as an "outrage" and a "disgrace." Murray emphasized the large wage increase included in the agreement, warned the delegates that "the eyes of the world are centered upon us," and appealed to them on patriotic grounds, urging them to "give all this coal to our country and to our allies." In November 1919 UMW leaders terminated a two-week-old national bituminous coal strike in the face of a sweeping federal injunction, federal plans to provide one hundred thousand troops to protect strikebreakers, a declaration of martial law in the coal-producing state of Wyoming, and a promise to the miners of a wage increase to be awarded by a presidentially-appointed commission. When the UMW convention delegates who had demanded that this strike be called reconvened to consider their decision, it was Murray who offered the resolution endorsing the officials' conduct.

Murray's favorable attitude toward federal intervention in labor disputes led president Harding to call on him in August 1921, when twenty thousand union miners, bearing arms and commanded by veterans of the First World War, marched on Logan County, West Virginia, and engaged in battle for a week with Baldwin-Felts mine guards, state police, and deputy sheriffs. The object of the marchers, who advanced in the face of machine-gun fire and bombing by light planes, was to free southern West Virginia miners from a company dictatorship backed by local authorities. The president responded by putting the entire state under martial law and asking Murray to help quell the conflict. "I went to Charleston, West Virginia, at the request of the president of the United States," Murray later recalled.

> I traveled from Charleston to Marmet, and from Marmet to Sovereign, a distance of some 60 miles, and met numbers of men patrolling the highways. The railroad running along that section of 60 miles had been taken over by the miners. Trains were commandeered and supplies were being run from commissaries by men who were fighting on the alleged battle front. . . . I succeeded, with the assistance of Major Hamilton of the United States Army, in persuading the mine workers to return to their homes, and so reported to brigadier General Barnholtz. . . . But had it not been for the threat of the presence of Federal troops in that scene, I am quite confident . . . there would have been a great amount of property destroyed and a considerable number of lives lost. It was all the outgrowth of a terrific and terrifying economic situation.

The logic of the United Mine Workers' situation pushed its leaders toward dependence on federal power. As their response to the 1919 bituminous strike and the 1921 march on Logan County made plain, federal authorities were perfectly willing to use the full force of the military and the law to crush coal miners' actions that they regarded as inimical to the national interest. "My friends, these are stern, real, cold facts that no body can hope to get away from," Murray asserted in defending the UMW leaders' 1919 capitulation to the Wilson administration. "When I made the motion that we . . . endorse the policy they have pursued, I did it with the feeling deep in my heart that it was the only course for the coal miners of this country to pursue under present day circumstances. There isn't a delegate in this convention who wants to . . . array the forces of his local union against the most powerful and strongly organized government in the world."

At the same time, the miners' union needed federal help. The UMW's economic problems—the rapid growth of nonunion coal fields in southern West Virginia and eastern Kentucky, the fierce resistance offered by authorities in these states to labor organization, and in the 1920s, the decline in demand for coal and the repudiation of UMW contracts by northern operators—forced all of the union's leaders to look for governmental aid. To John Brophy, the Socialists, and the Communists, federal ownership of coal mines combined with workers' control was the answer. Frank Farrington, president of the UMW's large Illinois district, which was isolated from nonunion competition, hoped to persuade that state's government to build huge new coal-consuming electric power and fertilizer plants on the Mississippi River. Unlike the radicals, Lewis and Murray had not the slightest faith in socialism. Unlike Frank Farrington, they had responsibility for North America rather than a single state. These men looked to the United States government to "stabilize" the coal industry, by which they meant that it should establish minimum and maximum coal prices, adjust railroad rates that discriminated against unionized coal-producing districts, standardize miners' wage rates across the country, and insist that all operators recognize the UMW.

After the 1921 march on Logan County, for example, Murray told the Senate Committee on Education and Labor that the report of the Bituminous Coal Commission, the federal agency that had settled the 1919 strike, should apply to all coal operators, nonunion as well as UMW-organized. "During the period of the strike," he declared, "the Government did not hesitate to use its great authority, under the war powers, against the United Mine Workers, even to the extent of placing its members in jail. Is there any reason why it should not have used its authority, under the same war

241

powers, to make the non-union operators observe the terms of a decision by a governmental tribunal?" If the Harding administration was unwilling to act, Murray told the senators, the legislators themselves should draw up an agreement, require the UMW and the operators' representatives to sign it, and request the chief justice of the Supreme Court to appoint an arbitrator "who will interpret and apply the agreement and pass upon grievances which may arise under its operation." Similarly, John L. Lewis collaborated with Secretary of Commerce Herbert Hoover in the winter of 1923–24 to secure the operators' consent to a contract—the Jacksonville agreement—that would give the industry four years of labor peace. In 1925, when the large Pennsylvania operators began to repudiate the Jacksonville agreement, Lewis demanded that Hoover stop them, arguing that since Hoover had helped negotiate the pact, he was responsible for its maintenance. In 1928, when the UMW had been driven out of all coal fields except Illinois, Senator James Watson of Indiana proposed a bill written by the UMW staff that would have created a new federal Bituminous Coal Commission, licensed coal-marketing cartels, and supported collective bargaining.

These pleas came to naught during the Republican-dominated 1920s, but after the Democrats captured the White House and Congress in November 1932, the UMW began to get results. Congress passed and president Roosevelt signed three bills—the National Industrial Recovery Act of 1933, the Guffey-Snyder Act of 1935, and the 1937 Guffey-Vinson Act—that sanctioned and encouraged the formation of a coal cartel. The Supreme Court invalidated the first two laws, but after the court shifted its position in 1937 under pressure from Roosevelt (backed in this effort by the UMW), the Guffey-Vinson Act was upheld. In the 1940s coal consequently was one of the few industries in which employers engaged in joint nationwide collective bargaining.

Even more important was the Wagner Act. This 1935 legislation, the purpose of which was to encourage labor peace through collective bargaining, changed the entire relationship between organized labor and the federal government. On the one hand, it created a powerful agency—the National Labor Relations Board (NLRB)—charged with ensuring that workers were free to choose to be represented by unions. In this way the act powerfully facilitated union growth. On the other hand, the law also gave the NLRB the power to define unions' jurisdiction, to certify (and, by implication, decertify) particular unions as representative of workers, and as time went on, to determine which union demands were legitimate and which employers could safely ignore.

The Wagner Act was only the beginning of federal regulation of organized labor. During the Second World War the Roosevelt administration created the National War Labor Board (NWLB), with the power to arbitrate all union-management disputes and regulate employers' labor policies. Unions grew spectacularly under the NWLB, but lost most freedom of action. This temporary step was followed by the Taft-Hartley Act of 1947, the Wage Stabilization Board during the war in Korea, and after Philip Murray had died, the Landrum-Griffin Act (1959), the wage guidelines of the Kennedy and Johnson years, the Nixon administration wage controls, and the 1974 pension reform act—all of which circumscribed unions' activities or subjected unions' internal affairs to federal control.

John L. Lewis and Philip Murray disagreed profoundly about the way to respond to the expansion under Franklin Roosevelt of federal power over labor. If it is an exaggeration to say that Lewis was a Republican just because he supported Republican presidential candidates in every election but one between 1924 and 1940, it is indisputable that Lewis retained, throughout his career, a mistrustful attitude toward federal intervention in economic affairs reminiscent of the Republican administrations of the 1920s. For this reason and because Lewis, like many Republicans of this era, thought that the United States' vital interests lay in the Western Hemisphere rather than Europe, he opposed Roosevelt's push toward American intervention in World War II. Wartime economic planning, Lewis predicted, would make the president a dictator and roll back labor's gains. Since he demanded for the coal industry the sort of federal intervention that he condemned in general, Lewis was inconsistent. (The attitudes of most businessmen toward the state were similar to Lewis's in this respect.) Lewis resolved this contradiction by doing everything he could to keep the organizations he headed independent of Washington. He poured union funds into FDR's 1936 reelection campaign, because the new group of industrial unions he was leading, the Committee for Industrial Organization (CIO), needed federal support, but he resisted pressures to merge labor's political machinery with the Democratic party and even speculated about forming a labor party four years hence. Lewis became increasingly wary of Roosevelt during the 1937 Little Steel strike, when the administration backed away from its earlier support of CIO organizing drives. Lewis was justifiably disappointed with the administration's performance on labor issues after that battle and by 1940 had concluded that the expansion of federal power under Roosevelt had to be stopped. After feigning interest in a left-wing coalition of the underprivileged, Lewis endorsed the Republican party's 1940 presidential candidate, the utilities magnate Wendell Willkie. To underscore his seriousness and maximize his influence in the event of a Willkie victory, Lewis announced that he would resign the presidency of the Congress of Industrial Organizations if Roosevelt was reelected.

Philip Murray's attitude was different and more consistent. Like Sidney Hillman of the Amalgamated Clothing Workers and other, less well known figures in the labor movement, Murray was convinced that semiskilled workers could only be organized into unions with the help of the federal government. These workers simply lacked the economic strength to beat corporations on their own. If federal authorities threatened to wield their powers against unions during wartime, that, to Murray, was all the more reason to cooperate with the government. Murray's outlook on foreign affairs also differed from Lewis's. Believing, as he put it at the 1924 UMW convention, that "dictatorships can have no place in the lives of free men whether it be either sovietism or fascism," he saw American liberties as bound up with the defeat of those systems in Europe. Although, like most labor leaders, he opposed American entry into the war in Europe in 1939 and 1940, he favored all-out aid to Britain—a stance that set him apart from many other American unionists of Irish-Catholic origin. Here, perhaps, Murray's upbringing in Scotland came into play. After the war he served as a member of the United States delegation to the San Francisco conference that established the United Nations. He also strongly supported the Marshall Plan, the North Atlantic Treaty Organization (NATO), and the Korean War.

Murray was a registered Republican in the late 1920s, but in Pennsylvania at that time, as David McDonald pointed out, that was a "simple political necessity—like being a Democrat in Alabama." By 1928, McDonald writes, Murray was "totally disenchanted" with Hoover and the Republicans, believing that they would never bring the coal operators to the bargaining table. Murray quietly endorsed Democrat Al Smith—a fellow Catholic—for president in 1928. In the summer of 1932, when Lewis headed a labor committee to reelect Hoover, Murray took a six-man UMW delegation to Albany, New York, to meet with Franklin Roosevelt.

Although Lewis had almost certainly given tacit approval to this meeting, it started a relationship between Roosevelt and Murray that ultimately drove a wedge between the two miners' leaders. "My mind goes back to the dark, bleak days of 1931 and 1932—days of privation, days of horror, days of sickness, yes, and death," Murray reminisced in 1944. "I can remember rather distinctly, together with a number of Mine Workers' leaders—not all of them, because there was one man missing—back in the year 1932 taking a train and going over to Albany, New York. . . . And those few Miners' leaders who attended that conference presented to the Governor of New York the condition of the Miners. You know the Miners in 1932 were eating garbage, yes, garbage, and getting $1.50 a day for a ten-hour day. . . . I lived with them, I worked with them. All my family were miners, and I felt that something ought to be done for them." "But one day," Murray declared, "they found a friend. He was sitting on the end of a divan in his library in the Executive Mansion in Albany, New York. He knew the miners and their problems, and he said he would help them. Another day he was found sitting at a desk in the White House, and he said: 'I will help you by giving you the means of helping youself.' The miner helped himself," Murray concluded, "and he shouted the name of Roosevelt as loudly as he shouted the words United Mine Workers."

As Clinton Golden, Murray's top advisor during the late 1930s and the war years, subsequently put it, "Philip Murray was immensely grateful to the New Deal, and he was not the type of person to repudiate friends ever." What's more, in 1940 Murray, unlike Lewis, still needed the Roosevelt administration's help. Murray had helped Lewis establish the Committee for Industrial Organization in 1935, arguing forcefully for the industrial-union principle at the AFL convention that year and accepting a CIO vice-presidency in addition to his UMW position. A year later, at Lewis's request, Murray also took on the job of chairman of the CIO's Steel Workers Organizing Committee (SWOC). This was a crucial post, for organizing the steel industry was the CIO's top priority. The SWOC secured contracts from United States Steel, Jones & Laughlin, and many smaller producers in 1937, but several of the largest firms—the so-called Little Steel companies—vowed to close down rather than to recognize the union.

The defeat of the 1937 Little Steel strike and the weakness of pro-union sentiment among workers at these companies led the steel union to turn to Washington for help. First, SWOC sought to use the Fair Wage Labor Standards Act of 1938 to raise the wage rates paid by Bethlehem and Republic—the most important Little Steel holdouts—on government work, thereby improving the competitive position of the unionized sector of the industry and gaining credit among nonunion workers for the wage increase. Then SWOC sought National Labor Relations Board orders banning discrimination against union members and securing reinstatement with back pay for the five thousand strikers fired by Republic Steel. Later, after the United States had entered World War II, SWOC sought to persuade the National War Labor Board to put a "union shop" clause in its agreements with the steel manufacturers. Such a provision, which requires workers to become union members after they have begun work, would have alleviated SWOC's problems with dues collection, which were chronic and serious. All these considerations forbade any break with the Roosevelt administration. As John Brophy remembered in the mid–1950s,

245

"the organizational need of the steel union was to maintain at least friendly relations with the Federal Government, if the union was to achieve its ends and break down the opposition of the great vested interests in the steel industry."

So Murray publicly supported FDR for a third term in 1940, while lesser UMW officials succumbed to pressure from Lewis to endorse Willkie. Yet after Roosevelt's reelection, Lewis chose Murray to succeed him as CIO president. Murray supported Roosevelt, Lewis reasoned, but he was not so interventionist as Sidney Hillman, the CIO's other top leader, who in Lewis's eyes had become virtually a federal agent in the labor movement. Moreover, Murray had been Lewis's docile aide for twenty years. Perhaps Lewis hoped to pull the strings behind a Murray presidency. According to Murray's aides, Lewis tried to get his daughter Kathryn appointed CIO secretary-treasurer, a move that would have made Murray a figurehead. For these reasons and more, Murray hesitated. He had always been a number-two man and wasn't sure he had the stuff to be number one. Even if he did, would Lewis let him be his own man? Lewis pledged to Murray his full support at all times, but Murray had seen Lewis break all his UMW rivals. Besides, the CIO was in bad shape: its treasury was empty; its membership far below its public claims; its leadership torn between the Hillmanites on the one side and Lewis's followers and the Communists on the other. But if Murray didn't accept the presidency, who else could hold the CIO together? As in western Pennsylvania in 1915, Murray was the indispensable conciliator. Murray agonized. The CIO presidency, he cried, would be his Gethsemane. Yet in the end, he took the job.

As CIO president, Murray led the nation's industrial unions—the garment, textile, and rubber workers, the shipbuilders, the auto and aircraft workers, longshoremen and sailors, the electrical, radio, and machine workers, his own steelworkers—toward a policy of full cooperation with the Roosevelt administration's war effort. "I have never quibbled about my attitude in the field of national defense. My attitude has always been, and I hope to God it will continue to be[,] one of supporting the president of the United States in the promotion of national defense in this country," Murray declared at the November 1941 CIO convention, his first as president. "The winning of this war . . . is paramount," Murray told the 1942 CIO convention. He added, "My belief in the trade union movement is such that I don't think we should have a trade-union movement in America unless that movement is prepared to render a service to its people and to its country." Murray stressed, "I am determined to support our Commander in Chief and I am going to support him."

As this last remark indicates, Murray's policy flowed in part from his love of Roosevelt and his esteem for the American political system and the office of the president. Both attitudes were commonplace among working-class immigrants of his generation. Indeed, Murray's enthusiasm for the war effort in 1941 and 1942 reflected the widespread feeling in CIO ranks that "This is *our* war!" The "brass hats"—the business executives who had flocked to Washington in 1941—were seen by many CIO leaders and activists as insufficiently devoted to mobilization and all-out victory. Hadn't they fought industrial unionism? Hadn't they appeased fascism? If America was going to beat the Nazis, such CIO activists reasoned, labor would have to roll up its sleeves. Here was a proletarian patriotism the roots of which go back to the days after the attack on Fort Sumter, when whole union locals disbanded to go fight the rebels, and to the bitter winter of 1778–79, when privates in the militia of Philadelphia, resentful of the fact that they "had bravely stepped forward" to defend the United States while "the monied men of the community" were "basking in the sunshine of monopoly," demanded the institution of price controls.

When he accepted the CIO presidency, Murray hoped that he could back Roosevelt without jeopardizing his friendship with Lewis. But this proved to be impossible. To Lewis, Murray's pro-Roosevelt, pro-war policy was more than a political mistake; it was a personal betrayal. Under great emotional strain, Lewis and Murray both suffered heart attacks in the first half of 1941. The two men met in Atlantic City in October 1941, while Murray was still recuperating, but were unable to compose their differences. Consequently, Lewis stayed away from the CIO's November 1941 convention. Murray persuaded the delegates to endorse the captive-mine strike—a strike at mines owned by the steel corporations—that Lewis was then leading, but the UMW delegation, which was headed by Lewis's younger brother Denny, went about hotel corridors slugging Hillman and Murray supporters. The miners' delegation also dissented from the majority's foreign-policy resolution.

Throughout the winter of 1941 Lewis maneuvered against Murray. Counterattacking, Murray likened Lewis to Republic Steel's dictatorial president, Tom Girdler. Finally, at a May meeting of the UMW's international executive board, Lewis gave Murray a brutal tongue-lashing, accusing him of betraying the union he has served since his youth. Murray could hardly speak. When he tried to rebut the charge, Lewis drew back his fist as if to slug his once-trusted aide—an uncanny reminder of the AFL convention in 1935 when Lewis had punched craft-union leader Bill Hutcheson as a symbol of his determination to break with AFL conservatism. At the end of three days, Murray left the UMW's basement chamber to confer with Roosevelt. While he was gone, the board declared the vice-presi-

Labor Leaders in America

dency vacant. "He was blue afterward," recalled Murray's aide Harold Ruttenberg. "Near depression. . . . He was very blue and somber for weeks
on time."

Murray's program for the war economy—the 1941 Industrial Council
Plan—envisioned the formation of councils for every major industry, consisting of equal numbers of union and management people and chaired by
a federal official. These councils would run the industries, determining
expansion needs, allocating orders, scheduling production, determining
priorities, and establishing labor policies. The plan was an amalgam of the
UMW's designs for the coal industry in the 1920s, the code planning procedures of the National Recovery Administration, and the vocational
group system advocated by Pope Pius XI in his 1931 encyclical *Quadragesimo Anno.* Indeed, throughout the late 1930s and early 1940s Murray
lent his name to plans for industry councils drafted by Monsignor John A.
Ryan and other Roman Catholic authorities. The teachings of the church
provided moral authority for the belief in interest-group cooperation under
federal supervision that Murray had acquired through his experiences in
the UMW and National Recovery Administration.

To managers and stockholders, however, the Murray industry-council
plan was radical, for it treated the industry, not the firm, as the basic economic enterprise and it elevated union officials to an equal footing with
management. The Roosevelt administration was also unsympathetic, for it
needed the cooperation of business interests alienated by earlier New Deal
policies. "Labor's chief difficulty in America today, as in days gone by,"
Murray protested in November 1941, "lies in the unwillingness, the obvious unwillingness of government and business to accept labor in good
faith." "I think that our government and the War Production Board particularly should call upon the genius, the vitality and the understanding of
labor," Murray told the 1942 CIO convention. "Labor doesn't want jobs;
it doesn't want people appointed to measly jobs with salaries attached to
them, where they are merely members of common, ordinary, so-called advisory boards. We do not want those jobs. We want to be placed in positions of trust and responsibility where we can render a service to our
nation."

"Why should the agencies of government in Washington today be virtually infested with wealthy men, men who are supposedly receiving one
dollar a year compensation?" Murray demanded to know late in 1941.
"What are we running in Washington?" Murray shouted. "A war production organization to win the war, or a war production organization to destroy labor?"

Philip Murray had many dissatisfactions during World War II: the cap placed on the wages of workers by the War Labor Board's "Little Steel" formula; the government's toleration of delaying tactics by industry when the steelworkers attempted to reopen their wage pact to catch up with inflation in 1943; Lewis's success in winning gains for his miners by defying the no-strike pledge; the loss of his key aides, Clinton Golden, Harold Ruttenberg, and Van Bittner, to the federal bureaucracy; and the way in which union staff were obliged to implement National War Labor Board decisions their organizations opposed. Yet Murray staked his authority and prestige, which by 1942 was immense, behind the no-strike pledge and the Roosevelt administration. Patriotism, his recognition that the CIO was growing enormously despite these problems, loyalty to Roosevelt, and the conviction that the defeat of nazism took precedence over everything else—all these factors influenced Murray. But in addition he was afraid that the unions faced destruction if they failed to cooperate. "The promotion of any kind of war economy . . . might easily lead to the conduct of campaigns that have for their purpose the destruction of unions in this country," Murray observed in November 1941. "Let us say, for example, you withdraw the no-strike pledge," he challenged a young delegate to the United Steelworkers' 1944 convention who had proposed doing just that.

> Isn't it true that your organization and its leaders would be required . . . to suddenly rush to Washington and combat the influence of a powerful anti-labor group who are hell bent upon the passage of no-strike legislation and national service legislation? . . . The withdrawal of your no-strike pledge here would be regarded as an insult to the armed forces and to the balance of our union-minded population. . . . It would only tend to create suspicion. It would encourage the enemies of the labor movement to press forward immediately toward the ultimate destruction of the United Steelworkers of America.

In a single sentence Murray caught the dilemma that American labor leaders faced in wartime: "You either accept the reasonable, voluntary method of doing business in the United States during the course of a war, or you accept regimentation or legislative compulsions of some description."

Murray's staunch support of the war effort plus the CIO's 1944 get-out-the-vote-for-the-Democrats campaign prevented the passage of the worst anti-union legislation proposed during World War II. But in 1946 and early 1947 an irresistible demand to "do something" about unions welled up among business executives and the broad middle class. The former felt their power threatened by growing union strength; the latter blamed unions for the huge 1946 strike wave and the shortages and soaring prices of consumer goods. Murray went on a speaking tour to try to turn the tide of public opinion. He met with dozens of groups of newspaper publishers and radio-station owners, making a brief pitch for the CIO's point of view, then taking questions. "It was rather like trying to sell ball bats in a china store," remembered David McDonald. "He handled himself well at these affairs, but the impact seemed to add up to absolute zero."

The 1947 Taft-Hartley Act was Congress's response to the demand for curbs on organized laobr. Among other things, it banned unions from making political contributions, outlawed the closed shop (under which only union members could be hired) and the secondary boycott (in which union members could boycott an employer other than their own), prohibited unions from organizing supervisors, denied access to the National Labor Relations Board to unions whose officers were unwilling to sign noncommunist affidavits, forbade strikes by federal employees, authorized the NLRB to cite unions as well as employers for "unfair labor practices," permitted employers to petition the NLRB for an election to decertify a union, allowed state governments to outlaw the union shop, revived the use of federal injunctions in the case of strikes that threatened "national emergencies," and permitted the president to halt such strikes for eighty days.

The Taft-Hartley Act turned unions into semipublic institutions, licensed by the state to perform a vital function—collective bargaining for workers—so long as they respected strict limitations on their behavior. As Van Bittner, who appeared for Murray at the March 1947 hearing of the House Education and Labor Committee, remarked, "Labor unions fear that this is the first step toward an attempt to regiment labor unions as instruments of the state such as corporations properly are. When this occurs we no longer have the free democratic institutions of our Nation. The threat of such a development prompts me to oppose, and oppose vehemently, the proposed legislation."

Confronted with this threat, Phil Murray began talking like Sam Gompers, who in his early years had urged labor to avoid entanglements with government. "I got a notion that may be rather old-fashioned, but I still think it is a pretty good formula. I got the idea that the American people are pretty much against these forms of legislative compulsions," Murray told Senator Wayne Morse in February 1947. "And when we get into the field of restrictive legislation of that character, legislation which directs itself against labor," he added pointedly, "then this Congress is paving the way for a system of national totalitarianism and many other bad things. It endangers the structure of our whole system of free enterprise in the United States."

The retreat to Gompers' philosophy of voluntarism was purely rhetorical, however. In point of fact, as leader of the United Steelworkers in the late 1940s and early 1950s, Murray relied more than ever on federal intervention. Although they would never admit it, steel union leaders consciously sought to involve the executive branch of the government in their disputes with management, believing—correctly—that this would benefit their cause. This was one reason why the union struck the industry as a whole in 1946, 1949, and 1952, rather than playing one firm off against another, as did the United Auto Workers. Given the centrality of steel in the economy, an industrywide strike automatically brought federal intervention. The strategy paid off, too, for in settling steel labor disputes the Truman administration consistently came down closer to the union than to the management side. The administration's choice resulted from many factors: its hostility to monopoly, its conviction that steel price hikes (which Truman blamed on corporate profiteering) were a major factor in inflation, the Republican affiliations of steel management, the strong backing that the CIO's political action committee gave to Roosevelt in 1944 and Truman in 1948, and the concentration of steelworkers in the electorally crucial states of Pennsylvania, Ohio, Indiana, and Illinois. Truman's intervention in the 1949 dispute over wages and pensions was particularly helpful to the United Steelworkers, for the old contract expired just as the industry was entering a slump, which weakened the union's bargaining position. The president of Bethlehem Steel denounced the Steel Industry Board appointed by Truman to resolve the 1949 dispute as "merely . . . a vehicle for forcing upon us important concessions to the unions."

The approach Murray took to assuage congressional opponents of labor and to slake the general postwar anti-union sentiment was to purge the Communist-led unions from the CIO. Murray had long fought "Russianized revolution," as he termed it at the 1924 UMW convention. In 1928, for example, he arranged for the Pittsburgh police to look the other way while UMW thugs smashed up a convention of the left-wing "Save the Union" movement, an action that resulted in the death of one radical and injury to five others. Murray made his acceptance of the CIO presidency in 1940 conditional on the organization's adoption of an anticommunist resolution. In 1942 he beat down an attempt from the floor to add the words "or political affiliation" to a clause in the United Steelworkers constitution that prohibited discrimination on grounds of "race, creed, color, or nationality." An indication of Murray's personal feelings in this area was his refusal to let his wife wear a fur coat that she had been given by the head of the Fur and Leather Workers Union, the reddest of the CIO's affiliates.

From the time of the German attack on the Soviet Union in June 1941 until the end of the war, however, Murray was allied with the Communists in the CIO. The alliance was based on their common conviction that the defeat of Hitler and support of the Roosevelt administration took precedence over all other considerations. Disturbed by Truman's 1946 request to Congress for the power to draft strikers and by his general failure to push ahead with the New Deal, Murray even briefly associated in 1946–47 with Communists and left-liberals in an effort to draft a more liberal Democrat for president.

The eruption of the cold war between the United States and the Soviet Union rendered this kind of cooperation impossible. A faithful Catholic, Murray was concerned about the suppression of the church in Soviet-occupied Eastern Europe and, in all likelihood, was being pushed by churchmen he knew to do something about it. Above all, as in 1918 and 1944, Murray felt that federal pressure and the generally insecure status of organized labor made it imperative to dispel all suspicions of disloyalty on the part of the labor movement. "While I have you together here, I am going to explode," Murray announced at the November 1946 meeting of the CIO's executive board. "I am not one of those who agree this is a Communistically dominated institution," Murray said. "I do believe that there are some of our unions whose judgments on matters of practical policy, particularly as they relate to international affairs, permit their judgments to be substantially influenced by the Communist Party." These unions offered "targets, targets that can be easily hit" by the CIO's enemies. "We must be pro-American in these trade union activities of ours."

Murray at first moved slowed against the Communist-led unions, thinking that precipitous action, such as expulsion, would damage the CIO by depriving the organization of almost a third of its membership. But while publicly assuming a conciliatory role between Left and Right, Murray secretly worked to undermine the Left. The full scope of his activities has yet to be uncovered, but Monsignor Charles Owen Rice, for one, has admitted that Murray used him as a conduit to funnel money to John Duffy, a tireless organizer against the officers of the United Electrical, Radio and Machine Workers (UE), the largest of the Communist-led unions. Murray turned a blind eye to other CIO affiliates' raids on the left-wing unions and, according to right-wing newspaper columnist Victor Riesel, attended the August 1946 meeting at which the UE Members for Democratic Action, the anticommunist caucus in the union, was established. Always a soft-soaper, he also put in long hours trying to convince individual left-wingers to switch to what he saw as the patriotic side. He would take left-wingers out for dinner, to a prize fight, or to a show, question their commitments, and explain his own view of labor's future.

In another attempt to impress the nation with labor's commitment to national values and goals and to convince dissenting delegates of the need to cooperate with federal authorities, Murray invited highly esteemed military and governmental figures to CIO conventions—General Eisenhower in 1946, Secretary of State George Marshall in 1947, Supreme Court Justice William O. Douglas in 1948. In 1949, the year the Communist-led unions were finally expelled, the CIO convention featured the chairman of the joint chiefs of staff, General Omar Bradley; the secretary of state, Dean Acheson; and the United States' special ambassador in Europe charged with overseeing the Marshall Plan, W. Averell Harriman. After Harry Truman complained to Murray that Communist propagandists in Europe were circulating a denunciation of the Marshall Plan issued by the CIO council in San Francisco, Murray pushed through new rules prohibiting state and local industrial union councils from making any statements on national or international affairs contrary to official national CIO policy. CIO staff men monitored the councils to see that they complied with the new policy; those that continued to denounce U.S. foreign policy lost their charters. Indeed, in 1948 Murray made support for Truman and the Democratic ticket the test of loyalty to the CIO. The irony of this decision was that Murray had a poor opinion of Truman and far greater regard for Truman's rival, former vice-president Henry Wallace. But Wallace was the candidate of the Communist-backed Progressive party.

The failure of the Wallace candidacy coupled with the boycott of the 1949 CIO convention by the UE, which was fed up with other CIO unions' raids on its membership, paved the way for the purge. Under Murray's leadership, the 1949 convention expelled the UE and a smaller Communist-led union, the Farm Equipment Workers. The convention also passed a constitutional amendment barring Communists from holding CIO office, doubled the dues paid by workers to finance a war with the Communist-led unions, chartered a rival to the UE, the International Union of Electrical Workers (IUE), and set up hearing boards—David McDonald later termed them "kangaroo courts"—to try ten other unions on charges of Communist domination. Fierce fighting ensued between the expelled unions and CIO affiliates, particularly the UE and IUE, but within several years the CIO had, in combination with the government and industry, largely eliminated radicals from the American labor movement.

In 1952, however, the steel corporations launched an all-out assault on the alliance between Murray and the White House that had made the United Steelworkers of America and, to a lesser extent, the CIO into such powerful organizations. Leading figures in the industry openly acknowledged their diagnosis of the problem. "It appears that we are on the eve of another election year and that some of our political leaders, and certain

253

pressure groups, are clearly attempting once again to make American industry their whipping boy in the coming presidential campaign," Benjamin Fairless, the president of United States Steel, declared on November 15, 1951, the day the steelworkers' union announced its twenty-two new contract demands on the industry. "Leaders of the union," Fairless asserted, "have publicly stated that their demands will be substantial and that they intend to upset the wage ceilings which have been established under the Government's wage stabilization program. . . . The negotiations, therefore, involve broad questions of public policy which go beyond the scope of collective bargaining in these days of wage and price control. . . . For my purposes . . . the important fact is that labor has possessed the economic and political power necessary to enforce its demands."

Although the Truman administration used Taft-Hartley injunctions repeatedly against Lewis's mine workers, it adopted a different course, one more favorable to labor, in dealing with emergencies involving CIO unions, particularly the steelworkers. Shortly before the 1952 battle began, Clarence B. Randall, the president of Inland Steel, wrote, "The procedure is quite simple. While an emergency is on, the union announces a paralyzing strike in a basic industry, and then the day before the catastrophe hits, graciously stands aside in the public interest at the request of the president to permit men from outside the industry who bear no responsibility for its welfare to determine what is best for it." Randall continued,

> The sequence is always substantially the same before a fact-finding board. Unions never lose. Of course, they don't get all of their demands, but they always get something. . . . Among the . . . factors that influence the decisions of public members of fact-finding boards let no one underestimate the importance of . . . their unwillingness to let an important labor personality lose face. It is known in management circles as the "Phil has got to have something" principle. It operates at every level of government mediation. . . . I have heard it personally in I can't tell how many government conferences.

The corporations' strategy followed logically from this analysis. The manufacturers made no response to the twenty-two demands issued by the steelworkers in November 1951. Their reasoning was that since the authorities would ultimately pick final terms partway between the positions of the union and the companies, it made no sense to volunteer concessions. To prevent an interruption of war production, Truman appointed a wage stabilization board to consider the issues in dispute. The manufacturers demanded unacceptably high price increases all the while the board was deliberating, then when the board issued its report, rejected its recommendations. Truman seized the mills to avert a strike, blaming the manufacturers for the impasse, but the industry screamed that he was abusing his power and secured a federal district court order and a Supreme Court decision invalidating the seizure. The corporations then took a strike—the longest in the industry since 1919—and withheld settlement until July 24, the day the Democratic National Convention nominated Illinois governor Adlai Stevenson as its presidential candidate.

Throughout the seven-month-long dispute Philip Murray railed at the companies' unwillingness to play by the government's rules. "The nation has its rules," Murray told the Steelworkers' May 1952 convention. "The Steelworkers in this situation respected the rules adopted for their guidance by their Government. The steel industry has not." Angered by the realization that the manufacturers' defiance of the government undercut his basic strategy for building up labor's strength, Murray resorted to language uncharacteristic of him in public: "The Wage Stabilization Board has already compromised your situation; it has given you much less than you hoped to get through collective bargaining. You protest the decision of the Wage Stabilization Board but you accept it in the national interest, and then the steel industry comes along and it says . . . 'Oh, no, we don't bargain with you on that basis, we are just meeting with you for the purpose of taking something away from you,' and I say to them, 'Go to hell.'"

The hard line taken by the steel industry in the 1952 negotiations exposed the limitations of the strategy for building union power pursued by Murray since the Wilson administration. Harry Truman did everything possible, including illegally seizing the steel mills, to bring the manufacturers to heel. He failed. The ultimate terms of the steel contract were satisfactory to the union, but by the time the union and the companies settled, the Truman administration was so weakened that the Republicans had their first real chance to capture the White House since Roosevelt's election in 1932.

The election of Dwight Eisenhower in 1952 is not ordinarily considered a watershed in American history, but to Philip Murray it was a frightening prospect, for Eisenhower was unencumbered by obligations to organized labor. Instead, he was indebted to Robert Taft, the author of the Taft-Hartley Act. As the astute political observer Samuel Lubell wrote at the time, "Many labor leaders are painfully aware that much of their following was recruited under the patronage of a friendly government, rather than through labor's own strengh. What if an unsympathetic administration came to power? What if that coincided with a recession? The still unexploded dynamite of the Taft-Hartley Law lies in those fears. . . . The real threat in the act lies in its union-busting potential during a period of unemployment, when labor's bargaining power is weak, and when a government hostile to labor might be in power."

Exhausted by the long battle over the steel contract, worried about the possibility of another major coronary, forbidden by his doctor from traveling by air, the sixty-six-year-old Murray nonetheless crisscrossed the country by train, imploring union members to defeat Eisenhower. He warned of a "raw deal," "vicious, dangerous amendements to the Taft-Hartley Act," and a "blitzkrieg against labor" if Stevenson was not elected. Eisenhower's landslide victory was "one of his biggest defeats[,] one of his saddest moments," recalled James Malone, Murray's nephew and a Steelworkers' staff member, who was with him when the returns came in. "That was a very hard blow to him. Because he banked everything on that. . . . The whole structure as far as he was concerned was depending on Adlai Stevenson becoming President of the United States." "That was hard, that was hard," remembered Murray's son, Joseph. "I think it broke his heart. I think it broke his heart."

The morning after the election a pale, dispirited Murray boarded a train for California, where he was to preside over the CIO's fourteenth constitutional convention the following Monday. He died four days later.

Bibliographic Notes

Finding sources for the study of Philip Murray's life and work is a problem. The only biography of Murray—Juanita Diffay Tate's 1962 New York University Ph.D. dissertation entitled "Philip Murray as a Labor Leader"—is thin and uninformative. Curious students would do better to consult Philip Taft's entry "Philip Murray," in John A. Garraty (ed.), *Dictionary of American Biography*, supplement 5 (1977), 509–11; or John Chamberlain's article "Philip Murray," *Life* 20, no. 6 (Feb. 11, 1946):78–90.

Murray is listed as coauthor (with Morris L. Cooke) of *Organized Labor and Production* (1940), a plea for combining scientific management with collective bargaining, and as the author of several articles, including "Labor and Responsibility," *Virginia Quarterly Review* 16, no. 2 (April 1940):267–78, and "If We Pull Together," *American Magazine* 145 (June 1948):21ff. However, the book was ghost-written and the articles most likely were as well. Murray was a man of some intellectual power, despite his lack of formal education, but he rarely expressed himself in writing. That is why the Philip Murray Papers at Catholic University disappoint every scholar who visits them. The collection is large, but it consists mostly of routine office memoranda and there are no finding aids. The John Brophy Papers, which are also located at Catholic University, are perhaps more valuable as a source of insight on Murray.

Philip Murray

Instead of pursuing his writing, researchers should look at Murray's speeches, particularly the remarkable addresses he gave as president of the CIO and the Steelworkers. These long, extemporaneous addresses reveal a great deal about Murray's feelings and convictions, not to mention his ability to manipulate men. Murray's remarks at the closed-door meetings of the CIO's executive board are valuable for the same reason. Minutes of the latter can be found in the CIO Secretary-Treasurer's Collection at Wayne State University's Walter Reuther Library. Records of the Steel Workers Organizing Committee and the United Steelworkers of America can be found at Pennsylvania State University's Pattee Library. This collection also contains transcripts of interviews with many union officials who knew Philip Murray.

Many published books discuss Murray. On Murray's career in the United Mine Workers, see John Brophy's autobiography *A Miner's Life* (1964); and Melvyn Dubofsky and Warren Van Tine, *John L. Lewis: A Biography* (1977). Given the absence of a history of the United Steelworkers of America, one must turn to Robert R. R. Brooks, *As Steel Goes, . . . Unionism in a Basic Industry* (1940); Clinton Golden and Harold J. Ruttenberg, *The Dynamics of Industrial Democracy* (1942); Lloyd Ulman, *The Government of the Steel Workers' Union* (1962); U.S. Department of Labor, *Collective Bargaining in the Basic Steel Industry: A Study of the Public Interest and the Role of Government* (1961); and David J. McDonald's unusually frank autobiography, *Union Man* (1969).

On Murray's efforts as CIO leader, see Walter Galenson, *The CIO Challenge to the AFL: A History of the American Labor Movement, 1935–1941* (1960); Len DeCaux, *Labor Radical: From the Wobblies to CIO* (1970); Nelson Lichtenstein, *Labor's War at Home: The CIO in World War II* (1982); Mary Sperling McAuliffe, *Crisis on the Left: Cold War Politics and American Liberals, 1947–1954* (1978); Harvey A. Levenstein, *Communism, Anticommunism, and the CIO* (1981); and James Caldwell Foster, *The Union Politic: The CIO's Political Action Committee* (1975).

Readers of secondary works should be wary, however, of historians' tendency to underestimate Philip Murray—to view him, as John Lewis did after 1940, as a weak figure who cooperated with the Roosevelt administration because he lacked courage. Though Lewis doubtless had insight into Murray's character, this view fails to reckon with the pressures Murray faced from Washington, the element of calculation in his thought, and his superpatriotism.

The interpretation of union-government relations presented in this essay builds on the work of Nelson Lichtenstein (cited above); Frederick H. Harbison and Robert C. Spencer's essay, "The Politics of Collective Bargaining: The Postwar Record in Steel," *American Political Science Review* 48, no. 3 (Sept. 1954):705–20; Christopher L. Tomlins's *State and the Unions: Labor Relations, Law, and the Organized Labor Movement in America, 1880–1960* (1985); and recent work by political scientists interested in liberal variants of corporatism, such as the essays in Philippe C. Schmitter and Gerhard Lehmbruch (eds.), *Trends Toward Corporatist Intermediation* (1979).

257

A. Philip Randolph, Black Workers, and the Labor Movement

11

William H. Harris

The lives of great men all remind us, we can make our lives sublime, and departing, leave behind us footprints on the sands of time.

—Henry Wadsworth Longfellow

At a meeting for labor leaders at the White House in 1969 to which George Meany, president of the American Federation of Labor-Congress of Industrial Organizations (AFL-CIO), had brought the entire executive council, President Richard M. Nixon went along with Meany from member to member saying hello. When he came to A. Philip Randolph, then eighty years old and white-headed, the president said, "Ah yes, A. Philip Randolph, the Grand Old Man of the labor movement." Meany responded, "there are two Grand Old Men of labor here. Phil and me." Such was the stature and reputation of A. Philip Randolph. Though he clearly never exercised the power and influence of Meany or several other leaders of the American labor movement, his reputation far exceeded his power. One of the most charismatic leaders of organized labor in the history of the United States, Randolph used quiet dignity and perseverance to claim a place among the elite of those who worked on behalf of the American laboring classes.

Though charisma denotes qualities that are difficult to define, it is clear without question that Randolph was a charismatic individual. A leading scholar defines charismatic leadership as "certain qualities of an individual personality by which he is set apart as endowed with supernatural, superhuman, or at least specifically exceptional powers and qualities." Such leaders usually originate under conditions of stress, show an absence of formal rules of routine administration, reject rational economic conduct, and usually prevail for short or intermittant periods. Moreover, charismatic leaders have the ability to issue statements clearly at variance with the facts and have their words accepted as truth, and they demonstrate at all times an air of personal incorruptability. Such individuals usually attain for themselves prestige and influence far out of proportion to the physical impact of their achievements.

Randolph possessed basic charismatic qualities. Handsome, almost exquisite in bearing, and a master of the arts of rhetoric and oratory, his speeches had a hypnotic effect upon his audiences. He carried himself with an air that exuded such confidence that his opponents found it almost impossible to deny the wisdom of his arguments and his supporters were loyal almost to his every word. So powerful was Randolph as a speaker that in 1926 Roy Lancaster, secretary-treasurer of the Brotherhood of Sleeping Car Porters, instructed district leaders to take up collections at mass meetings *before* Randolph spoke because "the Chief," as the porters called Randolph, "was sure to break up any meeting" and send the participants screaming into the streets, too excited to contribute to the cause. Yet, despite his ability to stimulate people, Randolph possessed few routine skills. He moved in the public realm, stirring up questions about black unionism and generating propaganda to publicize his view and the goals of the Brotherhood of Sleeping Car Porters (BSCP). He left the daily operations of the union to trusted lieutenants who were loyal to him personally and to his ideas.

Randolph first became a nationally recognized figure in 1925 when disgruntled porters of the Pullman Palace Car Company, stationed in New York City, decided to organize a union and invited Randolph to join their effort. Randolph agreed to join in the conversations with these men, and in August 1925, after several meetings, the New York group organized the Brotherhood of Sleeping Car Porters, with A. Philip Randolph as general organizer and his magazine, the *Messenger*, as the offical organ. In the absence of a constitution and given the strict rules of secrecy the union placed on its membership, Randolph embodied the BSCP and as general organizer had unlimited powers to act to ensure the union's success, a condition that permitted him to exploit his charismatic qualities. When the porters accepted Randolph as their leader, they did not get a man of proven leadership ability, nor one experienced in trade unionism. Randolph was already thirty-six years old in 1925, and aside from the confidence he inspired in others, there was little in his background that would make him attractive to a group of workers thinking of starting a union. Indeed, in the view of one observer, he seemed a man "whose time had passed him by." Born in Crescent City, Florida, in 1898, Randolph grew up in Jacksonville and moved to New York City in 1911. He spent his early years in New York as a roving bachelor, persuing his dream of becoming a Shakesperean actor. He attended classes in economics and history at City College and the Rand School of Economics and eventually joined the Socialist party. In 1917 Randolph joined another young Socialist, Chandler Owen, in founding *Messenger* magazine, a journal of black radical economic and social thought. The *Messenger*, which Langston Hughes later described as "God knows what," a magazine that "reflected the policy of whoever paid the best at the time," did well for a few years, but by 1925 its radicalism had faded and the magazine was experiencing deep financial trouble. In 1925 Randolph needed a job.

Randolph was poorly thought of in some black circles. He carried himself with such pride and dignity that some people considered him haughty and aloof. The English accent he affected, full of "maasses and claasses," did not help matters. In the view of one critic, Randolph's problem was a "bootleg superiority complex." Moreover, some black spokesmen distrusted him. Soon after the union's organizational drive got underway, one newspaper wrote that Randolph had failed in everything he had tried to do, and added that "the path of failures is said to be bedecked with shady deeds." Randolph, the claim went, was using the porters only to enhance sales of the *Messenger*—Randolph liked the reds and intended to take the porters' money and run off to Russia.

Whatever the criticisms, Randolph moved quickly to create a national organization of sleeping car porters and to personify what that union would be. Writing that "public opinion is the most powerful weapon in America," he was convinced that a favorable image, especially among influential whites, was as important to the success of the union as were the porters themselves. He spent much of his time trying to line up support for the BSCP among established black leaders and organizations and in soliciting aid and money from liberal whites. For example, his first action was aimed not at bringing in porters, but rather at attracting outside financial support. In September 1925 he appealed to the Garland Fund, a New York-based foundation that supported radical and unpopular causes. In the name of the "biggest and most significant movement among Negro workers ever started in America," Randolph asked for money not for organizational work among porters, but to subsidize the *Messenger*. He asked the fund to "relieve the financial embarrassment of the publication [because] all porters [accepted it] as their mouthpiece." The fund responded favorably, but made its check payable to the BSCP rather than to the *Messenger* or to Randolph.

Randolph's appeal to the Garland Fund was representative of how he

A. Philip Randolph

Moorland-Springarn Research Center, Howard University

was to function in coming years. He was to serve as a high moral force who would articulate the porters' aspirations and demands and serve as a symbol of their struggle. The chore of bringing in members fell to his lieutenants. Within months he had put together a network of agents across the country: Milton P. Webster at Chicago, Dad Moore at Oakland, Benjamin Smith at Detroit and Pittsburgh, and E. J. Bradley in St. Louis. Except in rare cases, those men remained in their positions throughout the long struggle for recognition and displayed strong personal loyalty to Randolph and his ideas. Likewise, Randolph secured money and endorsements from black and white groups and assembled a battery of white legal and economic experts to work for the union, many of whom served without compensation.

Randolph hungered for publicity and respectability for his struggling union, and he believed that the only way the BSCP would succeed would be to maintain discussion of the porters' grievances at a high volume. He filled the *Messenger* and favorable newspapers with derogatory comments about Pullman's labor policies and punctuated his speeches and other writings with attacks against his opposition, black as well as white. He was particularly caustic towards porters who would not immediately join the union, referring to them as "Uncle Toms" and in other uncomplimentary terms. Black opponents of the union were "conscienceless, crooked and corrupt, . . . mad dervishes" who used their "murderous fingers of graft and corruption" in efforts to destroy the union. The strategy did not contribute much to recruitment but it did gain press exposure for the union and marked Randolph as fearless and wholly committed to his cause. If much of the press opposed Randolph and what he was doing, his style made it impossible for newspapers to ignore his activities. Indeed, their opposition only added to Randolph's reputation. Because his organization was weak and without tradition, Randolph was able to operate on a hit or miss basis, formulating policy as he went along, projecting himself as a man of initiative, creativity, and daring.

BSCP leaders faced two problems. One was how to achieve the specific goals of the organization, which required impressing upon a large number of men the revolutionary idea that they could improve their standards of living through collective bargaining, to say nothing of easing their fear of Pullman reprisals. Moreover, in 1925 approximately twelve thousand porters worked for Pullman, making the company the largest single employer of blacks in the United States. This fact had gained Pullman widespread support among Afro-American spokesmen. During the same year, blacks were generally hostile toward organized labor. Thus the brotherhood saw its struggle in larger terms than simply confronting the Pullman Company. Indeed, the second problem for BSCP leaders involved changing the general economic and political awareness and status of black Americans.

Given his aim, Randolph's style had more effect on the public than on the porters. If BSCP sources and favorable newspapers reported large and enthusiastic crowds showing up to hear his speeches, attendance at rallies did not translate into union membership. Despite secret rolls, untiring efforts of BSCP organizers in various districts, and suspension of enrollment fees to encourage membership, fewer than half of the porters ever signed up. Of those who did, only thirty percent paid regular dues. And most porters maintained loyalty to local leaders rather than to Randolph.

Randolph was a living contradiction. Though his public rhetoric promised to bring Pullman to its knees and exuded militance and courage, privately he was a cautious individual who shrank from confrontation and sought to attain his goals by indirect means. As early as 1926 Randolph demonstrated the dichotomy between his public utterances and his private reluctance to meet Pullman head on, a development that was to recur in 1928. Some BSCP officials wanted to order member porters to boycott a Pullman company union election in 1926. Randolph disagreed. His refusal to go along caused grave consequences for the BSCP, both from within and outside the union. One organizer resigned in disgust and claimed that others threatened to join him. Randolph's continuous talk about action and his simultaneous failure to move led some observers to conclude that he was afraid and had no plan. Many argued that he should place more emphasis on organizing porters and less on public appearances.

Yet such critics did not understand Randolph and the way he functioned. Attaining recognition for the BSCP was Randolph's primary goal, but he also had in mind the additional aims of teaching trade unionism to the masses of black workers and of improving their condition within the labor movement. He intended to use the BSCP as a vehicle for his participation as a national spokesman and leader. In most of his speeches, Randolph emphasized that the problems of black people in the United States were essentially economic and that the remedy lay in organized labor, and he believed that if the BSCP succeeded the lesson would be driven home. If the union failed, his life-long goal of finding a way to improve conditions for the masses would fail with it. Randolph also recognized that his personal fortunes had become intertwined with the BSCP. If the union failed, so would he. Thus, although he talked big, he moved with caution, sacrificing immediate gains for long-range success.

At the same time, the disparity between Randolph's brave words and cautious behavior caused problems for the union. Some of his staunchest supporters took issue with his nonassertive policy, and the rank and file began to give up on the union. By summer 1928, conflicting views and a series of union failures led to a crisis in the brotherhood and threatened Randolph's career as labor leader. The union suffered three major defeats between August 1927 and June 1928. It failed to achieve a meeting with Pullman to discuss porters' grievances; it failed to raise porters' pay by having the Interstate Commerce Commission outlaw tipping; and it failed in its threat to stage a strike against Pullman. During the same period, the brotherhood lost the support of the Pittsburgh *Courier*, until then its staunchest defender. Placing full blame for the union's failure on Randolph, the *Courier*'s influential publisher personally demanded that Randolph serve the porters' cause by resigning.

Partly because of animosity between district offices and union headquarters, but also because of differences over Randolph's policies, BSCP officials took steps during late 1927 and early 1928 to decentralize operations and to reduce Randolph's control of brotherhood policy. The central figure in this reorganization was Milton P. Webster.

Unlike Randolph, Webster was a practical individual with few pretensions. Where Randolph was introspective and had a deep and abiding faith that justice eventually would prevail, Webster was a believer in action. An intelligent man of limited formal education, Webster was a minor functionary in Chicago Republican circles when he joined in organizing the BSCP in 1925. By 1928 he had succeeded in bringing officials from outside Randolph's New York group into the union's policy-making circle when power was transferred from the general organizer to the brotherhood's policy committee.

From his new position as policy committee chairman, Webster moved quickly to change the union's tactics. He had long argued that the only way the BSCP could extract recognition from Pullman was to strike, and he now led his colleagues in laying plans for the confrontation. Randolph supported his efforts reluctantly. Indeed, it appeared that Randolph had lost some of his old self-confidence. Much distressed about calling men off jobs they might be unable to regain, he clearly was afraid to call a strike in 1928.

In the end, the strike threat was only part of Randolph's policy of operating from a position of weakness, using his skills and contacts to bring influential individuals and organizations to support his cause. Characteristically, his announcement of an imminent strike was for public consumption. He wanted only to raise enough noise about the probability of a strike against Pullman to cause the federal government to intervene on the BSCP's behalf under provisions of the Watson-Parker Act of 1926. But on this occasion Randolph found himself caught between the need to appear militant and firm in the eyes of Pullman and the mediation board and at the same time allay the fears of porters about what they could expect from the strike. His actions during spring 1928—such as making a public statement to the porters that "a strike vote does not necessarily mean that the porters will strike"—convinced both the Pullman Company and the federal mediators that the whole episode was little more than gesture. Many porters also came to question his intent. The mediation board, recognizing the contradiction, called Randolph's bluff and refused to recommend emergency measures. The mediation board informed James Weldon Johnson, who as secretary of the National Association for the Advancement of Colored People (NAACP) had intervened on behalf of the BSCP, that there would be no disruption of rail service, and thus no emergency, if every Pullman car in the country stood idle. After the mediation board's decision, the BSCP, despite endorsement of the strike by a majority of the porters, did not carry through on its threat and instead "postponed" the strike. Randolph's activities of 1928 amounted to a bluff that failed.

Randolph's failure to act, though perhaps wise in light of elaborate plans the Pullman Company undertook to ensure that the strike would fail, nonetheless caused a severe crisis for the brotherhood and marked the end of a period in the union's development. Randolph's standing reached a low ebb even among fellow organizers, while rank-and-file members left the union in droves. Randolph's mood during the strike episode so troubled Webster that he believed Randolph, given his current state of emotional despair, would destroy the union. The Chicago leader took upon himself responsibility of maintaining the union's militancy and of increasing participation in policy making by organizers from outlying regions. Routine administrative functions were now much more crucial to the BSCP's survival than propaganda and publicity, for (as Webster wrote Randolph) the BSCP was clearly "past the point of stirring things up." At a meeting of brotherhood officials in July 1928, Webster insisted that in the future the policy committee would control BSCP decisions in fact as well as in name.

Although Webster left that meeting as the most influential organizer in BSCP circles, he recognized Randolph's superior abilities to articulate the union's goals and did not challenge Randolph's position of national leader. But just as important, Randolph understood Webster's talents for bringing in members and his standing among other brotherhood leaders. Above all, Randolph recognized that he must have a firm organizational base in order to continue to speak out on national issues. Thus, despite their differences in style, Randolph and Webster had mutual respect and trust, as well as recognition of the unique talents of the other, which they needed to harness their efforts to make BSCP an example for black Americans of the importance of union organization for economic advancement.

After 1928 the BSCP lost organizational rigidity as various organizers transcended their former roles and became a social group, a "unity of persons rather than technicians." Since close associations during shared failures had forged strong bonds among them, they were able to reach their new organizational relationship with a minimum of friction. Erosion of BSCP membership that began after the strike debacle of 1928 continued, and as the nation moved into the Great Depression the brotherhood became little more than a cell. Of the 4,632 members in the union in 1928, only 658 remained in 1933, and more than a third of those were in Webster's Chicago local. The BSCP could hardly consider itself a national organization. But its leaders were convinced that if they kept the doors open, the union would triumph in the end.

With the union's doors barely open, the period between the crisis of 1928 and the coming of the New Deal marked a hiatus in Randolph's style, as the needs of the union demanded that he take on routine functions. The BSCP changed it tactics and sought to attain its goal of recognition through the federal courts rather than through the press and propaganda. Indeed, Webster became the union's major figure and for all practical purposes brotherhood headquarters moved—as did Randolph—from New York to Chicago, from which site Webster directed the court fight and maintained the union's organizational structure. Randolph continued to devote full attention to the BSCP, but he utilized different methods than before, toning down his rhetoric and working through the American Federation of Labor (AFL).

Indeed, the BSCP's need in 1928, if it ever hoped to succeed, was to achieve legitimacy. Since there was no possibility at that point of gaining recognition from the Pullman Company, Randolph and his colleagues turned again to the AFL and applied for a charter. The AFL did not accept the BSCP's application for an international charter in 1928, but in 1929 the executive council of the federation chartered thirteen BSCP locals as federal unions directly affiliated with the AFL. Though fully aware of the Jim Crow nature of the charters they had received, brotherhood leaders believed that receipt of the charters marked the union with a certain legitimacy and respectability. But even more important for the relationship between black workers and the general organized labor movement, the charters granted Randolph and his BSCP colleagues access to the floor of the AFL meetings, from which they could challenge the racist attitudes and activities of member unions and fight for the rights of black workers.

From the strike fiasco to the coming of the New Deal, the brotherhood remained largely a paper organization, struggling simply to survive as its leader awaited an opportunity to reassert his rare abilities. Randolph's failure to perform a miracle in 1928 had dampened his followers' faith in his charismatic qualities and he had to await a victory before he could function as a symbolic figure again. The New Deal, with its liberalized labor laws and the emphasis the new administration placed on organized labor, opened new fields for Randolph and provided renewed opportunity for him to operate with the initiative and daring that had characterized his leadership of the BSCP in the days before June 1928.

The Amended Railway Labor Act of 1934 assured for the first time federal support of the BSCP's claim to the right to represent porters. Under protection of that legislation, Randolph convinced an overwhelming majority of porters, many of them nonmembers of the BSCP, to endorse the brotherhood as their bargaining agent in disputes with Pullman. After it won a bitter campaign with the Pullman Porters and Maids Protective Association—a company front—for endorsement from the porters, the BSCP gained recognition from Pullman as legitimate representative of porters and maids in 1935. The victory identified Randolph again as a major figure among black spokesmen.

Randolph's standing among black leaders derived from more than the BSCP's success in gaining recognition from Pullman. Long concerned about the impact of the AFL's discriminatory policies on the economic status of black workers, Randolph had made numerous appeals to AFL leaders to alter the federation's policies. After New Deal legislation in 1934 practically guaranteed the BSCP's success with Pullman, Randolph, capitalizing upon what he saw as his increased stature among both labor leaders and blacks, changed his action on the floor of AFL conventions from begging for improved opportunity for blacks within the federation to demanding that necessary changes be made. At the convention in 1934, with support from a few powerful industrial unions and a mass street demonstration by blacks under NAACP leadership, Randolph forced the AFL to establish a committee to study discrimination in federation affiliates and to report its findings to the convention the following year.

The hearings in 1935 of the Committee of Five on Negro Discrimination in the AFL brought enormous prestige to Randolph as he used every effort to make the sessions an event of importance to all blacks. He brought before the committee testimony from the NAACP and the National Urban League, other black spokesmen, and some Afro-American workers. When AFL leaders received the report in advance of the 1935 convention and tried to downplay its findings of widespread racial discrimination and its recommendations for remedy, Randolph enhanced his standing even more by the straightforward manner in which he carried to the floor the fight to save the report and make the federation responsive to the needs of black workers.

When the report of the Committee of Five on Negro Discrimination came before the convention for discussion in 1935, it came before one of the most significant meetings in the annals of American labor history. For not only did AFL delegates have to deal with what most of them considered to be the demands of militant blacks, but they faced as well the radical demands of industrial unions that the federation abandon its craft orientation and organize all workers regardless of skills or occupation. The federation, in effect, kicked out the industrial unions, and it attempted to sabotage the report on racial discrimination. But Randolph showed great courage as he eloquently objected to both efforts on the part of the leadership.

His main effort centered on the report on discrimination, which he excoriated as a "dignified, diplomatic camouflage." The problem for Randolph was that the original committee report had called for expulsion of racist unions, but the executive council had set those recommendations aside and submitted a report of its own. George M. Harrison, author of the executive council's draft, heatedly defended his position and maintained that organized labor had done more for the advancement of blacks than had any other institution in America. The convention supported Harrison's view and ended by angering a large segment of the black population. Walter White, executive secretary of the NAACP, wrote to John L. Lewis, of the United Mine Workers that the AFL had, by its action, "destroyed the last vestige of confidence" blacks had in that organization. But White went a bit too far. Though Randolph had sided with Lewis's position at the convention and had made himself obnoxious to white delegates, the 1935 convention of the AFL granted the Brotherhood of Sleeping Car Porters an international charter, marking it as the first black union to achieve that status. Although Randolph had written in *Messenger* magazine in 1919 that "the dissolution of the American Federation of Labor would inure to the benefit of the labor movement in this country . . . because it holds that there can be a partnership between labor and capital" and that the "American Federation of Labor is the most wicked machine for the propagation of race prejudice in this country," he accepted the charter. He did so because, as he told John L. Lewis, "you [CIO unions] organize Negro workers. My fight, the fight to organize Negro workers, is in the AFL. I must stay here and carry on that fight." But he also needed the legitimacy and prestige that an AFL charter brought, for the BSCP was still engaged in fierce negotiations with the Pullman Company.

A. Philip Randolph

Randolph's eloquent appeal for an end to discrimination in organized labor, the AFL's decision to grant the BSCP an international charter in 1935, the publicity surrounding the brotherhood's official talks with Pullman that commenced the same year, and the press coverage that followed this complex individual catapulted the BSCP president to prominence among black leaders and spokesmen. Randolph enjoyed wide name recognition. And though his actual accomplishments in organizing the BSCP touched only a small number of Afro-Americans—and his efforts before the AFL had resulted in moral victories at best—he had in fact attained a positive goal in the economic sector whereas others had contented themselves with theorizing. Moreover, Randolph possessed the ability to make the most routine "moral" victory appear as if he and his followers had achieved broad practical success, and he could turn the narrowest of activities into movements for advancement of the general black population. The masses of blacks, and some leaders, seemingly unaware of the nebulous quality of his achievements, looked on Randolph as *the* man to lead efforts to solve their social and economic problems. He was the one individual who combined articulate expressions of the hopes and desires of blacks with practical experience in trade union matters. In February 1936 representatives of approximately two hundred black groups from throughout the country met in Chicago to outline a program and to establish an organization that would more effectively pursue the economic interests of Afro-Americans. Some progressive white groups, particularly CIO unions, attended the sessions that resulted in the founding of the National Negro Congress (NNC). The congress elected A. Philip Randolph, president of the Brotherhood of Sleeping Car Porters, as its president and chose John P. Davis as executive secretary.

Randolph's tenure as president of the congress was one of failure, as the organization abandoned the broad base and endorsed the philosophies of the American Communist party and those of white unions associated with the Congress of Industrial Organizations. There is no simple explanation for this shift, though Randolph's activities were partly responsible. The BSCP leader was unable to devote much time to NNC affairs for two reasons. For the first two years of the congress, Randolph was deeply involved in BSCP-Pullman negotiations, trying to secure a favorable contract and gain support among nonmember porters. Moreover, Randolph was ill and did not have the physical energy to head two national organizations.

The fact is, then, that Randolph was president of the NNC, but he was not its leader. The actual leader was John P. Davis, the congress' executive secretary. It was Davis who as early as 1937 determined that NNC would concentrate on the Communist line. Randolph's relationship with Davis and the congress, a relationship in which the president desired to function largely as a symbolic leader of the NNC while others did the routine duties of running the organization—the manner in which he had operated in the BCSP—did not succeed. The failure underscores the importance of loyal supporters to the success of charismatic figures. Though Webster and other BSCP organizers argued with Randolph from time to time on both policy and tactics, in the end they maintained their loyalty to the common goals of the organization and did not attempt to sabotage Randolph's program. Unlike Randolph's experiences in the BSCP, Davis and others in NNC did not agree with his philosophies. Thus, in his absence from the daily activities of the organization, they pushed aside his views and substituted their own.

By the time the congress convened for its third session in 1940, the Davis element had succeeded in pushing the NNC into the Communist camp, and Randolph was forced to resign or be denied reelection to his post. Far from resigning in disgrace, Randolph mustered all his presence and oratorical powers and quit the NNC with remarkable dignity and aplomb. Ralph J. Bunche, who was present at the session, considered Randolph's resignation speech—in which he warned blacks against simplistic solutions to the problems of black people and of the inadvisability of depending upon whites for leadership and financing of their organizations—one of the most important statements ever made to black leaders and spokesmen. Yet though Randolph showed deep understanding of what was happening to NNC and to much of black leadership, the congress had reached that state largely because of the way he functioned. Moreover, Randolph did not even have his union's full backing in this endeavor. To the public, Randolph was the leader of the National Negro Congress, but power within the organization depended on delegates, and the Davis group had control of the delegates. Most NNC members did not recognize Randolph's charismatic qualities, and thus he exercised little influence over them.

Randolph's acceptance of the presidency of NNC was typical and defied the canons of charismatic leadership because he took a position to which he had been *elected* and did not himself respond to a crying need and devise a movement of his own. Charisma usually does not rest on vested authority, nor can charismatic figures function within limits that are set for them by others. Unlike his role in the BSCP in which he defined the premises and direction of the movement, in the NNC Randolph found his freedom to exercise his rare abilities constrained by the corporate structure. In no other sphere of his work was the failure as clear as this.

Despite his failure in NNC this man of enormous self-confidence and sense of mission remained undaunted and continued to press for equal economic and social justice for black people. Even before World War II, blacks had tired of talking about discrimination and had taken steps to force the government to ensure the rights of blacks to jobs, particularly in the burgeoning war industries. Blacks mounted many protests, the most important of which was the March on Washington Movement (MOWM), which Randolph and other officials of the Brotherhood of Sleeping Car Porters led. In late 1940 and early 1941, Randolph began talking increasingly about what many others had come to recognize: white workers were coming out of the depression because of new job opportunities while blacks remained on unemployment or relief rolls. Even the U.S. Employment Service had noted that blacks were being left out of training programs and new jobs. Randolph proposed that since blacks could improve their position only by showing mass strength, they should band together and march on Washington and demand that the president publicly support an end to racial discrimination in employment.

To give substance to his idea, Randolph announced the creation of the March on Washington Movement and promised that unless President Roosevelt issued an executive order ending racial discrimination in hiring by unions and employers, and eliminating segregation in the armed forces, ten thousand blacks would demonstrate in the streets of the national capital. Randolph's movement became even more frightening to white Americans when this formidable personality, following the position he had taken on resigning from the National Negro Congress, demanded that the march on Washington be all black. The time had come, he said, "when black people must fight their own battles."

Within weeks black newspapers, preachers, and other community leaders picked up the call for a march on Washington, and as the spring of 1941 rolled on, Randolph escalated the number of proposed marchers to fifty thousand. The March on Washington Movement was becoming the largest mass movement of blacks since the activities of Marcus Garvey's Universal Negro Improvement Association of the 1920s. As summer approached, Randolph began talking about one hundred thousand marchers coming to Washington, and federal officials began to worry even more. President Franklin D. Roosevelt sent several intermediaries, including his wife Eleanor and New York City mayor Fiorello LaGuardia, to talk Randolph into calling off the march. But the efforts came to no avail. Randolph declared that nothing less than a presidential executive order would stop the march.

A question that has perplexed scholars of the 1940s and of Randolph is whether the MOWM represented an actual threat to domestic tranquilty or was simply a "magnificent bluff." But in many ways that is not the crucial question. Of greater importance is why the bluff worked. If MOWM had chartered no buses or trains to transport marchers to Washington, if no arrangements had been made to provide food and toilet facilities for the expected masses, if leading black organizations offered only nominal support to the march effort, and if—as Eleanor Roosevelt warned—the Washington police were braced to clear the marching blacks out of Washington, a southern city, why did thousands of Afro-Americans still maintain that they intended to go to Washington at the appointed time? Moreover, given the enormous sources of information available to the president of the United States, why could not President Roosevelt ascertain that the march was a meaningless threat?

The answers to these questions lie in large part in the inspirational leadership and presence of A. Philip Randolph. People intended to march because he stood at the forefront of the movement. Embodying in himself the symbol of courage and perserverance, and tying together the twin essentials of jobs and justice, Randolph convinced the masses that the effort could end only in success. Likewise, his stalwart image of incorruptibility and righteousness apparently convinced even the president that the day was near when masses of blacks would be parading in protest on the malls of the capital.

When President Roosevelt's intermediaries failed to convince Randolph to call off the march, the president invited the leaders of the March on Washington Movement to the White House for direct talks. But even those conversations, in which the president himself participated, failed to convince Randolph to call of the march, and President Roosevelt gave in and issued Executive Order 8802, which one historian has called "the greatest single Negro victory since the Civil War." But that evaluation perhaps goes too far, for as with most political actions the president's decision to issue Executive Order 8802 was a compromise. Roosevelt, described by many as the consummate politician, had no intention of seeing thousands of blacks parade in protest on the malls of the national capital, particularly when German and Japanese propagandists were trying to exploit any evidence of American racial differences. In the end, he actually gave up little. Executive Order 8802 does not mention desegregation of the armed forces, a major MOWM demand in January, and the Fair Employment Practice Committee (FEPC) that it created was so weak as to have hardly any impact. Indeed, Randolph suffered considerable abuse from blacks who complained that he accepted far too little.

In accepting Roosevelt's FEPC in exchange for calling off the march,

Randolph did compromise on what he had demanded in January. Yet the important fact is that the March on Washington Movement had forced the federal government to admit publicly that blacks suffered from discrimination in employment and that the government had a responsibility to provide a remedy for that discrimination. Indeed, the March on Washington Movement accomplished the important result of putting the federal government officially on record for the first time against racial discrimination in employment. Though the action achieved little immediate results for black people, it forced an end to official racism in one important sector of American life. Of equal importance, Randolph emerged as a man of immense national stature.

Despite its questionable results, MOWM made Randolph one of the best known and most widely respected black leaders in the country. Many considered him willing to use militant leadership to mobilize the black masses in activities to improve their living conditions and self awareness as people. His name was a household word. Accolades and commendations, as well as offers of support for his work, poured in from across the country. Whatever one might say about the actual effectiveness of MOWM in the long run, the fact is that as long as it remained an *ad hoc* organization directed at stimulating the masses and obtaining a single goal, Randolph was able to function with style and effectiveness. And yet, even MOWM went into rapid decline when it took on routine institutional structure as the Permanent March on Washington Committee. By the end of 1942 much of Randolph's support had melted away, and he was once again just another among numerous black spokesmen in Harlem. Randolph's sudden and brief fame is a superb example of the ephemeral nature of charismatic leadership.

In some ways, Randolph's activities during the early 1940s mark a major interlude in his public life. Both the avowed reason for his resignation from the National Negro Congress—namely that blacks must finance and lead their own organizations—and the all-black emphasis he placed on the March on Washington Movement contradicted the importance of interracial cooperation that had characterized his past. Moreover, it contradicted the emphasis on class that had been his hallmark. Indeed, in 1925–26 when he emerged as an individual recognizable outside New York as a spokesman among blacks, Randolph stressed the community of interest among black and white workers. Convinced that all people of good will, black as well as white, should participate in improving conditions for the downtrodden, Randolph had made it a practice for the BSCP to depend heavily upon money and technical expertise gained from white sources. And he was committed in his efforts to establish black workers in organized labor and management. Randolph's announcement in 1941 (at the time of his all-black MOWM) of the creation of a National Citizens' Committee to Save the Jobs of Negro (Railroad) Firemen, under the nominal national leadership of Eleanor Roosevelt and Mayor LaGuardia of New York, underscores the contradiction even more. The fact is that though Randolph was undoubtedly sincere in his desire to mobilize the black masses, he never lost sight of the need to cultivate support among influential white individuals and organizations.

A striking feature of Randolph's entire career is the consistency with which he linked civil rights and economic security if black people would advance. In the early years he had maintained that in the United States' capitalist economy money was so important that if black people could only achieve good incomes, social barriers would soon disappear. But it did not take him long to see the folly of that idea. Thus, in the years following World War II he spent a great deal of time working to rid the organized labor movement of its vestiges of discrimination. In convention after convention Randolph took the floor to rail against union discrimination and to demand that the AFL expel those affiliates that permitted the insult to continue. And in convention after convention he stood almost alone, except for the stalwart Milton P. Webster, who remained consistent in his support of the chief.

The postwar years especially tested Randolph's leadership ability and his commitment to the labor movement, for events within organized labor set it apart from the interests of black workers. Under the influence of McCarthyism in the early 1950s, both the AFL and the CIO used red-baiting to get rid of Communist unions and union leaders. And far too often those expelled unions or leaders were those whose activities had been most supportive of blacks. Black unionists were particularly incensed when CIO red-baiting led to the deportation in 1951 of Ferdinand C. Smith, a long-time militant leader of the National Maritime Union. Moreover, when the AFL and the CIO merged in 1955, the leadership of the new federation went to the AFL rather than to the more militant CIO. Blacks were hardly mollified that two blacks, Randolph and Willard S. Townsend, sat on the executive council. Their anger was even heightened when the AFL-CIO began siding against blacks in the courts or before civil rights agencies in cases involving alleged union discrimination.

Randolph, as usual, was prepared to provide the leadership that would permit both continuation of the demands for equality of blacks within organized labor, on the one hand, and support from organized labor for the demands Afro-Americans were beginning to make for equal justice and civil rights on the other. His insistence from the floor of conventions that the AFL-CIO could not countenance racist unions began to hit home, though white labor leaders did not wholly accept Randolph's position. One particularly heated exchange took place at the AFL-CIO convention in San Francisco in 1959. George Meany, who had succeeded William Green as president of the AFL in 1952 and had become head of the AFL-CIO after the merger in 1955, engaged Randolph in a debate over the maintenance of segregated unions in some crafts. Meany alleged that some black workers wanted segregated unions and asked Randolph if segregation was permissable under such circumstances. When Randolph responded No, Meany—who professed warm feelings for the BSCP president—exploded, "That is not my policy. I am for the democratic rights of the Negro members. Who the hell appointed you as the guardian of all the [Negro members] in America?"

Meany's "who the hell" remark, though intended to intimidate Randolph, had the effect of only adding to his stature and influence, as the liberal white and black newspapers and organizations made it clear that Randolph, in the view of some, "speaks for millions of colored people throughout the nation," while another paper pointed out that blacks had accorded Randolph his "guardian" role because he had devoted "almost a half century of his life in freedom's cause." Ever ready to seize the moment, Randolph moved quickly to capitalize on the newly generated publicity. Shortly after the convention, he spearheaded efforts to create the Negro American Labor Council (NALC), an all-black group reminiscent of his March on Washington Movement. He intended to use NALC to "secure membership of Negro workers in the unions and employment and promotion on the job as well as participation in the executive, administrative and staff areas of the unions." NALC formalized its structure in 1960 and elected Randolph president, a post he held until 1966.

Randolph's opposition to union discrimination reached its peak during his years with NALC, and it was through this body that he achieved some major successes. But such success did not come without some suffering on his part. During the summer of 1961 Randolph charged several AFL-CIO unions with practicing racial discrimination, and at the meeting of the Negro American Labor Council later that year, he asserted that "under George Meany's leadership the AFL-CIO is guilty of moral paralysis, pessimism and defeatism." For those remarks, the AFL-CIO executive council, at its meeting in October 1961, censured Randolph for his "incredible assertions" and "false and gratiutous statements." Moreover, the resolution laid responsibility for "the gap that has developed between organized labor and the Negro community" squarely at his feet. All members of the executive council save one voted to pass the resolution of censure. Randolph stood alone.

Through all this, this amazing man remained undaunted and continued to push his fight for equal justice with increasing success. In 1963, for example, he forced the AFL-CIO to create a Special Task Force on Civil Rights. That panel, given that its members were George Meany, Walter Reuther of the United Automobile Workers, C. J. Haggerty of the AFL-CIO building and construction trades department, AFL-CIO secretary-treasurer William F. Schintzler, and Randolph, at least had sufficient high-level clout to have an impact on discriminating unions and civil rights issues beyond unions as well.

Randolph did cause both the task force and NALC to participate in one major international event. Since 1925, when Randolph first evolved as a leader, he had maintained that "public opinion is the most important force in America," and he tried numerous ways to rally public opinion to his cause. He was a great believer in the power of massive demonstrations and had long dreamed of leading a massive march on Washington so that national leaders could see black Americans trampling on the streets of the national capital in their demands for justice and equality. His big opportunity came when, after conversations with his lieutenant and trusted friend, Bayard Rustin, Randolph consulted with other national civil rights leaders and convinced them to endorse his call for a national March on Washington for Jobs and Freedom during the last week of August 1963. Randolph served as national director of the march, with Rustin as its organizer.

On August 28, 1963, after having overcome some significant obstacles, Randolph led more than two hundred thousand black and white marchers in a peaceful and well-organized demand for equal justice. Though Dr. Martin Luther King, Jr., president of the Southern Christian Leadership Conference, at his eloquent best that day, stole the show with his "I Have a Dream" speech, the march was a great day in the life of A. Philip Randolph. His dream of a massive march that would tie together his two demands of jobs and freedom had been realized. He told the assembled thousands, in part:

> Let the nation and the world know the meaning of our numbers. We are not a pressure group, we are not an organization or a group of organizations, we are not a mob. We are the advance guard of a massive moral revolution for jobs and freedom. . . . We know that real freedom will require many changes in the nation's political and social philosophies and institutions. For one thing, we must destroy the notion that . . . property rights include the right to humiliate me because of the color of my skin. The sanctity of private

property takes second place to the sanctity of the human personality . . . .
All who deplore our militancy, who exhort patience in the name of false
peace, are in fact supporting segregation and exploitation. They would have
social peace at the extent of social and racial justice. They are more concerned with easing racial tensions than enforcing racial democracy.

Though Randolph would live sixteen years more, his career peaked at
the time of the march on Washington. He continued to serve on the executive council of the AFL-CIO and maintained his insistence on justice for
all within the house of labor. When he died in 1979, in his ninetieth year,
his vision of a just society and his demand that the sanctity of private property takes second place to the sanctity of the human personality were as
clear and as firm as they had been in 1925.

Analysis of Randolph's leadership and activities as a leader reveals
much. His activities, particularly during the years before 1941—except
the BSCP-Pullman contract of 1937—usually resulted in "moral" victories, and his following was shallow, though at times quite broad. The temporary nature of his victories accounts in part for the various periods during
which numerous blacks and some whites supported his activities—for example during 1926–27, 1935–36, 1941, and 1961–63—and the rapidity
with which they deserted him. Part of the reason was that Randolph's appeal, except in the BSCP, was based on conditions other than firm organization. George Schuyler, a one-time colleague of Randolph's on the
Messenger, wrote of Randolph's leadership in 1942:

> Mr. Randolph knows how to appeal to the emotions of the people and to get
> a great following together, but there his leadership ends because he has no-
> where to lead them and would not know if he had. . . . He has the messianic
> complex, considerable oratorical ability, and some understanding of the
> plight of the masses, but the leadership capacity and executive ability re-
> quired for the task at hand simply is not there. The original March on Wash-
> ington move is now admitted to have been a failure else the current agitation
> would not be necessary. . . . Organization is not merely a matter of ballyhoo
> and oratory, it is a Science, and one that is largely a closed book to Mr.
> Randolph.

Far from reflecting unfavorably on Randolph's leadership, his inability
to organize the masses and to maintain a large following stemmed in part
from the times. Gunnar Myrdal, in his monumental study of blacks in the
United States, concluded that mass movements succeed only in organizations with limited and specific goals. Though undoubtedly fearful of Pullman, porters did rally to the side of the BSCP in the end. The March on
Washington Movement succeeded in attaining its limited goal of forcing

establishment of FEPC, but it fell apart when it took on wider aims. The march on Washington in 1963 was a major success though it did not result in a permanent organization. But more important than all that, Randolph used his charismatic personality, wonderful intellect, and dogged determination to force organized labor and organized employers to respect the basic dignity of black people. Moreover, it was largely because of A. Philip Randolph, who pioneered in mobilizing the masses to suffer to end injustice, that the government of the United States shifted its official policy from racist to antiracist. All in all his is a record of extraordinary accomplishment for a man whose institutional leadership in organized labor derived from his presidency of a union of pillow punchers.

The historian August Meier has suggested that while A. Philip Randolph pioneered in mobilizing the black masses, Martin Luther King, Jr., was the most charismatic individual that the civil rights movement has produced. Meier might be right in his assessment that King was the closest to a charismatic figure produced among blacks. Yet, it is interesting, though wholly academic, to speculate on what would have been Randolph's attainments had he reached his prime in the era of television and heightened political awareness in which blacks lived during the rise to prominence of Martin Luther King, Jr.

Bibliographic Notes

Any study of the life of A. Philip Randolph must begin with the papers of the Brotherhood of Sleeping Car Porters at the Chicago Historical Society. Those voluminous files can be augmented by a careful study of the *Messenger* magazine, the pages of which are particularly revealing for the early years of Randolph's life. The magazine is especially useful to efforts to understand the development of Randolph's radical philosophy and the shift to a more conservative position as he matured. Scholars of Randolph eagerly await the deposit of his papers at the Library of Congress, the archives that he designated to receive them before his death. Those documents will undoubtedly add to our understanding of this complex man.

Though growing, there is not a large collection of published works on Randolph. Jervis Anderson, *A. Philip Randolph: A Biographical Portrait* (1972), is the only full-length study of Randolph's life and, as the title suggest, it is not a thoroughgoing analytical biography. In addition to Anderson's study, two older books provide additional insight into his life; Julius Adams, *The Challenge: A Study in Negro Leadership* (1949), and Edwin R. Embree, *13 Against the Odds* (1944), each devote a chapter to Randolph's career.

There are several studies that discuss various aspects of Randolph's life. Theodore Kornweibel, *No Crystal Stair: Black Life and the Messenger, 1927–38* (1975)

A. Philip Randolph

is a good study of the place of that magazine among American publications and of Randolph's association with it. The pioneering study of the Brotherhood of Sleeping Car Porters, Brailsford R. Brazeal, *The Brotherhood of Sleeping Car Porters* (1946), is still quite a useful account. On the subject of the union, one might also see my book *Keeping the Faith: A. Philip Randolph, Milton P. Webster, and Brotherhood of Sleeping Car Porters, 1925–37* (1977). I also devote a major portion of *The Harder We Run: Black Workers Since the Civil War* (1982) to Randolph's activities and to those of the BSCP (see especially chapter 4).

Recently, several essays on Randolph have appeared. Benjamin Quarles's, "A. Philip Randolph: Labor Leader at Large," in John Hope Franklin and August Meier (eds.), *Black Leaders of the Twentieth Century* (1982), is a fine portrait of Randolph. See also two articles by me: "A. Philip Randolph: A Study in Charismatic Leadership," in *Journal of Negro History,* Summer 1980; and "Federal Intervention into Union Discrimination: FEPC and the West Coast Shipyards," in *Labor History,* Summer 1981.

Walter Reuther and the Rise of Labor-Liberalism

12

Nelson Lichtenstein

When Walter Reuther mounted the podium at the start of the United Automobile Workers' 1947 convention, he knew that power in the union had shifted decisively into his hands after almost a decade of factional strife. After a long, bitter fight the Reuther "caucus" had won the allegiance of the bulk of the tough, politically astute local union officers and shop stewards who composed the activist core of America's largest and most important trade union. More than any unionist of his time, Reuther represented that meeting of organized power and social vision so rare in the history of American labor. "We are the vanguard in America," the forty-year-old former socialist declared before nearly three thousand UAW delegates, "We are the architects of the future."

Reuther's bold assertion was not without foundation. As UAW president for almost a quarter of a century, Reuther dominated an institution that represented more than a million workers in the most quintessential of all American industries. From this strategically vital post he played a key role in determining the parameters of collective bargaining and the political shape of trade unionism in the post-depression era. Reuther began his union career as a socialist and a radical, then achieved national prominence as an aggressive proponent of a labor role at the highest level of corporate decision making. But Reuther was more than a trade union leader: he was one of the founders of mid-twentieth century liberalism and an architect of the American welfare state. As a sort of ideology, "Reutherism" came to combine the tactical approach of traditional business unionism with the political economy of liberal Keynesianism and the social vision of western European social democracy. As Reuther was so fond of saying, the UAW was not interested in just another nickel in the pay envelope. Instead, the UAW had an historic mission as the foremost organizer of social change.

Reuther's life is therefore the story of twentieth-century trade unionism's boldest effort to reshape the whole structure of society, but as we shall see his tenure as UAW president revealed as well the limits of Reutherism as political ideology and union practice.

Reuther's prominence as a trade union leader arose out of a compound of three elements: his socialist upbringing, his enormous energy and ambition, and his penchant for order and rationality. He was born the second of five children on September 1, 1907, in Wheeling, West Virginia, a medium-sized industrial city of iron and steel mills, glassworks, and riverboat shipyards. Tutored by their father, a socialist brewery worker and leader of unionism in the upper Ohio valley, the Reuther brothers—Theodore, Walter, Roy, and Victor—were Debsian socialists by the time they were adolescents. But their father, Valentine, a German immigrant from the Rhineland village of Edigheim, instilled in his sons a drive for self-improvement and success as well as a rebellious defiance of the established order. The eldest son, Theodore, became an accountant, while Walter mastered tool- and die-making in high school. As a skilled tradesman, Walter easily assimiliated the craftsman's characteristic devotion to order, economy of effort, and autonomous dignity on the job. These were values that would characterize Reuther's world view for many years.

In the 1920s the booming auto factories of Detroit beckoned ambitious youth from the farms, small towns, and coal mines of Appalachia. When Reuther heard this siren call in 1927, he packed his toolmaker's kit and set out for the Motor City. Reuther's combination of youthful industry and valuable skill assured him of work, first at Briggs Manufacturing Company, a low wage supplier firm with a reputation for dangerous working conditions and brutal foremen, and then at Ford when the giant River Rouge complex at Dearborn began the massive job of retooling to produce the Model A. The Rouge was then the industrial marvel of the world, employing upwards of eighty thousand workers in seventeen tightly coordinated production units; the splendidly equipped tool room where Reuther worked employed as many as seven thousand men in air-conditioned comfort. Hired in as a diemaker, and then rapidly advanced to quasi-foreman status, Reuther soon supervised an entire crew of skilled craftsmen and earned as much as $1.40 an hour, a rate of pay at least double that of ordinary Ford labor. Although Ford laid off more than two-thirds of its work force during the depths of the depression, Reuther never missed a day's work. His value as a skilled toolmaker charged with some supervisory responsibility afforded him an extraordinary degree of job security. Reuther's sense of his place in the world was certainly not unaffected by his good fortune. During the prosperous years of the late 1920s, he drank deeply of the spirit of the New Era. By working the evening swing shift, Reuther finished high school during the day, brought speculative property in Dearborn, and organized a student self-help club composed of other ambitious young workers. Reuther was certainly drifting away from his socialist roots in the late 1920s; had his more radical brother Victor not dropped out of college and joined him in Detroit in late 1930, Walter might well have followed a trajectory like that of his older brother Ted, who spent his entire working life as a minor official with Wheeling Steel.

Victor's influence and the deepening depression rekindled Walter's interest in politics. The Reuther brothers became student activists at Detroit City College (now Wayne State University), joined the Socialist party, and campaigned for Norman Thomas in the 1932 presidential election. Fired by Ford, probably for his political activity, Reuther and his brother Victor signed up for a year-long sojourn at the automobile factory the Ford organization had equipped for the Soviets in Gorki, a new industrial town 500 miles east of Moscow. Like many Socialists in the early 1930s the Reuther brothers were well disposed toward the Soviet Union and positively enthusiastic over its state planning experiments in heavy industry, so the impulse for this bold excursion came as much from a sense of political commitment as from their youthful curiosity to see a depression-era world in turmoil. After several months spent touring England, western Europe, and Germany, where they saw the brutal consolidation of Nazi power, the Reuther brothers arrived at Gorki. There Walter taught Russian peasants some of the finer points of tool- and die-making, and with the penchant for rationality, efficiency, and planning that would later win him fame in the United States, he bombarded the authorities in Moscow with suggestions for more smoothly scheduling the flow of work and increasing production. The Reuther brothers were *udarniks*, special workers with a high record of production achievement, whose regard for the Soviet industrialization effort was tempered only as the first signs of the Great Purge reached Gorki in late 1934.

Ironically, Walter Reuther's tooling experience in the Soviet Union was the last time he worked steadily in a factory, for when the brothers returned to the States in late 1935, jobs were scarce and his political enthusiasm high, so Walter plunged into virtually full-time work organizing a union of autoworkers. It was a propitious time. A series of quite militant strikes in 1933 and 1934 had signaled an important change in the consciousness of rank-and-file workers, and a number of unions—some based in a single plant, others representing a particular craft or skill—had taken the field. The Wagner Act had been passed in the spring of 1935, and in the fall John L. Lewis, Sidney Hillman, and other dissident trade union leaders set up

Archives of Labor and Urban Affairs, Wayne State University

a Committee for Industrial Organization (CIO) to wage a vigorous nation-wide union drive. But success in Detroit, Flint, Toledo, and other auto towns was by no means certain. The major auto corporations were determined to remain "open shop," while the CIO itself decided to first channel its resources toward organization of the steel industry. Moreover, auto-workers themselves did not exhibit any sustained, easily tapped commitment to organization. They were alternately fearful and courageous, doubtful and enthusiastic. Because of the uneven and episodic character of mass consciousness in the mid–1930s, the successful organization of these hundreds of thousands of autoworkers into a national organization capable of confronting their giant employers was heavily dependent upon the work of a corps of young radicals who saw the formation of a strong union as but one part of a larger social agenda designed to recast the social and political landscape. A Socialist and a friend of the Soviet Union, Walter Reuther was now one of several score of these dedicated, semiprofessional organizers who would play such a decisive role in building the UAW and shaping its early character.

Reuther devoted most of his attention to organizing workers on Detroit's West Side, a vast, crowded field of parts and assembly plants that stood almost in the shadow of the giant Rouge complex just across the city line in Dearborn. Aided by his new wife, May Wolf, a Russian-Jewish radical and experienced teacher's union activist in her own right, Reuther opened a store-front office and began slowly signing up workers, concentrating by the fall of 1936 on the Kelsey-Hayes Wheel Company, a Ford supplier employing about five thousand workers. Working with only a small corps of union activists in the plant, Reuther engineered a departmental stoppage that turned into a plantwide sit-down strike in mid-December 1936. Like the more famous General Motors (GM) sit-down strike that began two weeks later, the success of the Kelsey-Hayes stoppage hinged on the ability of a relative handful of workers to halt production and retain possession of the plant. Fortunately, the Kelsey-Hayes workers were in an unusually favorable situation. In the aftermath of the sweeping Democratic election victories of the previous November, the Detroit police felt constrained, while K-H management was anxious to avoid a long strike because they feared that the Ford Motor Company might turn to another supplier. Victor, who had helped instigate the strike from inside the plant, manned a sound truck, while Walter handled negotiations with management.

In late December an agreement was reached, nearly doubling wages, establishing a grievance procedure, and recognizing the UAW. Soon thousands of heretofore hesitant workers, many from other shops and factories on Detroit's West Side, rushed to join the new union. Led by the Reuther brothers and their radical allies, UAW Local 174 emerged as a giant "amalgamated local" representing upwards of thirty thousand workers within a year. Reuther, already a member of the UAW executive board, began work on the Ford organizing drive (during which his plummeling by company goons won him a photo spread in *Time*), and with other unionists campaigned, unsuccessfully, for a seat on the Detroit city council. A footloose world traveler only a year before, Reuther had become, to use the title of C. Wright Mills' later book, one of the "new men of power" made possible by the forward surge of the American working class in the Great Depression.

In the ten years that followed the great sit-down strikes that gave it birth, the UAW grew into the largest union in the nation and won a reputation for both rank-and-file militancy and bitter leadership factionalism. Because the union had been built by local activists, shop floor job actions and wildcat strikes retained a certain legitimacy, while local union leaders, many themselves politically ambitious, jealously guarded the autonomy and authority of their locals. Yet the UAW, like most other large industrial unions, could not successfully function as a series of individual locals. The UAW needed strong national leadership to coordinate the union's conflict with powerful multiplant corporations and to guide its increasingly important work in the political arena. Political factionalism, therefore, remained endemic to the UAW so long as the corporations resisted full recognition of the union, so long as the union's role in American politics remained open to debate, and so long as American autoworkers played a combative and autonomous role in shop floor conflicts with management.

As Reuther made the transition from radical organizer to nationally recognized union leader, he proved himself an adept participant in the UAW's complex factional politics. Although Reuther had been a Socialist party member who worked closely with the Communists during the sit-down strike era, he broke with both political groups in the years after 1938. The Communists became bitter enemies who correctly saw Reuther as a singular personality, a factionalist every bit as determined as themselves. From the Socialists, he merely drifted away, and in fact, Reuther retained the loyalty of most of the party's loosely organized UAW activists even when he took a political stance, such as his decision to support the Democratic candidate for governor of Michigan in 1938, which most Socialists opposed. Such an arrangement proved most useful, for it enabled Reuther to maintain a working relationship with a number of talented individuals without having to shoulder the responsibility that membership in an organized political group would require. In later years Socialists, former Socialists, and even a few Trotskyists became part of the informal circle of

Reuther advisors that gave the postwar UAW its distinctive political coloration.

Although Reuther's politics and programs would change over time, he had a keen understanding of the shifting character of rank-and-file consciousness. Thus in the immediate aftermath of the General Motors (GM) strike, Reuther defended many of the popular "wildcat" strikes that flared in company plants, even when these stoppages threatened to put into jeopardy the UAW's overall bargaining relationship with General Motors. But the insurgency of 1937 quickly turned to hesitancy, even fearful disaffection, following the onset of the sharp recession of 1937–38, and many corporations used a simultaneous outbreak of factional conflict among UAW leaders as an excuse to withdraw union recognition. When Reuther became the director of the union's General Motors department in early 1939 he recognized that the UAW could not rely on a mobilization of production workers to revive the union and rewin bargaining rights from GM and other key corporations. Turning to the more union-conscious skilled workers, Reuther organized a militant and highly successful strike of GM's tool and die shops that disrupted the corporation's 1940 car production schedule and eventually forced GM to again bargain with the UAW. Reuther's skillful handling of the GM "strategy strike" confirmed his standing as one of the UAW's most important officers.

Reuther could be as militant and resourceful a strike leader as any unionist of his time, but his remarkable rise to national political prominence in the early 1940s rested upon other grounds. He articulated a union strategy which recognized that in an era of wartime mobilization the state would serve as the key arena of struggle between the working class and its adversaries. This process had already begun in the 1930s when the New Deal had at least momentarily provided a politically benign climate in which unions could organize, but now Reuther could see that use of the strike weapon would become immensely more difficult, whereas the state's direct role in shaping the economic and social order would be vastly enlarged. The transforming of the economy to a war footing in 1940 and 1941 meant that traditional collective bargaining issues—wages, union recognition, and working conditions—had become thoroughly politicized. Labor would have to become political as well, not just in terms of its electoral activity, but as a planner and manager as well.

As a national political debate raged over the extent to which the United States should intervene in the war, Reuther captured newspaper headlines with a program to accelerate aircraft production by establishing an aircraft production board, composed of representatives of the government, management, and labor, that would have the power to reorganize auto/aircraft production facilities without regard for corporate boundaries, markets, or personnel. Reuther's December 1940 "500 planes a day" plan proposed to break the defense era bottleneck in American aircraft production by converting Detroit auto factories into one great production unit to fulfill President Roosevelt's ambition to manufacture 50,000 aircraft a year. "England's battles, it used to be said, were won on the playing fields of Eton," announced Reuther. "This plan is put forward in the belief that America's can be won on the assembly lines of Detroit." The proposal would have secured for the UAW at least a veto over a wide range of managerial decision-making powers. Winning wide support in the liberal, interventionist political community and among several influential members of the Roosevelt administration, the Reuther plan was ultimately delayed and then defeated by automobile executives hostile to social experimentation and jealous of management prerogatives.

The Reuther plan nevertheless cast a long shadow. By taking advantage of the statist tendencies inherent in the prewar mobilization process, Reuther helped link the union movement to a definition of modern liberalism that both sustained an activist foreign policy and endorsed a quantum leap in the power of the government to regulate labor-management relations and reorder economic life. Moreover, his "500 planes a day" plan contained hallmarks of a strategic approach that Reuther would use again and again: an assault on management's traditional power made in the name of social and economic efficiency, an appeal for public support in the larger liberal interest, and an effort to shift power relations within the larger political economy, usually by means of a tripartite governmental entity empowered to plan for whole sections of the economy. Thus later in the war Reuther proposed a peace production board that would preside over the reconversion of defense plants to ensure the mass production of railroad cars and working-class housing in the postwar era. Still merely a vice-president of the UAW, Reuther seemed a practical but imaginative planner who would link union power with government authority in what many historians today would label a "corporatist" framework designed to reorganize American capitalism within a more stable and humane framework. Yet because his program would limit the freedom and authority of individual corporate enterprise, it was bitterly resisted by most spokesmen for American business. As auto executive George Romney put it early in the war: "Walter Reuther is the most dangerous man in Detroit because no one is more skillful in bringing about the revolution without seeming to disturb the existing forms of society."

The rejection of Reuther's plan and the government's gradual imposition of a system of rigid wartime controls coincided with the renewal of an intense period of UAW factionalism that ultimately laid the basis for his succession to the UAW presidency. The internal union battles in which Walter Reuther participated during the next decade had a dual character. They were, of course, personal contests for office, money, and power, in which Reuther and a "caucus" of allied unionists jousted for control with their opponents, led for many years by a coalition headed up by the UAW's long-time secretary-treasurer, George Addes, and by Vice-President Richard Frankensteen. Addes and Frankensteen had the support of the sizable Communist group in the UAW, whose energy and organization made them a potent influence in UAW politics. In these contests, which often reached a climax of wholesale vote trading and bitter infighting at the UAW annual conventions, the Reuther group measured its strength and parcelled out the jobs over which it had control. His caucus represented a coalition of disparate elements ranging from the Association of Catholic Trade Unionists on the Right to socialist union militants on the Left. A tenacious builder of political and organizational influence, Reuther avoided the bars and all-night poker games frequented by some union politicos. Instead, as one opponent described him at a union convention in the mid–1940s, "For hours on end, the Redhead would come grimly downstairs, take up his stand near the UAW bookstore display and harangue little groups of delegates. . . . Certainly the indefatigable energy of the man paid off."

While other leaders of the UAW were just as ambitious, all knew that the Reuther group's drive for leadership in the union would bring profound changes that would permanently redistribute real power in the UAW. This largely explains why Reuther was never able to form a lasting alliance with any of the other major elements of the UAW leadership: not with Frankensteen who was as anticommunist as he; not with President R. J. Thomas, who needed his support; not with Addes, who was often as militant as Reuther on day-to-day trade union issues. Eventually all of Reuther's factional opponents coalesced into a caucus that opposed him: what is remarkable under these circumstances is how Reuther gained control of the union, and the story of his success here lies with the character of the political and social vision he offered the UAW rank and file.

Although Reuther was closely identified with the Roosevelt administration before the attack on Pearl Harbor, he had the political intelligence to recognize that the failure of the CIO's effort to link a progressive social program to the wartime mobilization effort would put the union on the defensive during the war. The government's gradual imposition of a rigid system of wartime controls, including a strike prohibition, laid the basis for a wartime period of turmoil in the UAW that was reminiscent of the era immediately after the sit-down strikes. Most workers were patriotic and backed the war effort, but they resisted the consequences of the wartime regimentation, especially if it appeared inequitably administered or entailed the sacrifice of union standards won in prewar years. In the words of one unionist, UAW locals found themselves "plagued by a malady of unsettled grievances" that undermined the solidarity and effectiveness of the union and gave management the chance to retake the initiative at the shop floor level. Despite the UAW's formal adherence to a no-strike pledge, therefore, a wildcat strike movement of large proportions swept through union ranks, peaking in 1944 and 1945 when over half of all workers in the auto industry participated in a work stoppage of one kind or another.

This insurgent movement had an important impact on the internal politics of the UAW and laid the basis for Reuther's accession to the UAW presidency. As the war neared its end, Reuther sought an accommodation with the militant and rebellious sentiment growing in UAW ranks, if only as a means of advancing his own power in the union. By 1943 he favored a more vigorous opposition to the government system of wage controls than other UAW leaders, and in 1944 he began to shift away from a blanket endorsement of the no-strike pledge. This turn toward political opposition proved popular with many key union activists, and it contrasted sharply with that of the Communist group in the UAW, which advocated strong support of the no-strike pledge as a domestic counterpart to the grand alliance forged by Churchill, Stalin, and Roosevelt on the international scene. In early 1945 Reuther urged that the CIO withdraw from the War Labor Board until that government agency was reorganized and adopted a more liberal wage policy, and a couple of months later he began a process of backing away from the rigid enforcement of the no-strike pledge, a political gambit that represented a growing break with the national CIO's more dependent relationship to the Roosevelt administration and the Democratic party. With the fall of Germany those in the union who had long fought for an end to the no-strike pledge insisted upon an immediate industrywide strike vote to demanded an end to all government wage ceilings. Alone among prominent members of the UAW leadership, Reuther back this proposal. By accommodating those local union activists who called for an immediate end to wartime wage controls, Reuther was laying the basis for both an aggressive defense of labors' interest in the postwar era and his own advancement to the UAW presidency.

Reuther's leadership of the UAW's 113-day strike against General Motors in 1945 and 1946 climaxed the UAW leader's accommodation to these insurgent forces at the same time that it offered the CIO's most far-reaching effort to use union power to effect far-reaching changes in the structure of the political economy. During the war full employment and plentiful overtime pay meant that the real wages of autoworkers had increased substantially, even though both prices and wages had been controlled by the government. Reflecting the contemporary fear that a postwar economic collapse might come if working-class income were not sustained, Reuther put forward the novel demand that General Motors raise wages by some 30 percent without increasing the price of its product.

While this program was formally directed against the giant automaker, it was in practice a union demand against the state as well, for its ultimate success rested upon the Office of Price Administration and other government agencies maintaining price and production controls well into the postwar era. Like the "500 planes a day" plan of 1940, the GM strike program also made a strong appeal to public interest, this time not in terms of rationalized production and democratic control, but in terms of the emerging Keynesian consensus that a substantial boost in mass purchasing power would be necessary to avoid a postwar depression. Thus Reuther and his many supporters consciously politicized the GM strike by challenging managerial control of product pricing and by emphasizing the stake that the consuming public had in the victory of the autoworkers. The UAW's bold demand that the corporation "open the books" to demonstrate its ability to pay forthrightly asserted the social character of business enterprise and questioned management's prerogatives in determining the relative distribution of its profits.

Although Reuther's closely watched leadership of the strike failed to win autoworkers a settlement much different from that negotiated by the rest of the CIO, it nevertheless capped his campaign for the top office in the UAW. At the March 1946 UAW convention Reuther won a narrow election victory over President R. J. Thomas, but his opponents secured control of the union's powerful executive board because many delegates were reluctant to offer any one faction full control of the organization. The stage was therefore set for twenty months of bitter internal union conflict. Reuther made union communism a central issue of his campaign, and he benefited from the growth of cold war tensions, which he used as a means of identifying his opponents with a set of politics that he considered destructive of the union and alien in the larger body politic. However, the success of his attack did not rest on the kind of reactionary and demogagic red-baiting that would soon characterize cold war political culture. Reuther did not ally himself with conservative anticommunist forces; in fact, he surrounded himself with radicals and socialists like Emil Mazey, the new UAW secretary-treasurer; Jack Conway, his administrative assistant; and Leonard Woodcock, later director of the union's General Motors department and UAW president. Combining his own reputation as a militant and politically astute union leader with thorough organization at the local level, the Reuther group made deep inroads among the corps of noncommunist UAW local leaders who had heretofore backed the Addes-Frankensteen caucus. The turning point came in the summer of 1947, when congressional passage of the anti-union Taft-Hartley Act convinced many union activists that only a staunch anticommunist such as Reuther could protect the UAW from further political attack.

Reuther's decisive victory at the UAW's 1947 convention, where his caucus captured almost every major post, proved a turning point in the political history of American labor. Within the CIO, the Reuther sweep shifted the balance of power decisively against the sizable group of unions, such as those in the longshore and electrical industries, whose leaders sought to maintain a working arrangement with the Communists, both within the labor movement and in the national political arena. His victory also reduced the political weight of those who might take issue with the emerging cold war foreign policy consensus, even though Reuther himself was often a liberal critic of the government's increasingly hard-line anticommunist posture. Thus Reuther's success in the UAW ensured that most CIO union leaders would both sign the anticommunist affidavits required by the Taft-Hartley Act and repudiate the 1948 third party presidential candidacy of the old New Dealer Henry Wallace, who campaigned with the close support of the Communist party, on a platform critical of U.S. foreign policy toward the Soviet Union.

Within the UAW Reuther easily consolidated his control of the union by purging his opponents, by creating an efficient bureaucracy, and by cultivating a political culture at the UAW that was at once politically liberal and ideologically monolithic. A nearly fatal assassination attempt by shotgun-welding Detroit gangsters (probably hired by an anti-union employer) dramatically enhanced Reuther's personal prestige in 1948. "Teamwork in the Leadership, Solidarity in the Ranks" became the new UAW watchword. The elimination of unionwide opposition substantially reduced the relative freedom local union officials had enjoyed when two factions competed for their allegiance. Radicals and important shop floor activists were either coopted onto the union staff or isolated by the sophisticated mobilization of the union's considerable organizational strength. Meanwhile, the growing UAW staff increasingly came to resemble a combination political machine and welfare bureaucracy that "serviced" the membership.

When opposition did bubble up from below, Reuther usually proved himself flexible enough to accommodate it. Thus during the inflationary surge of the Korean War, he successfully demanded that major auto corporations reopen their long-term contracts with the UAW after a series of wildcat strikes demonstrated growing discontent at many plants; and then later in the 1950s Reuther pushed through changes in the UAW constitution that would give skilled workers, who threatened to disaffiliate, a veto over contract ratification and a more secure craft status in the union. But even at the height of these internal conflicts, Reuther's moral and political standing was such that he faced no serious leadership challenge for the duration of his tenure as UAW president. As even one long-time opponent of the UAW president put it in the late 1950s, "Walter Reuther is qualified not only to be president of the UAW but of the United States of America."

Although it was far from his intention, Walter Reuther's consolidation of power in the UAW opened the way for the general alignment of his union and the industrial union wing of the labor movement with the more conservative, corporate-directed political and economic consensus emerging in the early cold war years. Certainly, Reuther's attack on corporate arrogance and wealth was still as sharp and pointed as that of any union leader at midcentury, and his defense of the living standard and dignity of the working class still echoed the socialist values of his earlier years. But Reutherism as a distinctive social ideology began to lose some of its dynamic quality even as its influence became most widespread. In the early years of his presidency, Reuther helped lay the foundations for the remarkably stable social compact between labor and capital that governed class relations in the United States during the first twenty-five years after the end of World War II. As the closely watched leader of the union that bargained for more than a million workers in the nation's most important industry, Reuther played the key role in advancing a uniquely American version of trade union social politics that both assured an increase in the standard of living of the organized working class while it simultaneously established rigid guideposts to the overall exercise of union power.

The preconditions for this social compact were as much political as economic. The late 1940s were an era of rightward drift in politics and growing business self-confidence. Although Reuther was a founding leader of the anticommunist, but left-liberal Americans for Democratic Action (ADA), efforts to revitalize a labor-liberal coalition were blunted by the political demobilization of many of the constitutent elements of the old Roosevelt coalition. Instead of using union power as a lever to widen the welfare state and to make demands upon the government that would alter the structure of the political economy, trade unionists increasingly adopted a defensive posture that looked first to the interests of their own immediate constituency. Growth of a business union mentality, even among sectors of the industrial union movement that had once been most radical, was facilitated by the realization that America was entering a period of unexpected economic prosperity. Though he still sought to make the UAW a vanguard of social reconstruction, Walter Reuther could not escape the political and economic logic of his era.

Reuther was, therefore, receptive in 1948 to the far-reaching proposals offered the UAW by the General Motors Corporation and its conservative but sophisticated president, Charles E. Wilson. Although GM had staved off the union's effort to link company pricing policy to a negotiated wage package in 1946, Wilson realized that disruptive strikes and contentious annual wage negotiations hampered the company's long-range planning and embittered shop floor labor relations. GM, therefore, sought to dampen the conflict with its workers engendered by the postwar inflationary surge and to negotiate multiyear contracts and assure management of a free hand in the postwar expansion and rebuilding of its automotive empire. In 1948 GM, therefore, offered the UAW a contract that included two pillars of the postwar social order: first, an automatic cost-of-living adjustment keyed to the general price index, and second, a two percent "annual improvement factor" wage increase designed to reflect, if only partially, the still larger annual rise in GM productivity. Reuther, in the hospital from gunshot wounds, endorsed the GM proposal; two years later he participated more actively in the negotiation of an even more elaborate contract that provided for a $125 a month pension, improved both the cost-of-living and the productivity factor adjustments, and most striking of all, provided for an unprecedented five-year contract.

The agreements reached by the UAW with GM and other auto industry employers were widely heralded, but they had important consequences not clearly apparent at the time. Most significantly these contractual arrangements represented a retreat from Reuther's earlier effort to use union power as a lever to limit managerial authority and begin economic planning. Although the UAW would long remain in the forefront of the labor-liberal coalition that sought an expansion of the welfare state, contracts of the sort negotiated with GM represented an accommodation by the UAW to the authority corporate management held in determining the general distribution of decision-making power in industry. The annual improvement factor explicitly linked the rank and file's standard of living to the industry's exceptional productivity growth, while the five year duration of the contract signaled the intention of both parties to inaugurate a social truce of virtually indefinite length. Combined with the pensions and health benefits the union also negotiated at midcentury, and the supplemental unemployment benefits won in 1955, the UAW program amounted to a sort of privatized welfare state that just about doubled the real standard of living of American automobile workers in the quarter century after 1945. But, unlike the Reuther "500 planes a day" plan or even the 1945 GM strike program, the collective bargaining compacts the UAW won during the 1950s and 1960s did not seriously threaten the way in which corporate management reshaped the industry. Thus *Fortune* magazine declared the 1950 UAW-GM contract the "Treaty of Detroit" because the promise of social peace that it contained provided the basis for a rebirth of managerial initiative. "GM may have paid a billion for peace" declared the magazine, "but it got a bargain. General Motors has regained control over one of the crucial management functions, . . . long-range scheduling of production, model changes, and tool and plant investment."

The social compact forged between the UAW and the auto corporations in the late 1940s required a routinization of the adversarial relationship not only across the bargaining table, but at the shop floor level as well. Because of the union's tradition of local union autonomy and assertive shop floor bargaining, such stability could not be achieved overnight, nor did Reuther and other top UAW leaders seek to directly impose the sort of autocratic internal regime that characterized unions in mining, steel, and trucking. Although Reuther had pioneered in the establishment of a grievance arbitration system, first at General Motors and then throughout the auto industry, shop floor conflict remained endemic in UAW organized shops during the prosperous years of the 1950s and 1960s. At Chrysler and International Harvester, wildcat strikes were actually more frequent in the 1950s than in the previous decade, and even at General Motors, where a tough management penalized unauthorized job actions, workers dramatically increased the number of grievances filed by their representatives. The difference between the 1930s and the 1950s was, therefore, not so much one of an ameloriation of shop floor conflict but of the ability of unionized workers to effectively project their fight onto a unionwide bargaining agenda. Although individual locals were often extremely militant, the UAW as an institution no longer sought a fundamental transformation of shop floor labor relations in the automobile industry.

Reuther and other national leaders of the UAW increasingly focused their attention on those elements of bargaining that could be most easily quantified and monetized, generally wage and fringe benefit improvements in the national contract. UAW locals still had the right to strike over those chronic, daily conflicts involving speed-up, work assignments, job content, and the like, and they did so with increasing frequency in the 1960s, but battles over these issues necessarily took a subordinate place on the bargaining agenda when Reuther and his team sat down with Ford or GM to hammer out a companywide settlement. After 1958 the UAW adopted an informal policy authorizing stoppages on such local issues, but only after the negotiation of a national contract had been completed, thereby severely limiting the effective power of local officials. From the international's perspective these strikes were politically useful, for they gave the rank and file a chance to blow off steam, and they enabled local officers to horsetrade difficult grievances that might otherwise fester during the remainder of the contract.

Despite the ambiguous character of the social compact Reuther negotiated with the major auto corporations, his ambition and broad social vision still marked him as the most exciting figure in the American labor movement: one survey in the late 1940s even ranked Reuther with Churchill and Stalin as among the ten most influential men in the contemporary world. Liberal Democrats often put Reuther's name forward as a possible candidate for a senate seat or a high administration appointment, but he never seriously considered any career outside of the union movement. Although his social and economic ambition narrowed in the 1950s and 1960s, Reuther nevertheless typified all that was attractive in postwar labor leadership. In virtually every speech, especially those delivered before nonunion audiences, Reuther declared that the UAW was not just another "nickel in the pay envelope" union; instead it sought to shape its bargaining program so as to make "progress with the community, not against it." And in a decade when many union leaders came under attack as flaccid and corrupt, Reuther and most of the UAW's lesser officers retained an almost spartan lifestyle. For many years his salary was the lowest of any major union president; moreover, Reuther found genuinely distasteful the lavish accommodations the AFL-CIO routinely rented for its winter meetings in Florida.

Upon the death of CIO president Philip Murray in 1952, Reuther won election as president of the industrial union federation, despite resentment by some rival union presidents that he had shouldered his way forward rather too forcefully. Because the CIO had lost much of its unity and élan by the early 1950s, Reuther viewed his new post as a part-time job. His only substantial accomplishment was to prepare the way for the CIO's long-delayed merger with the rival American Federation of Labor in 1955. Reuther was the guiding spirit behind the AFL-CIO's industrial union department (IUD), and he hoped that under the banner of a united labor movement the IUD would spark a massive organizing drive that would recruit millions of new union members. But such hopes were vain in the late 1950s. AFL-CIO president George Meany was uninterested in a bold new social initiative, the major unions had organized most of the key firms in each of their industries, and the legal framework for an organizing breakthrough remained problematic. Only maverick unions like the Teamsters, and later the teachers and municipal workers, showed much determination to expand the ranks of organized labor. Even the UAW, which sought to expand its constitutency by organizing small shops and white collar workers in the auto, aircraft, and metal fabrication industries, failed to increase its membership; the union lost its first place ranking to the Teamsters in 1958. Depending upon the number of workers on recessionary layoff, the UAW fluctuated at around 1.5 million members from the early 1950s until the late 1970s. Still, Reuther remained the union movement's most prominant advocate of "organizing the unorganized." In the mid–1950s the UAW spent millions of dollars on a multiyear, violence plagued, but ultimately successful effort to unionize the bitterly resistant Kohler Company of Sheboygan, Wisconsin. And in the 1960s Reuther took great personal interest in the struggle led by Cesar Chavez to organize California farm workers. Beginning in 1965, the UAW heavily subsidized the United Farm Workers and supported its boycott of nonunion grapes and lettuce.

In the larger realm of national politics, Reuther played a key role in shaping the relationship between the labor movement and the Democratic party, for it was in the same decade in which the UAW worked out a social compact with the major auto corporations that it also led the union movement onto new and more stable political terrain. Reuther's relationship to party politics can be conveniently divided into three stages. Although he had abandoned the Socialist party and voted for Roosevelt in 1940 and 1944, Reuther and most of his union allies initially favored maintenance of an "independent" relationship between the UAW and the Democratic party. Encouraging this perspective in the early postwar era was the persistance of labor party sentiment among many of Reuther's own supporters (including Emil Mazey and brother Victor), the massive example provided by the British Labor party's 1945 election victory, and President Harry Truman's postwar accommodation to antilabor conservatives within his own party. As a founding member of the ADA, Reuther and other liberals looked long and hard for a political alternative to Truman, and many in the new UAW leadership kept open the possibility that labor might form the core of an independent political party at some propitious future moment.

This period ended with the divisive Wallace candidacy in 1948, which seemed to tarnish the idea of a labor-backed third party, and with Truman's unexpected reelection in the same year. Thereafter Reuther sought a "realignment" of the Democratic party that would make it a genuinely effective vehicle for labor and liberal forces. From 1948 on the UAW played an active, organic role in the Democratic party's internal affairs, and Reuther developed close ties to labor-liberals like Hubert Humphrey and Michigan governor G. Mennon Williams. In Michigan and a few other industrial districts the UAW virtually took over the party apparatus, and Walter Reuther proved a forceful advocate of much that constituted the liberal Democratic program: negotiation with the Soviets to temper the arms race, protection of civil liberties and advancement of civil rights legislation, and an expansion of the welfare state combined with a vigorous Keynesian fiscal policy.

Although Reuther's political sentiments were certainly genuine, the increasing responsibility the UAW assumed for the maintenance of a multi-tendencied political party shifted him from the Left to the center of the Democratic party by the mid–1960s. This became clear even in his relationship to the growing civil rights movement of the early 1960s, a social movement of which Reuther was a strong proponent. The UAW provided Martin Luther King's Southern Christian Leadership Conference with substantial financial support and much public encouragement, and Reuther took sharp personal exception to the AFL-CIO executive council's decision not to endorse the 1963 march on Washington. The UAW sent a sizable contingent to Washington, and Reuther was by far the most prominent white to speak at the August 28 rally. But where the civil rights movement came in conflict with the institutional interests of either the UAW or the Democratic party, Reuther proved far more moderate. In Detroit the UAW often opposed the effort by a new generation of black activists to win influence in the local Democratic party, but Reuther's new sense of "realism" became most graphically apparent at the 1964 Democratic Convention, where President Lyndon Johnson and vice-presidential aspirant Hubert Humphrey used the UAW leader as their agent in the fight against the civil rights militancy of the Mississippi Freedom Democratic party (MFDP), which sought to oust the regular, racist Mississippi Democrats from their convention seats. Through UAW counsel Joseph Rauh, who was also the MFDP's lawyer, Reuther demanded that the MFDP accept a compromise that would liberalize future delegate selection guidelines, but allow the segregationists to retain the lion's share of delegate credentials at the 1964 convention. In a historically significant breech with the forces of labor-liberalism symbolized by Rauh and Reuther, the MFDP angrily rejected the offer and staged a disruptive sit-in. Humphrey later praised Reuther as a "practical liberal" in the emotional dispute, and in 1968 the UAW hierarchy backed the Democratic vice-president, both before and after the Democratic Convention in Chicago.

The last decade of his life was one of frustration and paradox for Walter Reuther. Although the 1960s were a prosperous era of Democratic party

297

ascendency, liberal ferment, and steady UAW contract improvements, Reuther and his union found themselves increasingly marginal to the political and social conflict of that turbulent decade. Reuther's brand of practical liberalism stirred few hearts in the 1960s; partisans of the decade's new movements for peace and civil rights saw the UAW president a distant sympathizer at best; even his old compatriots within the union movement distanced themselves from Reutherite politics.

Reuther's relative isolation was most graphically displayed during the course of his long feud with AFL-CIO president George Meany. Reuther, almost a generation younger than Meany, expected to be the next AFL-CIO president, so he was undoubtedly irritated that Meany clung to power well into his eighth decade. The AFL-CIO chief used his authority to thwart the UAW leader's restless ambition, both within the labor federation and in Washington, where Meany had enough political clout to deny Reuther even a presidential appointment to the American United Nations delegation. By the mid–1960s Reuther was both frustrated and disaffected, and he clashed repeatedly with Meany over what Reuther considered the labor federation's "complacency" at home and rigid anticommunism abroad. "The AFL-CIO lacks the social vision, the dynamic thrust, the crusading spirit that should characterize the progressive, modern labor movement," announced Reuther in 1966. He insisted that the union federation devote more energy and money to the organization of farm workers, to the advancement of civil rights, and to the war on poverty. Reuther called for an $87 million "national crusade" to organize white-collar employees, as well as migratory and other low paid workers.

Reuther supported President Lyndon Johnson's conduct of the Vietnam War in its early phases but favored greater efforts toward negotiations and a bombing halt in 1966 and 1967. Prodded by his brother Victor and by some of the other old radicals in the UAW leadership, Reuther distanced himself somewhat from the AFL-CIO's hawkish militancy. He denounced the federation's viewpoint on the war and domestic dissent as "intemperate, hysterical and jingoistic." Meanwhile relations between Reuther and Meany deteriorated still further, first after Victor Reuther used a 1966 UAW convention to denounce AFL-CIO cooperation with the Central Intelligence Agency in Latin America, and then when Meany abruptly withdrew American representatives from the International Labor Organization after a Polish Communist had been elected president of that organization. Reuther, who favored the broadest possible contacts with the Eastern Bloc, thought Meany highhanded in taking such unilaterial action.

Unfortunately, Reuther's critique of AFL-CIO policy failed to win him much support, even among his natural allies in the old CIO and the liberal community. By all accounts Reuther conducted his fight in an uncharacteristically maladroit fashion, never quite sure upon what issues to throw down the gauntlet. But even more importantly, Meany's politics seemed to reflect more accurately than Reuther's the stolid and complacent mood that came over much of the union bureaucracy. Thus Meany always controlled a large majority on the AFL-CIO executive council. Finally, Reuther lost touch with his long-time allies on the liberal Left. On the decisive Vietnam issue, Reuther was at best a moderate dove, unwilling either to break with the administration or to support antiwar politicians like Eugene McCarthy and Robert Kennedy.

UAW ties with the AFL-CIO unraveled in 1967 and 1968. After Reuther resigned his federation offices and the UAW ceased paying dues, the AFL-CIO suspended the 1.6 million member auto union: for the next fourteen years the UAW remained independent of the parent labor federation. Reuther's departure had little drama or political impact. No other unions departed the AFL-CIO with the UAW. Reuther tried to break out of this isolation in July 1968 when the UAW and the Teamsters formed an Alliance for Labor Action that Reuther hoped would "revitalize" the labor movement. However, this unlikely linkup with the powerful but conservative and corrupt Teamsters leadership could not last. It disintegrated in the early 1970s when the Teamsters raided the farm workers union in California and endorsed President Richard Nixon for reelection.

Although auto industry employment and real wages increased substantially during the 1960s, Reuther found leadership of his own UAW not without challenge and frustration. Reuther won sizable wage increases during the 1964 and 1967 negotiating rounds, but he also encountered an unusual degree of rank-and-file resistance to his bargaining priorities. After the wage pattern had already been set with Chrysler, contract talks with Ford and GM broke down over resolution of local plant disputes involving grievance procedures and working conditions. The Big Two automakers sought to absorb much of the new contract's increased labor costs through greater productivity, but local union negotiators resisted what they considered company "speed up." To head off a wildcat strike movement, Reuther authorized local stoppages and denounced GM working conditions as below "the minimum standards of human decency." Ford was shut down for twenty days and GM for thirty-one, but local disputes reflecting membership discontent with in-plant job problems continued to plague the UAW's top leadership throughout the 1960s and early 1970s. In February 1967 a wildcat strike by a GM local in Mansfield, Ohio, stopped much of the corporation's production, idling 174,000 men in over fifty-seven other plants. Reuther declared the strike illegal, called the local's leadership to

Detroit, and ordered a return to work. When the strike continued in March, Reuther obtained an executive board "seizure" of the local and ordered a resumption of work.

Internal union opposition from yet another quarter had an important impact on Reuther's handling of UAW wage negotiations in 1967. Skilled tool, die, and maintenance workers demanded wage parity with non-UAW craft unionists. Calling for a "dollar-an-hour" pay boost, the radical leadership of this group mounted one of the most effective unionwide mobilizations seen in postwar UAW history. To meet their criticism, Reuther won a special fifty cents an hour wage increase for skilled workers during the course of the UAW's seven-week Ford strike in the fall of 1967. But Reuther miscalculated during the contract negotiations, for he also agreed to a three-year ceiling of eighteen cents an hour on automatic cost-of-living payments. This "cap" cost autoworkers upwards of a $1,000 each over the life of the contract and set the stage for the lengthy GM strike of 1970.

Finally, Reuther's encounter with the insurgent black movement within his own union was also one of conflict and accommodation. In keeping with his national reputation as a civil rights advocate, Reuther did not hesitate to forcefully desegregate southern locals when they balked at UAW policy in the 1950s, but Reuther moved more slowly to accommodate black demands for more leadership authority within the union. His problem was an institutional one: in many urban plants blacks composed more than half of all production workers, but whites held an overall majority in the region that elected the executive board member. Since the UAW board was composed entirely of Reuther loyalists, he was unwilling to intervene, and it was 1962 before the UAW elected a black to a special at-large executive board seat. Five years later came the massively destructive Detroit riot of 1967 and the emergence of a "revolutionary union movement" among young black autoworkers. Reuther found their nationalist rhetoric unpalatable and their militancy disruptive; using tactics well honed since the 1940s UAW officials at the local and regional levels defused the movement by coopting some of these radicals, defeating or purging many others.

In early 1970, at the age of sixty-two, Reuther was looking forward to retirement, possibly a teaching post at a major university. Reuther's interests that spring had drifted from the day-to-day affairs of the UAW: instead his imagination was fired by construction of the union's $18 million Family Education Center on the shores of Black Lake in northern Michigan. Reuther, who had pushed the project from its inception, often visited the site. It was on one of these trips, on an evening flight to Black Lake in

May, that Reuther's chartered jet crashed in the Michigan woods, instantly killing the UAW leader, his wife, and four others aboard the plane. Walter Reuther's death almost precisely coincided with the end of a thirty-year boom in the history of American capitalism. He was the most exciting and influential trade unionist of that prosperous era because he defined the outer limits of liberalism's social and economic agenda. In the 1940s, his most creative time, Reuther seemed to have both the power and the will to restructure American capitalism's most important industry and lead the way toward a just and efficient planned economy. As this possibility faded, so too did the power and the appeal of the labor-liberalism for which Reuther was such a forceful spokesman. Although the UAW president presided over a progressive union that doubled the real income of autoworkers and vastly increased their security on the job and in retirement, his ability to coalesce a larger social constituency steadily diminished. After his death, the automobile industry found itself on difficult terrain, and these unstable times would sorely test the legacy he left to his loyal successors at the UAW.

Bibliographic Notes

Walter Reuther has been the subject of several biographies. The best is John Barnard's brief *Walter Reuther and the Rise of the Auto Workers* (1983). Victor G. Reuther's *Brothers Reuther and the Story of the UAWA: A Memoir* (1976) contains a warm and detailed account of the Reuther brothers' youth and their trip to the Soviet Union. This should be read in conjunction with the critical, socialist evaluation Irving Howe and B. J. Widick first offered in 1949, *The UAW and Walter Reuther* (1973). Two uncritical but useful book-length biographies published immediately after Reuther's death are Frank Cormier and William J. Eaton, *Reuther* (1970); and Jean Gould and Lorena Hickok, *Walter Reuther: Labor's Rugged Individualist* (1972). A hostile, right-wing attack is found in Eldorus L. Dayton, *Walter Reuther: Autocrat of the Bargaining Table* (1958).

The UAW has been a well-studied trade union, and twentieth-century labor histories focus much attention on the role played by Walter Reuther. See Jack Stieber, *Governing the UAW* (1962); Bert Cochran, *Labor and Communism: The Conflict that Shaped American Trade Unions* (1977); Roger Keeran, *The Communist Party and the Auto Workers Unions* (1980); and my, *Labor's War at Home: The CIO in World War II* (1982). The UAW factional fight receives much attention in two fine dissertations: Jack W. Skeels, "The Development of Political Stability within the United Automobile Workers Union," (Ph.D. dissertation, University of Wisconsin, 1957); and Martin Halpern, "The Disintegration of the Left-Center Coalition in the UAW, 1945–1950," (Ph.D. dissertation, University of Michigan, 1982). Two very useful studies of UAW automobile industry bargaining are Robert M. Macdonald, *Collective Bargaining in the Automobile Industry* (1963); and William Serrin, *The Company and the Union* (1973).

For those interested in further research, the first stop should be the Walter Reuther Collection at the Archives of Labor History and Urban Affairs, Wayne State University. The Reuther Library there, depository for a mass of UAW materials, also contains a complete file of the union's executive board minutes as well as the papers of such important UAW figures as George Addes, Richard Frankensteen, Victor Reuther, Nat Ganley, Henry Kraus, R. J. Thomas, Maurice Sugar, and Leonard Woodcock. Also vital for following Reuther's career are the papers of Local 174, the UAW-General Motors Department, and the UAW Research Department. The pages of the *United Automobile Worker* and *Solidarity*, the proceedings of some nineteen UAW conventions held during Reuther's life, as well as his separately printed reports to the convention are an indispensable printed source. Of course, these should be supplemented by a reading of newspapers and periodicals, such as the *Detroit Free Press*, the *New York Times*, and *Business Week*, but the weekly publications of the Left are also extremely valuable. These include the *Daily Worker*, *Labor Action*, and the *Militant*.

Jimmy Hoffa: Labor Hero or Labor's Own Foe?

13

Estelle James

In 1957 Jimmy Hoffa, a colorful and controversial labor leader, became head of the International Brotherhood of Teamsters (IBT). His tenure in office was a brief one, marked by charges of corruption and mismanagement by his enemies and political persecution by his friends. Nevertheless, he left his mark on the Teamsters and on the American labor movement to this date.

It was under Jimmy Hoffa that the Teamsters became a centralized bargaining unit, wielding life and death power over the transportation of the country, rather than an agglomeration of separate local fiefdoms, as it was previously. It was a consequence of Jimmy Hoffa that the IBT was expelled from the AFL-CIO, disrupting the unity of the labor federation both economically and politically. Finally, Hoffa won impressive wage and fringe benefit gains for his rank and file, maintaining a close rapport with many of them—and in that sense was the labor leader par excellence—but his tactics and underworld ties raised important (and as yet unresolved) questions about the role of unions in American society.

Hoffa's was a complex and paradoxical mentality, with both public image and self-image often a caricature of reality. He possessed a brilliant mind, but one which in many respects was nonintellectual. He built a well-deserved reputation for ruthlessness, but beneath the tough exterior was a genuine concern for others. He was a devoted family man, although his life centered about his work. He saw enemies and spies all around him, yet was unnecessarily trusting of new acquaintance. He viewed the world in terms of power relationships rather than in terms of right and wrong, yet he was motivated by a deeply instilled sense of morality. His behavior seemed unethical and uncouth to some, while in others his personal drive and magnetism aroused an unswerving loyalty. He brought substantial bread and butter gains to his members but ruthlessly suppressed their rights to control their own locals. He used violence freely, but his most effective weapons were his understanding of the economics of the trucking industry and the intricacies of labor law.

Hoffa's Early Days

James Riddle Hoffa was born on Valentine's Day, 1913, in the small midwestern town of Brazil, Indiana. His father, a coal driller of German-Dutch descent, died seven years later of coal poisoning, leaving a wife, two sons, and two daughters.

Hoffa's mother, a strong-willed Irish woman, first moved the family to nearby Clinton, Indiana, where she took in washing to earn their living. Young Jimmy helped after school by running errands and stringing clam lines in the river. In 1925 Mrs. Hoffa found a manufacturing job and settled down with her children on Detroit's West Side. Jimmy quit school at the end of the seventh grade and sought regular work.

Hoffa's trade union career began in the early years of the depression. At eighteen, he was working in a warehouse of Kroger's, a large midwestern food chain, unloading product cars. In later years, he frequently recalled the long hours and low pay that finally led the men to organize. "We would report in at 4:30 P.M. and stay around as long as they wanted us to. When a boxcar came in they would call a few of us to unload. The rest of the night we sat around gabbing and trying to keep warm. For that we got paid 32 cents an hour—but only for the time we actually worked."

Discontent was rampant among the workers, and their dissatisfactions were mobilized by Hoffa and his buddies, four of whom later rose with him through the Teamsters ranks in Detroit. One night, as a truck filled with strawberries pulled into the warehouse, Hoffa urged the men to refuse to work until management promised higher pay and better working conditions. Anxious to unload their perishable shipment, management capitulated within an hour, and Hoffa had won his first "collective bargaining" contract. Shortly afterwards the group received a charter from the American Federation of Labor (AFL) and in 1932 affiliated with the Teamsters. Hoffa had unpacked his last box of strawberries and became a full-time union official.

The Teamsters Union

The Team Drivers International Union had been chartered by the American Federation of Labor in 1899 to organize drivers of horse-pulled ve-

Photo by Robert E. Wilson, © Ralph James

hicles. When Hoffa joined the union in 1932, the Teamsters had only about eighty thousand members. Many were using powerdriven (rather than horsedriven) vehicles, but the membership was still primarily coal, ice, milk, and bread drivers—the specialized delivery "crafts," as they proudly called themselves.

General local cartage (platform loading and local delivery) was only sporadically unionized. Warehousemen, who at present comprise one-fourth of the membership, were not formally included, nor were a multitude of related production workers, whom Daniel Tobin, the powerful Teamsters president, called "rubbish" and considered outside Teamsters jurisdiction. Tobin did not desire to include the newly emerging highway drivers, a group that currently dominates the Teamsters and through which James R. Hoffa rose to power.

In contrast to Tobin's limited ambitions for his union, certain other leaders—notably old-timer Dave Beck on the West Coast and young Jimmy Hoffa in the Midwest—were anxious to expand the Teamsters' jurisdiction. This issue served as a source of great conflict within the union, with Beck and Hoffa eventually victorious. Today the IBT boasts truck drivers as its nucleus, but it also includes organized workers from a wide variety of other occupations and industries. In this way the Teamsters, with almost 2 million members, has become the largest union in the country, the bargaining representative for one out of every twelve organized workers.

Under Tobin, power was centered in the local unions. The local commanded jurisdiction over its craft within a single city, governed itself, and negotiated its contracts. If the local leaders paid their per capita tax (forty cents monthly for each member) to the international and had their own affairs under control, Tobin confined himself to pouring forth paternalistic advice in the international's monthly magazine.

When several Teamsters locals existed in the same locality, they banded together into a joint council for solving organizational, jurisdictional, and political problems—as they still do today. Tobin discouraged the growth of other intermediary bodies, fearing competition for the international and himself. By the 1940s a few states had established their own conferences, designed to accomplish on a broader scale what the joint councils did on the city level. However, the major trade union functions—negotiating and administering the collective agreement—continued to reside largely in the local until Hoffa gradually assumed control.

In contrast to his predecessors, Hoffa centralized collective bargaining power wherever he moved. As early as 1940, as negotiating chairman of the Central States Drivers Council (CSDC), he bargained for all midwestern highway drivers, the first and for many years the only example of areawide bargaining in the Teamsters. Later, as president of the IBT and as negotiator for the entire truck freight industry, he shifted the locus of authority away from local or regional bodies and toward the international.

Hoffa's Rise to Power

But this was all far in the future in the 1930s, when Hoffa was establishing his power base in Detroit. Teamsters organization in Detroit was weak during the early depression years. Locals were small, debt-ridden, and split by dissension. Fist fights, picket line brawls, and intensive interunion squabbles were standard operating procedure. The time was ripe for a leader who could take control and bring order out of chaos, and Hoffa was that leader.

Gradually he came to dominate the city's teamster movement; he became well known as "the man to call on if you want to get things done in Detroit." By the Second World War, already controlling the largest Teamsters local in Michigan's largest city, Hoffa was anxious to spread his domain over the rest of the state. In 1942 he organized and became the first chairman of the Michigan Conference of Teamsters, a loose federation of locals. Hoffa's grand scheme was to unionize the small outlying towns in Michigan and obtain a single statewide contract, for which he would negotiate, in place of the many independently bargained agreements that then existed. This was a harbinger of his future goals and techniques and of the mixed reception his schemes would evoke.

Both employers and local unions resented their potential loss of autonomy, a resentment with which Hoffa was to become better acquainted as he extended his bargaining power in the years to come. But with assistance from the international, which viewed Hoffa as a dynamic young leader, he forced through his plan. The employers were compelled to agree to his terms by means of a slowdown to 15 miles an hour (in place of an unlawful wartime strike). The following report from Ray Bennett, on a meeting of Kalamazoo rank and filers in December 1942, illustrates the local union antagonism toward Hoffa and the tactics used to over ride it:

> Cripe and one of the other Business Agents told the reasons why they had objected to the State-Wide Contract—namely; that he claimed Jimmy Hoffa was a dictator; also that the State-Wide Contract was being controlled and handled out of Detroit; . . . that they were going to put through their [own] contract. Just as the chairman was going to put the motion to a vote, I rose to my feet and told the membership and officers, in no uncertain terms, that I was at this meeting at the instructions of the International . . . and if they valued their organization, they had better change their mind and their attitude

then and there or there would not be any organization. A few of the more reasonable members soon grasped the meaning of this, and a motion was put on the floor that the question of the city contract be tabled.

Even before his control over Michigan was consolidated, Hoffa was ambitiously plotting beyond its borders. In 1937 the Central States Drivers Council had been set up by the Minneapolis Teamsters to organize and bargain centrally for all midwestern over-the-road drivers, a group that was just beginning its rapid growth. Hoffa was quick to see the potential in this body and threw the full support of Detroit behind the council, which met with opposition from many independent-minded locals.

In 1940, then only twenty-seven years old, Hoffa became negotiating chairman of the council and in 1941 vice-president as well, positions he continued to hold for the next two decades. However it was not until the postwar period, having control in Detroit and Michigan, that he began to dominate the CSDC. During the ensuing decade, Hoffa, who never drove a truck, became the bargaining champion of the tough highway driver and expanded his power throughout the central and southern states. In the late forties and early fifties his Detroit organizers were running strikes and locals as far afield as St. Louis and Kansas City, and Hoffa supporters were moving to the fore in Illinois and Indiana. In 1953 his areawide control was recognized when he became head of the new Central Conference of Teamsters, and by 1955 he was negotiating contracts for all midwestern and southern over-the-road and local cartage drivers. This accomplished, he directed his attention toward a takeover of the East and West, culminating in the 1964 national truck freight agreement.

Hoffa's Goals: Centralized Bargaining for Uniform Conditions

What were the principles and methods that guided Hoffa in his drive to power? As Hoffa spread his organizing campaigns to hostile areas, he carried with him an atmosphere of intimidation. Sabotaging of equipment, vandalism, gunshots in the night, and bricks thrown into the windshields of moving trucks were all part of his arsenal of weapons. Gangsters and thugs were part of the scene on both sides of the bargaining table, and Hoffa was proud of describing how he used them to his advantage. But, in retrospect, his most important modus vivendi, and his legacy for the future, was the use of ingenious leverage techniques, with the ultimate goal of centralized areawide bargaining designed to establish uniform wages, hours, and working conditions.

Hoffa inherited this goal and the basic technique for achieving it, from

Farrell Dobbs, a Minneapolis Teamsters leader who founded the Central States Drivers Council. A Trotskyite, Dobbs left the Teamsters abruptly in 1940 to head the Socialist Workers party, leaving a vacuum in the CSDS that was quickly filled by Hoffa. To Dobbs and Hoffa, organizing highway drivers, though the *sine qua non*, was not enough. Rather, they aimed at centralized areawide bargaining that would bring uniform working conditions to all truckdrivers. As Dobbs stated in 1938: "We have had sufficient experience to understand that the only solution to the problems of the over-the-road trucking industry lies in the establishment of uniform labor conditions for the trade areas. We are further aware that if we permit ourselves to be sidetracked into a maze of subregional and individual city negotiations that the only outcome will be to perpetuate the present chaotic conditions."

The basis for this point of view lies in the economic structure of the over-the-road trucking industry. Low capital requirements have meant easy entry, and intense competition has consequently prevailed among numerous small-scale entrepreneurs despite the restraining influence of government regulation. In such a setting the elasticity of demand for the trucking service—and thus for the labor that produces it—is significantly greater for a single firm than for the entire industry; that is, a price hike by a single firm would result in a much higher percentage loss of business than would obtain for the industry as a whole if all firms raised their prices together. In the former case customers could simply transfer their orders to a different company, but in the latter they would have to make the more difficult shift to another form of transportation to escape the new rates. Hence, the strong desire for standardized price-setting (which has successfully come to pass with government regulatory assistance) in such naturally competitive industries as trucking and agriculture.

Several other economic facts are also relevant. Profits are relatively low for many carriers, a condition that would undoubtedly be more widespread without government intervention. Labor costs consume the largest share of gross revenue. And in highway trucking the city in which a company hires its labor is subject to rapid change.

Under these circumstances a wage increase substantially raises costs, often at the expense of an already low level of profits. In the absence of centralized bargaining for uniform conditions, each individual carrier would find it very difficult to pass these higher costs along to the consumer, but very easy to shift its hiring base from a high- to a low-wage community. For example, on a run from city A to city B, with workers divided equally between the two initially, the operator could nullify a union's superior but localized negotiations in city A merely by relocating all its hiring in B.

Union members in A would then have to choose between no jobs at higher wages or unchanged wages at their old level of employment.

If locals in cities A and B bargain jointly for the same remuneration on a company-by-company basis, this effect is avoided. But the union will still meet extremely stiff resistance to wage increases on the part of individual carriers who fear their lower-cost competitors. The most reasonable solution, as recognized by Dobbs first and Hoffa after him, was centralized bargaining, covering all the employers in a broadly defined area. This automatically eliminated the type of employment shift described above. In addition, by acting together employers could expect little loss of business when they translated wage gains into higher prices (moving along the relatively inelastic industry demand curve)—and they were in a stronger position to convince the appropriate government authorities that a rate increase was necessary.* Thus, Dobbs's—and Hoffa's—goal of centralized bargaining was a logical development in a competitive, mobile industry.

Hoffa's Leverage Techniques

Besides setting the goals of the CSDC, Hoffa also developed its imaginative and singularly effective modus operandi, the systematic use of *leverage*. Broadly speaking, leverage implies the use of a stronger situation to advance an organizing or bargaining aim in a weaker situation. Hoffa and his cohorts evolved three major variants of the leverage device. The latter two have been increasingly constrained legally since 1947, but have not yet been completely eliminated.

The first example of leverage is the simplest. Employer X may have terminals in cities A and B. Perhaps he is organized only in A, or perhaps the union is merely stronger there. The union can take advantage of this situation by "sympathetic action," that is, by striking or threatening to strike in A until the employer capitulates in B, induces his workers to join, and signs the desired contract.

The second type of leverage involves two or more interrelated carriers. Because of its highly integrated nature the trucking industry is particularly susceptible to this classic form of secondary pressure—more so than any

*That Hoffa's bargaining strategy recognized the latter consideration was illustrated during a major negotiation in the summer of 1962. When asked if he anticipated a strike, he replied, "Only if we need one to convince the ICC [Interstate Commerce Commission] to grant a rate increase."

310

other industry except perhaps the construction and garment trades. Since no trucking line travels every route in the United States, no firm is wholly independent. Thus the right to "interline" is usually essential for survival; carrier X travels from city A to city B, where it transfer its freight to carrier Y, which engages in local pickup and delivery or continues onward to city C. Sometimes carrier Y would be put out of business if its relationship with X was broken. If X is more easily subject to direct union pressures than Y, a simple way of forcing Y's acquiescence to an organizing or bargaining demand is to compel X not to interline freight until Y agrees to the union's proposals.

A third kind of leverage may be employed against firms not in the trucking industry but dependent upon trucks for pickups and deliveries. Once local cartage is organized, drivers (in the absence of prohibitory legislation) may refuse to service establishments that are nonunion or fail to sign the desired contract. This can quickly place insuperable pressure upon companies that might otherwise be able to conduct their business for a prolonged period with nonunion labor or strikebreakers. Thus Teamsters support has been indispensable for certain weaker unions of relatively low-skilled workers, such as launderers, bakers, and retail clerks. Furthermore, Teamsters expansion into nontrucking industries, such as warehousing, canning, and brewing, has seemed too inviting to resist and has involved the union in numerous jurisdictional disputes.

The use of leverage for extending unionization is known within the Teamsters as "leapfrog organizing," a process that was widely employed during the formative stages of the CSDC. Using this technique, the Teamsters spread their domain from terminal to terminal of the same company, and then onward to different over-the-road carriers in the area.

The growing number of Teamsters highway drivers served as the strategic link for bringing local cartage into the fold. Unionized over-the-road drivers would refuse to accept freight from or turn shipments over to unorganized local cartage workers. And after local pickup, delivery, and dock men were successfully coerced, they provided the leverage by which to "leapfrog" into other industries and nontrucking occupations. As Hoffa was fond of saying, "Once you have the road men, you can get the local cartage, and once you have the local cartage, you can get anyone you want."

The leverage technique enables the union to choose the battleground. And once victorious against the first and weakest set of employers, it can use these for additional leverage against the next set, and so fan out. This was the method so carefully taught by Dobbs in the thirties and later ingeniously modified and perfected by Hoffa.

Leverage in Organizing: The Secondary Boycott

Hoffa used these techniques both in organizing and bargaining. In organizing, the secondary boycott was his major technique through the thirties and forties. Eschewing National Labor Relations Board-run secret ballot elections as the chief mechanism for determining whether a group of workers wished to be organized, Hoffa instead applied pressure directly on the employer to sign a collective bargaining contract.

Organized carriers were compelled, by a threatened strike, to cut off interlining with or making deliveries to nonunion firms, which were thereby induced to negotiate union-shop contracts that would compel all workers to join the IBT. On some occasions this top-down approach was chosen because employer opposition restrained the free expression of the workers' will. But in many cases it was simply cheaper, faster, and more effective to apply leverage against employers rather than to try persuading workers to vote for the Teamsters. The troublesome implications of this strategy for union democracy will be discussed later in this essay.

During the late forties and fifties, legislation combined with administrative-judicial rulings increasingly restricted organizing through secondary boycott in favor of employee self-determination through secret elections. For example, in 1947 the Taft-Hartley Act, Section 8b4, made it an unfair labor practice for a union to strike to force any "person to cease using, selling, handling, transporting, or otherwise dealing . . . with any other person." It seemed that the union could no longer compel an organized employer to break off his business relations with an unorganized firm. Section 8b4 taken by itself did not frighten Hoffa nearly so much as Section 303, which gave an injured employer the right to sue for damages.

However, a temporary respite quickly developed in the act's restrictions on secondary boycotts. Teamsters contracts, like those of many other unions, had long contained a clause enabling their members to "refuse to go through the picket line of a Union or refuse to handle 'unfair goods.'" The Democratic appointees to the National Labor Relations Board, which administers the Wagner and Taft-Hartley Acts, held that such "hot cargo" clauses in effect exempted the union from the Taft-Hartley secondary boycott prohibition. Thus Hoffa could legally apply his leverage power in an organizing or bargaining dispute during the most crucial period in his expansionary drive—the late forties to mid-fifties—simply by ordering his members and their employers to abide by the hot cargo clause and cease dealing with any company he designated.

Many truckers were happy to go along with the hot cargo clause, which helped to eliminate their lower-cost, nonunion, potentially rate-cutting competitors. The larger companies, in particular, seized the opportunity to buy the operating rights of their disappearing rivals. In some cases, the boycott was probably initiated by organized employers who encouraged Hoffa to use the hot cargo clause, thereby suppressing competition but avoiding antitrust violation.

A Republican administration in 1953 brought increased constraints on union activities. The new personnel of the National Labor Relations Board tightened their interpretation of the Taft-Hartley's secondary boycott proscription and reversed the board's earlier stand on hot cargo. Moreover, the Landrum-Griffin Act of 1959 outlawed hot cargo arrangements and tightened Taft-Hartley's secondary boycott restraints. Had these prohibitions come a little earlier, Hoffa's acquisition of power might have been seriously impeded. But by the late 1950s Hoffa was already firmly entrenched, and the Teamsters were well organized and were able to use other, still legal leverage techniques in their collective negotiations.

Leverage in Bargaining: Common Expiration Dates and Divide and Conquer

Hoffa's use of leverage was even more effective in the course of collective bargaining, once a firm was organized. One of his major techniques was the use of common contract expiration dates, which enabled him to utilize his power in a stronger situation to extend his influence where he was weaker. Since the passage of the Taft-Hartley Act and particularly since the National Labor Relations Board (NLRB) and Landrum-Griffin attacks on the hot cargo clause, this technique was used increasingly to evade the secondary boycott ban.

The device is simple enough to describe. Collective agreements with employers in "controlled" sectors, where Hoffa was strong, were manipulated to terminate at the same time as contracts in "uncontrolled" sectors. Since this was no easy matter to arrange, the dates were sometimes close, rather than identical. Once Hoffa had the contract dates in line, he refused to sign in the controlled sector until the uncontrolled sector capitulated.

Hoffa's use of this technique is probably best illustrated by his movement into the South shortly after World War II. The number of organized southern over-the-road drivers was small, wages were low and not uniform. As a result, employers tended to move their headquarters to the South and operate from there into the Midwest, instead of vice versa. In some cases they hired southern Teamsters; usually, they hired nonunion labor. In either event, the CSDC appeared to be pricing itself out of the market and losing jobs for its members.

One of the first tasks faced by Hoffa at the close of World War II was the elimination of this deleterious effect on employment by organizing highway drivers in the South. The "leapfrogging" technique was effectively used. Carriers operating in the central states found themselves struck and picketed, unable to pursue their activities in the highly organized Midwest unless they hired Teamsters members in the South as well. Next Hoffa maneuvered a common expiration date for the southern contracts and the CSDC and refused to sign the latter until a comparable agreement was reached with the former. Again unwilling to take a strike in the powerful Midwest, which was a fulcrum point for interstate shipping, the employers agreed to raise southern wages to the central states' level within five years. A series of short strikes, buttressed by secondary hot cargo pressures from interliners, brough the intrastate long-line carriers of the Deep South into the Teamsters uniform agreement by the early 1950s.

Closely related to Hoffa's use of the leverage principle was his "divide and conquer" strategy, a technique that was extremely effective because of the great diversity within trucking. Because of the disparity of interests and attitudes on the employers' side of the table, Hoffa was able to play one off against the other. For example, carriers on short hauls wanted to keep the drivers' daily guarantee low, while those on long runs were more concerned about the basic mileage and hourly rates. Private carriers, for whom Teamsters wages were only a small fraction of total costs, were particuarly anxious to avoid a strike that would shut down their entire business. The numerous labor relations associations into which these employers are organized were likewise antagonistic and competitive toward each other. Thus, on several occasions, Hoffa was able to reach his desired goal with one group of carriers and then proceed to impose these terms on the others.

When entering a new area, such as New England or the West in 1961, Hoffa sometimes found himself confronted with a hostile and seemingly united group of employers intent upon opposing his program for uniformity with the CSDC. To counteract this resistance on one occasion, a transcontinental line threatened to withdraw from the statewide truckers' association, thereby cutting off its large contribution of per capita dues, unless the other members capitulated to Hoffa's demands. In another case, much to the dismay of the local association, transcontinental carriers were "persuaded" to negotiate as "independents" and to settle on Hoffa's terms. If the local truckers refused to accept the same conditions, Hoffa warned they would be struck and their accounts assumed by the "independents" who had signed the contract and thus would continue to operate. Anticipating a long strike, in which their drivers might be working for their competitors and some shipping customers permanently lost, the resentful local truckers were almost invariably afraid to resist.

The Open-End Grievance Procedure

Hoffa's use of the open-end grievance procedure for leverage became increasingly important as legal restrictions on secondary boycotts tightened. As a general practice in American unionized industries, when a worker feels wronged by management, he files a grievance, which is then evaluated by union and management representatives.

Almost all grievance procedures are "closed"—that is, the terminal stage consists of arbitration by an impartial third party, and the union agrees not to strike to enforce its point of view. Most labor leaders strongly favor arbitration as the final stage of the grievance procedure for it helps ensure that justice rather than power is the basis for settlement and relieves their obligation to call a work stoppage over a grievance involving only one individual.

Hoffa stood virtually unique among American labor leaders in opposing this sytem. Instead, he preferred what he called an "open-end grievance procedure," in which there is no arbitration and the union retains the right to strike without exposure to damage suits under Section 301 of the Taft-Hartley Act. Thus, under Hoffa, grievances were settled in a context of power. Furthermore, the open-end grievance procedure became a major Hoffa control mechanism between negotiations, for it permitted him to threaten a strike whenever he wanted to, anywhere in the country. Hoffa's regulation of grievance decisions also buttressed his domination of the union and helped explain why many local officials went along with his drive toward centralized bargaining despite the resultant lessening of their own status and authority.

What were some of the ways in which Hoffa gained an advantage through the open-end grievance procedure? He used it occasionally to renegotiate a contract, obtaining more favorable terms as interpretive problems arose. Also, in a collective bargaining structure that stresses uniformity, he used it to reap the benefits of a discriminating monopolist. A contract could be enforced more stringently against employers who could affort to provide better conditions, while retaining the advantages derived from apparent equality.

Indeed, a belief in uneven enforcement pervaded many central states carriers. But the major reason was not the discriminating monopolist rationale, nor was it necessarily evidence of corruption and personal payoffs. To further his collective bargaining goals, Hoffa found it helpful to buy good will on both sides of the table, and he did so by granting or withholding favors through the grievance procedure.

For example, employers were induced to break ranks with the other carriers in Hoffa's divide-and-conquer bargaining technique by the implicit promise of grievance procedure benefits. Conversely, an employer was warned that if he failed to cooperate, Hoffa would throw the book at him in the grievance meetings. When a carrier incurred Hoffa's wrath, locals were instructed to "dig up grievances, bring them to the JAC [Joint Area Committee] and we'll deadlock them and strike." Similarly, an organized carrier knew that if he voluntarily refused to tender freight to a nonunion firm or one with which the Teamsters had a bargaining dispute, he would receive friendly treatment on grievances. Or, if he failed to do so, Hoffa could "induce" him to reconsider by threatening to deadlock and strike over upcoming cases. If necessary, the work stoppage ensued, strategically placed to cut off interlining with the unorganized company.

Leverage Against Recalcitrant Locals

Under Tobin, Teamsters chiefs jealously guarded their local autonomy and resented any encroachment by the international or intermediate bodies. And the negotiation process, often the most interesting part of the job and the most rewarding in terms of popularity and prestige among the membership, was not easily surrendered. Hoffa's power over the "controlled" group of employers helped him overcome this internal union pressure for local autonomy.

If a particular local refused to go along with his uniform area pact and tried to hold out for higher compensation, Hoffa conveyed his displeasure to friendly employers operating out of his home territory. He urged the carriers to stand firm against the local's "excessive" demands and to route their trucks around the city in question, breaking freight at another point if a strike should occur. He assured management representatives that the local was being pressured to capitulate and informally warned the employers of retaliation elsewhere if they failed to cooperate with his scheme.

Uncooperative locals were sometimes consolidated into larger units, under friendly leadership, of course. The desire to move toward a uniform areawide contract in local cartage in the Midwest helps explain the merger movement that Hoffa pressed for in the interest of greater efficiency in the early fifties. In other cases, he threatened recalcitrant locals that, unless

316

they towed the line, they would lose grievances in the Teamsters' open-end procedure.

Union opposition in the New York-New Jersey and San Francisco-Oakland areas in the early 1960s was successfully countermanded by this device. Such behavior, of course, antagonized local officials and rank and filers. To those who cried "dictator" or "sellout," Hoffa would retort that he could not permit the selfishness of the few to interfere with the welfare of the many. He argued that his system of centralized negotiations and uniform contract demands would, in the long run, bring maximum wages and employment to the entire group.

In fact, a study of the wages and working conditions won by Hoffa shows that he almost always raised wages when he took over an area. Initially he raised CSDC earning relative to other Teamsters contracts and other industries. During the fifties he was busy organizing southern drivers and obtaining for them the same conditions he had won earlier in the Midwest. The relative advantages won for the Midwest and South were dispelled in the early sixties when Hoffa moved into the East and West and did for them what he had already accomplished in the central states. Consistent with his emphasis on uniformity, differentials among job classifications were also narrowed or eliminated, thereby disrupting traditional status distinctions and hurting certain groups, but most truck freight workers had higher wages by the earlier sixties because of Jimmy Hoffa.

A National Agreement—1964

Constantly exploiting and building upon his various leverage techniques, Hoffa worked toward a national agreement for trucking in 1964. Article 49 of the CSDC's 1961 road contract declared that "the parties in this Agreement accept the principle of a National Over-the-Road Agreement and are willing to enter into negotiations for the purpose of negotiating such National Agreement." A similar clause appeared as Article 42 of the CSDC's local cartage agreement and in practically every other major road and cartage contract in the country, virtually all of which were to expire between January 31 and August 3, 1964.

In addition, most contracts were already modeled after those of the CSDC, to facilitate conversion to nationwide bargaining. As early as the spring of 1962, Hoffa was calling meetings of "friendly" employers so that they could study how to overcome resistance to a national contract. Thus, by the end of 1963 the stage was set for national negotiations, led by Hoffa and his CSDC, to encompass virtually the entire truck freight industry.

The 1964 master contrast was qualified by numerous regional supplements and local riders (or exceptions); beset by legal and political difficulties, Hoffa made no further effort to standardize conditions. To an impressive degree, however, by 1964 he had established the national agreement and wage uniformity that he had set his sights on almost three decades before.

Hoffa's Downfall

In October 1957 Hoffa was elected IBT president. Already well on his way to controlling negotiations in trucking throughout the nation, Hoffa planned to combine the roles of collective bargaining chief and political head of state—in contrast with his two presidential predecessors, Dan Tobin and Dave Beck, who were largely uninterested in bargaining. But just as he reached the apex of his power, his downfall had also begun. Ironically, the same "life is a jungle" philosophy, the wheeling and dealing, willingness to skate close to the law, and use of violence and unsavory friends that brought him success also contained the seeds of his ultimate destruction.

The Senate Select Committee on Improper Activities in the Labor Management Field (popularly known as the McClellan Committee), with an energetic young counsel named Robert Kennedy, had recently begun investigations into "vice and corruption" in labor unions, and the Teamsters quickly caught their attention. The government's attack on Hoffa began in March 1957, with his arrest for allegedly attempting to bribe a congressional investigator. It continued for over two years, with Hoffa appearing as a frequent witness, during which time his darker side was vividly exposed to public scrutiny.

The McClellan Committee charges against Hoffa fell into two broad categories. The first involved allegations of financial malpractice, including the misuse of union funds and the acceptance of payoffs from employers; the second, the resort to undemocratic procedures, racketeering, and violence. For example, Hoffa had encouraged Teamsters members to buy lots in Sun Valley, a land development-retirement community near Orlando, Florida. He had placed $500,000 from the treasury of his home local, No. 299 of Detroit, in an Orlando bank, to induce the bank to grant a loan to the project's promoter, Henry Lower. When Lower diverted this loan to other uses, Sun Valley went bankrupt, the bank refused to return Local 299's money, and Robert Kennedy revealed that Hoffa owned a forty-five percent option on the property.

A more lucrative financial venture involved a truck-leasing company, Test Fleet, which was jointly owned by Hoffa's wife and the wife of his associate, Bert Brennan. Kennedy argued that the firm that leased these trucks did so as a payoff for Hoffa's cooperation in settling a Teamsters strike several years before.

Hoffa was also accused of steering the union's health and welfare fund to an insurance company that was not the most favorable bidder. He forced this decision on his fellow trustees, Kennedy claimed, at a cost of over a million dollars to the fund, in order to help his friends and strengthen his underworld ties.

In other cases, Hoffa was charged with using hoodlums to extend his control. One such incident allegedly occurred in New York City in 1955–56, when Hoffa induced Dave Beck, then president of IBT, to charter seven new locals, said to be dominated by underworld elements, just in time for them to cast their votes for his preferred candidate in a close contest for the presidency of the city's joint council. Kennedy dubbed these groups "paper locals" because they had practically no members. Close Mafia connections were alleged to exist in other incidents as well.

The McClellan Committee investigations precipitated two indictments against Hoffa during 1957–58—the congressional bribery case and a wiretap conspiracy case, in which Hoffa was prosecuted for spying on his subordinates with illegal listening devices. Both ended in acquittal. In addition, he was indicted in November 1960 for mail and wire fraud in connection with Sun Valley, an indictment that was eventually dropped.

The interest of the Justice Department in Hoffa intensified after John F. Kennedy became president and appointed his brother, Robert, attorney general. A "get Hoffa squad" was established that, Hoffa believed, followed him wherever he went, tapped his phone, opened his mail, and beamed listening devices on him. In addition, he believed that Robert Kennedy used pressure tactics to force others to move against him; that, with this purpose in mind, the Internal Revenue Service combed the tax returns of Teamsters officials and key employers; that the Federal Bureau of Investigation stole Teamsters records and then accused the union leaders of destroying them; and that Pension Fund borrowers were indicted on a variety of charges. In each case, he claimed, the Justice Department threatened prosecution unless the individual broke with Hoffa or testified against him or his associates. Whether these alleged civil liberties violations are valid we do not know for sure, but we do know the final outcome of this classic struggle between two fiercely competitive antagonists, one believing it was his responsibility to root out evil and corruption, the other believing he was the victim of political persecution and hypocrisy.

In 1962 Hoffa stood trial for accepting illegal payments from an employer in the Test Fleet case. The jurors split 7 to 5 in Hoffa's favor, thereby enabling him to avoid conviction, but this merely set the stage for another indictment, in which Hoffa and several associates were charged with jury tampering; in March 1964 he was convicted and sentenced to eight years in prison. Four months later he was convicted and sentenced to five years in jail for mail and wire fraud growing out of his activities as trustee of the Teamsters' $300-million Central and Southern States Pension Fund and his long involvement with Sun Valley. After extensive unsuccessful appeals that went all the way to the Supreme Court, Hoffa finally entered Lewisburg Prison in March 1967.

The End

By 1968 the political tides were turning once again. In November the Democrats lost the national election and the following January Richard Nixon, whom Hoffa had supported since his race against Kennedy in 1960, took office as president of the United States. Negotiations immediately began for Nixon to release Hoffa from prison, and they bore fruit three years later.

In December 1971, after Hoffa had been in prison for four and one-half years, Nixon signed an executive grant of clemency, commuting his sentence and making him eligible for immediate release. The commutation required that Hoffa resign the various union offices that he had continued to hold while in prison and that he agree not to engage in any "direct or indirect management of any labor organization prior to March 1980."

Announcing that he would devote himself to prison reform efforts, Hoffa began traveling around the country on speaking engagements. Speculation centered on whether he would regain his former control of the Teamsters and he did indeed initiate legal proceedings to overturn the restrictions in his commutation order. But Hoffa's health and energy had been impaired by his years in prison. Moreover, he had reemerged to a world very different from the one he had left four and one-half years earlier. The Teamsters were now led by his former friend, Frank Fitzsimmons, who had assumed the presidency as a "caretaker" but who was not anxious to give up his position of power. New political connections, new working relationships had been forged. People were comfortable with the status quo; there seemed no room left for Hoffa in the tight structure that he had so carefully built. It was only a matter of time until some of his previous associates began to wonder if he could be trusted; he knew too many secrets; he was a dangerous enemy.

On July 30, 1975, on his way to a meeting with a leading underworld figure, perhaps intending to iron out his future comeback plans, Hoffa was seen getting into a maroon car allegedly driven by his foster son, Chuckie O'Brien (with whom he had recently had a falling out). He was never heard from again, nor has the mystery of his disappearance ever been solved.

So faded from the scene one of the strongest and most controversial labor leaders of our day.

How can we assess the legacy that he left us? Hoffa, in effect, reshaped the Teamsters Union and, beyond that, the trucking industry. The industry is undoubtedly less chaotic, less competitive, and more costly than it was before Hoffa appeared on the scene. Teamsters bargaining is more centralized and wages more uniform than would have been the case without his leadership.

The labor movement as a whole, however, is more fragmented than it would have been without the McClellen Committee revelations and their aftermath. Hoffa had never been "one of the boys" in the AFL-CIO, and the federation was embarrassed by the publicity about financial malpractice and labor racketeering. Based on a detailed report by the AFL-CIO's Ethical Practices Committee, which accepted all the unfavorable congressional findings, the labor federation voted in December 1957 to expel the Teamsters. Veteran Teamsters officials smarted with outrage and declared they were being used as scapegoats to prevent antilabor legislation and investigations of other unions. But George Meany insisted that the IBT was not acceptable to the federation. The Teamsters remain outside of the AFL-CIO to this day.

The rise and demise of Jimmy Hoffa also raises basic questions about the desirability of multiemployer bargaining, the relative importance of bread-and-butter gains versus participatory democracy, and the trade-off between group welfare and individual rights.

Centralization of power went hand-in-hand with Hoffa's trade union gains. Is such centralization good or bad? This issue arises in the labor movement, in corporate agglomerations, and even more so, in government. As an economist, I am tempted to do a benefit-cost analysis. On the credit side, centralization permits a union to take advantage of certain economies of scale—for example, in negotiating and collecting information. Industrywide bargaining may make employers more amenable to settling, since they know that all their competitors will be facing the same wage increase, eventually to be passed along to their customers in the form of higher prices. A uniform expiration date, furthermore, gives the union the power to strike selectively the weakest link in the chain. These arguments apply especially to the over-the-road truck driver, where the competition is mainly nationwide, rather than to cartage and warehousing, where the market is local. However, the latter groups can benefit in their negotiations from ties to the former, who can refuse to "interline" with recalcitrant local employers. Thus, from a strategic bargaining point of view, Hoffa's drive for centralization made sense. Centralized bargaining may be even more important to the union and the industry in the current deregulatory environment, since it achieves some of the same (anticompetitive) ends as does regulation.

While many Teamsters benefited from the centralization brought about by Hoffa, others lost. The latter include those (e.g., on the West Coast) whose particular local situation made it possible for them to do better under conditions of pure local bargaining. These members constitute a clearly identifiable and vociferous anti-Hoffa group. Another, less identifiable group also suffered: people who lost their jobs as employer costs rose and people who might have obtained Teamsters jobs if Hoffa had not raised wages as much as he did. This wage-employment trade-off was especially significant in the South, where Hoffa unionized, in part, to preserve Teamsters jobs up North. Thus the higher southern wages were gained at the expense of expanded southern employment.

Finally, a third group lost out—those who cared deeply about local control and participatory democracy. Centralization may give the union increased control over employers, but it also gives workers decreased control over their own union. For those who want to run their own affairs, control their own destinies, and make their own mistakes, this is an important cost of Hoffa-style unionism.

Such people, however, are in the minority in American unions. Most workers appear to value bread-and-butter gains over the opportunity to participate. Indeed, many do not bother to attend union meetings or to vote in elections, nor do most union leaders encourage more participation. In this respect, the Teamsters are not very different from the typical "respectable" American union. The large majority of Teamsters may have been getting exactly what they wanted out of Hoffa's leadership, and that may help explain why he was able to retain the loyalty of hundreds of thousands of rank and filers despite the disclosures brought out by the McClellan Committee and the trials.

Closely related to the centralization issue was Hoffa's consistent willingness to submerge the interests of the individual for the welfare of the group. This was particularly apparent in his suppression of local dissidents, who were squashed (sometimes literally) if they interfered with Hoffa's plans for the union as a whole. This was clear in his extensive leapfrog organizing whereby, in order to benefit those already in the Teamsters, nonunion workers were forced to join without the benefit of choice through secret ballot. Another example was Hoffa's wheeling and dealing with employers through the open-end grievance procedure. It may have been in the group's interest for Hoffa to reward cooperative and punish recalcitrant employers, but this also meant that some of his members received less job protection than others; unequal enforcement of contract on employers meant an unequal contract for workers.

The distinction between individual and group welfare and between minority rights and majority rule are central to an evaluation of Hoffa's overall role and merit. Those who would emphasize the individual will be shocked and repelled by many of these techniques, while those who would rank the group as supreme are more likely to pay him deference for skillfully and imaginatively using every means at his disposal to enhance the power of his union and, concomitantly, himself.

Bibliographic Notes

For a fuller development of the themes introduced in this essay see Ralph and Estelle James, *Hoffa and the Teamsters* (1965), which was drawn on heavily (with permission from Van Nostrand) for this essay. The book is based on extensive access to Teamsters files, numerous interviews with union officials and critics, and personal observations of Jimmy Hoffa in action by the authors. It also contains an analysis of the huge Teamsters pension fund, which Hoffa so mismanaged that Congress passed regulatory legislation. Robert D. Leiter, *The Teamsters Union* (1957), is valuable in outlining the union's economic impact prior to Hoffa's presidency, and Sam Romer, *The International Brotherhood of Teamsters* (1962), describes the union's form of governance.

There are several books that focus upon corruption within the union and Hoffa's problems with the law. The two most recent works are Dan Moldea, *The Hoffa Wars* (1978), and Stephen Brill, *The Teamsters* (1978). Walter Sheridan, an investigator for the McClellan Committee, presented most of the committee's findings in *The Fall and Rise of Jimmy Hoffa* (1972). Robert F. Kennedy, the committee's chief counsel, revealed his feelings toward Hoffa in *The Enemy Within* (1960), while the Teamsters' leader presented his side of the case, as well as a sense of how he would like to be remembered, in *Hoffa: The Real Story* (1975).

George Meany: Labor's Organization Man

14

Robert H. Zieger

George Meany was an organization man. For almost sixty years he acted as a business agent, administrator, lobbyist, and spokesman. He never walked a picket line, organized a local, or led a strike. A product of ancient, exclusivist traditions of craft unionism, he climbed the bureaucratic ladder to become in 1955 the dominant figure in a national labor movement embracing all sorts of workers and members of every race and occupation. During his twenty-four-year tenure at the center of labor's world, Meany articulated a public philosophy of American exceptionalism, laborite Keyneseanism, and adamant anticommunism. Within the labor movement itself—Meany's most comfortable arena—his greatest achievement lay in engineering the merger of the American Federation of Labor (AFL) and the Congress of Industrial Organizations (CIO) in 1955 and subsequently, as he put it in 1970, "holding the boys together." His emphasis on laborite political and legislative action and his own forceful personality helped bring the labor movement into public life as never before, both during his leadership of the New York State Federation of Labor and his presidency of the AFL-CIO. Critics found him judgmental, dogmatic, and disdainful of the masses of unorganized workers and sometimes of his own membership. They accused him of rigid adherence to sterile formulas and of remoteness from the real world of work and protest. Meany, however, largely ignored such judgments, as he did those of conservatives who condemned him as a power-hungry subversive. With each year of leadership that passed he became ever more convinced that his blend of practicality and principle reflected accurately the values and aspirations of American workers.

324

William* George Meany was born August 16, 1894, the second of eight surviving children. His parents, Michael Meany and Anne Cullen Meany, were native-born children of the pre–Civil War Irish immigration. When he was five, the family moved from Harlem to the sparsely-settled Port Morris section of the Bronx, a neighborhood of small factories and single-family dwellings populated by Irish, German, and Anglo-Scots mechanics, building tradesmen, and craftsmen. Formal schooling for George ended at age fourteen after a childhood of close family relationships and stereotypical—almost bucolic—pleasures. From his grade school days onward, young George earned pocket money running errands and making deliveries. On leaving school, he took a job with a Manhattan advertising firm. Determined, however, to follow in the footsteps of his father, a plumber and local union official, he signed on as an unskilled helper at age sixteen. At his father's insistence, he attended trade school at night to prepare for the journeyman's test.

Union affairs, politics, Irish nationalism, and Roman Catholicism infused the neighborhood and family in which George Meany matured. The family's little house near 133d Street served as a meeting place for union members and officials. Michael Meany, president of the large Bronx plumbers' local, was active also in Democratic party precinct politics. The highly intelligent young George did well in school, but drill and routine bored him. He received his real education, he later recalled, on the streets and in the neighborhoods of St. Luke's parish and Port Morris. He spent many childhood hours fascinated by the endless talk about the affairs of the "Organ-I-zation"—the plumbers' local—that accompanied the steady stream of Sunday visitors to the Meany household.

Soon after passing his journeyman's test and gaining entry into the local union in January 1916, the twenty-one-year-old plumber had to shoulder heavy family responsibilities. His father, weakened by pneumonia, died suddenly of a heart attack later that year. In April 1917, older brother John enlisted in the United States Army, leaving George as sole support for his mother and the six younger children. Journeymen's wages of over thirty dollars per week sufficed when he could find work, but the building trades were notoriously seasonal. The young man worked at building sites throughout the New York area, often boarding in remote locations. He supplemented his income by playing semiprofessional baseball, earning local fame as a burly, but nimble catcher. For four years he courted Eugenia McMahon, a clothing worker and member of the International La-

---

*Neither he nor his family ever used this name. In fact, Meany did not know that it was on his birth certificate until he got working papers as a teenager.

dies' Garment Workers' Union. They married in 1919 and settled down in the Bronx.

In 1920, at age twenty-six, Michael Meany's son ran successfully for a slot on the executive board of the Bronx local. Two years later, he was elected business manager, a decisive advance since the position was full-time. From that point onward, he never again worked as a plumber and was never off the payroll of a labor organization. New York's plumbers in the 1910s and 1920s were proud, hard-working, well-trained, and economically insecure. Union-negotiated wages were high, but the weather and the vagaries of the business cycle created chronic unemployment. Determined to preserve their status as solid home-owning breadwinners, plumbers relied on the union to regulate the supply of labor. The enemy was not usually the contractor but rather nonunion workers or rival building tradesmen who stole plumbers' jobs. Indeed, the insecurity and hard physical work of the trade initially caused Michael Meany to discourage his son's ambition to become a plumber.

The New York City plumbers' unions were ingrown and provincial. Bronx Local No. 463 had 3,600 members, making it one of the largest in the United Association of Journeymen and Apprentices of the Plumbing and Pipe Fitting Industry of the United States and Canada. Its leaders struggled constantly to resist the international union's assaults on local union autonomy and to police the trade by rigorous enforcement of contractual provisions and by limiting the supply of plumbers. Its function was not to organize the unorganized but rather to preserve the privilege of union membership for a relative handful of favored men. Indeed, some members of the Bronx local had opposed young George's membership, despite the young man's pedigree, fearing to open the membership books for any reason lest an oversupply of plumbers undermine hard-won union standards.

As a budding labor bureaucrat, George Meany never dreamed of challenging these trade union values. As business agent, he toured the job sites, keeping careful tabs on the work performed, the ratio of helpers to journeymen, and the pattern of job assignments. He scrutinized the materials and methods employed, constantly mindful of the demarcations among the various crafts, encyclopedic in his knowledge of contracts, union jurisdictions, and work classifications. When confronted with nonunion workers performing tasks falling under the local's jurisdiction, Meany did everything possible to take the work away from them. Years later he recalled the prevalent attitude: "We didn't want the people . . . ; we merely wanted the work. So far as the people who were on the work were concerned, for our part they could drop dead."

George Meany Memorial Archives, AFL-CIO

With a growing family—by 1930, the Meanys had three young daughters—George found the secure salary of the business agent a blessing. He earned a reputation for good judgment, fairness, and probity in financial matters. Innovative leadership of a 1927 job action, in which he scandalized old-time laborites by resorting to a court injunction to defeat a lockout, marked him as a comer. He became active in the influential New York City Building Trades Council, gaining its secretaryship in 1923. Compensation for the post was nominal, but the council's activities brought him into contact with influential politicians and powerful local and even national labor leaders. By all accounts, young Meany was a consummate union functionary—shrewd, articulate, honest, and always respectful of the labor movement's protocols and rituals of deference and influence. "A plumber with brains," judged one observer. "No," corrected another, "all plumbers have brains. The difference is that Meany *uses* his."

In the late 1920s and early 1930s, these attributes carried Meany to the top of New York State's labor hierarchy. His service on the Building Trades Council won him election in 1932 as one of thirteen vice-presidents of the New York State Federation of Labor. When the president suddenly resigned the next year, Meany made a bold grasp for the remainder of the term, only to lose in a narrow vote of the executive board. But in 1934 he waged a skillful campaign to defeat a veteran rival, thus attaining the top position in the AFL's largest state federation at the youthful age of forty.

The AFL's forty-odd state federations were the stepchildren of the labor movement. Dependent entirely on their constituent unions for financial and political support, they played sharply restricted roles in the affairs of the labor movement. State federation officials served at the pleasure of the powerful national and international unions that had local unions in a given state. Financed by the per capita tax that these locals paid on the basis of their membership, the state federations enjoyed no autonomy, especially since local unions were not compelled to join or remain in the state federation. Thus, although Meany presided over a body that in theory spoke for New York's 800,000 unionists, he had to tread carefully. His dependence on the dominant unions required tact and caution. Successful state federation functionaries mastered the inner world of organized labor, skillfully seeking consensus, balance, and cooperation among sometimes-warring union chieftains. They played no role in the labor movement's primary activity, collective bargaining, nor did they lead organizing campaigns, which remained the province of the national and local unions. In the affairs of the AFL itself, even the most powerful state federation president was a "one-lunger"—that is, a man with only one vote in a convention with a weighted delegate electorate that usually numbered over twenty-five thousand.

Meany soon found, however, that a state federation president was very much in the public eye, especially in newspaper-saturated New York. The state federation served as labor's political arm, its legislative watchdog, its lobbyist, and its public voice. Meany spent much of his time testifying at legislative hearings, making public speeches, and matching wits with reporters at press conferences. An effective state federation leader soon became a prominent figure in the state capital. He wielded political endorsements and promises of campaign assistance to further labor's legislative goals. Reporters and editors, often ignorant of the locus of "real" power in the labor movement, looked to the state federation president as labor's spokesman, thus bestowing on him recognition unjustified by the formal powers of his office.

Meany flourished in these circumstances. He impressed lawmakers, reporters, and lobbyists as well-informed, straightforward, and resourceful. He mastered the intricacies of the lawmaking process in Albany and revelled in the give-and-take of legislative hearings, press conferences, and public meetings. His ascendancy to the state federation presidency coincided with the depth of the depression—and also with the coming to office of liberal administrations in Washington, Albany, and New York City. Meany worked adeptly with Democratic governor Herbert Lehman and a slim Democratic majority to secure passage of seminal workmen's compensation, unemployment insurance, and health and safety legislation.

He also won high marks from New York unionists in the performance of other duties that befell a state federation president. He bargained astutely and tenaciously with city and federal authorities in disputes over wage rates for publicly-funded workers. He marshalled support for Roosevelt's 1936 reelection and for reform mayor Fiorello LaGuardia's electoral campaigns. He kept the peace among New York's notoriously rough-and-tumble building trades and goods-handling unions. Recalled Meany late in life, "I was about as busy as a man could be—and enjoying every minute of it."

By 1939 Meany had achieved remarkable influence and esteem. In collaboration with Lehman, LaGuardia, and indirectly, Franklin Roosevelt, he had come to enjoy a kind of public influence denied to men who did the things normally associated with labor's central concerns, namely organizing and collective bargaining. Of his success in the state federation, Meany later remarked, "I worked hard, but I was damn lucky." The depression, the presence of sympathetic political figures in high office, and the renewed labor activity that the New Deal had set in motion created opportunities that Meany exploited.

This combination of ability and good fortune also lay behind Meany's entry into the AFL national hierarchy. By 1939 the old federation had recovered from the initial shock of the CIO challenge. The AFL's affiliates grew rapidly, often outstripping those of the rival federation in the drive for new members. Yet its central bureaucracy remained creaky and unresponsive, of little use in the escalating rivalry with the CIO. AFL president William Green, in office since 1924, was safe from challenge, but federation leaders had soured on the number-two man, secretary-treasurer Frank Morrison. A veteran member of the printers' union, Morrison had been a fixture at headquarters since 1896. Now approaching his eightieth birthday, Morrison ran the AFL office by nineteenth-century methods. His plodding responses to requests for information and assistance, once quaint, were now infuriating. Morrison, decided key AFL leaders, would be pensioned off. But who would take his place?

The inner dynamics of the AFL made Meany an obvious choice. A secretary-treasurer should not be too closely identified with any of the federation's dominant power blocs. He should be adept in the political realm, an area in which few unionists could claim much experience. He should be vigorous, efficient, and perhaps innovative. Because most ambitious unionists identified the national and international unions as the most likely avenues for advancement, few harbored designs on the secretary-treasurer's position. Thus when AFL power brokers weighed the possibilities, Meany's name stood out. At age forty-six he was perhaps too youthful to suit some leaders in an organization noted for its geriatric cast, but he had no plausible rival. Indeed, it took heavy pressure and fast talking on the part of powerful union leaders to persuade the New Yorker to make the move from Albany to Washington. Eugenia Meany, with three young daughters to tend, had no desire to uproot the family. Colleagues in New York pointed out that the secretary-treasurer slot could well prove a dead end for Meany, who had achieved power and influence in the nation's largest state. The salary—$10,000—was the same for the two jobs. "But," recalled Meany later, "the more I thought about it, the more I felt it was something I just couldn't say no to." It was, he told his wife, "the second biggest job in the labor movement. This is my life, you know."

Meany remained secretary-treasurer for twelve years. He annually gained reelection at AFL conventions without serious challenge. From the start, his vigor, willingness to entertain new ideas, and articulateness contrasted with the stodgy mediocrity normally characteristic of the AFL's national officers. The role of secretary-treasurer, however, brought its share of frustrations to the energetic New Yorker. The AFL's constitution seemingly gave the secretary-treasurer little autonomy or power. Morrison had been largely an office manager and bookkeeper, with little substantive role in the federation's affairs. Moreover, President William Green, increasingly feeble with his advancing years, seemed suspicious of Meany, viewing him as a rival, even as he relied on the younger man to conduct more and more of the AFL's business. Meany had naturally assumed that one of his main jobs would be the preparation and delivery of testimony before congressional committees, but Green sharply limited Meany's role in this important task.

Nonetheless, the war and postwar years provided Meany with outlets for his abilities. During World War II, for example, he was a permanent AFL representative on the twelve-member National War Labor Board. With Green frequently unable to participate fully, Meany emerged as the AFL's most prominent voice. He clashed repeatedly with the board's "public" members and on several occasions dramatically threatened to resign from the agency to protest its rigid opposition to wage increases. Utterly loyal to the war effort, Meany nonetheless spoke bluntly in behalf of workers' rights, challenging the Roosevelt administration's anti-inflation program, which, he claimed, penalized workers and led to deterioration of their standards of living.

During the war years Meany also became deeply involved in the foreign policy aspects of the AFL's operations. Staunchly anticommunist throughout his career, Meany sharpened his hostility to the Soviet Union and to the presence of Communists within the American labor movement. Regarding the alliance with the Soviets as a necessary evil in the crusade to destroy Hitler, Meany drew closer to those AFL figures, such as David Dubinsky and Jay Lovestone of the International Ladies' Garment Workers' Union and Matthew Woll, a veteran AFL functionary, to whom the Soviet threat internationally and the Communist menace domestically posed the next critical challenge for the country and for the labor movement.

As the war ended, Meany spoke up. In 1945 he led the AFL's boycott of the founding meeting of the World Federation of Trade Unions (WFTU). This organization, supported by the CIO and by the prestigious British Trades Union Congress (TUC), included unions from the Soviet Union in its ranks and sought to maintain the antifascist alliance in the postwar world. In September 1945, Meany addressed the TUC, explaining the AFL's hostility to the WFTU and chiding the British (and the CIO) for collaborating with the Soviet labor organizations. Amid jeering and cat-calls—for Soviet prestige among laborites of almost all persuasions was at a peak in the wake of the Russian role in the defeat of Germany—Meany ridiculed the notion that democratic trade unionists could usefully cooperate with state-controlled Soviet bodies. What, he asked, could a democratic unionist possibly find to discuss with official representatives of the Stalinist state? "The latest innovations being used by the secret police to ensnare those who think in opposition . . . ? Or perhaps, bigger and better concentration camps for political prisoners?" In short, the AFL did not "concede that the Russian worker groups are trade unions." Meany's blunt language marked him for many leftists and laborites as a strident anticommunist, determined to foment postwar hostility among the wartime allies.

In the crisis-plagued postwar years, Meany grew ever more vociferous in his anticommunism. He worked closely with Lovestone, Dubinsky, and AFL European representative Irving Brown to undermine Communist labor unions in western Europe. He hailed the Truman administration's anti-Soviet foreign policy, arguing with some justification that the administration was following the AFL's lead in responding to the Soviet threat. He supported the decision in 1950 to intervene in Korea and soon emerged as the AFL's leading spokesman and representative in the complex dispute-resolution and wage-determination machinery with which the Truman administration sought to combat war-related inflation.

Meany made his mark in political and interunion affairs as well. Throughout 1946 and early 1947, he served as point man in the AFL's unsuccessful efforts to prevent passage of sweeping antilabor legislation. In June 1947, shortly before final passage of the Taft-Hartley Act, Meany pulled out the stops in a mass rally in Madison Square Garden in New York. The impending law, he asserted, was "only one phase of an all-out war against the common people of America." Greedy industrialists, he charged, were "attempting to destroy workers' organizations as the first step in their plan to control the economic life of America." In more neutral forums—at a college symposium, for example—Meany eased off on the class-conscious rhetoric and stressed the disruptiveness likely to follow in the wake of repressive legislation. Without union security provisions (which the new law threatened to undermine), union officers would have no way to get "rid of individual troublemakers and agitators who are bent upon . . . fomenting wild-cat strikes," he warned.

After passage of Taft-Hartley in June 1947, Meany led in revamping the AFL's political action machinery. Determined to secure repeal of Taft-Hartley, Meany drafted plans for establishing Labor's League for Political Education (LLPE), which the AFL adopted in December 1947. Under Meany's hand-picked director, LLPE worked aggressively in the 1948 congressional races to punish legislators who had voted for Taft-Hartley. The league collaborated with Democratic party strategists for the election of President Truman as well. In Meany's view, the creation and activities of LLPE did not depart from traditional AFL nonpartisanship, for the new political arm did not formally align with the Democrats. The AFL had simply responded to the growing tendency of Republican politicians to join in the assaults on organized labor launched by corporate America. On the other hand, the AFL's level of financial and organizational support to its chosen candidates and the vigor with which the LLPE operated were new, reflecting Meany's grasp of the permanent importance of political action.

For many AFL leaders, it was not Meany's anticommunism, his leadership in the Taft-Hartley struggle, or his innovative role in political action that ensured his status as Green's eventual successor. Rather, it was his widely publicized clash with the fearsome John L. Lewis at the AFL's 1947 convention. In 1946 Lewis had reaffiliated his 400,000-strong United Mine Workers with the AFL. Increasingly hostile to governmental regulation of labor affairs, he had joined in the crusade against Taft-Hartley. One of the most noisome provisions of the law required that officers of unions using the services of the National Labor Relations Board sign affidavits affirming that they were not Communists. This repressive and insulting provision angered unionists, but most swallowed their resentment and duly signed the noxious affidavits, fearing that if they refused, their local unions would forfeit important NLRB privileges. Lewis, however, would not sign and thus threatened to thwart the AFL's efforts to comply with the law in the most painless way possible. At the December AFL convention in San Francisco, delegates listened in rapt silence as the eloquent and contemptuous Lewis lashed out at the members of the AFL executive council, denigrating their manhood and questioning their courage. For nearly an hour, Lewis rolled on, attacking Taft-Hartley, to be sure, but reserving his choicest rhetoric for the AFL leadership. "The welkin is filled with the outcries and the lamentations of our great leaders of labor . . . calling upon high heaven" and preparing "to grovel on their bellies." Labor's cowardly leadership, thundered the mine workers' chief, was composed of "fat and stately asses." The AFL, he sneered, had no head—"I think its neck has just grown up and haired over."

Even the most self-assured laborites feared Lewis's matchless thrusts. Recalled one veteran observer of labor gatherings, "Lewis had a tongue like a butcher's knife, and he could chop a man to little pieces, and enjoyed doing so." Thus, when Meany, who had never led a union or organized a local, arose to rebut the mine workers' fabled chief, delegates were prepared to see yet another victim eviscerated. But the confident Meany gave

333

a remarkable performance. Deflating Lewis's histrionics with a careful, factual recounting of the consequences of refusal to sign the affidavits, he reminded the convention that the new law confronted workers with a "very practical problem." Nor did he believe that "we are going to solve it by impugning the integrity of men who feel that they can best represent their membership by complying with the law of the land." Having defused Lewis's attack, Meany unleashed a strident anticommunism that caught Lewis off guard. To be sure, he acknowledged, Lewis had barred members of the Communist party from the United Mine Workers; but in his capacity as leader of the CIO in the 1930s he had opened the gates to Communists, employing the "comrades" as organizers and officials in the rebel labor federation. As for himself, Meany declared, "I am prepared to sign a non-Communist affidavit. I am prepared to go a step further and sign an affidavit that I was never a comrade to the comrades" as, he broadly implied, Lewis had been. Grateful delegates, at last finding a champion against the impregnable Lewis, responded enthusiastically. "Meany," recalled an AFL official, "this building tradesman from New York, not a Shakespearean actor by any means, knock[ed] the stuffing out of Lewis."

According to Jay Lovestone, a veteran of thousands of union and radical meetings, Meany's demolition of the Lewis mystique made his eventual elevation to the AFL presidency inevitable. "George 'elected himself' in San Francisco," Lovestone believed. "Thereafter it was a matter of time." Thus when Green, just short of his eightieth birthday, died in November 1952, Meany faced only ceremonial opposition when the executive council chose him interim president and none at all at the 1953 convention.

Thus, at age fifty-eight, George Meany joined the pantheon of America's twentieth-century top labor leadership. Unlike his predecessors and counterparts, he had made his way to the top not through dynamic organizing or innovative collective bargaining. Nor was he a founding father, as Samuel Gompers had been, or a quiet functionary, like Green. Unlike Green, Lewis, Walter Reuther, and Philip Murray, he had no primary identification with a powerful international union. For over thirty years, Meany had been an administrator, lobbyist, and bureaucrat. While he had never led a strike or even stood on a picket line, he had maneuvered skillfully amid scores of legislative committees, dozens of government regulatory bodies, and hundreds of press conferences. He knew the inner world of union politics intimately. Meany, better than anyone else, appreciated both the limits and the possibilities inherent in executive office in the world of American labor.

As AFL president, Meany had as his highest priority reunification of the labor movement. Exhausting and unproductive raiding among affiliates of the AFL and CIO, together with the mounting conservative political threat highlighted by the Republican victory in the 1952 elections, made merger seem imperative. The deaths of Green and CIO president Philip Murray in November 1952 and the diminishment of ideological conflict and differences in approaches to organizing made merger now more possible than ever before. In engineering merger talks, Meany cut loose from old-time AFL leaders, who still nursed grievances against the CIO dating back twenty years. At the same time, well aware of the deep fractures within the CIO, he exploited the growing sentiment for unification within the once-dissident body. Merger proceeded step-by-step, from a no-raiding compact signed in 1953 through the drafting and revision of a constitution in 1954 and 1955.

While the new constitution for the joint American Federation of Labor-Congress of Industrial Organizations (AFL-CIO) retained the basic structure and guarantees of individual union autonomy that both organizations had separately featured, it contained innovations as well. In particular, Meany supported CIO demands that it empower the executive to move against affiliates tainted with corruption. As AFL president, Meany had broken with AFL tradition to secure suspension of the racket-ridden International Longshoremen's Association (ILA) in 1953. Fearing that anti-labor forces would harm the labor movement in general unless the new AFL-CIO cleaned up its own house, Meany insisted on granting the merged federation the power to require affiliates to comply with a stiff ethical conduct code. Of course, these provisions both provided retrospective sanction for Meany's actions against the ILA and added importantly to the power of the merged union body's chief executive.

At a joint convention in December 1955, the merger was consummated. Since the AFL outstripped the CIO in membership by over two to one, few doubted that Meany would serve as the first president of the AFL-CIO. For Meany, to whom the CIO rebellion in 1935 had been little more than an exercise in power-seeking on the part of John L. Lewis (and perhaps, he sometimes darkly hinted, Franklin D. Roosevelt), unification of the two federations removed all obstacles to labor's onward march. "The merger of the AFL and CIO—reuniting the house of labor," he later declared, was "the accomplishment I take the most pride in."

For twenty-four years, until his retirement in 1979, George Meany dominated the AFL-CIO. Despite his age—he was sixty-one at the time of the merger—and serious health problems (a severe hip ailment afflicted him with constant pain), he survived would-be rivals and remained a vigorous and outspoken public figure until the end of his career. His stewardship of the labor movement was controversial. Supporters viewed him as straightforward and courageous, whether he was expelling corrupt affiliates, iso-

335

lating visionary rivals, bluntly correcting American presidents, or facing down self-proclaimed militants and radicals. They pointed to the merger itself and the ending of twenty years of internecine conflict as a brilliant achievement. Organized labor's vastly increased political operations, its successful electoral campaigns, and its positive impact on civil rights, social welfare, and labor legislation provided almost daily evidence of Meany's strength and determination. Meany's anticommunism served as a constant reminder of the essentially moral and ethical nature of the East-West confrontation. The AFL-CIO leader's easy access to a generation of presidents and his vigorous advocacy of labor's cause in the press and in other public forums testified to organized labor's coming of age. For over two decades, in the words of an admiring biographer, he was "the unchallenged strong man of American labor."

Even Meany's critics—of whom there were many, both on the Left and the Right—agreed that his stress on political action paid off in power and influence for the AFL-CIO. Soon after the merger, the new labor body created a Committee on Political Education (COPE) to conduct its electoral efforts. COPE quickly demonstrated vigor and effectiveness in helping to elect scores of liberals to Congress and to gain the presidency for John F. Kennedy in 1960, Lyndon B. Johnson in 1964, and Jimmy Carter in 1976. It pioneered in techniques of voter registration, political mobilization, and canvassing, providing a model for other groups. Meanwhile, the AFL-CIO's legislative department, directed by the highly respected Andrew Biemiller, gained an enviable reputation on Capitol Hill and played a major role in extending New Deal reforms during the conservative Eisenhower years and securing passage of civil rights, social welfare, and labor legislation in the more favorable atmosphere of the 1960s. This strong commitment to electoral and legislative activity directly reflected Meany's sense of priorities and both Biemiller and COPE director Al Barkan enjoyed privileged access to the AFL-CIO chief.

Throughout his tenure, Meany used the forums that congressional hearings and political campaigns offered to articulate his (and the AFL-CIO's) approach to economic policy and foreign affairs, his two legislative and political priorities. In a thousand hearings, speeches, and press conferences, he advanced a laborite Keyneseanism that called incessantly for full employment and economic growth. Of course, success in these areas increased workers' living standards and provided the bases for fuller participation in society. More than that, however, Meany believed that full employment and the growth that could alone guarantee it provided the acid test of American capitalism. He never wavered in his adherence to capitalism; he never flirted with even the most moderate forms of socialism. He believed that America's socioeconomic system provided working people with freedom, material well-being, and opportunity. "We have long ago gotten over the idea that workers were a class apart," he told the AFL-CIO convention in 1957. "Whatever the faults of our nation," he asserted in 1973, "it is still mankind's last hope for freedom."

Yet the system did not run automatically. The Great Depression had discredited laissez-faire once and for all. Government had to stimulate economic growth. Tax policies should benefit lower-income families. Strong minimum wage provisions, generous public assistance and unemployment programs, and publicly funded job training and employment initiatives were needed to buoy mass purchasing power and thus to fuel economic growth. Government expenditures to build schools, highways, parks, roads, and housing expanded employment and kept open the doors of opportunity. Indeed, Meany declared in 1967, "the government itself must become the employer of last resort as well as the landlord of last resort." Meany lashed out at those who would sacrifice workers by "accepting" widespread unemployment as a means of dampening inflation. His view of the American economy was bullish, for it envisioned endless expansion, perpetual growth, and widening opportunities for all, without any need for basic redistribution of income or power.

And it was organized labor that most vigorously and effectively championed the economic growth that stood at the heart of the American way of life. Labor insisted on collective bargaining, resisted the armchair theories of conservative economists, and exposed the short-sighted actions of greedy corporations. "We cannot preserve this system," he warned repeatedly, "unless we can step up our economic growth."

Linked to Meany's commitment to growth and to American exceptionalism was his intense anticommunism. He saw the Soviet Union as irremediably totalitarian. Its cynical and ruthless quest for world power threatened American values at their most basic level. "The Communist conspiracy," he warned in a typical speech, "overshadows everything else that we may think of." He consistently urged increased military expenditures and cooperated cheerfully with the American government's often-successful efforts to undermine allegedly Communist-influenced Third World regimes. His support of American military actions in Korea and Vietnam was unstinting and categorical. "I would rather fight the Communists in South Vietnam than fight them here in the Chesapeake Bay," he vowed in 1966. His speeches directly connected the necessity for economic growth and social reform at home with the desperate struggle to outpace the USSR and thus provide an anti-Communist alternative for the poverty-stricken masses of the underdeveloped nations. Under Meany's leadership, the AFL-CIO spent about a quarter of its annual budget on international projects encouraging anti-Communist unionism around the world.

Meany's anticommunism per se was not remarkable in the American context. Few workers or labor activists looked to the Soviet Union, its client states, or the People's Republic of China for inspiration. Life in post-Stalinist Russia remained repressive and barren, even if terror and mass imprisonment had given way to more bureaucratic and indirect forms of control. What was remarkable about Meany's often-expressed views was their intensity and stridency of rhetoric. Although he did support measures such as the 1962 Test Ban Treaty and never joined those who dreamed of "rolling back" the advance of Soviet tyranny, he did condemn even the most gingerly gestures toward accommodation with the Communist states. Increasingly, the vociferousness of his anticommunism separated him and the AFL-CIO from all but the most bellicose elements. Thus, in 1971, he blasted President Nixon and Secretary of State Henry Kissinger for pursuing a policy of détente with the Soviet Union and for making overtures to China. Nixon, he told a labor audience, had once declared himself "the No. 1 anti-Communist." Given Nixon's red-baiting past, Meany remarked, he himself had been willing to concede the title to the president, but he insisted that "I was No. 2." Now, however, he implied, Nixon's sudden discovery of the virtues of life in Russia and China had elevated Meany to the top ranking.

Meany had ample opportunity to drive home these views to a generation of American presidents. His appearances before congressional bodies and his frequent press conferences broadcast his statements widely. In addition, for nearly thirty years he enjoyed frequent access to the Executive Mansion.

The relocation of the federation's headquarters in 1955 to Sixteenth Street, just across Pennsylvania Avenue from the White House, symbolized labor's arrival at the seat of power. After an initial falling out with the Eisenhower administration over the secretaryship of labor, Meany got along well with the general, supporting many of his foreign policy initiatives while bolstering moderate Republicans in their struggles against the party's extreme right wing. Indeed, in 1956 Meany even suggested that the AFL-CIO executive council refrain from endorsing either candidate in the presidential contest between Eisenhower and Democratic nominee Adlai E. Stevenson.

Meany's access to the White House expanded dramatically under John Kennedy and Lyndon Johnson. Seeing the young Irishman as a surrogate for the son he never had, Meany basked in Kennedy's deference to the wisdom of age in matters relating to appointments and labor policies. True, the AFL-CIO had differences with the administration. Laborites regarded its tax-cutting approach to economic stimulation as overly pro-business and deplored the Democrats' timidity in civil rights and social welfare legislation. Still, Meany combined broad support for the administration's foreign and domestic policies with both admiration and affection for Kennedy. Near the end of his days, Meany said that the single most memorable event of his life had been when he stood behind Kennedy on the platform in Berlin on June 26, 1963, and heard the young president declare in fervent (if ungrammatical) German, *"Ich bein ein Berliner."* Kennedy's murder plunged him into despair. "Washington is never going to be the same town again," he brooded. "I don't know if I want to keep on working here."

Curiously, Meany enjoyed perhaps his most intimate personal relationship with Kennedy's successor, Lyndon B. Johnson. Laborites had opposed Johnson's nomination for the vice-presidency in 1960. Meany and his colleagues viewed the then-Senate majority leader as a ruthless manipulator, little concerned with progressive legislation and steeped in the reactionary traditions of the South. In his cutthroat rise to power in Texas, Johnson had cultivated antilabor oil and corporate interests. He had voted for the Taft-Hartley Act.

As president, however, Johnson expanded on the Kennedy program in civil rights and social reform legislation, revealing an unexpected and admirable genuineness in pushing through the two great legislative monuments of the civil rights movement, the acts of 1964 and 1965. Following his overwhelming election to a full term in 1964, Johnson used the bloated Democratic majorities in Congress to gain pathbreaking legislation in education, urban renewal, medical care, housing, and other areas of special concern to the AFL-CIO. Not only did labor's political operatives work closely with the administration on Capitol Hill, but in addition Johnson and Meany developed a close personal relationship. On more than one occasion, the president summoned the labor leader late at night to the White House. There, as Meany sipped root beer, Johnson would talk into the night, detailing his plans and venting his frustrations.

It was in foreign policy, however, that the Meany-Johnson relationship most fully flourished. As a vigilant anticommunist, Meany welcomed the Kennedy presidency as much for its determination to beef up American military capabilities and to challenge Communist advances as for its domestic agenda. Meany regularly steered resolutions fully endorsing escalation of American intervention in Vietnam through the AFL-CIO executive council and conventions. As the war ground on in the second half of Johnson's administration, liberals turned against it and a besieged president felt increasingly isolated in the White House. Yet Meany and the AFL-CIO remained steadfast, pledging anew support for the war even in the dark days of 1968.

Meany's relationships with the last three presidents who served during his tenure were less intimate. Richard Nixon had been labor's nemesis since his days in Congress in the 1940s. Meany, while continuing his support of American policy in Vietnam, accumulated many grievances against Nixon. The administration's 1971 wage-price freeze and subsequent efforts to curb inflation through direct government action caused Meany to deepen his distrust of the motives and stratagems of Nixon and his advisors. On several occasions, Meany felt that the president tried to embarrass him publicly, once at the 1971 AFL-CIO convention. But of all the issues that divided the two men, it was the Nixon-Kissinger policy of détente with the Soviet Union and friendship with the People's Republic of China that most antagonized Meany. Yet at Meany's insistence the AFL-CIO did not oppose Nixon's successful 1972 reelection bid, so appalled was labor's top leadership by liberal George McGovern's antiwar Democratic candidacy and by the seeming capture of the party by countercultural and new left elements. When the Nixon administration sank into the slough of Watergate, however, Meany and the AFL-CIO were quick to condemn the treachery and cynicism behind Nixon's cover-up. The executive council of the federation was the first major body to call for Nixon's impeachment.

The Carter administration was something of an anticlimax for Meany. Though Carter and his aides went through the motions of consultation with organized labor's leadership, the Georgian prided himself on his distance from traditional power brokers such as Meany. Organized labor did exert some influence in economic policy and had the administration's support in efforts to reform the country's basic labor laws. But the Carter White House, with its deliberate provincialism the order of the day, was not nearly so hospitable a place for George Meany as the executive mansion of the Kennedy-Johnson years had been.

For traditional laborites, ongoing access to the centers of power was heady. They remembered labor's long struggle for recognition and its long-term status as an outcast element. And Meany's behavior with the presidents with whom he dealt was the opposite of sycophantic. He spoke frankly to the chief executives, exhibiting a strong sense of pride and dignity. He did not hesitate to dissent publicly, and he frequently blew the whistle on manipulation—as, for example, in Nixon's efforts to maneuver Laborites into open-ended support for his wage control plans. On national television, the heavy, cigar-chomping, gravel-voiced Meany, bluntly assessing the successes and failures of presidential policies—even awarding grades to evaluate performance in office—was a familiar feature of the evening news.

Yet, critics argued, Meany's AFL-CIO had, in the end, disappointingly little real impact on politics, legislation, or government policies. To be sure, the gruff Meany exposed the limitations of the domestic policies of each administration; but when it came to foreign policy, and especially the war in Vietnam, Meany and the labor leadership offered carte blanche endorsement for the increasingly dubious venture. Moreover, even on domestic matters, Meany often appeared more the spokesman for a special interest group than the leader of the working class. Politicians increasingly distanced themselves from identification with organized labor and public regard for labor leaders began to rival that awarded to used car salesmen. Often Meany's well-publicized confrontations with the presidents appeared to contain more show than substance.

Nor did the AFL-CIO's political and legislative operations retain their luster through the 1970s. Successful in helping to elect Democrats, COPE seemed unable to prevent the party from drifting ever rightward. Labor's political operatives increasingly found themselves forced to support candidates—including Carter himself—whose liberal credentials were at best marginal. On the legislative front, labor's operatives thwarted some conservative initiatives, spearheaded the rejection of questionable federal appointees, and even gained passage of mild social welfare reforms. But on the issues closest to the hearts of laborites themselves—repeal of Taft-Hartley or, at least, substantial revision of that hated legislation; labor law reform designed to counteract the rightward drift of the National Labor Relations Board; liberalization of restrictions on construction and public employees unions; protection of unions from punitive legislation—the AFL-CIO failed time after time.

Meany's reputation as rebuilder of the house of labor also raised questions. To be sure, the merger itself had moderated the more blatant forms of internecine union conflict. Meany's ability to get dozens of imperious labor chiefs to put aside differences, however temporarily, was impressive. But what was the purpose of merger if not to create a more vigorous, progressive, and dynamic labor movement? On the face of it, Meany's record of stewardship did seem spotty. Despite important breakthroughs in recruitment of public employees beginning in the early 1960s, the percentage of workers organized dropped substantially during Meany's tenure. Thus in 1955 about one-third of the country's nonagricultural labor force was enrolled in unions, while in 1980 the figure had shrunk to less than a fourth. Yet Meany expressed little concern with this development, declaring in the midst of this decline "At no time, within my memory, has labor been better equipped and prepared to deal with its problems . . . than is the case today."

Moreover, he ridiculed those who urged that the AFL-CIO launch bold and aggressive organizing campaigns. At times, indeed, he even appeared indifferent to the unorganized majority of the American working class. "Why should we worry about organizing groups of people who do not appear to want to be organized?" he asked in 1972. As for UAW president Walter Reuther's plea in the late 1960s that the AFL-CIO reach out to organize the poor by creating community unions, Meany was flatly disdainful. Reuther's proposals to bring the message of organization to masses of unemployed and sporadically employed workers—most of them in the low wage, marginal employment sectors—evoked only contempt: "Well, good luck on that one," was Meany's only response to Reuther's initiative.

Indeed, critics wondered, how successful was merger itself if two of the AFL-CIO's largest and most dynamic organizations, namely the Teamsters and the UAW, were outside the sanctified House of Labor. The Teamsters, ousted in 1957 for failure to comply with the AFL-CIO's ethical standards strictures, flourished throughout the 1960s and 1970s apart from the federation. Despite sometimes questionable motives and recruitment methods, the Teamsters, almost alone among traditional American unions, exhibited organizing dynamism in the Meany era. As for the UAW, its disaffiliation from the AFL-CIO in 1968 robbed the federation of its most progressive and principled voice. Meany loyalists blamed president Walter Reuther for the UAW's departure, some in fact hinting that Reuther had grown weary of waiting for Meany to die or retire so that he himself could claim labor's most prestigious post. Throughout the 1960s, however, as Reuther's always-earnest and often-perceptive critiques of the AFL-CIO's lassitude in organizing, compromises in civil rights, and uncritical support for U.S. foreign policy became more frequent, Meany responded with legalistic maneuvering. He marshalled sycophantic majorities on the executive council of the AFL-CIO and resorted to crude public ridicule rather than addressing the substance of Reuther's calls for reform.

Meany also drew a mixture of criticism and approval in his treatment of the single most significant domestic issue of his tenure, civil rights. As the assault on segregation gained force in the 1950s, organized labor stepped forward as a major public voice in behalf of civil rights. Despite rampant discrimination within many unions, notably AFL craft and building trades organizations, both pre-merger federations aligned themselves with the effort to strike down legal barriers that blacks encountered in quest of education, suffrage, and public accommodations. Meany, despite his provincial background in a racially discriminatory building trades union, had worked with civil rights organizations during his presidency of the New York State Federation of Labor and during his term as AFL secretary-treasurer. Not even critics accused him of personal bigotry, although his quick intolerance for any but the most orderly and restrained forms of protest did suggest insensitivity to the depths of outrage and bitterness that millions of black Americans felt. In his capacity as AFL president, Meany endorsed the goals of the standard civil rights organizations and quietly encouraged AFL affiliates to abandon the racial disabilities and overtly discriminatory practices that some continued to practice.

This pattern of support for the formal demands of civil rights groups and muted efforts to effect change within the labor movement continued after Meany assumed the AFL-CIO presidency. Labor lobbyists played important roles in the passage of the 1957, 1960, 1964, and 1965 civil rights acts. Indeed, the seminal 1964 measure included far-reaching language barring discrimination by employers and by unions. Not only did Meany and his legislative corps support this controversial feature, they insisted on its inclusion. In 1969 and 1970 AFL-CIO forces joined with those of civil rights and liberal groups to defeat two successive Supreme Court nominees, Clement Haynesworth and G. Harold Carswell, partly on the grounds of their racial views. When it came to public accommodations, voting rights, education, legal standing, and related matters, Meany's AFL-CIO was a stalwart ally of the civil rights movement.

Yet while Meany spoke out against discrimination in hiring, he opposed all but the most marginal programs of recruiting black workers for high-wage employment. The building trades unions, whose powerful chiefs constituted a major bloc within the AFL-CIO, defended their discriminatory records in recruitment and apprenticing, yielding only grudgingly to governmental pressure to seek out minority applicants. Meany regularly defended their half-hearted efforts and countered potentially far-reaching programs with support for underfunded and notoriously ineffective alternatives. Despite the AFL-CIO's vigorous support for federal legislation and for economic policies favorable to the black community, Meany's foot-dragging and apologetics in the matter of hiring and apprenticing embittered black activists and traditional allies of labor within the civil rights movement.

Meany's impatience with black activism was sometimes harsh and insulting. His refusal to sanction official AFL-CIO participation in the magnificent 1963 march on Washington contrasted with the leading role played by his long-term critic, UAW president Walter Reuther, who shared the podium with Martin Luther King, Jr., and other black leaders. Black leaders such as King attempted to extend the civil rights struggle into a broad progressive coalition to challenge the nation's distribution of wealth and power, only to find Meany adhering to a narrow and legalistic definition of civil rights. Too often the AFL-CIO president seemed unaware of the intensity of black rage, equating the experiences of blacks under slavery with the tribulations of the nineteenth-century Irish and eastern European peasantry. At the AFL-CIO convention in 1959, he interrupted A. Philip Randolph's principled critique of the federation's continuing toleration of Jim Crow practices in several affiliates. "Who the hell appointed you as the guardian of all the Negroes in America?" he barked at the elderly black unionist.

Randolph himself insisted that he viewed Meany as a champion of civil rights. "I don't know of anyone who is the head of an organization . . . who has fought as vigorously as he has," he declared. Yet to a new generation of activists coming of age in the 1960s and 1970s, Meany epitomized all that was wrong with the labor movement. As the ghettoes exploded into rebellion and as the campuses erupted with antiwar dissent, labor's leadership grew more and more closed and defensive. Environmental activists often found unions disdainful of ecological dangers and protective of corporate polluters. In May of 1970 hard-hatted construction workers assaulted antiwar demonstrators in New York City, deepening organized labor's reputation for mean-spirited conservatism. True, Meany and the AFL-CIO did support civil rights laws, but Meany frequently voiced his fears that the civil rights movement was slipping out of the control of the veteran leaders of such organizations as the National Association for the Advancement of Colored People (NAACP) and into the grasp of a new generation of "wild men of the NAACP" and fire-eating "black militants." Of youthful activists in general, Meany charged in 1970 that "There is more venereal disease among them. . . . There are more of them smoking pot and . . . they have long beards and look dirty and smell dirty." He defended the behavior of the Chicago police in the savage assaults on dissidents at the 1968 Democratic convention that nominated Hubert Humphrey. Virtually alone among putatively liberal figures, Meany declared that "the Chicago police did not overreact." The protestors were, he said, a "dirty-necked and dirty-mouthed group of kooks."

Nor did Meany seem to be in close touch with rank-and-file workers. By 1970, of course, he was almost fifty years away from his days as a working plumber. Since 1934 he had been an administrator and lobbyist uninterruptedly. Unlike leaders of international unions, he lacked even the secondhand knowledge of life on the shop floor that periodic contact with local union activists and officers provided. The media and government officials looked to him for expertise on matters such as the quality of working life, specific collective bargaining goals, worker dissatisfaction, health and safety, and the general mood of unionized America. Meany could cite AFL-CIO surveys that documented the changing profile of the union membership, showing it to be younger, better educated, more suburban than its earlier counterparts. He could speak eloquently about the economic pinch of the late 1960s, as real income slowed for the first time in a generation and even began to diminish. But his words were often accompanied by disdainful references to the affluence of contemporary union members and by unfavorable comparisons between workers of his generation and those he now led.

He often spoke as if he did not trust workers to know what their interests were. Perhaps, he speculated in the late 1960s at a time of increasing strike action and escalating rank-and-file rejection of union-negotiated contracts, the time had come to supplant the strike weapon with a system of voluntary arbitration. Workers in the past, he recollected, had been willing to man the picket lines; they had little to lose. But "now the workers have a little home," he noted in 1972, "they may have a couple of kids going to college. You put them on strike, they're overboard within a week." In remarks that appeared to legitimate the traditional conservative charge that unions were self-perpetuating bureaucracies and not democratic extensions of workers' choice, Meany in 1969 urged further centralization of union governance. He deplored the fact that many union constitutions required rank-and-file ratification of contracts negotiated by the leadership. Rising rank-and-file opposition to these contracts, he believed, usurped the legitimate functions of union officials. A wave of contract rejections that peaked in the late 1960s, he believed, stemmed not from any real grievances or genuine militancy but from petty jealousies and interpersonal rivalries. Those sympathetic to the assertion of democratic rights by union members pointed to the declining real standard of living of the late 1960s and to employers' efforts to bend work rules so as to increase productivity, but for Meany— who, he frequently reminded auditors, had never walked a picket line in his life—this development was merely another example of the fecklessness of modern workers.

As Meany neared and then passed his eightieth birthday in 1974, muted suggestions that he contemplate retirement cropped up more frequently. No one connected with the AFL-CIO dared openly call for him to step down. And indeed his leadership in the campaign to impeach Nixon and his shrewd and trenchant statements on the country's economic problems in the 1970s won him a new audience. In 1974 on a national television show Meany told a shocked Dick Cavett that he had been wrong about Vietnam. Elaborating at subsequent press conferences, he said that Nixon, Kissinger, and possibly Johnson had deceived him. "I didn't know that they were going to bomb the civilian population. If I had known that," he declared, "I wouldn't buy that. I didn't know about the secret bombing of Cambodia and many other things." In 1976, he argued for more critical scrutiny of foreign policy and military initiatives; no longer, he believed, would labor automatically support the government in these matters as the AFL-CIO had during his reign. This rather startling change of heart included no apology for the distainful epithets and charges of disloyalty he had regularly hurled at antiwar critics during the war itself. Nor did he appear to acknowledge any responsibility for the role his now-admittedly uncritical support may have played in legitimating and prolonging the bloody conflict. Nonetheless, his reversals revealed a new openness and did offer sanction for a more independent role for organized labor in foreign and military policy than had been the case during Meany's tenure.

Despite his distaste for talk of retirement, he soon had to give in to physical afflictions. In March 1979 Mrs. Meany died, ending an unusually close and sustaining marriage of sixty years. Later that spring and in the summer, Meany suffered serious respiratory ailments and a savage attack of bursitis. He had to use a wheelchair when he emerged from the hospital. In 1966 he had undergone a risky operation to correct a painful and debilitating hip condition. The surgery and his spartan program of rehabilitation had given him a new vigor and strength that carried him into his mid-eighties. But clearly now the time had come for him to step down. In an emotional farewell, he turned over the reins of leadership to his hand-picked successor, Lane Kirkland, at the November 1979 AFL-CIO convention. Shortly after, on January 10, 1980, the anniversary of his enrollment in the Bronx plumbers' local, he died. In a eulogy, Monsignor George Higgins recalled something that Meany had confided to him almost thirty years earlier when assuming the AFL presidency: "I have no other interest in life outside my family and the federation."

Bibliographic Notes

The George Meany Memorial Archives, soon to be housed on the campus of the George Meany Center for Labor Studies in Silver Spring, Maryland, has recently made available to scholars a collection of materials relating to the Office of the Secretary-Treasurer (1939–52) and the Office of the President (1952–60). When completed, the archives will contain a vast array of additional material on the life and times of George Meany. I have not had the opportunity to consult these records.

There are two full-length biographies of Meany. Joseph C. Goulden, *Meany: The Unchallenged Strong Man of American Labor* (1972), was written with the benefit of Meany's cooperation. It is an able interim report and a reliable guide to Meany's career up to the date of publication. Archie Robinson, *George Meany and His Times: A Biography* (1981), is eulogistic but its copious verbatim quotations from Robinson's interviews with Meany and his associates make it useful. I found two periodical articles particularly helpful in understanding the Meany method. They are John Corry, "The Many-Sided Mr. Meany," *Harper's*, March 1970, and Byron E. Calame, "Labor's Durable King of the Hill," *Wall Street Journal* (Oct. 23, 1973). Jerry Flint, "George Meany Is Dead; Pioneer in Labor Was 85," *New York Times* (Jan. 11, 1980), contains basic factual information.

Meany wrote little. The best way to trace his views and activities is to read his speeches and other public statements. The proceedings of the annual conventions of the New York State Federation of Labor, 1932–39, are valuable. The proceedings of the annual conventions of the American Federation of Labor (1939–55) and the joint American Federation of Labor-Congress of Industrial Organizations (1955–79) provide a basic record. Many of the Meany's speeches and interviews were reprinted in such publications as *Vital Speeches of the Day, U.S. News and World Report, Congressional Digest*, and the *New York Times Magazine*.

Published secondary works and autobiographies provide needed contextual material. Martin Segal, *The Rise of the United Association: National Unionism in the Pipe Trades, 1844–1924* (1970), contains abundant information on the tempestuous New York City plumbers' locals. General works on the labor movement during Meany's career include Philip A. Taft, *Organized Labor in American History* (1964), and Taft, *The A.F. of L. from the Death of Gompers to the Merger* (1959), which are standard references. My own *American Workers, American Unions, 1920–1985* (1986) is a recent synthesis.

For the 1930s, see Walter Galenson, *The CIO Challenge to the AFL: A History of the American Labor Movement, 1935–1941* (1960); James O. Morris, *Conflict Within the AFL: A Study of Craft Versus Industrial Unionism, 1901–1938* (1958); and especially Irving Bernstein, *The Turbulent Years: A History of the American Worker, 1933–1941* (1969). For World War II the standard works are Joel Seidman, *American Labor from Defense to Reconversion* (1953), and Nelson Lichtenstein, *Labor's War at Home: The CIO in World War II* (1982). There is no fully adequate treatment of Taft-Hartley as yet, but see James Gross, *The Reshaping of the National Labor Relations Board: National Labor Policy in Transition, 1937–1947* (1981), and Howell J. Harris, "The Snares of Liberalism? Politicians, Bureaucrats, and the Shaping of Federal Labour Relations Policy in the United States, ca. 1915–47," in Steven Tolliday and Jonathan Zeitlin (eds.), *Shop Floor Bargaining and the State: Historical and Comparative Perspectives* (1985).

Conflicting assessment of the AFL and AFL-CIO record in foreign policy are given in Roy Godson, *American Labor and European Politics: The AFL as a Transnational Force* (1976), and Ronald Radosh, *American Labor and United States Foreign Policy: The Cold War in the Unions from Gompers to Lovestone*

Labor Leaders in America

(1969). Meany's encounters with Lewis are dealt with ably in Melvyn Dubofsky and Warren Van Tine, *John L. Lewis: A Biography* (1977). His running conflict with Walter Reuther is discussed in John Barnard, *Walter Reuther and the Rise of the Auto Workers* (1983) and, more pointedly, in Victor G. Reuther, *The Brothers Reuther and the Story of the UAW: A Memoir* (1976).

Meany's efforts to combat corruption can be seen in Vernon Jensen, *Strife on the Waterfront: The Port of New York Since 1945* (1974), and John Hutchinson, *The Imperfect Union: A History of Corruption in American Trade Unions* (1970). The limits to Meany's commitment, however, are interestingly suggested by the discussion of his handling of the problem in an international setting in David Kwavnick, *Organized Labour and Pressure Politics: The Canadian Labour Congress, 1956–1968* (1972).

The civil rights record of Meany and the AFL-CIO is sharply criticized in Philip S. Foner, *Organized Labor and the Black Worker, 1619–1973* (1976); William B. Gould, *Black Workers in White Unions: Job Discrimination in the United States* (1977); Herbert C. Hill, *Black Labor and the American Legal System* (1977); and Jervis Anderson, *A. Philip Randolph: A Biographical Portrait* (1972). General critiques of the state of organized labor during the period of Meany's stewardship include Stanley Aronowitz, *False Promises: The Shaping of American Working Class Consciousness* (1973); Burton Hall (ed.), *Autocracy and Insurgency in Organized Labor* (1972); Paul Jacobs, *The State of the Unions* (1963); and Haynes Johnson and Nick Kotz, *The Unions* (1972). See Derek Bok and John Dunlop, *Labor and the American Community* (1970) for a more favorable assessment.

Organized labor's political efforts in the Meany era are ably analyzed in J. David Greenstone, *Labor in American Politics* (1969), and David Brody, "The Uses of Power II: Political Action," in Brody, *Workers in Industrial America: Essays on the Twentieth Century Struggle* (1980), 215–57. For a ringing critique from the left, see Mike Davis, "The Barren Marriage of American Labour and the Democratic Party," *New Left Review* (1980): 43–84; and from the right, Terry Catchpole, *How to Cope with COPE: The Political Operations of Organized Labor* (1970).

There is no adequate analysis of organized labor's post–World War II efforts to shape economic policy and articulate what I have called "labor Keyneseanism." Everett M. Kassalow, "The Great Depression and the Transformation of the American Labor Movement," Industrial Relations Research Association Reprint No. 234 (reprinted from U.S. Congress, Joint Economic Committee, *The Business Cycle and Public Policy, 1929–1980*; Nov. 28, 1980), gives a succinct overview. The AFL and AFL-CIO publication *American Federationist* contains most important statements on economic policy. The Goulden and Robinson biographies, as well as many of the speeches and statements alluded to above, present Meany's words on this subject.

Finally, suggestive in establishing a context for Meany's career in the labor movement are Warren Van Tine, *The Making of the Labor Bureaucrat: Union Leadership in the United States, 1870–1920* (1973); C. Wright Mills, *The New*

Men of Power: America's Labor Leaders (1948); Walter Licht and Hal Seth Barron, "Labor's Men: A Collective Biography of Union Officialdom During the New Deal Years," *Labor History* (1978): 532–45; and especially Gary Fink, "Introduction: The American Labor Leader in the Twentieth Century: Quantitative and Qualitative Portraits," in Fink (ed.), *Biographical Dictionary of American Labor* (rev. ed., 1984): 3–79.

Cesar Chavez and the Unionization of California Farm Workers

15

Cletus E. Daniel

It was, Cesar Chavez later wrote, "the strangest meeting in the history of California agricultue." Speaking by telephone from his cluttered headquarters in La Paz to Jerry Brown, the new governor of California, Chavez had been asked to repeat for the benefit of farm employers crowded into Brown's Sacramento office the farmworker leader's acceptance of a farm labor bill to which they had already assented. And as the employers heard Chavez's voice repeating the statement of acceptance he had just made to the governor, they broke into wide smiles and spontaneous applause.

That representatives of the most powerful special interest group in California history should have thus expressed their delight at the prospect of realizing still another of their legislative goals does not account for Chavez's assertion of the meeting's strange character. These were, after all, men long accustomed to having their way in matters of farm labor legislation. What was strange about that meeting on May 5, 1975, was that the state's leading farm employers should have derived such apparent relief and satisfaction from hearing the president of the United Farm Workers of America, AFL-CIO, agree to a legislative proposal designed to afford farmworkers an opportunity to escape their historic powerlessness through unionism and collective bargaining.

Beyond investing the state's farmworkers with rights that those who labored for wages on the land had always been denied, the passage of California's Agricultural Labor Relations Act (ALRA) was a seismic event, one that shattered the foundation upon which rural class relations had rested for a century and more. For the state's agribusinessmen, whose tradition it had been to rule the bounteous fields and orchards of California with a degree of authority and control more appropriate to potentates than mere employers, supporting the ALRA was less an act of culpable treason against their collective heritage than one of grudging resignation in the face of a suddenly irrelevant past and an apparently inescapable future. For the state's farmworkers, whose involuntary custom it had always been to surrender themselves to a system of industrialized farming that made a captive peasantry of them, the new law made possible what only the boldest among them had dared to image: a role equal to the employer's in determining terms and conditions of employment. Yet if the ALRA's enactment was a victory of unprecedented dimensions for California farmworkers as a class, it was a still greater personal triumph for Cesar Chavez.

More than any other labor leader of his time, and perhaps in the whole history of American labor, Cesar Chavez leads a union that is an extension of his own values, experience, and personality. This singular unity of man and movement has found its most forceful and enduring expression in the unprecedented economic and political power that has accrued to the membership of the United Farm Workers (UFW) under Chavez's intense and unrelenting tutelage. Indeed, since 1965, when Chavez led his then small following into a bitter struggle against grape growers around the lower San Joaquin valley town of Delano, the UFW has, despite the many crises that have punctuated its brief but turbulent career, compiled a record of achievement that rivals the accomplishments of the most formidable industrial unions of the 1930s.

While this personal domination may well be the essential source of the UFW's extraordinary success, it has also posed risks for the union. For just as Chavez's strengths manifest themselves in the character of his leadership, so, too, must his weaknesses. Certainly the UFW's somewhat confused sense of its transcending mission—whether to be a trade union or a social movement; whether to focus on narrow economic gains or to pursue broader political goals—reflects in some degree Chavez's personal ambivalence toward both the ultimate purpose of worker organization and the fundamental objective of his own prolonged activism.

Had his adult life followed the pattern of his early youth, Cesar Chavez need not have concerned himself with the task of liberating California farmworkers from an exploitive labor system that had entombed a succession of Chinese, Japanese, Filipino, Mexican, and other non-Anglo immigrants for more than a hundred years. Born on March 31, 1927, the second child of Librado and Juana Chavez, Cesar Estrada Chavez started his life sharing little beyond language and a diffuse ethnic heritage with the Chicano—Mexican and Mexican-American—workers who constitute nearly the entire membership of the United Farm Workers of America. Named after his paternal grandfather Cesario, who had homesteaded the family's small farm in the north Gila River valley near Yuma three years before Arizona attained statehood, Chavez enjoyed during his youth the kind of close and stable family life that farmworkers caught in the relentless currents of the western migrant stream longed for but rarely attained. And although farming on a small scale afforded few material rewards even as it demanded hard and unending physical labor, it fostered in Chavez an appreciation of independence and personal sovereignty that helps to account for the special force and steadfastness of his later rebellion against the oppressive dependence into which workers descended when they joined the ranks of California's agricultural labor force.

It is more than a little ironic that until 1939, when unpaid taxes put the family's farm on the auction black, Chavez could have more reasonably aspired to a future as a landowner than as a farmworker. "If we had stayed there," he later said of the family's farm, "possibly I would have been a grower. God writes in exceedingly crooked lines."

The full significance of the family's eviction from the rambling adobe ranch house that had provided not only shelter but also a sense of place and social perspective was not at once apparent to an eleven year old. The deeper meaning of the family's loss was something that accumulated in Chavez's mind only as his subsequent personal experience in the migrant stream disclosed the full spectrum of emotional and material hardship attending a life set adrift from the roots that had nurtured it. At age eleven the sight of a bulldozer effortlessly destroying in a few minutes what the family had struggled over nearly three generations to build was meaning enough. The land's new owner, an Anglo grower impatient to claim his prize, dispatched the bulldozer that became for Chavez a graphic and enduring symbol of the power that the "haves" employ against the "have-nots" in industrialized agriculture. "It was a monstrous thing," he recalled: "Its motor blotted out the sound of crickets and bullfrogs and the buzzing of the flies. As the tractor moved along, it tore up the soil, leveling it, and destroyed the trees, pushing them over like they were nothing. . . . And each tree, of course, means quite a bit to you when you're young. They are a part of you. We grew up there, saw them every day, and they were alive, they were friends. When we saw the bulldozer just uprooting those trees, it was tearing at us too."

The experience of the Chavez family fell into that category of minor tragedy whose cumulative influence lent an aura of catastrophe to the greater part of the depression decade. The scene became sickeningly familiar in the 1930s: a beleaguered farm family bidding a poignant farewell to a failed past; setting out for California with little enthusiasm and even less money toward a future that usually had nothing but desperation to commend it.

Cesar Chavez

Dave Evans, Stockton *Record*

353

"When we were pushed off our land," Chavez said, "all we could take with us was what we could jam into the old Studebaker or pile on its roof and fenders, mostly clothes and bedding. . . . I realized something was happening because my mother was crying, but I didn't realize the import of it at the time. When we left the farm, our whole life was upset, turned upside down. We have been part of a very stable community, and we were about to become migratory workers."

Yet if Chavez's experience was in some ways similar to that of the dispossessed dustbowl migrant whose pilgrimage to California was also less an act of hope than of despair, it was fundamentally unlike that of even the most destitute Anglo—John Steinbeck's generic "Okie"—because of virulent racial attitudes among the state's white majority that tended to define all persons "of color" as unequal. For the Chavez family, whose standing as landowners in a region populated by people mainly like themselves had insulated them from many of the meanest forms of racism, following the crops in California as undifferentiated members of a brown-skinned peasantry afforded an unwelcome education. To the familiar varieties of racial humiliation and mistreatment—being physically punished by an Anglo teacher for lapsing into your native tongue; being in the presence of Anglos who talked about you as if you were an inanimate object—were added some new and more abrasive forms: being rousted by border patrolmen who automatically regarded you as a "wetback" until you proved otherwise; being denied service at a restaurant or made to sit in the "Mexican only" seats at the local movie house; being stopped and searched by the police for no reason other than your skin color announced your powerlessness to resist; being cheated by an employer who smugly assumed that you probably wouldn't object because Mexicans were naturally docile.

But, if because of such treatment Chavez came to fear and dislike Anglos—*gringos* or *gabachos* in the pejorative lexicon of the barrio—he also came to understand that while considerations of race and ethnicity compounded the plight of farmworkers, their mistreatment was rooted ultimately in the economics of industrialized agriculture. As the family traveled the state from one crop to the next, one hovel to the next, trying desperately to survive on the meager earnings of parents and children alike, Chavez quickly learned that Chicano labor contractors and Japanese growers exploited migrants as readily as did Anglo employers. And, although the complex dynamics of California's rural political economy might still have eluded him, Chavez instinctively understood that farmworkers would cease to be victims only when they discovered the means to take control of their own lives.

The realization that unionism must be that means came later. Unlike the typical Chicano family in the migrant stream, however, the Chavez family included among its otherwise meager possessions a powerful legacy of the independent life it had earlier known, one that revealed itself in a stubborn disinclination to tolerate conspicuous injustices. "I don't want to suggest we were that radical," Chavez later said, "but I know we were probably one of the strikingest families in California, the first ones to leave the fields if anyone shouted "Huelga!"—which is Spanish for "Strike!" . . . If any family felt something was wrong and stopped working, we immediately joined them even if we didn't known them. And if the grower didn't correct what was wrong, then they would leave, and we'd leave."

Chavez had no trouble identifying the source of the family's instinctive militancy. "We were," he insisted, "constantly fighting against things that most people would probably accept because they didn't have that kind of life we had in the beginning, that strong family life and family ties which we would not let anyone break." When confronted by an injustice, there "was no question. Our dignity meant more than money."

Although the United Cannery, Agricultural, Packing and Allied Workers of America, a CIO-affiliated union, was conducting sporadic organizing drives among California farmworkers when Chavez and his family joined the state's farm labor force at the end of the 1930s, he was too young and untutored to appreciate "anything of the real guts of unions." Yet because his father harbored a strong, if unstudied, conviction that unionism was a manly act of resistance to the employers' authority, Chavez's attitude toward unions quickly progressed from vague approval to ardent endorsement. His earliest participation in a union-led struggle did not occur until the late 1940s, when the AFL's National Farm Labor Union conducted a series of ultimately futile strikes in the San Joaquin valley. This experience, which left Chavez with an acute sense of frustration and disappointment as the strike inevitably withered in the face of overwhelming employer power, also produced a brief but equally keen feeling of exhilaration because it afforded an opportunity to vent the rebelliousness that an expanding consciousness of his own social and occupational captivity awakened within him. Yet to the extent that unionism demands the subordination of individual aspirations to a depersonalized common denomination of the group's desires, Chavez was not in his youth the stuff of which confirmed trade unionists are made. More than most young migrant workers, whose ineluctable discontent was not heightened further by the memory of an idealized past, Chavez hoped to escape his socioeconomic predicament rather than simply moderate the harsh forces that governed it.

To be a migrant worker, however, was to learn the hard way that avenues of escape were more readily imagined than traveled. As ardently as the

Chavez family sought a way out of the migrant orbit, they spent the early 1940s moving from valley to valley, from harvest to harvest, powerless to fend off the corrosive effects of their involuntary transiency. Beyond denying them the elementary amenities of a humane existence—a decent home, sufficient food, adequate clothing—the demands of migrant life also conspired to deny the Chavez children the educations that their parents valiantly struggled to ensure. For Cesar school became a "nightmare," a dispiriting succession of inhospital places ruled by Anglo teachers and administrators whose often undisguised contempt for migrant children prompted him to drop out after the eighth grade.

Chavez's inevitable confrontation with the fact of his personal powerlessness fostered a sense of anger and frustration that revealed itself in a tendency to reject many of the most visible symbols of his cultural heritage. This brief episode of open rebellion against the culture of his parents, which dates from the family's decision to settle down in Delano in late 1943 until he reluctantly joined the navy a year later, was generally benign: *mariachis* were rejected in favor of Duke Ellington; his mother's *dichos* and *consejos*—the bits of Mexican folk wisdom passed from one generation to the next—lost out to less culture-bound values; religious customs rooted in the rigid doctrines of the Catholic church gave way to a fuzzy existentialism. In its most extreme form, this rebelliousness led Chavez to affect the distinctive style of a *pachuco*, although he never really ventured beyond dress into the more antisocial ways in which that phenomenon of youthful rebellion manifested itself in the activities of Mexican gangs in urban areas like Los Angeles and San Jose. In the end, Chavez reacted most decisively against the debilitating circumstances of his life by joining the navy, a reluctant decision whose redeeming value was that it offered a means of escape, a way "to get away from farm labor."

The two years he spent in the navy ("the worst of my life") proved to be no more than a respite from farm labor. If Chavez had hoped to acquire a trade while in the service, he soon discovered that the same considerations of race and ethnicity that placed strict limits on what non-Anglos could reasonably aspire to achieve at home operated with equal efficiency in the navy to keep them in the least desirable jobs. Without the training that might have allowed him to break out of the cycle of poverty and oppression that the labor system of industrialized agriculture fueled, Chavez returned to Delano in 1946 to the only work he knew.

Finding work had always been a problem for farmworkers due to a chronic oversupply of agricultural labor in California. The problem became even more acute for migrant families after the war because agribusiness interests succeeded in their political campaign to extend the so-called

Bracero program,* a treaty arrangement dating from 1942 that permitted farm employers in California and the Southwest to import Mexican nationals under contract to alleviate real and imagined wartime labor shortages.

For Chavez, the struggle to earn a living took on special urgency following his marriage in 1948 to Helen Fabela, a Delano girl whom he had first met when his family made one of its periodic migrations through the area in search of work. Being the daughter of farmworkers, and thus knowing all too well the hardships that attended a family life predicated upon the irregular earnings of agricultural work, did nothing to cushion the hard times that lay ahead for Helen Chavez and her new husband, a twenty-one-year-old disaffected farm laborer without discernable prospects.

Chavez met the challenge of making a living, which multiplied with the arrival of a new baby during each of the first three years of marriage, in the only way he knew: he took any job available, wherever it was available. Not until 1952, when he finally landed a job in a San Jose lumberyard, was Chavez able to have the settled life that he and Helen craved. The Mexican barrio in San Jose, known to its impoverished inhabitants as Sal Si Puedes—literally "get out if you can"—was a few square blocks of ramshackle houses occupied by discouraged parents and angry children who, in their desperation to do just what the neighborhood's morbid nickname advised, too often sought ways out that led to prison rather than to opportunity. Long before it became home to Chavez and his family, Sal Si Puedes had earned a reputation among the sociologists who regularly scouted its mean streets as a virtual laboratory of urban social pathology. In the early 1950s, however, the area also attracted two men determined in their separate ways to alleviate the powerlessness of its residents rather than to document or measure it. More than any others, these two activists, one a young Catholic priest, the other a veteran community organizer, assumed unwitting responsibility for the education of Cesar Chavez.

When Father Donald McDonnell established his small mission church in Sal Si Puedes, he resolved to attend to both the spiritual need of his destitute parishioners and their education in those doctrines of the Catholic church relating to the inherence rights of labor. To Cesar Chavez, the teachings of the church, the rituals and catechism that he absorbed as an obligation of culture rather than a voluntary and knowing act of religious faith, had never seemed to have more than tangential relevance to the hard-edged world that poor people confronted in their daily lives. But in the

---

*The *Bracera* program—the word root means "arm" in Spanish—continued in force until the end of 1964, when political pressures finally led the federal government to abolish this "emergency" measure.

militant example and activist pedagogy of Father McDonnell, Chavez discovered a new dimension of Catholicism that excited him precisely because it was relevant to his immediate circumstances. "Actually," he later said, "my education started when I met Father Donald McDonnell. . . . We had long talks about farm workers. I knew a lot about the work, but I didn't know anything about economics, and I learned quite a bit from him. He had a picture of a worker's shanty and a picture of a grower's mansion; a picture of a labor camp and a picture of a high-priced building in San Francisco owned by the same grower. When things were pointed out to me, I began to see. . . . Everything he said was aimed at ways to solve the injustice." Chavez's appetite for the social gospel that McDonnell espoused was insatiable: "[He] sat with me past midnight telling me about social justice and the Church's stand on farm labor and reading from the encyclicals of Pope Leo XIII in which he upheld labor unions. I would do anything to get the Father to tell me more about labor history. I began going to the bracero camps with him to help with Mass, to the city jail with him to talk to prisoners, anything to be with him so that he could tell me more about the farm labor movement."

More than anyone else, Father McDonnell awoke Chavez to a world of pertinent ideas that would become the essential source of his personal philosophy; introduced him to a pantheon of crusaders for social justice (Gandhi among them) whose heroic exertions would supply the inspiration for his own crusade to empower farmworkers. Yet the crucial task of instructing Chavez in the practical means by which his nascent idealism might achieve concrete expression was brilliantly discharged by Fred Ross, an indefatigable organizer who had spent the better part of his adult life roaming California trying to show the victims of economic, racial, and ethnic discrimination how they might resist further abuse and degradation through organization.

Drawn to Sal Si Puedes by the palpable misery of its Chicano inhabitants, Ross began to conduct the series of informal house meetings through which he hoped to establish a local chapter of the Community Service Organization (CSO), a self-help group that operated under the sponsorship of radical activist Saul Alinsky's Chicago-based Industrial Areas Foundation. Always on the lookout for the natural leaders in the communities he sought to organize, Ross at once saw in Chavez, despite his outwardly shy and self-conscious demeanor, the telltale signs of a born organizer. "At the very first meeting," Ross recalled: "I was very much impressed with Cesar. I could tell he was intensely interested, a kind of burning interest rather than one of those inflammatory things that lasts one night and is then forgotten. He asked many questions, part of it to see if I really knew, putting me to the test. But it was much more than that." Ross also discovered that Chavez was an exceedingly quick study: "He understood it almost immediately, as soon as I drew the picture. He got the point—the whole question of power and the development of power within the group. He made the connections very quickly between the civic weakness of the group and the social neglect in the barrio, and also conversely, what could be done about that social neglect once the power was developed." "I kept a diary in those days," Ross said later. "And the first night I met Cesar, I wrote in it, 'I think I've found the guy I'm looking for.' It was obvious even then."

The confidence that Ross expressed in Chavez's leadership potential was immediately confirmed. Assigned to the CSO voter registration project in San Jose, Chavez displayed a natural aptitude for the work; so much in fact that Ross turned over control of the entire drive to him. And if his style of leadership proved somewhat unconventional, his tactical sense was unerring. While Ross had relied upon local college students to serve as registrars for the campaign, Chavez felt more could be gained by using people from the barrio. "Instead of recruiting college guys," he said, "I got all my friends, my beer-drinking friends. With them it wasn't a question of civic duty, they helped me because of friendship, and because it was fun." With nearly six thousand new voters registered by the time the campaign ended, Chavez's reputation as an organizer was established.

As exhilarated as he was by the challenge of organizing, Chavez was also sobered by the personal attacks that the local political establishment unleased against anyone who presumed to alter the balance of power in the ghetto. Since it was the heyday of McCarthyism, the charge most frequently lodged against him was that he was a Communist. It seemed not to matter that such charges were preposterous. Even the vaguest suggestion of radicalism was enough to cause the more cautious members of the Chicano community to regard Chavez with growing suspicion. "The Chicanos," he said, "wouldn't talk to me. They were afraid. The newspaper had a lot of influence during those McCarthy days. Anyone who organized or worked for civil rights were called a Communist. Anyone who talked about police brutality was called a Communist."

> Everywhere I went to organize they would bluntly ask, "Are you a Communist?"
> I would answer, "No."
> "How do we know?"
> "You don't know. You know because I tell you."
> And we would go around and around on that. If it was somebody who was being smart, I'd tell them to go to hell, but if it was somebody that I wanted to organize, I would have to go through an explanation.

359

Before long, however, Chavez became an expert in turning the cultural tendencies of his Chicano neighbors to his own advantage. When his detractors wrapped themselves in the flag, Chavez countered, with the help of Father McDonnell and other sympathetic priests, by cloaking himself in the respectability of the Catholic church. "I found out," he recalled with apparent satisfaction, "that when they learned I was close to the church, they wouldn't question me so much. So I'd get the priests to come out and give me their blessing. In those days, if a priest said something to the Mexicans, they would say fine. It's different now."

In the course of raising the civic consciousness of others, Chavez broadened and deepened his own previously neglected education. "I began to grow and to see a lot of things that I hadn't seen before," he said. "My eyes opened, and I paid more attention to political and social events." And though his emergence as a trade union activist was still years away, Chavez the community organizer felt a sufficient affinity with his counterparts in the labor field that he adopted as texts for his self-education "biographies of labor organizers like John L. Lewis and Eugene Debs and the Knights of Labor."

After watching his protégé in action for only a few months, Fred Ross persuaded Saul Alinsky that the CSO should employ the talents of so able an organizer on a full-time basis. Becoming a professional organizer, however, was a prospect that frightened Chavez nearly as much as it excited him. Helping Fred Ross was one thing, organizing on his own among strangers was quite another. Yet in the end, his desire to oppose what seemed unjust outweighed his fears.

From the end of 1952 until he quit the organization ten years later to build a union among farmworkers, the CSO was Chavez's life. He approached the work of helping the poor to help themselves in the only way his nature allowed, with a single-mindedness that made everything else in his life—home, family, personal gain—secondary. For Chavez, nothing short of total immersion in the work of forcing change was enough. If his wife inherited virtually the entire responsibility for raising their children (who were to number eight in all), if his children became resentful at being left to grow up without a father who was readily accessible to them, if he was himself forced to abandon any semblance of personal life, Chavez remained unshaken in his belief that the promotion of the greater good made every such sacrifice necessary and worthwhile.

The years he spent as an organizer for the CSO brought Chavez into contact, and usually conflict, with the whole range of public and private authorities to which the poor were accountable and by which they were controlled. The problems he handled were seldom other than mundane, yet each in its own way confirmed the collective impotence of those who populated the Chicano ghettos that became his special province. "They'd bring their personal problems," Chavez said of his CSO clients: "They were many. They might need a letter written or someone to interpret for them at the welfare department, the doctor's office, or the police. Maybe they were not getting enough welfare aid, or their check was taken away, or their kids were thrown out of school. Maybe they had been taken by a crooked salesman selling fences, aluminum siding, or freezers that hold food for a month."

In the beginning, helping people to deal with problems they felt otherwise powerless to resolve was an end in itself. In time, however, Chavez saw that if his service work was going to produce a legacy of activist sentiment in Chicano neighborhoods, it was necessary to recast what had typically been an act of unconditional assistance into a mutually beneficial transaction. And, when he discovered that those whom he was serving were not just willing, but eager, to return the favor, Chavez made that volition the basis upon which he helped to build the CSO into the most formidable Mexican-American political organization in the state. "Once I realized helping people was an organizing technique," he said, "I increased that work. I was willing to work day and night and to go to hell and back for people—provided they also did something for the CSO in return. I never felt bad asking for that . . . . because I wasn't asking for something for myself. For a long time we didn't know how to put that work together into an organization. But we learned after a while—we learned how to help people by making them responsible."

Because agricultural labor constituted a main source of economic opportunity in most Chicano communities, many of those whom Chavez recruited into the CSO were farmworkers. Not until 1958, however, did Chavez take his first halting steps toward making work and its discontents the essential focus of his organizing activities. This gradual shift from community to labor organization occurred over a period of several months as Chavez struggled to establish a CSO chapter in Oxnard, a leading citrus growing region north of Los Angeles. Asked by Saul Alinsky to organize the local Chicano community in order that it might support the flagging efforts of the United Packinghouse Workers to win labor contracts covering the region's citrus-packing sheds, Chavez embarked upon his task intending to exploit the same assortment of grievances that festered in barrios throughout the state.

His new clients, however, had other ideas. From the beginning, whenever he sought to impress his agenda upon local citizens, they interrupted with their own: a concern that they were being denied jobs because growers in the region relied almost entirely on braceros to meet their needs for farm labor. It proved to be an issue that simply would not go away. "At every house meeting," Chavez recalled, "they hit me with the bracero problem, but I would dodge it. I just didn't fathom how big that problem was. I would say, 'Well, you know, we really can't do anything about that, but it's a bad problem. Something should be done.'" An apparently artless dodger, he was, in the end, forced to make the bracero problem the focus of his campaign. "Finally," he admitted, "I decided this was the issue I had to tackle. The fact that braceros were also farmworkers didn't bother me. . . . The jobs belonged to local workers. The braceros were brought only for exploitation. They were just instruments for the growers. Braceros didn't make any money, and they were exploited viciously, forced to work under conditions the local people wouldn't tolerate. If the braceros spoke up, if they made the minimal complaints, they'd be shipped back to Mexico."

In attacking Oxnard's bracero problem, Chavez and his followers confronted the integrated power of the agribusiness establishment in its most forceful and resilient aspect. While farm employers around Oxnard and throughout the state were permitted under federal regulations to employ braceros only when they had exhausted the available pool of local farmworkers, they had long operated on the basis of a collusive arrangement with the California Farm Placement Service that allowed them to import Mexican nationals without regard to labor market conditions in the region.

Although Chavez and the large CSO membership he rallied behind him sought nothing more than compliance with existing rules regarding the employment of braceros, the thirteen-month struggle that followed brought them into bitter conflicts with politically influential employers, state farm placement bureaucrats, and federal labor department officials. Yet through the use of picket lines, marches, rallies, and a variety of innovative agitational techniques that reduced the Farm Placement Service to almost total paralysis, Chavez and his militant following had by the end of 1959 won a victory so complete that farm employers in the region were recruiting their labor through a local CSO headquarters that operated as a hiring hall.

Chavez emerged from the Oxnard campaign convinced that work-related issues had greater potential as a basis for organizing Chicanos than any that he had earlier stressed. The response to his organizing drive in Oxnard was overwhelming, and he saw at once "the difference between that CSO chapter and any other CSO up to that point was that jobs were the main issue." And at the same juncture, he said: "I began to see the potential of organizing the Union."

What Chavez saw with such clarity, however, the elected leadership of the CSO, drawn almost exclusively from the small but influential ranks of middle-class Chicanos, was unwilling even to imagine. Determined that the CSO would remain a civic organization, the leadership decisively rejected Chavez's proposal to transform the Oxnard chapter into a farmworker's union. "We had won a victory," Chavez bitterly recalled, "but I didn't realize how short-lived it would be. We could have built a union there, but the CSO wouldn't approve. In fact, the whole project soon fell apart. I wanted to go for a strike and get some contracts, but the CSO wouldn't let me. . . . If I had had the support of the CSO, I would have built a union there. If anyone from labor had come, we could have had a union. I think if the Union of Organized Devils of America had come, I would have joined them, I was so frustrated."

Even though he remained with the CSO for two years following his defeat over the issues of unionism, Chavez's devotion to the organization waned as his determination to organize farmworkers increased. Finally, when the CSO once again rejected the idea of unionism at its annual convention in 1962, Chavez decided that he had had enough. He resigned as the convention ended and left the organization on his thirty-fifth birthday. "I've heard people say," he later explained, "that because I was thirty-five, I was getting worried, as I hadn't done too much with my life. But I wasn't worried. I didn't even consider thirty-five to be old. I didn't care about that. I just knew we needed a Union. . . . What I didn't know was that we would go through hell because it was an all but impossible task."

Based on the often heroic, but inevitably futile, efforts of those who had earlier dared to challenge the monolithic power of industrialized agriculture in California—the Industrial Workers of the World before World War I; the communist-led Cannery and Agricultural Workers Industrial Union during the early 1930s; the CIO in the late thirties; the AFL in the 1940s; and a rich variety of independent ethnic unions over the better part of a century—Chavez's assertion that organizing the state's farmworkers was "an all but impossible task" hardly overstated the case. Farm employers, assisted by a supporting cast representing nearly every form of public and private power in the state, had beaten back every attempt by workers to gain power while assiduously cultivating a public image of themselves as beleaguered yeomen valiantly struggling against the erosive forces of modernity, including unionism, to preserve the nation's Jeffersonian heritage.

To the task of contesting the immense power and redoubtable prestige of the agribusiness nexus, Chavez brought nothing more or less than an intensity of purpose that bordered on fanaticism. And while he would have rejected the disdain that the remark reflected, Chavez was in essential agreement with the cynical AFL official who declared in 1935: "Only fanatics are willing to live in shacks or tents and get their heads broken in the interest of migratory labor." In Chavez's view, nothing less than fanaticism would suffice if farmworkers were to be emancipated from a system of wage slavery that had endured for a century. When a reporter observed during one of the UFW's later struggles that he "sounded like a fanatic," Chavez readily admitted the charge. "I am," he confessed. "There's nothing wrong with being a fanatic. Those are the only ones that get things done."

In many ways, Chavez's supreme accomplishment as an organizer came long before he signed up his first farmworker. Attracting disciples willing to embrace the idea of a farmworkers' movement with a passion, single-mindedness, and spirit of sacrifice equal to his own was at once Chavez's greatest challenge and his finest achievement. By the fall of 1962, when he formally established the National Farm Workers Association (NFWA) in a derelict Fresno theater, Chavez had rallied to "La Causa"—the iconographic designation soon adopted by the faithful—an impressive roster of "co-fanatics": Dolores Huerta, a small, youthful-looking mother of six (she would have ten in all) whose willingness to do battle with Chavez over union tactics was exceeded only by her fierce loyalty to him; Gilbert Padilla, like Huerta another CSO veteran, whose activism was rooted in a hatred for the migrant system that derived from personal experience; Wayne Hartimire and Jim Drake, two young Anglo ministers who were to make the California Migrant Ministry a virtual subsidiary of the union; Manuel Chavez, an especially resourceful organizer who reluctantly gave up a well-paying job to join the union when the guilt his cousin Cesar heaped upon him for not joining became unbearable. Most important, there was Helen Chavez, whose willingness to sacrifice so much of what mattered most to her, including first claim on her husband's devotion, revealed the depth of her own commitment to farmworker organization.

Working out of Delano, which became the union's first headquarters, Chavez began the slow and often discouraging process of organizing farm laborers whose strong belief in the rightness of his union-building mission was tempered by an even deeper conviction that "it couldn't be done, that the growers were too powerful." With financial resources consisting of a small savings account, gifts and loans from relatives, and the modest wages Helen earned by returning to the fields, the cost of Chavez's stubborn idealism to himself and his family was measured in material deprivation and emotional tumult. Had he been willing to accept financial assistance from such sources as the United Packinghouse Workers or the Agricultural Workers Organizing Committee (AWOC), a would-be farmworkers' union established in 1959 by the AFL-CIO, the worst hardships that awaited Chavez and his loyalists might have been eased or eliminated. Yet, following a line of reasoning that was in some ways reminiscent of the voluntarist logic of earlier trade unionists, Chavez insisted that a farm-workers' union capable of forging the will and stamina required to breach the awesome power of agribusiness could only be built on the sacrifice and suffering of its own membership.

During the NFWA's formative years there was more than enough sacrifice and suffering to go around. But due to the services it provided to farm-workers and the promise of a better life it embodied, the union slowly won the allegiance of a small but dedicated membership scattered through the San Joaquin valley. By the spring of 1965, when the union called its first strike, a brief walkout by rose grafters in Kern County that won higher wages but no contract, Chavez's obsession was on its way to becoming a functioning reality.

Despite the studied deliberateness of its leaders, however, the struggle that catapulted the union to national attention, and invested its mission with the same moral authority that liberal and left-wing activists of the 1960s attributed to the decade's stormy civil rights, antipoverty, and anti-war movements, began in the fall of 1965 as a reluctant gesture of solidarity with an AWOC local whose mainly Filipino membership was on strike against grape growers around Delano. Given the demonstrated ineptitude of the old-time trade unionists who directed the AFL-CIO's organizing efforts among California farmworkers, Chavez had reason to hesitate before committing his still small and untested membership to the support of an AWOC strike. But the strike was being led by Larry Itliong, a Filipino veteran of earlier agricultural strikes and the ablest of the AWOC organizers, and Chavez did not have it in him to ignore a just cause. "At the time," he recalled, "we had about twelve hundred members, but only about two hundred were paying dues. I didn't feel we were ready for a strike—I figured it would be a couple more years before we would be—but I also knew we weren't going to break a strike." The formal decision to support AWOC, made at a boisterous mass meeting held in Delano's Catholic church on September 16 (the day Mexicans celebrate the end of Spanish colonial rule), produced twenty-seven hundred workers willing to sign union cards authorizing the NFWA to represent them in dealing with area grape growers.

The Delano strike, which soon widened beyond the table grape growers who were its initial targets to include the state's major wineries, was a painful five-year struggle destined to test not only the durability of agricultural unionism in California but also the wisdom and resourcefulness of

Chavez's leadership. Because growers had little difficulty in recruiting scabs to take the place of strikers, Chavez recognized immediately that a strike could not deny employers the labor they required to cultivate and harvest their crops. Even so, picket lines went up on the first day of the strike and were maintained with unfailing devotion week after week, month after month. Chavez emphasized the need for picketing because he believed that no experience promoted a keener sense of solidarity or afforded strikers a more graphic and compelling illustration of the struggle's essential character. "Unless you have been on a picket line," he said, "you just can't understand the feeling you get there, seeing the conflict at its two most acid ends. It's a confrontation that's vivid. It's a real education." It was an education, however, for which pickets often paid a high price: threats, physical intimidation, and outright violence at the hands of growers and their agents and arbitrary arrests and harassment by local lawmen who made no effort to mask their pro-employer sympathies. Yet, no matter how great the provocation, no matter how extreme the violence directed against them, strikers were sworn by Chavez not to use violence. Chavez's unwavering commitment to nonviolence was compounded from equal measures of his mother's teachings, the affecting example of St. Francis of Assissi, and the moral philosophy of Gandhi. In the end, though, it was the power of nonviolence as a tactical method that appealed to him. Convinced that the farmworkers' greatest asset was the inherent justice of their cause, Chavez believed that the task of communicating the essential virtue of the union's struggle to potential supporters, and to the general public, would be subverted if strikers resorted to violence. "If someone commits violence against us," Chavez argued, "it is much better—if we can—not to react against the violence, but to react in such a way as to get closer to our goal. People don't like to see a nonviolent movement subjected to violence. . . . That's the key point we have going for us. . . . By some strange chemistry, every time the opposition commits an unjust act against our hopes and aspirations, we get tenfold paid back in benefits."

Winning and sustaining public sympathy, as well as the active support of labor, church, student, civic, and political organizations, was indispensable to the success of the Delano struggles because the inefficacy of conventional strike tactics led Chavez to adopt the economic boycott as the union's primary weapon in fighting employers. Newly sensitized to issues of social justice by the civil rights struggles that reverberated across the country, liberals and leftists enthusiastically embraced the union's cause, endorsing its successive boycotts and not infrequently showing up in Delano to bear personal witness to the unfolding drama of the grape strike. Many unions—from dockworkers who refused to handle scab grapes to autoworkers, whose president, Walter Reuther, not only pledged generous financial assistance to the strikers but also traveled to Delano to join their picket lines—also supported the NFWA. Even the AFL-CIO, which had been sponsoring the rival Agricultural Workers Organizing Committee, ended up embracing the NFWA when Bill Kircher, the federation's national organizing director, concluded that the future of farmworker unionism lay with Chavez and his ragtag following rather than with the more fastidious, but less effective, AWOC. Kircher's assessment of the situation also led him to urge a merger of the UFWA and AWOC. And although their long-standing suspicion of "Big Labor" impelled many of the Anglo volunteers who had joined his movement to oppose the idea, Chavez and the union's farmworker membership recognized that the respectability and financial strength to be gained from such a merger outweighed any loss of independence that AFL-CIO affiliation might entail. With Chavez at its helm and Larry Itliong as its second-in-command, the United Farm Workers Organizing Committee (UFWOC) was formally chartered by the AFL-CIO in August 1966.

The public backing the farmworkers attracted, including that of Senator Robert F. Kennedy, who became an outspoken supporter of the union when the Senate Subcommittee on Migratory Labor held its highly publicized hearings in Delano during the spring of 1966, indicated that large segments of the American people believed that grape strikers occupied the moral "high ground" in their dispute with farm employers. To an important degree, however, public support for the farmworkers' cause also reflected a willingness among many Americans to believe and trust in Cesar Chavez personally; to see in the style and content of his public "persona" those qualities of integrity, selflessness, and moral rectitude that made his cause theirs whether or not they truly understood it. And if Chavez was more embarrassed than flattered by such adoration, he was also enough of an opportunist to see that when liberals from New York to Hollywood made him the human repository of their own unrequited idealism or proclaimed his sainthood, it benefited farmworkers.

"Alone, the farm workers have no economic power," Chavez once observed, "but with the help of the public they can develop the economic power to counter that of the growers." The truth of that maxim was first revealed in April 1966, when a national boycott campaign against its product line of wines and spirits caused Schenley Industries, which had 5,000 acres of vineyards in the San Joaquin valley, to recognize the farmworkers' union and enter into contract negotiations. For Chavez, who received the news as he and a small band of union loyalists were nearing the end of an arduous, but exceedingly well-publicized, 300-mile march from Delano to

Sacramento, Schenley's capitulation was "the first major proof of the power of the boycott."

Chavez's tactical genius, and the power of a national (and later international) boycott apparatus that transformed an otherwise local dispute into a topic of keen interest and passionate debate in communities across the country, prompted one winery after another to choose accommodation over further conflict. For two of the biggest wine grape growers, however, the prospect of acquiescing to UFWOC's brand of militant unionism was so loathsome that they resolved to court a more palatable alternative: the giant International Brotherhood of Teamsters. And although they had no apparent support among farmworkers in the region, the Teamsters, under the cynical and oportunistic leadership of William Grami, organizing director of the union's western conference, eagerly sought to prove that theirs was indeed the type of "businesslike" labor organization which anti-union farm employers could tolerate. Yet as good as the idea first seemed to the DiGiorgio Fruit Corporation and then to Perelli-Minetti Vineyards, consummating such a mischievous liaison with the Teamsters proved impossible. In the end, neither the companies nor the Teamsters had the will to persist in the face of intensified UFWOC boycotts, angry condemnations by the labor movement, and a rising tide of public disapproval. The controversy was finally resolved through secret ballot elections, which resulted in expressions of overwhelming support for Chavez and UFWOC.

The victories won during the first two years of the Delano struggle, while they propelled the cause of farmworker organization far beyond the boundaries of any previous advance, left Chavez and his followers still needing to overcome table grape growers in the San Joaquin and Coachella valleys before the union could claim real institutional durability. The state's table grape industry, comprised for the most part of family farms whose hardworking owners typically viewed unionism as an assault on their personal independence as well as a threat to their prerogatives as employers, remained unalterably opposed to UFWOC's demands long after California's largest wineries had acceded to them. Thus when Chavez made them the main targets of the union's campaign toward the end of 1967, table grape growers fought back with a ferocity and tactical ingenuity that announced their determination to resist unionism at whatever cost.

While the boycott continued to serve as the union's most effective weapon, especially after employers persuaded compliant local judges to issue injunctions severely restricting picketing and other direct action in the strike region, the slowness with which it operated to prod recalcitrant growers toward the bargaining table produced in farmworkers and volunteers alike an impatience that reduced both morale and discipline. It also undermined La Causa's commitment to nonviolence. "There came a point in 1968," Chavez recalled, "when we were in danger of losing. . . . Because of a sudden increase in violence against us, and an apparent lack of progress after more than two years of striking, there were those who felt that the time had come to overcome violence by violence. . . . There was demoralization in the ranks, people becoming desperate, more and more talk about violence. People meant it, even when they talked to me. They would say, 'Hey, we've got to burn these sons of bitches down. We've got to kill a few of them.'"

In responding to the crisis, Chavez chose a method of restoring discipline and morale that was as risky and unusual as it was revealing of the singular character of his leadership. He decided to fast. The fast, which continued for twenty-five painful days before it was finally broken at a moving outdoor mass in Delano that included Robert Kennedy among its celebrants, was more than an act of personal penance. "I thought I had to bring the Movement to a halt," Chavez explained, "do something that would force them and me to deal with the whole question of violence and ourselves. We had to stop long enough to take account of what we were doing." Although the fast's religious overtones offended the secular sensibilities of many of his followers, it was more a political than a devotional act; an intrepid and dramatic, if manipulative, device by which Chavez established a compelling standard of personal sacrifice against which his supporters might measure their own commitment and dedication to La Causa, and thus their allegiance to its leader. The power of guilt as a disciplinary tool was something Chavez well understood from his study of life and philosophy of Gandhi, and he was never reluctant to use it himself. "One of his little techniques," Fred Ross said of Chavez's style of leadership, "has always been to shame people into doing something by letting them know how hard he and others were working, and how it was going to hurt other people if they didn't help too."

Those in the union who were closest to Chavez, whatever their initial reservations, found the fast's effect undeniably therapeutic. Jerry Cohen, the union's able young attorney, while convinced that it had been "a fantastic gamble," was deeply impressed by "what a great organizing tool the fast was." "Before the fast," Cohen noted, "there were nine ranch committees [the rough equivalent of locals within the UFW's structure], one for each winery. The fast, for the first time, made a union out of those ranch committees. . . . Everybody worked together." Dolores Huerta also recognized the curative power of Chavez's ordeal. "Prior to that fast," she insisted, "there had been a lot of bickering and backbiting and fighting and

369

little attempts at violence. But Cesar brought everybody together and really established himself as a leader of the farm workers."

While a chronic back ailment, apparently exacerbated by his fast and a schedule that often required him to work twenty hours a day, slowed Chavez's pace during much of 1968 and 1969, the steadily more punishing economic effects of the grape boycott finally began to erode the confidence and weaken the resistance of growers. With the assistance of a committee of strongly pro-union Catholic bishops who had volunteered to mediate the conflict, negotiations between the union and the first defectors from the growers' ranks finally began in the spring of 1970. And by the end of July, when the most obdurate growers in the Delano area collapsed under the combined weight of a continuing boycott and their own mounting weariness, Chavez and his tenacious followers had finally accomplished what five years before seemed impossible to all but the most sanguine forecasters.

The union's victory, which extended to eighty-five percent of the state's table grape industry, resulted in contracts that provided for substantial wage increases and employer contributions to UFWOC's health and welfare and economic development funds. Even more important, however, were the noneconomic provisions: union-run hiring halls that gave UFWOC control over the distribution of available work; grievance machinery that rescued the individual farmworker from the arbitrary authority of the boss; restrictions on the use of pesticides that endangered the health of workers; in short, provisions for the emancipation of workers from the century-old dictatorship of California agribusiness.

After five years of stuggle and sacrifice, of anguish and uncertainty, Chavez and his followers wanted nothing so much as an opportunity to recuperate from their ordeal and to savor their victory. It was not to be. On the day before the union concluded its negotiations with Delano grape growers, Chavez received the distressing news that lettuce growers in the Salinas and Santa Maria valleys, knowing that they would be the next targets of UFWOC's organizing campaign, had signed contracts providing for the Teamsters' union to represent their field workers. In keeping with the pattern of the Teamsters' involvement with agricultural field labor, no one bothered to consult the Chicano workers whose incessant stooping and bending, whose painful contortions in the service of the hated short-handle hoe, made possible the growers' proud boast that the Salinas valley was the "salad bowl of the nation."

Except for one contract, which the union acquired in 1961 through a collusive agreement with a lettuce grower scheming to break a strike by the Agricultural Workers Organizing Committee, the Teamsters had been content to limit their interest to the truck drivers, boxmakers, and packing-shed workers of the vegetable industry. The Teamsters' decision to expand their jurisdiction to include field labor was a frontal assault on UFWOC. Still weary from the Delano struggle and confronting the complex job of implementing the union's newly won contracts, Chavez and his staff rushed to Salinas in order to meet the challenge.

If William Grami and his Teamsters cohorts discovered that the specter of a UFWOC organizing drive put Anglo lettuce growers in an unusually accommodating frame of mind, they found that Chicano farmworkers in the Salinas and Santa Maria valleys were unwilling to accept a union other than of their own choosing, especially after Chavez launched his boister-ous counterattack. As thousands of defiant workers walked off their jobs rather than join a union of the employers' choice, the Teamsters' hierarchy, inundated by a rising tide of liberal and labor criticism, decided that Grami's tactics were inopportune from a public relations standpoint, and therefore ordered him to undo his now inexpedient handiwork. Grami du-tifully, if reluctantly, invited Chavez to meet with him, and the two men quickly worked out an agreement providing the UFWOC would have ex-clusive jurisdiction over field labor, and that the Teamsters would renounce their contracts with lettuce growers and defer to the workers' true prefer-ence in bargaining agents. For a few of the largest growers in the Salinas valley, those who felt most vulnerable to the boycott Chavez had threat-ened, abandoning Teamsters contracts in favor of agreements with UFWOC provided a welcome escape from a misadventure. Yet when the Teamsters asserted that they were "honor bound" to respect the wishes of 170 growers who refused to void their contracts, Chavez had no choice but to resume hostilities.

Although the more than five thousand workers who responded to UFWOC's renewed strike call brought great enthusiasm and energy to the union's rallies, marches, and picket lines, their capacity to disrupt the fall lettuce harvest declined as the influence exerted by a ready supply of job-hungry *green carders* (Mexican nationals with work permits) combined with aggressive strikebreaking by violence-prone Teamsters "guards," hos-tile police, politically influential employers, and injunction-happy local judges. As strike activities diminished and boycott operations intensified, employers obtained a court order declaring both types of union pressure illegal under a state law banning jurisdictional strikes.* Chavez later spent

*Two years later the California State Supreme Court overturned the order, cit-

three weeks in jail for instructing his followers to ignore the order, but the publicity and additional support his brief imprisonment generated made it one of the few positive developments in an otherwise discouraging slide into adversity.

The challenge presented by the Teamsters-grower alliance in the lettuce industry forced UFWOC to divert precious resources into the reconstruction of its far-flung boycott network. It also distracted Chavez and his most competent aides at a time when the union was in the process of transforming itself from an organization expert in agitation into one equipped to administer contracts covering thousands of workers in the grape industry. Meeting the demands of the hiring hall and the grievance process, which were the union's greatest potential sources of institutional strength, also became its most worrisome and debilitating problem as ranch committees composed of rank-and-file members struggled against their own inexperience, and sometimes powerful tendencies toward vindictiveness, favoritism, and a residual servility, to satisfy the labor requirements of employers and to protect the contractual rights of their fellow workers.

Although Chavez instituted an administrative training program designed by his old mentor Fred Ross, he rejected an AFL-CIO offer of assistance because of his stubborn conviction that a genuinely democratic union must entrust its operation to its own members even at the risk of organizational inefficiency and incompetence. And when he shifted the union's headquarters fifty miles southeast of Delano to an abandoned tuberculosis sanitorium in the Tehachapi Mountains that he called La Paz—short for Nuestra Senora de la Paz (Our Lady of Peace)—Chavez claimed the move was prompted by a concern that his easy accessibility to members of the union's ranch committees discouraged self-reliance. "It was my idea to leave for La Paz," he explained, "because I wanted to remove my presence from Delano, so they could develop their own leadership, because if I am there, they wouldn't make the decisions themselves. They'd come to me." But the move intensified suspicions of internal critics like Larry Itliong, who left the union partly because Chavez's physical isolation from the membership seemed to enhance the influence of the Anglo "intellectuals" while diminishing that of the rank and file. The greatest barrier to broadening the union's leadership and administrative operation, however, was posed neither by geography nor the influence of Anglo volunteers, but by Chavez himself, whose devotion to the ideal of decentralization was seldom matched by an equal disposition to delegate authority to others. Journalist

---

ing the collusive relationship between the employers and the Teamsters and the latter's lack of support among farmworkers at the time the contracts were signed.

Ron Taylor, who observed Chavez's style of leadership at close range, wrote: "He conceptually saw a union run in the most democratic terms, but in practice he had a difficult time trying to maintain his own distance; his tendencies were to step in and make decisions. . . . Even though he had removed himself from Delano, he maintained a close supervision over it, and all of the other field offices. Through frequent staff meetings and meetings of the executive board, he developed his own personal involvement with the tiniest of union details."

If Chavez's deficiencies as an administrator troubled sympathetic AFL-CIO officials like Bill Kircher, they tended to reinforce the suspicion privately harbored by such trade-union traditionalists as federation president George Meany that viable organization was probably beyond the compass of farmworkers, no matter how driven and charismatic their leader. Indeed, what appeared to be at the root of Meany's personal skepticism was Chavez's eccentric style of leadership and somewhat alien trade union philosophy: his well-advertised idealism, which uncharitably rendered was a species of mere self-righteousness; his overweening presence, which seemingly engendered an unhealthy cult of personality; his extravagant sense of mission, which left outsiders wondering whether his was a labor or a social movement; his apparently congenital aversion to compromise, which, in Meany's view, negated the AFL-CIO's repeated efforts to negotiate a settlement of UFWOC's jurisdictional dispute with the Teamsters. None of these reservations was enough to keep the AFL-CIO in early 1972 from changing the union's status from that of organizing committee to full-fledged affiliate—the United Farm Workers of America—but in combination they were apparently enough to persuade Meany that Chavez was no longer deserving of the same levels of financial and organizational support previously contributed by the federation.

Yet if trade union administration of an appropriately conventional style was not his forte, Chavez demonstrated during the course of several legislative battles in 1971 and 1972 that his talents as a political organizer and tactician were exceptional. When the Oregon legislature passed an anti-union bill sponsored by the American Farm Bureau Federation, Chavez and his followers, in only a week's time, persuaded the governor to veto it. Shortly thereafter, Chavez initiated a far more ambitious campaign to recall the governor of Arizona for signing a similar grower-backed bill into law. And while the recall drive ultimately bogged down in a tangle of legal disputes, Chavez's success in registering nearly one hundred thousand mostly poor, mostly Chicano voters fostered fundamental changes in the political balance of power in Arizona.

It was in California, however, that the UFW afforded its opponents the most impressive demonstration of La Causa's political sophistication and clout, and Chavez revealed to friends and foes alike that his ability to influence public debate extended well beyond the normal boundaries of trade union leadership. With the backing of the state's agribusiness establishment, the California Farm Bureau launched during 1972 a well-financed initiative drive—popularly known as Proposition 22—designed to eliminate the threat of unionism by banning nearly every effective weapon available to the UFW, including the boycott. Having failed the year before to win legislative approval for an equally tough anti-union measure, farm employers were confident that they could persuade the citizens of California, as they had so often before, that protecting the state's highly profitable agricultural industry was in the public interest. Aware that the UFW could not survive under the restrictive conditions that Proposition 22 contemplated, but without the financial resources needed to counter the growers' expensive media campaign, Chavez and his aides masterfully deployed what they did have: an aroused and resourceful membership. In the end, the growers' financial power proved to be no match for the UFW's people power. In defeating Proposition 22 by a decisive margin—58 percent to 42 percent—the UFW not only eliminated the immediate threat facing the union, but also announced to growers in terms too emphatic to ignore that the time was past when farm employers could rely upon their political power to keep farmworkers in their place.

The political battles that occupied Chavez and the UFW during much of 1972 involved issues so central to the union's existence that they could not be avoided. But even in the course of winning its political fights with agribusiness, the union lost ground on other equally crucial fronts. Organizing activities all but ceased as the UFW turned its attention to political action, and further efforts aimed at alleviating the administrative problems that plagued the union's operation in the grape industry and increasing the pressures on Salinas valley lettuce growers were neglected. At the beginning of 1973 the UFW was in the paradoxical situation of being at the height of its political strength while its vulnerability as a union was increasing.

Just how vulnerable the union was became apparent as the contracts it had negotiated in 1970 with Coachella valley grape growers came up for renewal. Chavez had heard rumors that the Teamsters were planning to challenge the UFW in the region, but not until growers made plain their intention to reclaim complete control over the hiring, dispatching, and disciplining of workers did he suspect that a deal was already in the making. The UFW retained the allegiance of a vast majority of the industry's workers, but neither the growers nor the Teamsters seemed to care. As soon as the UFW contracts expired, all but two growers announced that they had

signed new four-year agreements with the Teamsters. Hiring halls, grievance procedures, and protections against dangerous pesticides disappeared
along with the workers' right to a union of their own choice.

Unlike their earlier forays into agriculture, which reflected the opportun-
ism of lower level functionaries interested in advancing their own careers,
the Teamsters' move into the grape industry was only the leading edge
of a grandiose new strategy by the union's top leadership to rescue farm
employers from the UFW in return for the exclusive right to represent
farmworkers. Teamsters president Frank Fitzsimmons, with the strong
encouragement of the Nixon administration, had suggested such an arrangement late in 1972 when he appeared as the featured speaker at the
annual convention of the American Farm Bureau Federation. The Teamsters provided further evidence of their revived interest in agriculture by
announcing a few weeks later that the union had renegotiated contracts
with 170 growers operating in the Salinas, Santa Maria, and Imperial valleys even though the existing five-year agreement still had nearly three
years to run.

The Teamsters' special appeal to California's agribusiness community
was obvious: while the UFW insisted that farm employers share power
with their workers, Teamsters contracts required only a sharing of the industry's wealth in the form of higher wages and other economic benefits.
That the Teamster never contemplated a kind of unionism that would permit Chicano farmworkers to gain a measure of control over their own lives
was confirmed by Einar Mohn, director of the Western Conference of
Teamsters, who said shortly after the union announced its coup in the grape
industry: "We have to have them in the union for a while. It will be a couple
of years before they can start having membership meetings, before we can
use the farm workers' ideas in the union. I'm not sure how effective a
union can be when it is composed of Mexican-Americans and Mexican
nationals with temporary visas. Maybe as agriculture becomes more sophisticated, more mechanized, with fewer transients, fewer green carders,
and as jobs become more attractive to whites, then we can build a union
that can have structures and that can negotiate from strength and have
membership participation."

In the face of the Teamsters onslaught, the UFW, reinforced by familiar
coalition of religious, student, liberal, and labor volunteers, resorted to its
customary arsenal: picket lines, rallies, marches, boycotts, and appeals to
the public's sense of justice. Yet with hundreds of beefy Teamster goons
conducting a reign of terror through the region, and UFW activists being
jailed by the hundreds for violating court orders prohibiting virtually every
form of resistance and protest the union employed, the Chavez forces

never had a chance of winning back what they had lost in the Coachella valley, or of stopping the Teamsters when they later moved in on the UFW's remaining contracts with Delano-area table grape growers and the state's major wineries. George Meany, who described the Teamsters' raids as "the most vicious strikebreaking, union-busting effort I've seen in my lifetime," persuaded the AFL-CIO executive council to contribute $1.6 million to the UFW's support. But the money could only ease the union's predicament, not solve it. After five months of bitter struggle, more than thirty-five hundred arrests, innumerable assaults, and the violent deaths of two members—one at the hands of a deputy sheriff who claimed that his victim was "resisting arrest," the other at the hands of a gun-toting young strikebreaker who said he felt menaced by pickets—Chavez, his union in ruins, called off any further direct action in favor of the UFW's most effective weapon: the boycott. The UFW, which only a year before had more than one hundred fifty contracts and nearly forty thousand members, was reduced by September 1973 to a mere handful of contracts and perhaps one-quarter of its earlier membership.

In the wake of the UFW's stunning defeat in the grape industry, writing the union's obituary became a favorite pasttime not only of its long-time adversaries but of some of its traditional sympathizers as well. Most acknowledged the irresistible pressures that a Teamsters-grower alliance unleashed against the union, but many also found fault with the leadership of Cesar Chavez, especially his real or imagined failure to progress from unruly visionary to orderly trade unionist. Chavez's "charisma," said one sympathizer, was no longer "as marketable a commodity as it once was." Another observer concluded that "the charisma and the cause are wearing thin." The "priests and nuns" were losing interest; "the rad-chics from New York's Sutton Place to San Francisco's Nob Hill are bored with it all." "I admire him," George Meany said of Chavez: "He's consistent, and I think he's dedicated. I think he's an idealist. I thinks he's a bit of a dreamer. But the thing that I'm disappointed about Cesar is that he never got to the point that he could develop a real viable union in the sense of what we think of as a viable union."

Yet if Chavez left something to be desired as a union administrator, his alleged deficiencies scarcely explained the UFW's precipitous descent. The union's battered condition was not a product of its failure to behave conventionally, or of Chavez's disinclination to abandon his assertedly quixotic proclivities in favor of the pure and simple ethic that informed the thinking and demeanor of the more typical trade union leader. Rather, the UFW's sudden decline was, for the most part, not of its own making: grape growers had never resigned themselves to sharing power with their workers, and when the Teamsters proffered an alternative brand of unionism that did not impinge upon their essential prerogatives they happily embraced it.

It was precisely because Chavez was "a bit of a dreamer" that the idea of farmworker organization gathered the initial force necessary to overcome the previously insurmountable opposition of employers, and it was because he remained stubbornly devoted to his dream even in the face of the UFW's disheartening setbacks that those who had rushed to speak eulogies over the momentarily prostrated union were ultimately proven wrong. The resources available to him after the debacle of 1973 were only a fraction of what they had been, but Chavez retained both the loyalty of his most able assistants and his own exceptional talents as an organizer and agitator. As the nationwide boycotts he revived against grape and lettuce growers and the country's largest wine producers, the E. and J. Gallo Wineries, slowly gained momentum during 1974, Chavez reminded his Teamsters-employer adversaries in the only language they seemed to understand that the UFW was not going away no matter how diligently they conspired to that end.

The same message was communicated through the union's greatly intensified political activity in 1974. The union relentlessly lobbied the state assembly to win passage of a farm labor bill providing for secret-ballot union-representation elections. Although it later died in the agribusiness-dominated senate, Chavez still demonstrated that the UFW had lost none of its political prowess. The union also brought considerable pressures to bear on Democratic gubernatorial nominee Jerry Brown to win a promise that, if elected, he would make the passage of an acceptable farm labor bill one of his top legislative priorities. The UFW had no real hope of achieving its legislative aim as long as the anti-union administration of Governor Ronald Reagan dominated the state government, but in the youthful Brown, who had actively supported the UFW's grape boycotts while he was a seminary student, Chavez recognized a potential ally.

Because they could not have the kind of explicitly anti-union law they had promoted through their unavailing campaign in support of Proposition 22, the state's farm employers, in a significant reversal of their longstanding position, sought to undermine the UFW by joining with both the Teamsters and AFL-CIO in support of federal legislation extending the National Labor Relations Act (NLRA) to include farmworkers. Chavez, who had years before supported such an extension, strongly opposed NLRA coverage for farmworkers both because of its diminished effectiveness in guaranteeing workers' rights and because it banned the secondary boycotts upon which the UFW had become so dependent.

377

With Brown's election in November 1974, a legislative solution to the conflict that had convulsed the state's agricultural labor relations for nearly a decade appeared to be at hand. But given the mutual rancor and distrust that existed between farm employers and Teamsters on the one hand and Chavez and his followers on the other, drafting legislation compelling enough in its composition to induce compromises required both unfailing patience and an uncommon talent for legerdemain. Brown, however, was persuaded that a combination of good will and resolve could produce such a "vehicle for compromise." The new governor recognized that almost ten years of constant hostilities had not only rendered the combatants less intransigent, but had also created public enthusiasm for legislation that might restore labor peace to California's fields and vineyards.

Though none of the parties affected by Brown's compromise bill was fully satisfied in the end, each found reasons to support it. For the Teamsters' union, whose reputation as labor's pariah was reinforced by its anti-UFW machinations, supporting the Agricultural Labor Relations bill was a belated act of image polishing. For the state's agribusinessmen, who were finally discovering that preemptive arrangements with the Teamsters would not protect them from the UFW's seemingly inexhaustible boycott organizers, accepting Brown's proposal promised to restore order to their long unsettled industry. For the UFW, whose leaders were hopeful that legislation might do for La Causa what it had earlier done for the civil rights movement, going along with the governor's bill was a calculated risk that had to be taken.

The Agricultural Labor Relations Act, which went into effect during the fall harvest season of 1975, established a five-member Agricultural Labor Relations Board (ALRB) to implement the law, the most important provisions of which guaranteed the right of farmworkers to organize and bargain collectively through representatives chosen by secret-ballot elections. The ALRB, which faced problems not unlike those confronted by the National Labor Relations Board forty years earlier, was forced to operate under exceedingly difficult circumstances, particularly after disgruntled growers provoked a bitter year-long political confrontation with the UFW by blocking the special appropriations the agency needed to support its heavier than expected workload. Yet despite attacks from all sides, an inexperienced staff, and the administrative miscarriages that inevitably attended the discharging of so controversial and exceptional a mandate, the ALRB doggedly pursued the law's essential intention of ensuring that farmworkers were free to decide questions of union affiliation without undue interference.

Whereas Chavez was often frustrated by the ALRB's plodding pace and periodic bungling, and at times criticized its operation in language as caustic and intemperate as that used by the most aggrieved farm employer, he considered the law a "godsend . . . without question the best law for workers—any workers—in the entire country." Chavez and the UFW, notwithstanding their sporadic fulminations, had good reasons to consider the ALRA in providential terms. Within two years of its passage, the UFW, with a membership approaching forty thousand, had regained its position as the dominant union in California agriculture. Even more important, the union's success persuaded the Teamsters, who had faltered badly in the heated competition for the allegiance of farmworkers, to sign a five-year pact that effectively ceded jurisdiction over agricultural labor to the UFW.* The ALRA became, in short, the means by which the UFW accomplished its own resurrection, the instrument by which Cesar Chavez redeemed his stewardship of La Causa.

But for the tenacious idealism and organizational virtuosity of Cesar Chavez, there is no reason to believe that the circumstances which fostered the ALRA's enactment would have arisen. Before he arrived on the scene, agribusinessmen in California were as secure in their power and authority as any employers in the country. Yet only ten years after Chavez and his followers first challenged their supremacy, farm employers were acquiescing to a law that augured the demolition of their one-hundred-year-old dominion over labor.

The law, however, imposed obligations as great as the benefits it promised. Beyond forcing the UFW to prove that the support it had always claimed to enjoy among farmworkers was actual rather than imagined, the ALRA had also challenged the capacity of Chavez and his lieutenants to take their organization into a new and different phase, one that rewarded abilities more closely associated with conventional trade union leadership than with the boycotting, marching, and other forms of social proselytism that the UFW had emphasized up to that time. Once the ALRA created the machinery whereby farmworkers might secure their rights to organize and bargain collectively, the conflicts that remained between themselves and employers had much less to do with elemental questions of justice than with arguable issues of economic equity and job control. The law enabled the UFW to make its presence felt in California's industrialized agriculture; it did not ensure that the union would either prevail in the short run or endure in the long run.

As from the beginning, the UFW's future as an organization is inextricably linked to Cesar Chavez's success as a leader. And since 1975 the

*Early in 1982 the pact was extended for another five-year period.

union's record testifies to a mixed performance on Chavez's part. After reaching a membership of approximately fifty thousand by the late 1970s, the union has slowly dwindled in size, comprising roughly forty thousand members by the early 1980s, nearly all of whom, except for isolated outposts in Florida, Arizona, and a couple of other states, are confined to California. The union's continuing failure to make greater headway among the 200,000 farmworkers who are potential members in California alone is attributable, in part, to the growing sophistication of employers in countering the UFW's appeal to workers through voluntary improvements in wages and conditions; to the entry into the farm labor force of workers without strong emotional ties to or knowledge of the heroic struggles of the past; and to the inability of an increasingly politicized ALRB to enforce the letter and the spirit of its mandate in a timely fashion, especially following the election in 1984 of a governor allied with the union's fiercest opponents.

It is also the case, however, that the UFW's drift from vitality toward apparent stagnation is partially rooted in a web of complex factors related to the sometimes contradictory leadership of Cesar Chavez: a sincere devotion to democratic unionism that is undermined by a tendency to regard all internal dissidents as traitors at best and anti-union conspirators at worst; a professed desire to make the UFW a rank-and-file union governed from the bottom up that is contradicted by a strong inclination to concentrate authority in his own hands and those of close family members; a commitment to professionalize the administration of the UFW that is impeded by a reliance on volunteerism so unyielding as to have caused many of the union's most loyal and efficient staff members to quit.

In fairness, however, Chavez's performance must be assessed on a basis that encompasses far more than the normal categories of trade union leadership. For unlike most American labor leaders, who had stood apart from the traditions of their European counterparts by insisting that unionism is an end in itself, Chavez has, in his own somewhat idiosyncratic way, remained determined to use the UFW and the heightened political consciousness of his Chicano loyalists as a means for promoting changes more fundamental than those attainable through collective bargaining and other conventional avenues of trade union activism. In defining the UFW's singular mission, Chavez once declared: "As a continuation of our struggle, I think that we can develop economic power and put it in the hands of the people so they can have more control of their own lives, and then begin to change the system. We want radical change. Nothing short of radical change is going to have any impact on our lives or our problems. We want sufficient power to control our own destinies. This is our struggle. It's a lifetime job. The work for social change and against social injustice is never ended."

When measured against the magnitude of his proposed enterprise, and against his extraordinary achievements on behalf of workers who were among the most powerless and degraded in America prior to his emergence, Chavez's real and alleged deficiencies in guiding the UFW across the hostile terrain of California's industrialized agriculture in no way detract from his standing as the most accomplished and far-sighted labor leader of his generation. Whether or not he has it in him to be more than a labor leader, to turn the UFW into an instrument of changes still more profound and far-reaching than it has already brought about, remains to be proven.

The history of American labor is littered with the wreckage of workers' organizations—the Knights of Labor and the Industrial Workers of the World among them—that tried and failed to combine the immediate purposes of trade unionism with an ultimate ambition to alter the fundamental structure of American society. Indeed, in an era when many labor leaders are preoccupied with nothing so much as the survival of their organizations, Chavez's pledge before the UFW's 1983 convention to lead the union in new and even bolder assaults against the economic and political status quo seems distinctly unrealistic. Unrealistic, that is, until one recalls the implausibility of what he has already accomplished.

Bibliographic Notes

The richest variety of primary sources relating to Chavez's career are in the official records of the UFW, which can be found in the Archives of Labor and Urban Affairs at Wayne State University. Jacques Levy's *Cesar Chavez: Autobiography of La Causa* (1975) is an important and readily accessible source of personal recollections contributed by Chavez, and by many other individuals who participated in or otherwise influenced the union's development.

Although there is no first-rate biography of Chavez, his career is the subject of a large and instructive body of popular and scholarly literature. Among the many books that may be profitably consulted are: John Gregory Dunne, *Delano* (rev. ed., 1971); Peter Mathiessen, *Sal Si Puedes: Cesar Chavez and the New American Revolution* (1969); Joan London and Henry Anderson, *So Shall Ye Reap: The Story of Cesar Chavez and the Farm Labor Movement* (1970); Ronald B. Taylor, *Chavez and the Farm Workers* (1975); Dick Meister and Ann Loftis, *A Long Time Coming: The Struggle to Unionize America's Farm Workers* (1977); Eugene Nelson, *Huelga* (1966); Sam Kushner, *Long Road to Delano* (1975); Jean Maddern Pitrone,

Chavez: Man of the Migrants (1972); and Mark Day, *Forty Acres: Cesar Chavez and the Farm Workers* (1971).

Because of La Causa's prominence in the broader movement for social justice in the 1960s and 1970s, articles on Chavez and the UFW can be found in a wide variety of periodical sources. Such left-of-center magazines as the *Nation*, the *New Republic*, *Ramparts*, and *Dissent* are particularly good contemporary sources on Chavez and the UFW's struggles, as are such liberal religious periodicals as *Christian Century*, *Christianity in Crisis*, *America*, and *Sojourners*. The attitudes of California farm employers toward Chavez and the UFW are available in the *California Farm Bureau Federation Monthly*,the *California Farmer*, and the *Farm Quarterly*. Newspapers also constitute an indispensable source of information on Chavez and the farmworkers' movement. The reporting of Harry Bernstein in the *Los Angeles Times*, Ron Taylor in the *Fresno Bee*, Dick Meister in the *San Francisco Chronicle*, and Sam Kushner in the *People's World* constitute an invaluable chronicle of the UFW's perilous passage from ambitious idea to established union. The UFW's newspaper, *El Macriado*, is also useful, although it should be used with caution.

For historical background on agricultural unionism in California, see: Carey McWilliams, *Factories in the Field* (1939); Stuart Jamieson, *Labor Unionism in American Agriculture*, U.S. Bureau of Labor Statistics Bulletin No. 836 (1945); my own *Bitter Harvest: A History of California Farmworkers, 1870–1941* (1981); Ernesto Galarza, *Merchants of Labor: The Mexican Bracero Story* (1964); and H. L. Mitchell, *Mean Things Happening in This Land* (1979).

Additional sources relating to the evolution of the UFW and the career of Cesar Chavez may be found in: Beverly Fodell (ed.), *Cesar Chavez and the United Farm Workers: A Selected Bibliography* (1974); and *Selected Bibliography: United Farm Workers, 1973–1976*, Walter P. Reuther Library of Labor and Urban Affairs, Wayne State University (1977).

Notes on Contributors

JOSEPH R. CONLIN is a professor of history at California State University, Chico. He has written several books on the history of labor and radicalism, including *Big Bill Haywood and the Radical Union Movement* and *Bread and Roses Too*. His current research focuses on the social history of diet and food customs.

CLETUS E. DANIEL teaches at the New York State School of Industrial and Labor Relations at Cornell University. Among his publications are *The ACLU and the Wagner Act* and *Bitter Harvest: A History of California Farmworkers, 1870–1941*.

MELVYN DUBOFSKY is currently chairman of the history department at the State University of New York at Binghamton. He has authored numerous books on American labor history, including *We Shall Be All*, *Industrialism and the American Worker, 1870–1920*, and *John L. Lewis: A Biography* (with Warren Van Tine). He is now completing a study of labor and the state in modern America.

STEVEN FRASER is a senior editor for Basic Books. He has published several articles on Sidney Hillman and the Amalgamated Clothing Workers and is now at work on a biography of Hillman.

WILLIAM H. HARRIS is an historian now serving as president of Paine College. Among his major publications is *The Harder We Run: Black Workers Since The Civil War*. He is currently researching a biography of H. Philip Randolph.

ESTELLE JAMES is a professor of economics and chair of the economics department at the State University of New York at Stony Brook. Author of *Hoffa and the Teamsters*, she is currently working on two topics—a study of the role of nonprofit organizations around the world and an analysis of the public-private division of responsibilities for education, in comparative perspective.

ALICE KESSLER-HARRIS is a professor of history at Hofstra University and author of several books and articles in the areas of women's and labor history, including *Women Have Always Worked* and *Out To Work: A History of Wage Earning Women in the United States*.

JOHN H. M. LASLETT is a professor of history at UCLA. In 1984 a second of edition of *Failure of a Dream? Essays in the History of American Socialism*, coedited with Seymour Martin Lipset, was published. His most recent monograph is a comparative study of coal mining towns in Scotland and the United States entitled *Nature's Noblemen: The Fortunes of the Independent Collier in Scotland and the American Midwest, 1855–1889*.

NELSON LICHTENSTEIN teaches history at the Catholic University of America. He is the author of *Labor's War at Home: The CIO under the No-Strike Pledge* and is currently preparing a biography of Walter Reuther.

DAVID MONTGOMERY is Farnam Professor of History at Yale University and author of "The Fall of the House of Labor: The Workplace, the State, and American Labor, 1865–1925" (forthcoming) and *Workers' Control in America: Studies in the History of Work, Technology, and Labor Struggles*.

RICHARD OESTREICHER is on the history faculty at the University of Pittsburgh. He is author of *Solidarity and Fragmentation: Working People and Class Consciousness in Detroit, 1875–1900* and is currently researching a social history of American working class formation, development, and recomposition from 1800 to 1980.

CRAIG PHELAN is on the faculty of Worchester Academy and is writing a biography of William Green.

NICK SALVATORE is a professor at the New York State School of Industrial and Labor Relations at Cornell University. His first book, *Eugene V.*

384

Debs: Citizen and Socialist, was awarded the Bancroft Prize in History (1983) and the John H. Dunning Prize (1984). He is currently working on a biography of Samuel Gompers and a study of black workers in the late nineteenth century North.

RONALD SCHATZ is on the history faculty at Wesleyan University. He is the author of *The Electrical Workers: A History of Labor at General Electric and Westinghouse, 1923–60* and is currently researching such topics as Catholic clergy, corporatism, and labor.

WARREN VAN TINE is chair of the Department of History at the Ohio State University. He is author of *The Making of the Labor Bureaucrat: Union Leadership in the United States, 1870–1920* and coauthor with Melvyn Dubofsky of *John L. Lewis: A Biography*.

ROBERT H. ZIEGER is professor of history at the University of Florida. His books include *Republicans and Labor, 1919–1929, Rebuilding the Pulp and Paper Workers' Union, 1933–1941* (winner of the 1984 Philip Taft Labor History Award), and *American Workers, American Unions, 1920–1985*.

Index

Acheson, Dean, 253
Adamic, Louis, 202–3
Addams, Jane, 210–11
Addes, George, 288, 291
Address of the National Labor Congress to the Workingmen of the United States, 14, 22
Agricultural Workers Organizing Committee (AWOC), 364, 367, 371
Alinsky, Saul, 358, 360–61
Alliance for Labor Action (ALA), 299
Amalgamated Association of Iron, Steel and Tin Workers, 83–84
Amalgamated Clothing Workers of America (ACWA), 176, 211–33, 244
Amalgamated Society of Carpenters and Joiners, 73
Amalgamated Society of Engineers, 73
Amended Railway Labor Act (1934), 267
American Coal Shipping Co., 205
American Farm Bureau Federation, 373–75
American Federation of Labor (AFL), x, xii, 31, 53–56, 62–63, 64–88, 100, 104–5, 112–14, 124, 126, 134–38, 142–59, 164–65, 171–82, 185, 188–90, 193–97, 204, 211, 215, 222–25, 228, 231, 238, 245, 247, 267, 269, 274, 304, 324, 331–33, 363
American Federation of Labor-Congress of Industrial Organizations (AFL-CIO), xii, 258, 274–77, 295–99, 303, 321, 324, 335–46, 365, 367, 372–73, 376–77

American Federationist, 74, 148
American Labor party, 175
American Labor Union, 105
American National Stove Manufacturers' and Iron Founders' Association, 11
American Railway Union (ARU), 64, 89–94, 102–4
American Workers party, 152–53
Americans for Democratic Action (ADA), 292, 296
Ameringer, Oscar, 59
Anderson, Mary, 161
Anthony, Susan B., 18, 24–28
Appeal to Reason, 121
Arthur, P. M., 100–101
Ashley, W. J., 140
Association of Catholic Trade Unionists, 288

Baker, Newton, 213
Baltimore and Ohio Railroad, 96–97
Barkan, Al, 336
Barry, Tom, 52–55
Baruch, Bernard, 217–18
Beck, Dave, 306, 318–19
Bell, Daniel, 62, 64, 69
Bellanca, Dorothy Jacobs, 161
Bennett, Ray, 307
Benson, Allan, 107, 125
Berger, Victor, L., 94, 103, 105–6, 122–25
Bethlehem Steel Co., 245, 251

387

Index

Biemiller, Andrew, 336
Bill Haywood's Book (Haywood), 115
Bisno, Abraham, 59
Bittner, Van, 238, 249–50
Bituminous Coal Operators' Association, 204
Blatch, Harriot Stanton, 175
Borah, William, 200
Boyce, Ed, 117, 119
Bracero program, 357, 362
Bradley, E. J., 262
Bradley, Omar, 253
Brandeis, Louis, 210, 212
Brennan, Bert, 319
British Trades Union Congress, 14, 230, 331
Brody, David, 188
Brophy, John, 138, 194, 238, 241, 245
Brotherhood of Locomotive Firemen, 95, 97–100, 103–4
Brotherhood of Sleeping Car Porters, 259–78
Brotherhood of the Kingdom, 139
Browder, Earl, 229
Brown, Geoffrey, 135
Brown, Irving, 332
Brown, Jerry, 350, 377–78
Brown, John, 102
Bruere, Henry, 218
Bryan, William Jenning, 200
Bunche, Ralph J., 270
Burlington Railroad strike (1888), 100–102
"Business unionism," x, 71, 74, 85
Byrnes, James, 229

California Agricultural Labor Relations Act, 350, 378–80
Cameron, Andrew, 11, 13, 21
Campbell, Alexander, 17–18
Cannery and Agricultural Workers Industrial Union, 363
Carey, Henry, 4
Carruthers, William, 115
Carter, Jimmy, 336, 340–41
Cary, Samuel, 15, 19
Central Intelligence Agency, 298
Central Labor Federation of New York, 72

Central States Drivers Council (CSDC), 306, 308–11, 314, 317
Chaplin, Ralph, 114, 128, 131
Chavez, Cesar, xii, xiii, xiv, 296, 350–82
Chavez, Helen Fabela (wife of Cesar), 357, 364
Chavez, Juana (mother of Cesar), 351
Chavez, Librado (father of Cesar), 351
Chavez, Manuel (cousin of Cesar), 364
Childs, Marquis, 201
Christman, Elizabeth, 161, 178
Chrysler, Walter, 220
Churchill, Winston, 230, 289, 295
Cigarmakers International Union (CMIU), 67, 70, 72–73, 76, 78–79, 85
Cigarmakers Progressive Union, 79–80
CIO News, 186
Citrine, Sir Walter, 230–31
Civil War, 7, 11, 13, 17, 22, 36–37, 46, 66
Claflin, Tennessee, 70
Clayton Anti-Trust Act, 82
Cleveland, Grover, 93, 200
Coeur D'Alenes strike (1899), 119–20
Cohen, Jerry, 369
Cohen, Sophie, 114–15
Cohn, Fannia, 161
Committee for Industrial Organizations, 178, 179, 193, 243, 284
Committee of Thirty-four, 20
Committee on Political Education (COPE), 336, 341
Commons, John R., 63, 73, 85, 140
Communist party, 108–9, 134, 153, 179, 229–30, 241, 246, 251–53, 269–70, 274, 285, 288–91, 331, 334
Community Service Organization, 358–64
Conference for Progressive Political Action, 86
Congress of Industrial Organizations (CIO), xi, 78, 127, 155–58, 185, 194–204, 216, 220–32, 234, 244–56, 269, 288, 290–91, 324, 363
Congressional Union, 168
Conlin, Joseph R., xi
Conway, Jack, 290
Cook, Cora, 175
Cooke, Morris, 213, 217

388

Coolidge, Calvin, 192–93
Cripple Creek strike (1903), 82, 119–20

Daniel, Cletus, xii
Darrow, Clarence, 92, 121, 210–11, 219
Darwin, Charles, 208
Das Kapital (Marx), 94, 118
Daughters of St. Crispin, 27
Davey, Martin, 199
Davis, John P., 269–70
Davis, John W., 86
Day, Horace H., 18
Debs, Daniel (father of Eugene), 94
Debs, Eugene, xi, xiii, xiv, 64, 80, 89–110, 121, 125, 360
Debs, Marguerite (mother of Eugene), 94
DeCaux, Len, 186
Delaware and Hudson Railroad, 32, 37, 41
Delaware, Lackawanna, and Western Railroad, 37, 38, 41, 44
DeLeon, Daniel, 80–81
Dennison, Henry, 218
Dewey, Thomas, 229
Dickson, James P., 32, 36
Dickson, Thomas, 32, 37
Dickson Manufacturing Co., 32
Dietz, Peter, 136
DiGiorgio Fruit Corp., 368
Dobbs, Farrell, 309–11
Dodge, Mabel, 122, 125
Dolan, Pat, 236
Douglas, William O., 253
Drake, Jim, 364
Dreier, Mary, 172
Dubinsky, David, 177, 331–32
Dubofsky, Melvyn, 118
Duffy, John, 252
Durant, Walter, 132

Ehmann, John, 55
Eisenhower, Dwight D., 158, 253, 255–56, 336, 338
Emancipation Proclamation, 22
Engels, Friedrich, 67, 72
English, William, 3
Espionage Act (1917), 114, 128, 130
Ettor, Joe, 129

Fagan, Pat, 236
Fair Employment Practice Committee (FEPC), 228, 230, 272, 278
Fair Labor Standards Act (1938), 220, 245
Fairless, Benjamin, 254
Farm Equipment Workers, 253
Farrington, Frank, 241
Federal Council of Churches of Christ in America, 136
Federal Fuel Board, 144
Federation of Organized Trades and Labor Unions (FOTLU), 64, 69, 100
Feehan, Francis, 236
Fehrenbatch, John, 42–44
Ferral, John, 3
Filene, Edward, 212, 218
Filene, Lincoln, 212, 218
Fincher, Jonathan, 13, 21
First International (International Working-men's Association), 14, 67–68, 70–73, 85
Fisher, Dorothy Canfield, 160
Fitzsimmons, Frank, 320, 375
Flint Sit-Down strike (1937), 186, 197–98, 284
Flynn, Elizabeth Gurley, 129
Foner, Philip S., 63, 69
Ford, Henry, 111, 112, 148
Ford Motor Co., 153, 223, 281–85, 294, 299–300
Foster, William Z., 117
Frankensteen, Richard, 288, 291
Frankfurter, Felix, 210, 213, 217
Fraser, Steven, x, xi
Freedman's Bureau, 23
Fur and Leather Workers' Union, 251

Garland Fund, 260
Garvey, Marcus, 271
General Electric, 225
General German Workers Association, 14
General Managers Association, 92
General Motors (GM), 148, 153, 156, 186, 197–98, 286, 289–90, 293–94, 299–300
George, Henry, 69
Gerber, Julius, 175
Gibson, William, 14, 18
Girdler, Tom, 247

389

Index

Gitlow, Benjamin, 131
Gladden, Washington, 139
Golden, Clinton, 245, 249
Goldman, Emma, 131
Goldmark, Pauline, 170
Gompers, Samuel, x, xii, xiii, xiv, 30, 62–
   88, 104–5, 112, 124, 144, 154, 157,
   164, 175, 182, 190, 215, 250, 334
Gompers, Solomon (father of Samuel), 66
Gorman, Francis, 135
Gould, Jay, 47, 58, 100
Gowen, Franklin, 38
Grami, William, 368, 371
Grant, U. S., 24
Green, Duff, 23
Green, Hugh (father of William), 138
Green, Jane Oram (mother of William),
   138
Green, Jenny Mobley (wife of William),
   139
Green, William, xii, xiii, xiv, 134–59,
   180, 196, 275, 330–35
Green Compulsory Workingmen's Com-
   pensation Act (1913), 141
Greenbackism, 17–18, 23, 25, 39, 43–44,
   69–70
Gross, Ignatius, 24
Guffey-Snyder Act (1935), 242
Guffey-Vinson Act (1937), 242

Haggerty, C. J., 276
Hanna, Mark, 84
Hapgood, Hutchins, 122
Hard Rock Miners (Lingenfelter), 118
Harding, Warren G., 108, 240
Harding, William, 13, 242
Hardman, J. B. S., vii, ix, x, xi, xiv
Harriman, W. Averell, 253
Harris, William H., xii
Harrison, George M., 268
Hart, Schaffner and Marx, 210, 212
Hartimire, Wayne, 364
Hay, John, 200
Hayes, Frank, 144, 238
Hayes, John W., 55
Hayes, Max S., 148
Haymarket Square Riot (1886), 50–54,
   116

Haywood, William D. "Big Bill," xi, xiii,
   xiv, 59, 105–6, 111–33
Hibernians, 38, 236
Higgins, George, 346
Hill, James J., 89–90
Hillman, Sidney, x, xi, xiii, xiv, 153, 207–
   33, 244, 246–47, 282
Hillquit, Morris, 103, 105–6, 122–25
Hirsch, David, 67–69
Hoffa, James R., xi, xii, xiv, 303–23
Hogan, Thomas, 3
Holland, James, 173
Homestead strike (1892), 82
Hoover, Herbert, xi, 149, 191, 192–93,
   200, 204, 242, 244
Howat, Alex, 240
Huerta, Dolores, 364, 369
Hughes, Langston, 260
Hulman, Herman, 95, 98–99
Humphrey, Hubert, 297, 344
Hutcheson, William L., 196, 247

Industrial Brotherhood, 44–45
Industrial Congress, 24
Industrial Workers of the World (IWW),
   77, 81, 104–7, 112–15, 117, 122–33,
   156, 211, 363, 381
Inland Steel Corp., 254
International Association of Machinists,
   156, 196
International Brotherhood of Teamsters,
   131, 195–96, 296, 299, 303–22, 342,
   368, 370–79
International Federation of Trade Unions,
   173
International Federation of Working
   Women, 173
International Labor Organization, 298
International Ladies' Garment Workers'
   Union (ILGWU), 162, 165–70, 212,
   218, 325–26
International Longshoremen's Association,
   335
International Socialist Review, 123
International Typographical Union, 27–28
International Union of Electrical Workers,
   253

Iron Molders' International Co-operative and Protection Union, 12–13
Iron Molders' International Union, 4, 8–13
Itliong, Larry, 365, 367, 372
Ives, H. M., 76–77

Jacksonville Agreement (1924), 192, 242
Jacobstein, Meyer, 213
James, Estelle, xii, xiii
Jessup, William, 13–16, 18
Johnson, C. Ben, 13
Johnson, James Weldon, 265
Johnson, Lyndon, 297–98, 336, 338–39, 346
Jones & Laughlin Steel Corp., 245
Journeymen Stove and Hollow-Ware Moulders' Union of Philadelphia, 8
Julian, Sophia, 66

Kaufman, Stuart, 62, 69
Kelley, Florence, 213
Kelley's Army, 116
Kellogg, Edward, 25
Kelsey-Hayes Wheel Co., 284
Kennedy, John F., 336, 338–39
Kennedy, Robert, 299, 318–19, 367, 369
Kennedy, Tom, 198
Kessler-Harris, Alice, xii
Keynesian economics, 217–19, 224, 227–28, 280, 290, 297, 324, 336
King, Martin Luther, Jr., 276, 278, 297, 343
Kircher, Bill, 367, 373
Kirkland, Lane, 346
Kirstein, Louis, 212–13
Knights of Labor, xii, 21, 28, 30, 39, 41–61, 63, 69–70, 77–80, 85, 100–101, 115, 127, 134, 136, 139, 381
Knights of Pythias, 45
Knights of St. Crispin, 46
Knudsen, William, 224
Korean War, 234, 244, 291, 332, 337

Labor and Democracy (Green), 156
Labor Forward Movement, 136, 144
Labor's League for Political Education (LLPE), 157, 332–33
Labor's Non-Partisan League, 221

Labriola, Antonio, 117
LaFollette, Robert M., 86, 126, 200, 215–16
LaFollette, Robert, Jr., 186, 200, 217
LaGuardia, Fiorello, 271, 274, 329
Lancaster, Roy, 259
Landis, Judge Kenesaw Mountain, 129–34
Landrum-Griffin Act (1959), 243, 313
Lane, Emma, 27
Laslett, John H. M., xi, xii
Lassalle, Ferdinand, 67–68, 80, 208
Lauck, W. Jett, 193
Laurell, Ferdinand, 68
Leach, Ebeneazer, 40
Leach, Joshua, 95
Lehman, Herbert, 329
Leiserson, William, 213
Levinson, Edward, 194
Lewis, Augusta, 27–28
Lewis, Denny, 247
Lewis, John L., xi, xiii, xiv, 144–45, 155–56, 179, 185–206, 220–23, 238–39, 242–49, 254, 268, 282, 333–35, 360
Lewis, Kathryn, 246
Lewis, Myrta Bell (wife of John L.), 189
Lichtenstein, Nelson, x
Lincoln, Abraham, 102, 188
Lippman, Walter, 107, 122, 210, 213
Litchman, Charles, 54
Little, Frank, 114, 126–28
Little Steel Formula, 229, 243, 249
Little Steel strike (1937), 198–200
Littlefield, Charles E., 81
Lloyd, William Bross, 130
Locomotive Foremen's Magazine, 97, 99
Love, George, 204
Lovestone, Jay, 331–32, 334
Lubell, Samuel, 255
Luce, Henry, 230
Lucker, Henry, 18, 25

McCartney, John, 236
McClellan Committee (Senate Select Committee on Improper Activities in the Labor Management Field), 318–19, 321–22
McDonald, Alexander, 138
McDonald, David, 235, 244, 250, 253
MacDonald, Mary A., 25

Index

MacDonald, Ramsay, 122
McDonnell, Father Donald, 357–58, 360
McDonnell, J. P., 68
McGovern, George, 340
McGuire, Peter, 71, 99
McKeen, William Riley, 97–99, 102
McKinley, William, 56
McNeill, George, 42–43
McNutt, Paul, 227
McParland, James J., 120–21
Malone, James, 256
Malthus, Thomas, 4
Mandel, Bernard, 62
March on Washington for Jobs and Freedom, 276
March on Washington Movement, 281–85
Marcy, Mary, 130–31
Marot, Helen, 167
Marshall, George, 253
Marshall Plan, 244, 253
Marx, Karl, 63, 67–69, 72, 84, 208
Masons, 45, 138
Mazey, Emil, 290, 296
Meany, Anne Cullen (mother of George), 325
Meany, Eugenia McMahon (wife of George), 325, 330, 346
Meany, George, xi, xii, xiii, xiv, 157, 258, 285–86, 295, 298–99, 321, 324–48, 373, 376
Meany, John (brother of George), 325
Meany, Michael (father of George), 325
Meier, August, 278
Messenger, 259, 260–62, 268, 277
Michels, Robert, xiii
Militia of Christ for Social Service, 136
Mill, John Stuart, 4, 208
Mills, C. Wright, 285
Mine Owner's Protection Association, 120
Miner's Fight for American Standards (Lewis), 192
Miner's Magazine, 119, 123
Minneapolis Teamsters' strike (1934), 186
Minor, Nevada Jane, 116, 118, 132
Mississippi Freedom Democratic party, 297
Mitchell, John, 83–84, 143
Mohn, Einar, 375
Molly Maguires, 38, 120

Montgomery, David, xi, xii
Moore, Dad, 262
Morgan, J. P., 83–84, 195
Morrison, Frank, 330–31
Morse, Wayne, 250
Mortimer, Wyndham, 153
Moyer, Charles, 119–24
Mullaney, Kate, 25–26
Muller vs. Oregon (1908), 170
Murphy, Frank, 186, 197–99, 202
Murray, Joseph (son of Philip), 256
Murray, Liz Lavery (wife of Philip), 236
Murray, Philip, xi, xiii, xiv, 203, 223, 229, 234–57, 295, 334–35
Murray, Rose Ann Layden (mother of Philip), 235
Murray, William (father of Philip), 235
Mussolini, Benito, 198, 201
Muste, A. J., 152–53
Myers, Isaac, 24
Myrdal, Gunnar, 277

National American Women's Suffrage Association, 168
National Association for the Advancement of Colored People (NAACP), 265, 266–68, 344
National Association of Manufacturers, 119, 217
National Bank of Washington, 205
National Civic Federation, 59, 76, 82–84, 86
National Coal Policy Conference, 205
National Consumers League, 213
National Defense Advisory Committee, 223
National Farm Labor Union, 355
National Farm Workers Association, 364–65, 367
National Industrial Recovery Act (NIRA, 1933), 150–51, 193, 218–19, 242
National Labor Reform party, 19
National Labor Relations Board (NLRB), 242, 245, 250, 312–13, 333, 341, 378
National Labor Union (NLU), xi, 13–29, 44–45, 85
National Maritime Union, 274
National Negro Congress, 269–71, 273

National Recovery Administration (NRA), 177, 182, 218–20, 248
National Urban League, 267
National War Labor Board (NWLB), 86, 243, 245, 249, 298, 331
Negro American Labor Council, 275
Nestor, Agnes, 161
New Deal, 86, 151, 177, 186, 193, 213, 216, 221–22, 227, 230, 245, 248, 252, 266, 267, 286
New York City Building Trades Council, 328
New York City Central Trade and Labor Council, 174
New York City Workingmen's Union, 13
New York State Federation of Labor, 173, 174, 324, 343
New York Times, 92, 132, 229
Newman, Pauline, 165
Nixon, Richard M., 258, 299, 320, 338, 340, 345
Norris, George, 126, 200, 217
North American Aviation Co., 214
North Atlantic Treaty Organization, 244

O'Brien, Chuckie, 321
Odd Fellows, 45, 138
Oestreicher, Richard, xii
Office of Production Management, 224, 226
Ohio Federation of Labor, 141
Ohio Manufacturers' Association, 141
Ohio Workingmen's Compensation Act (1911), 141
Olney, Richard, 92–93
Orchard, Harry, 120–22
O'Reilly, Leonora, 161
Owen, Chandler, 260

Padilla, Gilbert, 364
Paine, Thomas, 102
Parker, Julia O'Connor, 161
Pennsylvania Railroad, 30
People's (Populist) party, 70, 103
Perkins, Charles E., 100–101
Perkins, Frances, 149, 177, 217
Perlman, Seleg, 85
Pettibone, George, 121

Phelan, Craig, xii
Phelps, Alfred, 22
Philadelphia Garment Cutters Association, 45
Philadelphia General Trade Union, 3, 4
Pinkerton Detectives, 38, 120–21
Plasterers' International Union, 15
Political Action Committee (PAC), 228, 230–31
Pouget, Emile, 117
Powderly, Hugh (brother of Terence), 32
Powderly, Joseph (brother of Terence), 32
Powderly, Margery (mother of Terence), 31
Powderly, Terence, Sr. (father of Terence), 31
Powderly, Terence V., xii, xiii, 30–61, 69, 79
Progressive Miners' Union, 139
Pullman, George, 89, 90–94
Pullman Palace Car Co., 89–94, 259, 262–69, 277
Pullman Porters and Maids Protective Association, 267
Pullman strike (1894), 64, 68, 82, 89–94, 102, 104
Putnam, Mary Kellogg, 25

Quadragesimo Anno (Pope Pius XI), 248

Randall, Clarence B., 254
Randolph, A. Philip, xii, xiii, xiv, 258–79, 344
Rauh, Joseph, 296
Rauschenbusch, Walter, 139
Reading Railroad, 37, 38
Reagan, Ronald, 377
Red Scare (1919), 86, 129–30
Reed, John, 125
Reed, Warwick, J., 24
Republic Steel Co., 153, 245, 247
Reuther, Mary Wolf (wife of Walter), 284
Reuther, Roy (brother of Walter), 281
Reuther, Theodore (brother of Walter), 281–84
Reuther, Valentine (father of Walter), 281
Reuther, Victor (brother of Walter), 281–82, 296, 298
Reuther, Walter, xi, xiii, xiv, 235, 276, 280–302, 334, 342–43, 367

Index

Revolution, 25, 27
Reynolds, Pat, 115
Rice, Charles Owen, 239
Riesel, Victor, 252
Robins, Margaret Dreier, 171–72
Romney, George, 287
Roosevelt, Eleanor, 171, 176–80, 271–72, 274
Roosevelt, Franklin D., 150–51, 176, 186, 188, 193–204, 207, 216–30, 235, 243–52, 255, 271–72, 287–89, 292, 329–31, 335
Roosevelt, Theodore, 56, 106, 121, 200, 235
Ross, Fred, 358–60, 369, 372
Rustin, Bayard, 276
Ruttenberg, Harold, 248–49
Ryan, John A., 248, 252

St. John, Vincent, 118, 123, 125
Salvatore, Nick, xi
San Francisco General Strike (1934), 186
Sandburg, Carl, xiii, 114
Saniel, Lucian, 80
Sargent, Frank P., 101
Schaffner, Joseph, 211
Schatz, Ronald, xi
Schenley Industries, 367–68
Schnitzer, William F., 276
Schneiderman, Rose, xii, xiv, 160–84
Schuyler, George, 277
Schwab, Charles, 83
Scott, Melinda, 167
Scranton, William, 37, 39
Second International, 59, 112, 122
Sedition Act (1918), 128
Senior, Nassau, 4
Serviss, Elizabeth, 132
Seward, William Henry, 200
Shaw, Anna Howard, 167–68
Sherman Anti-Trust Act, 82
Shirtwaist-makers strike (1909–10), 165–67
Simons, Algie, 122–25
Siney, John, 13, 41
Smith, Al, 244
Smith, Benjamin, 262
Smith, Ferdinand C., 274

Smith, Paul, 148
Smith-Connelly Act (1943), 157, 204
Socialist Labor party (SLP), 41, 71–72, 80–81
Socialist Party of America, 81, 103–10, 112, 121–26, 166–68, 213–15, 241, 260, 281–85, 290, 296
Socialist Trades and Labor Alliance, 80–81
Socialist Workers party, 309
Sorel, George, 117
Sorge, Friedrich, 70, 72, 118
Southern Christian Leadership Conference, 276, 297
Spencer, Herbert, 208
Stalin, Joseph, 198, 289, 295
Standard Oil of New Jersey, 82
Stanton, Elizabeth Cady, 18, 25, 27, 168
Steel strike (1919), 64, 86
Steel Workers' Organizing Committee (SWOC), 186, 198, 245
Steinbeck, John, 354
Stephens, Uriah S., 21, 44–46, 48
Stephenson, George, 36
Steunenberg, Frank, 120–22, 130
Stevenson, Adlai, 158, 255–56, 338
Steward, Ira, 42–43
Strasser, Adolph, 68, 71–73, 75, 78
Survey, 213
Swartz, Maude, 172, 176–77
Swope, Gerard, 220
Sylvis, Maria Mott (mother of William), 3
Sylvis, Nicholas (father of William), 3
Sylvis, William H., xi, 3–29, 127
Syndicalism, 117

Taft, Robert, 255
Taft, William Howard, 106
Taft-Hartley Act (1947), 157, 204, 243, 250, 254–56, 291, 312–13, 315, 332–33, 339, 341
Taylor, Myron, 198
Taylor, Ron, 373
Test Fleet Corp., 318–19
Textile Workers Organizing Committee (TWOC), 220
Thirty Years of Labor (Powderly), 57
Thomas, Amelia, 6
Thomas, Norman, 282

Thomas, R. J., 288, 290
Thorne, Florence, 63
Tobin, Daniel, 149, 195–96, 306, 316, 318
Toldeo Auto-Lite strike (1934), 152–53, 186
Toledo Central Labor Union, 152–53
Townsend, Willard S., 274
Trevellick, Richard, 13, 18, 19
Triangle fire (1911), 170
Tridon, Andre, 121
Troup, Alexander, 19
Truman, Harry S., 157, 229–31, 234, 251–55, 296, 332–33
Tugwell, Rexford, 199, 217

United Association of Journeymen and Apprentices of the Plumbing and Pipe Fitting Industry of the United States and Canada, 326
United Automobile Workers (UAW), 186, 198, 220, 224, 251, 276, 280, 281–301, 342
United Brotherhood of Carpenters and Joiners, 157, 196
United Cannery, Agricultural, Packing and Allied Workers, 355
United Cigar Manufacturers Association of New York, 79
United Cigarmakers, 68, 76
United Cloth Hat and Cap Makers' Union, 164
United Electrical, Radio and Machine Workers (UE), 252, 253
United Farm Workers, 296, 350–82
United Garment Workers, 211, 212
United Hebrew Trades, 162
United Mine Workers' Journal, 140
United Mine Workers of America (UMW), xi, 78, 83, 136–44, 151, 156, 189–94, 197, 201, 203–5, 218, 234, 236–48, 268
United Nations, 228, 231, 244, 298
United Packinghouse Workers, 361, 364
United States Steel Corp., 82–84, 156, 186, 197, 245, 254
United Steelworkers of America, 234, 249, 251, 253–56
United Textile Workers, 135

Universal Negro Improvement Association, 271

Vandalia Railroad, 94, 96
Vanderveer, George, 129–30
Vietnam War, 298–99, 337, 339–41, 345–46
Vogt, Hugo, 80

Wade, Benjamin F., 27
Wage Stabilization Board, 234, 243, 255
Wagner, Robert, 186, 217
Wagner Act (1935), 204, 242, 282, 312, 377
Walker, Edwin, 92
Wallace, Henry, 229, 230, 253, 291, 296
Wallbridge, Martha, 27
Walls, H. J., 8
War Manpower Commission, 227
Ware, Norman, 59
Washington, Booker T., 77, 87
Watson, James, 242
Watson-Parker Act (1926), 264
Webster, Milton P., 262, 264–65, 270, 274
Western Federation of Miners, 80, 105, 117–23
Western Labor Union, 105
Whaley, John C. C., 14, 16–18
Wharton, A. P., 196
White, John P., 142–43, 144, 236–38
White, Walter, 268
Willard, Mrs. E. O. G., 27
Williams, G. Mennon, 297
Willkie, Wendell L., 201–2, 243, 246
Wilson, Charles E., 293
Wilson, Woodrow, 62, 81, 86, 106, 125, 128, 189–91, 200, 238, 241, 255
Woll, Mathew, 146, 331
Women Suffrage Association of America, 27
Women's Bureau, 173, 179
Women's suffrage, 166, 168–70, 173
Women's Trade Union League, xii, 160–84, 210
Woodcock, Leonard, 290
Woodhull, Victoria, 70
Woodstock County jail, 93–94, 102

Workingmen's Benevolent Association, 38–39, 41
World Federation of Trade Unions, 231, 331
World War I, 62, 64, 74, 82, 84, 86, 107, 111–15, 126, 143, 189, 190, 213, 239, 240

World War II, 157, 204, 207, 222, 243, 245, 248–49, 271, 274, 292, 307, 331

Young, Owen, 225

Zieger, Robert H., xii, xiii

Books in the Series The Working Class in American History

Worker City, Company Town: Iron and Cotton-Worker Protest in Troy and Cohoes, New York, 1855-84   DANIEL J. WALKOWITZ

Life, Work, and Rebellion in the Coal Fields: The Southern West Virginia Miners, 1880-1922   DAVID ALAN CORBIN

Women and American Socialism, 1870-1920   MARI JO BUHLE

Lives of Their Own: Blacks, Italians, and Poles in Pittsburgh, 1900-1960 JOHN BODNAR, ROGER SIMON, AND MICHAEL P. WEBER

Working-Class America: Essays on Labor, Community, and American Society   EDITED BY MICHAEL H. FRISCH AND DANIEL J. WALKOWITZ

Eugene V. Debs: Citizen and Socialist   NICK SALVATORE

American Labor and Immigration History, 1877-1920s: Recent European Research   EDITED BY DIRK HOERDER

Workingmen's Democracy: The Knights of Labor and American Politics LEON FINK

The Electrical Workers: A History of Labor at General Electric and Westinghouse, 1923-60   RONALD W. SCHATZ

The Mechanics of Baltimore: Workers and Politics in the Age of Revolution, 1763-1812   CHARLES G. STEFFEN

The Practice of Solidarity: American Hat Finishers in the Nineteenth Century   DAVID BENSMAN

The Labor History Reader   EDITED BY DANIEL J. LEAB

Solidarity and Fragmentation: Working People and Class Consciousness in Detroit, 1875-1900   RICHARD OESTREICHER

Counter Cultures: Saleswomen, Managers, and Customers in American Department Stores, 1890-1940   SUSAN PORTER BENSON

A Generation of Boomers: The Pattern of Railroad Labor Conflict in Nineteenth-Century America   SHELTON STROMQUIST

The New England Working Class and the New Labor History EDITED BY HERBERT G. GUTMAN AND DONALD H. BELL

Labor Leaders in America EDITED BY MELVYN DUBOFSKY AND WARREN VAN TINE

Barons of Labor: The San Francisco Building Trades and Union Power in the Progressive Era   MICHAEL KAZIN